IN CONTROL
The Rebirth of an NFL Legend

Thomas Hollywood Henderson
with Frank Luksa

THOMASHENDERSON
Publishing

IN CONTROL
The Rebirth of an NFL Legend

Published by

THOMASHENDERSON
Publishing

Book design and cover art by Dick Reeves Design Group, Austin, Texas

Library of Congress Control Number: 2004095810

ISBN: 0-9759890-0-6

Manufactured in the United States of America
Published simultaneously in Canada

Proceeds from this book will support Eastside Youth Services and Street Outreach a 501c3 non-profit

ESYSSO built and supports a Football Stadium, a 7 lane track and little league football teams in Austin, Texas, including Pop Warner.

Our facilities have been open since 1992.
Our outreach programs assist recovering individual and families.

For more information:
www.HollywoodHenderson.com
tehenderson@earthlink.net

DEDICATION

This book is dedicated to my mother, Violet Faye, my daughters, my grand-children, Wyetta and my biggest fan and love, Linda. It is also dedicated to all the individuals and families who are in the recovery process.

Sponsors and friendships that have helped me along the way:

Dr. Joseph Pursch
Chuck Denmark
Frank O.
Chuck C.
George Benedict
Father Martin
Bill O'Donnell
Jimmy Daniels
Fred Ferriell
Robert and Margaret Spellings
Ted and Page Ashley
Howard and Marie Burttschell
Amie Gold
Roger Staubach
Ed (Too Tall) Jones
Drew Pearson
Beasley and Paula Reece
Peter and Jane Knobler
Frank and Lisa Weimann
Judy and John McCaleb
Tom and Lynn Meredith
Gigi and Sam Bryant
Marcus Wilkins
Jimmy Vaughn

Marcello and Allison Grasso
Steve and Michelle Bartholomew
Derrick Britt
Nat Moore
Barry and Lucy Cox
Pete and Danielle Carry
Robert Page
Adrian Burrough
Veana Clay
Mary Peck
Sabine Fulcher
Attorney Bruce Fox
Attorney Tony Alexander
Duane and Ellen Bell
C.B. Banks Jr.
Mike and Gwen Murray
Darrell and Edith Royal
Congresswoman Eddie Bernice
Johnson
Treatment Centers:
Sierra Tucson
Father Martin's Ashley
Seafield Center

This book is not about me. It is about us. We who clean up our lives are not vic-tims; we are survivors. When we live clean and sober, we enrich ourselves, our children, family, friends, neighbors, employers, society and those seeking to change their own lives. I don't have enough fingers or toes to count my friends. You know who you are and I love all of you.

Special Thanks to
Mr. and Mrs. Lou Bantle
Mr. and Mrs. Don Riddle
Elizabeth Brisco
Thank you NFL Charities for contributing $10,000 to ESYSSO
and the Youth of Austin, Texas.

"Without any thought at all I began a curious relationship with alcohol and other drugs, never knowing or thinking of the possible consequences. Looking back now I was in trouble the moment I began."

CONTENTS

THOMAS HOLLYWOOD HENDERSON

Sports writers describe Thomas "Hollywood" Henderson as outrageous, witty and a talented athlete. He was a first-round draft pick of the Dallas cowboys and a Pro Bowl linebacker. He has been called the most flamboyant football player of the seventies. Thomas, however, simply describes himself as a miracle. Because, despite all the fame, glory and talent, he almost lost his life to alcohol and drugs,

During his colorful seven-year career as a top NFL player, Thomas played in three Super Bowls. On the field he could woo the crowd with rare talent. Off the field, he attracted the masses with humor and wit. This combination of talent and flair landed him on the cover of a 1979 issue of Newsweek. He was one the stars of America's Team. Alcohol and drug abuse, however, quickly brought his brilliant career to a stunning halt. He lost it all. He lost his career, his family, his friends and because of alcohol abuse and drug addiction, Thomas lost his freedom.

Fortunately, in 1983, Thomas's life began to change. Through therapy and twelve step programs, Thomas established a new way of living. He has been clean and sober since November 8, 1983. Today, he travels the world, openly sharing his story. He is a lecturer, an educational filmmaker and a promoter of recovery programs throughout our nation's colleges, high schools and criminal justice systems.

Thomas has also become a community philanthropist in his hometown of Austin, Texas. As founder and chairman of East Side Youth Services and Street Outreach, he has built a stadium in East Austin complete with a 7-lane track – all for the recreational enjoyment of East Austin's youth. He is also president and owner of Thomas Henderson Films, an educational video visual aid distribution company that provides the incarcerated community with much needed information on prevention, recovery and sobriety. Thomas has devoted his new life to the prevention of substance and alcohol abuse by helping the youth and incarcerated individuals of today understand that sobriety is an option,

On March 22, 2000, Thomas won a 28 Million dollar jackpot from the Texas Lottery. Thomas understands now that to one who is given much...much is expected. He believes his winning is a direct result of his giving. Because of his recovery from drugs and alcohol he is now fully prepared to finally handle success.

Thomas' speaking tour has taken him to high schools, college campuses, treatment centers, companies and prisons. Always an interesting and eloquent speaker, Thomas shares his firsthand knowledge of the pain, suffering and helplessness one encounters in the midst of an alcohol or drug dependency. He has been from Super Bowl to cell block with many horrifying stops along the way. Today he is a new man sharing his story of hope, courage and change – one day at a time.

FOREWORD

This is not only a book about one man's recovery, it is also a clinical guide to recovery.

The goal of recovery is more than just being clean and sober. (There are alcoholics and other addicts who are clean and sober but are not in recovery.)

Clinically, the goal of recovery is to remain clean and sober ~ and function successfully in the mainstream of life as a member of society. That means to take care of your family, get along with your friends, not create legal problems, handle your financial obligations, live a healthy lifestyle and pull your own weight in the workplace. (A good way to diagnose addiction is to ask, "are any of the above areas of your functioning impaired by your addictive behavior?" If the answer is yes, you've got a problem.)

Re-entering the mainstream of life is the hard part of recovery. How difficult it will be depends on (1) the severity of your addiction, (2) the quality of people you hang out with (3) the power of your brain to accept that you have a problem and to work at correcting it.

For example, let's assume that former President Jimmy Carter is hospitalized with severe injuries from an accident and getting heavy doses of morphine injections for a month. If at this point we suddenly (cold turkey) stop the medication, he will have withdrawal symptoms because his body and his brain have become dependent on morphine. But if we "wean" him off the medications over several days and discharge him clean and sober, he will re-enter the mainstream of life with relative ease. Why? Because he already had an orderly, productive, spiritual life prior to getting on the drugs.

By contrast, if a street addict undergoes detoxification (notice that with addicts we don't use the word "wean") and we discharge him clean and sober a few days later, the street addict's re-entry into the mainstream of life will be difficult because of the kind of life he had before detox.

In some cases, re-entry is the wrong word to use, because the patient was never in the mainstream of life to begin with. Such a case was Thomas Henderson. He tells us in this book that prior to getting clean and sober he enjoyed fame, fortune and Super Bowl physical health. But he had never learned how to live.

Psychosocially, Thomas was always at the bottom because the only life skills he had were the standard survival tools that are used by practicing addicts: getting by, getting high, cutting corners, rationalizing, minimizing, lying and stealing. Those were the tools he was using to make it in the "easier, softer" lane on the road to addiction.

His addiction became undeniable when his safety net of enablers (his toxic family, Hollywood type friends, sound bite hungry media, the money-driven NFL, the "benefits"-oriented Players Union, the selfish fans etc.) dissolved and left him crashing into the penitentiary. Why did his enablers bail out? Because he had become an addict who was financially broke, too sick to play ball and charged with a sex crime.

At this point, Thomas started his recovery. He told me early on "I'm gonna stay clean and sober by always scoring 100% on the first Step of AA and work the other Steps later." The idea is this: You are not powerless over alcohol when you are no longer drinking; you become powerless again when you start drinking again. And there are no gradations. You are not just powerless over alcohol "most of time" you are powerless over alcohol 100% of the time - because you have become an unpredictable drinker.

Thomas discovered something for himself that we now know from functional MRI studies of the brain. Psychologically speaking, when your brain is drug-impaired, the Frontal lobe of your brain - the seat of your reasoning/evaluating/executive functions - is overpowered by your Middle lobe - the seat of your lust/murder/mayhem drives. When that happens, you might do bad things; things that later have to be rationalized with remarks like "that wasn't me talking - that was whiskey talking;" or your attorney is telling the judge "Your Honor, my client has no recollection of killing his ex-wife."

"Change" became Thomas' new mantra. This idea is based on the seemingly simplistic notion that if you don't change ~ your life stays the same. The underlying notion is that suffering addicts begin to change when they no longer want to stay the same.

In 1981, after an unsuccessful attempt at recovery in a clinic in Arizona, Thomas asked himself the question many addicts ask themselves: Why should I change? What for?

He learned the answer in rehab by watching us "rehabilitate" alcoholic airline pilots. The idea is to let go of the things your addiction took from you, and focus on the things sobriety can bring you. (That's probably why alcoholic airline pilots have a 90% recovery rate. They realize that they have everything to lose and everything to gain, i.e. if they don't recover, they lose their wings.)

Recovery starts when your Frontal lobe begins to manage more and more of your life on a daily basis. That's when you start taking direction, learn new things, and follow the good examples of those recovering addicts and non-addicts who are successful role models. (In 12-Step work, it's called "stick with the winners".)

Today Thomas says that every good idea he has ever used, he stole from functional people – not from addicts who are still suffering. (Addicts who are still suffering can only teach you what NOT to do.) Today he remembers how, as a sick but still "successful" Dallas Cowboy, he'd be listening resentfully to the 'harangues' of Tom Landry and Roger Staubach. He didn't hear the true meaning of their words because he was sullen, angry and resentful. But he must have learned a lot subliminally, because the ideas they expressed are still helping Thomas make changes in his attitudes and in his actions on a daily basis.

In recovery, as you change your attitudes, you are, in effect, modifying/changing the neurotransmitter functions in your brain. Over time, we can see that your Frontal lobe is gradually taking charge and you are getting better at the task of restraining and containing the self-destructive, murderous urges of your Middle lobe. This can be accomplished through daily application of your 12-Step program, without the use of medications.

Most people don't believe that this is possible, but brain imaging studies clearly show the changes in brain activity that take place in the obsessive-compulsive patients who are in psychotherapy – the talking cure – without using medication. One can infer that similar neurochemical changes are taking place in the brain of addicts through 12-Step recovery. We see the evidence clinically. If AA were a drug, it would be FDA (Food & Drug Administration) approved.

There is no magic here. What happens is that you rebuild your Fontal lobe by slowly incorporating the examples and attitudes of your sponsors, your therapists and other positive role models. You do it in the same way that normal, healthy people build their Frontal lobe in their early childhood, i.e. by incorporating the examples and attitudes of their parents, teachers, coaches, clergy, etc. (That's how all human beings end up somewhere on a wide spectrum of psychosocial functioning – from Jimmy Carter to Charles Manson.)

As a therapist, I can tell how you, as a recovering patient, are progressing in your brainwork when I listen to the contents of your relapse dreams. For example: One night in your early, struggling sobriety, you have a dream. You dream that "somehow you got talked into having" a drink, but then - still in your dream-you decide that you might as well keep on drinking -

since you already broke your sobriety. What's really going on here is that you are enjoying that drinking dream so much that when your wife bumps you accidentally and you wake up you yell at her to let you go back to sleep. Why? Because you want to keep enjoying that dream. This means that the memory remnants or trigger areas in your brain are still fresh and powerful; or, putting it psychologically, your unconscious mind is still in the grip of drinking urges. That's why, in your waking hours, you are barely able to hang on to your conscious resolve not to drink again.

As you progress in your sobriety, your dreams change because they reflect your struggle with sobriety. For example: You dream that a drink is offered to you... and you drink a part of it, but you don't enjoy it. You wake up with a racing heart, feeling sweaty, scared and guilty... because you will have to tell your sponsor, your spouse, etc. that you broke your sobriety. A few minutes later, when you are fully awake, you feel relieved because you realize that it was only a dream, that you didn't really break your sobriety.

You are even farther along in your recovery if you dream that a drink is offered to you, and you refuse it... and you wake up, amused and relieved because even in your dream, you made the right decision.

Thomas says that today, I can't get high even in my dreams. He has had dreams where there is cocaine available, but he somehow can't quite reach it.., or he doesn't have a light .., or it drops out of his hand.., or he is already handcuffed, with cops standing over him. In one such dream he asked the cop to let him use his cell phone to tell his sponsor about the incident (When you can make only one call, whom do you call? Your sponsor or your lawyer?)

Recovery means that you are starting to take care of business, i.e. family, friends, legal problems etc. It also means giving back and becoming a useful part of the community. (This book tells of such incidents in which recovering Thomas has practiced this principle.)

All of us, not just recovering addicts, are judged every day by how we handle our good and our bad fortunes. In March 2000 Thomas was presented with a double-edged fortune: he won the 28-million dollar jackpot in the Texas Lottery. From the next morning on, I got phone calls from people who knew my treatment connection with Thomas, and Thomas got a great many such calls. All the phone calls and e-mails essentially asked the same question: Is Thomas still clean and sober? "Come on," they said, "A coke addict with 28 million dollars – you gotta to be kidding? Or "I'm worried for him."

Well, unlike many lottery winners ~ who are in serious trouble in less than a year – Thomas continues to handle the stress of that challenge by living the life he has learned to live, and by applying the principles of the program. He chooses to stay clean and sober by saying "I am not the mistakes of my past – I am the person I have become;" and "my wealth is not my money – my wealth is my recovery." Also, even though Thomas is now a wealthy man, he continues to learn profound lessons from the overdose suicides of some of his old friends, people he had known intimately, people who could not refrain from "just one more time," setting up a situation in which their drug-impaired Frontal lobe was overpowered by their Neanderthal Middle lobe.

I like to look at recovery as a process of re-building the life skill areas one by one, using the Steps of the program as the rungs of the recovery ladder. With your feet firmly planted on the first rung of the ladder, you leave your "bottom" and keep your eyes and your ears on your sponsors, your therapists and other positive role models. And from the top (the 12th) rung of the ladder you carry the message to those alcoholics/addicts/co-dependents/the community who are still suffering.

Thomas starts this book with the statement: "This story could have turned out quite differently." He is right of course. If in 1983 he had been an addict who still had lots of money and his athletic skills, America would have witnessed another prolonged TV trial – a network media circus/psychodrama/court room soap opera – starring a famous athlete and a mixed-up nation. His safety net of high-priced lawyers and cheering fans would have saved him once more. But over time he would have gotten sicker and lost it all.

Thomas ends the book with the note: "To be continued."

When I asked him how the book of his life will continue, he said "I can choose to stay clean, and my hope is that I can keep on doing it."

"In Control", is a document about an individual recovery that every alcoholic, addict and families touched by this disease should read.

Joseph A. Pursch, MD.
Psychiatric Consultant
Sober Living by the Sea, Newport Beach, CA

"Every experience in my life for over twenty (20) years has a direct link to my recovery from alcoholism and crack addiction. This is who I've become. I function on certain principles as a way of life. My life and story therein is redundant because every step I take and every act is tied to decisions made while clean and sober, one day at a time. Therefore this habit is a chosen lifestyle.

So, over and over again, I tie everything to my being clean and sober. Forgive my redundancy."

Thomas Henderson

INTRODUCTION

"When we walk to the edge of all we have, and take the step into the darkness of the unknown, we must believe one of two things will happen... there will be something solid for us to stand on, or we will be taught to fly."
S. Martin Edges

Around noontime on October 15, 1986, I was saying goodbye to the State of California Correctional System, Norco Branch, and to prisoner number C-87983. I was saying hello to the greatest challenge I'd ever face, living a sober life. The second half of my life. The Sober Bowl. I was starting over, totally over, with little money, no job and no prospect for one, and really, really scared.

Seven months prior to being sentenced to prison, I made a decision to try sobriety as a lifestyle. I had prepared myself for staying off alcohol and drugs, and changing the way I functioned. Fear often overwhelmed me because I didn't know whether I had the strength, courage, or faith to do it, or whether I would make the right choices, or whether, in a hundred lifetimes, I could ever live down my sordid past.

I am an alcoholic and a drug addict. I did a lot of shit to many people self included, for too many years. Never knowing that sobriety was an option I relentlessly lied, cheated, stole, bullied, and controlled.

When I got into trouble most thought I was an immoral dog. I got busted and charged with sexual misconduct. The shame itself almost killed me.

I had a horrific history and an uncertain future. Sometimes I felt as though my questions, doubts, fears, and shame were going to devour me.

1

Most of those feelings had to do with what you thought of me rather than what I thought of me. Just how was I going to pull this off? How was I supposed to stay sober one day at a time when today was uncomfortable?

It is now almost twenty years since that prison cell door opened. It's been over 20 years since I've had a drink or a drug. This book is about the solutions, change, and comfort I've found in the Sober Bowl. It's about a man who found his inner child by looking inside for love. About a sick man who found a way of living that's better than anything he'd ever had or seen.

New questions, fresh doubts come along. That just means life's in session. Those searing, frightful questions I had as I started over have gone away. There was hard work, soul searching and long lingering fear. And there was struggle, plenty of it. But gratitude and a glow I never thought was possible have supplanted the struggle.

I'm a pragmatic guy. I deal in facts. One fact there's no escaping is that sobriety works. Sobriety is also an option.

Sobriety, for me, is everything. On November 8, 1983, I admitted, surrendered, and accepted that I was an alcoholic and drug addict. I admitted to other character defects and shortcomings as I got better. To admit it was one thing, but to say it out loud among strangers was the difficult part. Ego, self will, fear, pride and denial were but a few of the committee members in my head telling me "It isn't so." Luckily, I said it, I believed it, and I accepted it. My name is Thomas Henderson and I'm an alcoholic and drug addict. When I found myself among strangers who had the same afflictions as mine and I admitted to them that I was indeed one of them... I was finally home. I was home among recovering people. Like a lost puppy, I wandered through life not knowing where I belonged, wagging my tail at shit I didn't even understand. Didn't know who I was, what I was, what feelings were or how I should act. At thirty years old, I found my team, my home. I found recovery from alcohol and other drugs.

It wasn't the Dallas Cowboys. It was recovering alcoholics and addicts. These folks taught me that on a schedule of "one day at a time," I could and would be happy, joyous and free if I worked for it. I've been working. I was exposed to my feelings by listening to feelings expressed by others. I was introduced to honesty by hearing lies from a liar: me. I found God by accepting a Higher Power in my life. My life before recovery was like working on a high wire without a net. Absent was a relationship with a higher power. I didn't know how to live, be a friend or how to treat a woman. Fortunately, I realized that a new life in recovery could be an opportunity rather than a sentence to a square-assed life.

If I had looked at recovery any other way, I'm sure I wouldn't still be sober. Listening to others rather than myself has been the single most important lesson I've learned. I decided that I had done a fine job of screwing up my life and the lives of many others with my thinking.

It was time to learn all that I didn't know. I knew nothing. With that attitude, I was open to change and growth. Change is remarkable. The only pain I've had with change has been my resistance to it. I'm convinced I was functioning on human power. I went as far as I could go on that fuel with nothing but fumes at the end.

I was godless, amoral, angry, afraid, confused, and without questions, a liar. I had these character defects and shortcomings without knowing what to call them. I believe this is how one lives until they learn how to live.

I did the best I could. That's all anybody can do. I did the best I could with what tools and information I had. When I break my anonymity and admit to folks on airplanes, buses, golf courses, bars and hotels that I'm an alcoholic and addict, it's a prideful disclosure. I'm serious.

When I think of a recovering person, I think of change, courage, commitment, honesty, credibility and a person who is learning how to live. We learn how to treat ourselves so we could then know how to treat others. More and more, alcoholism and all addictions are touching all people and all families. Slowly, people are giving recovery the patience, respect and credibility it deserves.

Addiction recovery is becoming a normal and common part of all American families. It's because America and the world are pretty much dysfunctional places to grow up in. Whether it's drugs, alcohol, co-dependency, food or sex addiction, depression, abuse, incest, or lying, it's with all of us all day long. I didn't know that sobriety was an option until I was thirty years old.

I believe everyone should have access to this simple idea. Too many of us grow up believing that in order to have fun in life, you must have a drink or a drug. This belief is killing individuals and family systems by the thousands.

I know today that some of us are allergic to alcohol and drugs. Today, I know I'm one of those folks. Drugs and alcohol don't work for me. I've invested a bunch of emotional sweat into my recovery, and the evidence is plain to see; the investment has reaped me a damn windfall. I've got a new life. When I first got sober, one thing was promised to me: If I didn't drink or use drugs, my life would get better. I looked at the mess my life had become and I said, "What the heck I'll try it."

I was about the most hopeless case I've ever known. A lost cause, and then some. Plenty of people had given up on me. Even I had given up on me. I was lucky that I didn't die. If I had died before my recovery, it would have been from alcoholism, pure and simple.

The promise was fulfilled. Where there was once hopelessness, now there is hope. Where there was despair, there is contentment. If drugs, alcohol, sex, food, relationships, or whatever are kicking your butt and the hurt is too much and it seems useless and hopeless and worthless, please hear me: You can change and feel good about yourself. Recovery is real! If I can change my life the way I have, I'm convinced anyone can.

That's why I'm writing this book. My first book was about the problem. This book is about the solutions. No matter how bad you think your case is, you too can recover to a place of freedom and happiness. Why am I writing this book? To paraphrase Thoreau, I write about myself because there is no one else I know as well. Fortunately, I am confined to the narrowness of my own experience. That's all I've got. That's all I share. My experience is my knowledge.

Today my life is rich. I'm green and growing, not ripe and rotten. Life is meaningful now. It's so much simpler and healthier than it has ever been and it's just getting better and better.

And so now, all those questions and doubts that descended on me the day the door opened have been answered. Now I know. I know that every step has had a purpose, a wonderful purpose. I had to endure a lot of suffering on my way to recovery. But I have to tell you one thing — all the pain, the struggling, the suffering, the heartache, the seemingly endless battles, ALL OF IT, has been worth it.

CHAPTER ONE

WHEN DID I KNOW?

In 1979, I was clearly addicted to everything, didn't matter what it was. My life consisted of doing drugs, drinking, taking pills, and whatever else I could abuse. Why? I had grown up in a dysfunctional family, and now I was totally dysfunctional too. I had no idea of how to live. I was beyond sad. I was pathetic. Forget the fame and wealth. I was living in a nightmare. I've often wondered how such a thing could happen when, on the surface, life had never been better. Anyone looking on probably thought I had it all. In recovery, I've discovered the answer was pretty simple. I had everything I wanted, but nothing I needed. I was starting to acknowledge that I had a problem. Doesn't mean I did anything about it. I believe all of us who finally recover knew we had problems for a long time.

Eventually, I sunk much lower but I didn't know how to fix what was wrong. So I was a strong man and stuck it out for as long as I could — and almost died in the process. My true bottom would not come until four years after my first notion of a problem. If I'd recognized my problem earlier, I would've saved myself a few hundred thousand dollars, a felony conviction and a prison term. But it wasn't to be.

There's no underestimating the power of an addict's denial. More than anything else, denial is what makes drug addiction and alcoholism the killer diseases they are. Denial is as much a symptom of this sickness as a runny nose and boogers are to a cold or cocaine use. We wall ourselves off from reality, because often the reality is too painful. We will go to whatever lengths necessary to avoid accepting or acknowledging that we have lost control. We will lie, run, point fingers, hide, and have temper tantrums. You name it. An addict's capacity for self-deception is virtually unlimited. You actually con and lie to yourself.

People said I was fast on the football field, but damn, that wasn't anything compared to how I ran from my addictions, my shame, and my misery. I ran because I didn't know what else to do. There are a million rationalizations. You tell yourself, "I can stop any time I want to." Or, "I'm just going through a hard time right now." Or, "If they would stop fucking with me and screwing me over, everything would be fine." Your disease pipes a tape into your brain, and the tape never stops. It's them, not me. I put a freebase pipe in my mouth and never stopped. It says, over and over, "There isn't any problem here." It tells you, "What's wrong with feeling good now and then? What's wrong with a little escape? I'm in control here. Here now, have another. You'll feel better..."

You keep hearing the message and you want desperately to believe it. So you do. That's what I call 'human power'. It's some weak shit. You keep using. And even though on a deeper level you know something is awfully wrong, your life keeps heading directly down the toilet. A rush and then a flush. You're shit. It got so I was denying the existence of every complication in my life. Got a problem. Punt it. It will go away. Light the pipe. Use the blissful ignorance method of handling it.

Late in my using days, the IRS wanted to talk to and audit me. They sent me a yellow envelop asking/warning me to repay and comply. I got at least half dozen of these yellow things, maybe more, and I never did anything more than throw them away. Barely gave it a thought. Nobody can catch me. Nobody can run with me. I'm bulletproof. Or so I thought. Pass the pipe. It wasn't a calculated risk so much as the work of a diseased mind. The yellow envelopes stopped, but only after the IRS seized my mother's house (which I bought for her and left in my name), evicted her, and auctioned my Super Bowl ring and a bunch of other prized possessions. I was held responsible for my actions. Denial was beginning to hurt.

It chills me to think about my denial. I pulled all kinds of stuff. Sick, crazy stuff. But you didn't dare try to tell me I was out of control. You didn't dare. In Houston, after the Oilers had released me in 1980, I'd spent all my money freebasing, and I was out of coke. So, I gave this dealer my full-length beaver coat for seven grams of cocaine. A $4,000 coat for a few hundred dollars of shit. Addiction makes you stupid as hell. It's dope.

I was at his apartment with him and his girlfriend. The place was on the third floor. The complex must have been a big dealer haven. It had security guards, alarms, iron gates, cameras, German Shepherds, and a few other features to discourage criminals. Should've been named Nostril Village or Boogerland or something.

We smoked and snorted and they'd been going for a couple days, and finally they said they wanted to go to bed. I saw them take Quaaludes. They asked me to leave. "Okay, thanks for the stuff. Good night." Before I left, I slipped away and unlocked the sliding glass door by their terrace. My plan was to hole up in a motel for a couple of hours, finish the rest of the cocaine I had, then come back when they were conked out and get some of theirs. So what's a little breaking and entering between friends? And so what that the guy's place was stocked with enough weapons to arm a small militia. I had to have his cocaine. That was the only issue on the table. I was out of money, so it was time for plan B: robbery.

About 4:00 a.m., I called and let the phone ring forty times. No answer. Perfect. I drove over, parked my car, then climbed up over this 20-foot iron fence. There was barbed wire at the top. I ripped my hands up. Now I was in the complex. The guard dogs started barking. I didn't know where the guards or cameras were. These were rent-a-cops anyway.

I was hiding in a bush, sweat pouring out of me, heart pounding, hands bleeding. I was afraid. I was thinking, "Is one of these dogs gonna bite my ass off tonight?" I pushed the fear aside. No German Shepherd was stopping this mission. Cocaine was on my mind. I sneaked over to their section and hoisted myself up, barely reaching the iron railing they had on the terrace. One slip and I would have been a heap on the ground and the mutts and guards would have been all over my butt.

I made it to the third floor. The dogs were barking louder now. A neighbor's light came on. Too late, I was entering. I slid over to the door. It was just as I had left it. I walked in and called their names, trying to wake them. No chance of that though. They were comatose.

I took the freebase pipe and rocks from their nightstand and smoked in their kitchen as they slept. If they had awakened, I would have been a dead man. Didn't matter. I smoked a little more. I ransacked the living room and kitchen, found a few more ounces and then exited. I took the stairs. A couple of days later, the guy called me up and said, "Hey, guess what, man? While me and my woman were sleeping, somebody came in here and robbed us." "No shit," I said.

7

Denial obscures everything. Your thinking becomes totally warped. You get paranoid. People in recovery sometimes call it 'stinking thinking.' My thinking really stunk. Ripe, Grade A shit. Like most alcoholics, I was convinced I was Mr. Indestructible. There was no way Tangueray or cocaine or marijuana or anything else was ever going to get the better of me. Hooked? Powerless? Get the hell out of here! Hey, I was a professional athlete. Will power was as much a part of my uniform as my helmet. I got to the NFL by rising above pain and pushing myself to my physical limits. My body was lean and strong. My will was supreme. I believed with everything I had that it was beyond the realm of possibility. Everybody thinks that.

My working definition of alcoholism was that it's a terrible thing that happens to other people. My life was unmanageable. But I was still running. You don't have to look far to see the tragic wreckage of denial. Don Rogers (a former Cleveland Brown) died of cocaine poisoning. So did Len Bias and David Croudip. And yet, hardly a week or month goes by that we don't hear of a positive test, drunk driving or suspension in pro sports. How about Stanley Wilson bolting from the Cincinnati Bengal's the night before the Super Bowl for cocaine, throwing a career into the trash can in the process. I can identify.

Hadn't they heard the news? Cocaine is killing people! Any more questions? That shit can happen to anyone... including you. And what about the relentless parade of DWI cases you hear about? Hadn't those people heard about Bruce Kimball, the Olympic diver who's now the Olympic inmate, who killed with his car because of alcohol? Hadn't they heard about the thousands of people dying every year because somebody got behind the wheel loaded or a little impaired. One drink can impair you, you know. Of course they heard. Their denial did a beautiful job. Convinced them, "That won't happen to me. I can handle it." It happens to other people.

Another pro athlete and recovering alcoholic was telling me how his denial kept him drinking for years after the problem became apparent. Drinking and using cost him his baseball career, his family, and about $500,000. "I thought to be an alcoholic, you had to be wearing two raincoats and living on the streets or under a bridge," he said. It's supposed to be something that only happen to skid row types. If you're a respectable sort with a mortgage and a microwave and nice lawn furniture, you're supposed to be safe. Sorry. That's plain bullshit and the worst kind of denial.

A football player and friend of mine went into a 30-day rehabilitation center. At first, he was sure he wasn't an alcoholic because he wasn't missing practice or going on extended drinking binges or falling off barstools at 3 a.m. nightly. He was a classic weekend warrior, a blackout drinker. The most dangerous breed of boozer there is. Weekend warriors are usually loud, violent and unpredictable. They're convinced they've got nothing to worry about because they report to work on Monday morning and pay their bills on time. This guy came up with all kinds of rationalizations even as his life was getting wrapped more and more tightly around the bottle. "I'm functioning fine," he said. "I pay my bills. You don't see me guzzling liquor in the morning. I don't have any problem."

The prerequisites for the diagnosis of alcoholism are not so much how much or how often you drink. The question is what happens when you do drink? Is it creating problems in your life? Do you use it to get away from your troubles for awhile? I sure did. Is it a compulsion you feel powerless over? Is the compulsion getting worse?

I had my own rationalizations when my drinking got out of control. I was totally broke and had hustled, borrowed and swindled from all the sources I could hit. I couldn't afford coke right then. I needed a more economical way to get off. Alcohol was down the street. I was with a management recruiting firm doing a lot of liquor-lubricated two hour lunches with the coat and tie set, and a lot of happy hour time a few hours later. What a breeding ground for alcoholism. Most nights, I'd go home when the happy hour traffic cleared up, usually around 2 a.m. Don't want to mess with traffic. I'd have a minimum of twenty Tangueray and tonics in me by then.

A drinking problem? I would never stumble or fall. I felt I was stronger than alcohol. That was all there was to it. "I'm into freebasing," I told myself. This stuff is Kool-Aid compared to that. I'm in total control.

I went into treatment for the first time in 1981. I was the first NFL player to go public with my cocaine problem. It was a few days after Super Bowl XV, the Eagles and the Raiders in New Orleans. I had seen Charlie Jackson, the NFL director of security, during the telecast. My freebasing was out of hand. The next day, I called Jackson and Rozelle at a hotel in New Orleans. I wedged the phone between my shoulder and ear. I had to. I needed my hands for my bic lighter and freebase pipe. I could not stop using long enough to talk. Couldn't really talk.

Sometimes my lips would move but no words would or could come out. Cocaine paralysis. Crack and coke addicts know what I'm talking about. My lungs were hot with smoke. I could barely talk. My words were gurgling, nearly incoherent. This is Thomas Henderson. I'm freebasing cocaine right now. I can't stop. I need help! Please help me! Pain and fear enabled me to reach out for help that day. "You hold on," he said. "We'll get right back to you. "Two days later, I entered treatment at a center in Scottsdale, Arizona.

I stayed in the center for more than sixty days, and it did me no good at all. It wasn't their fault, though. It was mine. I went in because my denial was slowly getting chipped away, and even I could see I wasn't going to be in this world for long if things kept up. But I also went in with the firm conviction that my problem was cocaine. Just cocaine, nothing else.

They would talk to me about total abstinence, about how if you were hooked on one mind-altering drug, you need to stay away from all of them. If you just switch substances, you'll wind up in the same shit a little farther down the line. I didn't want to hear it. I had a hidden agenda. Just get me off cocaine. My problem is with cocaine. Period. I was there for damage control that's all. They would show films and have lectures about different substances, and I'd totally ignore the parts about alcohol, marijuana and the rest. It was only when they started talking about cocaine that I'd listen up. "Okay, here's my part," I'd say. That denial, stupidity and hidden agenda caused me to fail yet again.

This facility would let me have four or eight hour passes, and I would go out and have a few beers and smoke grass, and come back and tell them my pass was a success because I didn't use cocaine. I was doing it my way. It didn't work.

Maybe the other patients there had to be totally abstinent. Their problem was probably bigger than mine was. I felt all I needed was a way to stay off cocaine. Nobody ever punished me or took me to task for any of this. I just went along using and doing my thing.

When I left that program, I had a friend bring my car and some grass to ride with. As we left Scottsdale getting on the highway headed east toward Texas, I rolled a big, fat joint of marijuana. I lit it, took a big hit off of it and said to my friend in a held breath, "I believe this program's gonna work."

Stay off cocaine, stick with just the other stuff, and things will be just fine. I'm no alcoholic. I had tried to tell them that a million times. And marijuana? Hell, the only thing that ever did to me was make me eat a family size bag of Oreo's. No big deal. Yeah, I was sure everything would be fine.

The pink cloud era lasted a week. By then, I was back freebasing, beginning a spiral downward to my ultimate bottom. It never occurred to me to stop drinking and using other drugs. My underlying disease, my craving and compulsion to use drugs was raging on. My misery, defectiveness, fear, shame, and guilt were all intact. For two more years, I drank, smoked dope, and freebased. My existence became a sick, destructive whirl that included nothing but ingesting chemicals. I was out of control.

I see now that I could have spent six hundred days in that facility in Scottsdale and it wouldn't have made a bit of difference. I wasn't ready to accept help. I was overwhelmed with denial, thought the doctors and therapists were a bunch of meddling alarmists. I understand anyone who feels like this upon entering treatment. I wasn't powerless over drugs and alcohol, and I would promptly cuss anyone out who suggested otherwise.

Recovery for most alcoholics doesn't come until they totally accept that they are powerless. There are a few who may be able to get jolted enough by a close call or an arrest or a confrontation with their boss or family: "Clean up your act or we're gone," to begin getting sober before things get too ugly. Seems most of us get our asses kicked real good before we surrender. We need to have our denial, the entire arsenal of excuses and rationalizations, blown to bits. Coming face-to-face with the terrifying truth we've been trying so hard to avoid is tough. But until we accept the hard, cold fact that we're in trouble and need help, nothing's going to get better. No one can want it for us. We have to want it for ourselves.

The absolute lowest point in my life came in November 1983. I was freebasing cocaine, drunk, and not far from dead. My nerves were totally shot. My life was worthless. No morals, no God, and very much alone. My clothes were dirty, tattered, and smelly and all I cared about was the next pipeful. The final crushing and shaming blow came after I'd been arrested and charged with one count of sexual assault and two counts of false imprisonment. I was smoking crack with two teenage girls. It was wrong. I was wrong. I will never make an excuse for that incident. It happened. But for an addict like me, that behavior didn't seem out of the ordinary. Clear environmental insanity at the time.

I was accused of other things that I didn't do. That's not my shame. The lies were all over the news and in the papers, and I was portrayed as the lowest form of life, which at that time wasn't far from wrong.

It's been over twenty years since that horrible incident and I've always wanted to set the record straight, but who would have believed me back then? Enough time had to pass before I would have any credibility. Today, I finally have a chance to set a twenty-year-old lie straight. I'm not trying to defend myself. I don't have to anymore. The simple truth is that I'm free and at peace with myself now. Unlike most celebrities who claim to be innocent...I was guilty as charged – one count of sexual assault and two counts of false imprisonment.

Yes, I smoked crack with two teenagers. That was par for my course. Yes, I made a grave mistake in judgment. But, NO, I did not then, nor have I ever had sex with anyone in a wheelchair! It was the Long Beach police department and the press who fabricated and suggested that story. It never happened! What really happened was bad enough. What you thought happened hurt me more than you'll ever know. I did time in prison and paid my debt to society. I've carried that miserable shame with me for what seems like an eternity. Today, I give it back. In spite of it all, I survived. I survived the pain, the heartache, the heartbreak, the lies, my behavior, EVERYTHING! I was still wrong. All of this was dark and sordid. I had never knowingly or consciously sexually assaulted anyone in my entire life. And I had had a lot of sex. Crack wacked me out. I was crazy – known crack behavior.

The following day, I woke up and I didn't know what it was, but this bleakness descended on me. This utter bleakness and it wouldn't lift. I was alone in my apartment in Long Beach, California, waiting for my attorney to come by to get me into treatment again. Slowly but surely, the weight of all my self-destruction was sinking my rocky boat. I felt like a waste.

Defective. Ashamed. Alone. How could it have come to this? How is it possible to feel this much pain? I wanted to die, but didn't have the nerve or courage to do it. You know what they say; suicide is a permanent solution to a temporary problem.

I was huddled in the corner. The room was cold and bare. I was sucking on the pipe, sucking desperately trying to flee reality, getting nowhere fast. My head was down. So was my life. The phone was ringing and ringing. I never answered it. Who would call? Who would want to? Leave me alone. Let me die. Please, just let me die.

I felt hollow. I picked up my head and looked at the state of my life. A box spring sat in the middle of the room. That was my furniture. The closet was empty. Clothes were heaped on the floor. They were dirty. Next to them was a pile of football trophies, plaques, my Newsweek cover, awards, and other momentous. The walls were gray and empty. The place was filthy and so was I. I hadn't showered in at least three days. The repugnant stench that emerged like thunder from my abandoned body would have killed ten horses. Everywhere I looked, I saw nothing but despair and hopelessness. Ragged remnants of a life that once was. From the Super Bowl to this? Why? How? Then, I didn't know. I just hurt. Intense, unrelenting hurt had taken control. I wept in my pain.

My attorney arrived and found me huddled in my bedroom wired out of my mind. I had bailed out of jail and bought more cocaine and had been smoking all day long. When I saw him, I began to cry. I didn't know what to do. The pain inside was heavier than any I'd ever known in my life. Everything was assaulting me at once. I had had it. I kept crying and whining this mournful whine, and whenever I would pull myself together for a moment, I would stick the pipe in my mouth. It was all I knew.

"Thomas, you're disgusting. Get up!" he said. "Let me finish this little bit," I said. I sucked one more time and the pipe was done. He walked over to me, glared at my condition and me. He grabbed the pipe from my hand and then he fired it against the wall. It shattered. No one was going to sweep it up. No one ever swept here. This was a dump. I lived here.

My mind began to fill, nonstop, with all the wreckage that had brought me to this point. It was like credits of a movie, a horror movie, rolling on before me. Some of my friends in recovery have told me about their bottoms, calling it their moment of clarity. Me, I call it my moment of "Thomas, don't you see? Don't you see what this disease has wrought, what your life has become, what you need to do before you do anything else? Don't you see that it was the cocaine? And the marijuana? And the alcohol?" It was the worst day of my thirty year old life, but in a sense, it was also the best because it had to happen just the way it happened. If I was going to change, it had to happen.

It was November 5, 1983. I call it the day I saw, the day I understood what the problem was. I saw where alcohol and drugs had landed me. I realized I needed help, a lot of it, and fast.

I will never forget how it felt to be hopeless and helpless and a total slave to alcohol, drugs, and a dysfunctional life. I won't allow myself to ever forget. Since the moment my attorney took the pipe from my dirty, blackened hands and flung it away, I have not taken any cocaine, crack, grass, alcohol or any other mind-altering substance.

The day of my rebirth was November 8, 1983. On that day, I found the willingness and desire to give sobriety a chance. My attorney took me to a treatment center in Orange, California. I had no money and no insurance. All I had was my name, "Hollywood." They took me in because a doctor named Joseph Pursch gave me the gift of free treatment. He looked me squarely in the eye when we met. He said, "You're Thomas Henderson?" "Yes," I said. "Thomas, I will take you into this hospital, but if you make one mistake, you're out of here." He paused and said, "Now, you're an alcoholic and an addict, is that right?" I said, "Well, no Doc. I'm really just a cocaine abuser. That's what my main problem is with." One more time, denial was trying to sabotage me. He said, "You have no insurance and no money?" "No." "Aren't you an alcoholic?" I said, "Yeah. Yeah! You're damn right. I'm an alcoholic." I wanted to stay.

Whatever he wanted me to say was fine by me. The teacher had appeared. The student was ready. Joe Pursch literally saved my life. If I had been turned away that day, God only knows where I'd be today. This time was totally different from my first go around in treatment. Gone were any half-baked notions of learning to drink or use in moderation, or of believing I merely needed to deal with my cocaine addiction and that would suffice. I had given that approach a try and it had been a raging failure. I was a broken man with a broken spirit. I was ready to listen. God, was I ready. I pulled the cotton out of my ears and stuffed it in my mouth.

Before then I don't think I had ever used the word 'sober' in my entire life. I had no sense of what getting sober was about, and I had no real sense of having a disease. I knew I had something wrong with me. I didn't know what I had. I just knew that if these people could help me get well, I was going to be a willing subject.

I was ready. I had had enough. For the first time in my life, I was crying and pleading for help. I was in a strange, new place with counselors and doctors and other people I had never seen before, and they were going to have to be my lifeline. I needed them in a way I had never needed another human being before. I had to trust their intentions for me. It was the only way to deal with the terror I felt.

It was tough to trust the process. Even tougher to process the trust. I knew I had to get better. Had to stop using everything, or my life was literally over. This time, I was ready. And that's why I was so afraid. I was ready, but was I able?

Now I see very clearly how your prospects for recovery are intertwined totally with the frame of mind you bring into it. My greatest fear as my Care Unit treatment began was that they would kick me out. I'd been kicked out of everywhere else I'd ever been. Whenever one of the staff would pass by or look at me, I'd freeze with the horrible thought that at any moment, someone was going to ask me to leave. The thought of leaving was mortifying.

I had no place to go. That was clear to me. It also inspired my recovery. When I got there, I had nowhere else to go. For me, the outside world was a place where I could not function. When you have nowhere to go, you usually have a chance of getting and staying sober.

I was more than worried that I wouldn't be able to stick with their program. Ego, pride, and denial were on their mark, ready, and set to go. I had spent most of a lifetime challenging authority. From my childhood, to college, to the Cowboys, I was one of the all-time greatest rule benders. I always wanted to do it my way. I'd charm you or curse you or lie to you or do whatever I needed to do so I would get my way. If it were a black tie affair, I'd wear a red T-shirt. I had to be different.

I was always creating trouble. I took a strange pride in getting away with things. That's not normal. It was about some powerful childhood stuff, I see now. I craved attention, wanted to be special. I wanted to mat-

15

ter and if that meant being team hell raiser, well, that was okay. Attention is attention.

So there I was Mr. Rule Bender, in a rigid place where things were spelled out and rules were not to be fooled with. It was their way or the highway. At the very beginning, when I was still on Valium in the detox unit, I tried things my way. They had a rule about turning off the television at 11:00 p.m. In my best sabotage effort, I tried to get kicked out. "Fuck that," I said. "If you turn off this TV, I'm walking out of here!" They let me leave it on. They let me stay. It's a damn good thing because I had nowhere to go.

After a few days, I came down and calmed down. I was afraid to break another rule. I'd already been allowed one more mistake than Dr. Putsch had said I would get. After that, I was obedient. For once, I wasn't looking to be a special case. The stakes were too high for any more bullshit rebellion. I needed this place. Bad.

The treatment process itself was anything but easy. I had been destroying myself for a long time. I had no idea where or how to begin the rebuilding, no idea of how to live. I was angry. Angry at what I had become and what I had lost. The fog was still dense. I just kept thinking, "How will I ever find my way out?" I also thought, "What the hell is the use? Why even bother? What is there to get sober for?" The present was too dark, the past too ugly. Reality was sordid. I riffled through my head for some sliver of hope to hang on to, for a reason to believe things could get better. I found none, and yet there must have been something buried somewhere because I didn't walk out the door and I didn't stick cocaine up my nose and I didn't kill myself. As much as I loathed myself, a message, a truth, was sinking in, however slowly.

Miracles do happen. God entered my life. Early on, I went to 12-step support group meetings. It was in a hospital cafeteria, with maybe fifty people. There were long, linoleum tables and bright lights overhead, and things were just starting when somebody got up and asked if there were any newcomers on hand. A few people raised their hands. I looked around. I squirmed in my seat. Cautiously, I edged up my hand. They asked the newcomers to stand up and introduce themselves. One by one, they stood. "My name is Joe and I'm an alcoholic." "My name is Diane and I'm an addict and alcoholic." Now it was my turn. I stood up. I was anxious. Uncomfortable. I could feel the shame overwhelming me. I didn't want to say it. Didn't want to accept it or admit it. My mind raced with more dread – if I don't do this, I'm out of here.

I used to be this rich, famous linebacker in the National Football League and now I was standing in front of a room full of strangers and feeling weak and beaten and helpless. And I was exactly where I was supposed to be. I wanted to run, but knew there was no place to run to. I knew intuitively that I was in the right place, even if I still didn't want to be there. The room was still. My head was cloudy. And then the words came to me. Acceptance came and I let it. I wasn't thinking anymore, I was feeling. It was as though I was automated, following the crowd. The words just came. I heard my voice: "My name is Thomas, and I'm an alcoholic and drug addict."

There, it was done. I sat down and I felt okay. The ceiling hadn't fallen, no one laughed, and nobody was saying, "You're too disgusting and we don't want to help you." I looked around and I saw nodding heads and small, knowing smiles. I saw these strangers looking at me, and the looks were saying, "Welcome. You've come to the right place. You're home."

I've spoken those words a few thousand times by now. It has become very easy, back then it was a huge breakthrough. I was sick and I was saying so, with no hedging or excuses or extenuating circumstances. It was the official burial of my denial. No more running or hiding. No more lies.

When the arrest happened and I was charged, I knew I had to change or die. At this point, while under the influence of crack, I knew I was capable of murder. When I realized that, I knew I had to quit getting high.

DR. JOSEPH A. PURSCH
(Psychiatric Consultant, Sober Living by the Sea, Newport Beach, CA)

I went to the hospital to meet Thomas the morning he was admitted Right away he started on a grandiose plan with me. We were going to be partners He just couldn't fathom what was going on except he had been in a county jail and now he was in a hospital That's when we had our one-on-one confrontation

You know he's a very bright man. I could see that, but he was still toxic. He couldn't understand what rehab was all about. He talked black talk to me. Like, 'Doctor, you're jivin' me. You're giving me all this 'whitey' talk that don't make no sense."

I tried to tell him that "if you are sober ~ anything is possible, but if you're not sober, nothing was possible." He latched on to that later, but he couldn't get it right then. I realized I couldn't get through to this man in a medical or academic sense. So I did a word picture for him.

"Look at it this way," I said. "You could conceivably become (and I popped up one finger after another as I was talking) the first black (my thumb went up) ex-convict (I lifted my index finger) former athlete and recovering alcoholic... (now I was down to my little finger and it popped up when I said),.. President of the United States, you dumb shit!"

By now I was getting a little impatient. I got carried away, which is why I resorted to "dumb shit" He interrupted me and said, "Yeah, I could do that. That could happen. "

I said, "Wait a minute. Sure, you can do that but only if you are clean and sober. Let's imagine now that you get elected and you are in the White House, and you are clean and sober ~ but you decide to go back to drinking gin, or do some coke. You know what would happen if you are the President and you start using drugs again?"

That's when I became impressed with this man. He cut me off in mid-air and said, "Oh, yeah, I see what you mean. If I'm in the White House and started using that stuff again, they will impeach my black ass."

I said, "Well, I'm glad you said that. I couldn't say that As a doctor, I am supposed to be dignified; and as a white man I can't use words like those. But that is the general idea."

He probably didn't hear anything else I said that morning, but he did latch on to that part.

*We treated him for the next 56 days, and he learned remarkably well
He learned so fast that by the time he got to prison he knew enough. I 'd
talk to him from prison every week at first. He'd call long distance collect
(You know they can't make a call from prison unless it's collect, and for a
good reason)*

*We talked about the psychiatrists he was seeing in prison. I had to agree
with him that he knew more about rehab and addictions by then than these
psychiatrists who only knew about addiction what they learned in medical
school, which wasn't very much.*

*I sent him an occasional shipment of self-help books. I also talked two
or three times with the psychiatrists who were treating him, and that kept
them off his back. They were suspecting all kinds of diagnostic possibilities*

*I also knew if this man could stay sober, he would be safe in prison. The
doctors who were treating him were glad to cover his butt and let him do
his rehab. In that way, Thomas was exemplifying what people in my field
call self-help. He helped himself in prison by not screwing himself over. He
didn't use the drugs that were available in prison.*

*All I did was help Thomas help himself. Nobody saves people like
Thomas. They save themselves by applying the lessons they are learning.*

*Some doctors like to go around and say, 'I saved so and so..." Some
sponsors like to say, 'I sobered up Thomas..." All of that is bullshit People
who are bright as this guy, they either grab the ball and run and save themselves or they figure the ball you passed them is not worth having, then they
throw the ball out of the game and willfully run on their own until the disease tackles them again.*

*Today, we still talk occasionally because in my practice some of the peo-
ple who get well become friends or acquaintances (The people who don't get
well avoid me. They don't call me anymore. If I call them they don't return
my calls.)*

*One of my recent contacts with Thomas was second hand. I did a semi-
nar in Germany at a rehab center in a place called Bad Herrenhalb near
Karisruhe. When I got there, people asked if I knew a guy named
Hollywood Henderson? I said, you mean Thomas Henderson? They said
yes, and I asked how do you know about him?*

*They said, well, he was here and he spoke a couple of years ago. They
still remember him in Germany. I thought what a small world, and how the
cycles complete themselves. If you are an addict, people also remember the
good things you do.*

*"Every man, woman and child on earth should know
that never drinking alcohol or using any drugs is an option
and choice they should exercise."*

CHAPTER TWO

ROAD LESS TRAVELED

This story could have turned out quite differently.

I had spent seven months among the sorriest collection of drunks and drug addicts you could imagine – ex-drunks and ex-drug addicts, bar flies who would exchange sex for gin fizzes and corporate executives who had sat in their own body waste on street corners begging for quarters. That sorry collection included me.

I was Thomas "Hollywood" Henderson, former Pro Bowl linebacker for the Dallas Cowboys, a man who played in three Super Bowls and had been cheered by millions, who'd had pockets full of cash and women throwing themselves at me offering to do whatever I desired. In the end, all I desired was to free-base cocaine, over and over and over again, until there was little of the "Hollywood" left.

My football career was gone. So were the fancy homes and the full-length furs. The money and big flashy diamond rings I'd bought were gone. The rich and famous no longer invited me to their homes. "Hollywood" Henderson himself was gone, and in his place was just Thomas H., alcoholic and drug addict, spending a quiet weekend at a 12-step retreat in Palm Springs, California, struggling to find sobriety one day at a time as a lifelong commitment.

I had been sober for seven tenuous months, ever since I'd been arrested for sexual misconduct. I was traveling with a friend, Tom, a fellow recovering drug addict who was having a hard time staying clean. The next day, June 10, 1984, would be my last day of freedom for more than two years. I would be sentenced to prison within the next 24 hours. It was during those remaining few hours of freedom that my disease of alcoholism and drug addiction tried to reclaim a foothold on my life.

21

I sat quietly among a crowd of 300 during that last meeting. No one knew me except Tom, a carrot-topped, freckled faced accountant who reminded me of Howdy Dowdy. He and I had met at an Orange County drug treatment center and we'd spent the last few months traveling to 12-step meetings, sort of the black and white version of The Odd Couple.

Tom often abused the recovery system. He would leave the treatment center on a pass and return drunk. As he habitually relapsed, I had a front row seat to his behavior. I liked him. He was funny and intelligent, but what he was dealing with scared me to death. It related to something I told a friend of mine much later.

"I think over the last 20 years I've been lucky in the process of being sober, of staying sober by not drinking in hotels, airplanes or out of mini bars. By not smoking marijuana or snorting crack. I think I've just been lucky," I said.

My friend replied with a most powerful thought. He disagreed and came closer to the truth about my motivation to stay clean.

"No," he said, "you're afraid of you."

Now a different sort of fear was growing inside of me: about where I would go next. I'd already been to so many dark, sordid places. Alleys and $10 hotel rooms, places I couldn't believe I was standing, sitting or even being there. It was like being in the first rehab when I looked around the room and thought, "Hell, these people are crazy!"

Then it dawned on me. I'm in the group now. The others are thinking, "Here's a black guy who thinks he's a Dallas Cowboy." So we're all crazy.

That Thomas Henderson was financially and spiritually bankrupt. But I figured, never mind, I'll go to Palm Springs for a last weekend. The attorneys had already told me that I was going to get a couple of years in jail and that was something I'd accepted. It was a relief actually, like when I broke a cervical vertebrae in the my neck with the Miami Dolphins and the doctor said to me: "You can't play any more." I felt the same sort of relief when the lawyer said, "You're going to do about two years."

At this point in my journey it had become apparent to me that consequences were something I had to face. I'd gotten away with so much rotten behavior, things I couldn't repeat or was allowed to slide on, that there had been no consequences in my life. So maybe that was the first time I was going to be held accountable.

But how was I going to handle it? I had no money, no property and no prestige. The Internal Revenue Service had taken everything I had left. The bondsman gave my Super Bowl ring to the IRS. I was in Palm Springs with a bunch of alcoholics and nobody knew I was going to prison the next day. No one said, "Oh, good luck." No one said, "Oh, you'll be fine." I was carrying this knowledge within myself, and I felt all right about it.

I didn't want pity. I didn't really need comforting to do what had to be done. My friend Tom served as a disturbing reminder of where I'd been and who I didn't want to be anymore.

Tom was near my age, 31, and out of New York. A few months earlier he'd gone with me one night to watch Bob Hope shoot a Texaco commercial. We were in the drug rehab center together but Tom went to the liquor store and bought a pint of vodka. What I saw in him was the sickness of the disease or addiction, whatever you want to call it. I saw him caught up in it- where the choice to drink was more powerful than the choice not to.

So he was mentoring me in a sordid way on this disease. I saw it front and center. I'd heard about it, we'd talked about it in groups and counseling by psychiatrists, during chalk talks and lectures about alcoholism. Here I had the real thing.

I was privately wrestling with another issue beside sobriety. I was struggling with the shame of the sexual assault and what people thought about me. I was suffering in the core of my soul.

How do you take something back that isn't you? How do you explain that you never sexually assaulted anyone? I've never raped anyone in my life. How did I get here? Is this shame going to be with me the rest of my life? It is worth picking up my raggedy-ass life and moving on?

So I was dealing with something completely different from Tom. I was dealing with degradation. What I got charged with was an out-of-body experience. It was a unique, lone combination of hookers and cocaine whores and me buying the junk and having it and giving it away and in return I received favors. Self-disgust reminded that I had been involved in these same episodes for a long, long time without repercussions.

But the public thought that I had brutalized someone. I wasn't dealing with cocaine now. I wasn't even dealing with alcohol or marijuana. I was dealing with, "Can I go on from this?"

Do I give up? Did it matter? Did it make any difference that I didn't drink or do drugs anymore? I was still a sex offender so did it really matter? There were times that my pride and constitution wanted to just end it.

I've never told anyone before, but I had many plots and plans about suicide. How was I going to go out? I'm Thomas Henderson, so you know I have to go with a bang. How about a lot of cameras, downtown Dallas, and from the tallest building I just take off from the top of that sucker? Call a press conference and take a spectacular swan dive into the middle of Commerce Street. Or go to Dealy Plaza, where President Kennedy was shot. Get on a high perch there, call a press conference and do a jackknife swan, a Greg Louganis-dive onto the pavement.

I'd heard all the slogans of the recovery process. "Easy does it." Or "Let go and let God." And "Don't give up before the miracles happen." But I'm Thomas Henderson, and I was ashamed. How do I get past shame?

That weekend in Palm Springs I didn't sit in the back of the room, napping behind a pair of dark glasses as I had in my Dallas Cowboys days during Coach Tom Landry's team meetings. I sat somewhere in the middle, alert, listening to the speakers: the skinny white doctor with wire rim glasses, his pinched owl face becoming grim and then cheerful as he spoke of his drug abuse and subsequent recovery; the flashy redhead who had spent three years locked in her bedroom washing down Valiums with red wine.

Despite our obvious differences, we were all very much alike. Addiction didn't care about black or white, rich or poor, male or female. Addiction was an equal opportunity disease, and we were all there because we were its indiscriminate victims. I felt a great fellowship with the people there. For once in my life, I felt like I was with people who accepted me for who I was, who didn't judge me by my sordid past, but were there to encourage me onward to a brighter future.

A sense of anxiety crept through me as the last speaker spoke, because these people were my safety net. I'd had a safety net before, with the Dallas Cowboys, but it was the kind of safety net an addict didn't need. The Cowboys protected and covered for me. They were my enablers, propping me up and not letting me fall. But in spite of their protective circle my illness grew stronger and took me to the bottom of despair. In the end I admitted that it was me, that my powerlessness over drugs and alcohol had brought me to my desperate state, and by admitting my powerlessness and asking for God's help I was able to begin the long process of healing.

Each of us in that room in Palm Springs had suffered comparable degradation in our lives and together, by sharing our experiences, we were all getting better. The last speaker stepped down and we all bowed our heads in one final prayer. God, grant me the serenity to accept things I cannot change, the courage to change the things that I can, and the wisdom to know the difference.

Most of the guests left quickly, but I waited for the sun to do down before heading for my car. Crossing the desert toward the coast would be cooler after dark, I told myself, though the real reason for delay was embarrassment about the vehicle I was driving. This was Palm Springs after all: educated, well-heeled addicts driving expensive cars. I stared into the employee parking lot where I'd hidden my vehicle, a $200 Datsun that I was struggling to make payments on. A far cry from those stretch limos, I thought with amusement.

There was a time when all that stuff mattered – the fame, the money and all that it could buy – but now it was my tenuous sobriety that I valued. Despite its obvious shortcomings, the car suited me just fine even if it was an embarrassment. Old teammates like Roger Staubach, Danny White and Too Tall Jones would have laughed if they'd seen me now.

Tom Landry would not have laughed. He rarely laughed. He would have shaken his head and said, "Thomas, Thomas, Thomas. You wouldn't follow my playbook. You had to do things your own way, and look where it got you." But I was tired of doing things my way. I was finally listening to others.

My friend Tom was standing beside the ugly, gray Datsun, his freckled face now looking older and more haggard as evening shadows creased his cheeks. Yet he still had a touch of that boyish Howdy Dowdy look.

"Come on, Thomas. We got to hit the road," he said.

I truly liked Tom. I called him Carrot Top, C. T. for short. When we had first met in detox, he and I were both shuffling around like zombies, wearing nothing but blue paper slippers and throwaway gowns. He was a two-time loser, a speedball freak shooting heroin and cocaine between bouts of sobriety. He was working on his last chance at sobriety when we met because treatment centers are expensive and their resources are limited. They don't like to waste those limited resources on drunks and addicts who, once released, just go back to their old habits. Conventional thinking was, three strikes and you're out.

Carrot Top had swung twice and missed, and I was with him now trying to help him stay in the game. Despite his shortcomings, his failures, I respected Carrot Top for what he had accomplished, that while embroiled in the madness of addiction he had still managed to go to college and become an accountant. I admired that part of him.

A huge biker guy stepped from the shadows and approached across the parking lot. He stretched his tattooed arms, grabbed and then hugged me. "Good luck, Thomas," he said. "You have my number. Call me if you need anything."

"Thanks," I replied. "Same to you, man."

I no longer had a pocket full of cash, but I had something more valuable: a pocket full of paper slips, phone numbers from addicts who were eager to talk to me, to help firm my resolve whenever the disease tried to drag me down the steps to hell.

In the distance, the final stragglers drove away from the parking lot. Some were heading out to start new jobs, the weekend in Palm Springs having instilled them with new confidence – " Man, this time I'm going to make it." Others were headed back to families that still did not trust them, that watched their every move looking for a sign that they were drinking or drugging again. Hell, the family had a right to be that way. We'd lied and cheated our way through life for so long that only another drunk could understand that that was not the real us, that by just not drinking and drugging we had become changed people.

"Come on, come on," Carrot Top urged, and I broke into a trot. "You got to be in court tomorrow."

Unlike the others, I wasn't headed to join a family or start a new job. I had to leave Palm Springs on that hot June night and cross a desert so that I could appear in court the following morning, June 11, 1984, for a hearing before a judge who had already decided to send me to prison. I was told that to have a successful recovery I would have to make amends. Prison, paying for my past, was going to be the first step in making many amends and accepting the consequence of my actions.

C. T. struggled to open the passenger car door. Like most of the parts on my car, the door was not original but had been salvaged from some other make or model. I started the Datsun and a stream of blue smoke poured from the rattling exhaust pipe; just another poor drunk leaving a posh resort. Once we got moving the staff would probably call the pollution police. I looked out into the empty parking lot, then over to Carrot Top sitting beside me. It was just the two of us now: a bad imitation of Howdy Dowdy and a washed up Dallas Cowboy hitting the long dusty trail to sobriety.

Only one of us would make it.

I ground the gears forward and headed into the desert. The evening air temperature still hovered near 100 degrees and my car lacked air conditioning. I had plenty of air flow, however, because in addition to the open windows there was a large hole rotted through the floorboard that offered an unwelcome view of the asphalt below. Hot air plus the aroma of steaming asphalt flooded the car through the hole that C. T. and I tried to offset by chain-smoking cigarettes.

I once mentioned to a fellow addict that I might try smoking cigarettes as a substitute habit. He warned me off that idea.

"Worry about your sobriety," he told me. "You go back to drugs and drinking, you lose your family, your career, your home – everything – then finally your life. At least with cigarettes you only lose your life."

Drunken logic, we call it, but somehow it worked and I learned to listen to guys who had stayed sober the longest. Yet I got my inspiration from people who stayed sober the least, like Carrot Top. Any time I got to thinking that a little moonshine might not taste too bad, I only had to remember the night in detox when C. T. robbed the treatment center pharmacy. I was sleeping when the alarms went off. I thought the building was burning down and stumbled into the hallway in my underwear.

But it was only Carrot Top sprawled on the floor with two big orderlies pinning him to the tiles, both his hands clenched in fists that refused to release a generous assortment of pills. His normally red face had turned purple, and I could tell he was dying. I knelt down and started pounding his chest, but I could see that wasn't working.

CPR was needed but that required that I kiss him. I looked down and saw rancid crud on C. T.'s lips, slime flowing from his mouth and my stomach did a flip-flop. I probably had put my lips against worse mouths when I was free-basing but I was reasonably sober now and hesitated, thinking, "Oh, man, I can't do this." Carrot Top was dying, though, so I dove in and performed mouth-to-mouth until I heard sirens outside and knew the paramedics had arrived.

Any time thereafter when I thought that a little moonshine or a toot of coke might not be too bad, I recalled that image of Carrot Top sprawled on the floor, his purple face contorted and sputtering slime, him willing to die for a few pills. I prayed that I wasn't going back to that madness.

Now we were rolling on the highway. It felt like we were going 100 miles an hour, but the Datsun couldn't go that fast downhill with a tail-wind. C. T. sat beside me fiddling with the radio knobs, cursing softly as he tuned in nothing but static.

"You need a new radio," he said.

"Hell, I need a new car," I replied.

We were nearing the coast, taking the scenic route out of San Juan Canyon, when Carrot Top spoke again. He picked his words carefully as if they weren't actually his words but some voiced talking through him.

"You know, Thomas, you're going to prison tomorrow."

"Yeah, I know."

"Well, I was thinking. It's your last night of freedom so what would be the harm of us going to Santa Ana for a little fun?"

"Santa Ana? What's in Santa Ana?" I said, and glanced at C. T. Even in the darkness I could see his face had changed. Gone was the look of calm serenity that the weekend had brought him. In its place was that hungry, haunted look I had seen in my own face and eyes back when my disease was in full control of my life.

"I know a couple of girls there," he said, wetting his lips. "You're going to prison. There won't be any girls there."

"C. T., I've had enough ladies in my lifetime to get me through a couple of years in prison," I said. "I'm going to do this one straight. Whatever it brings me, I'm going to do it straight."

He wet his lips again and the haunted look spread. Panic filled his eyes. We were on Route 5 and our turnoff was just a few miles up the high-way. Santa Ana lay straight ahead. To the left lay Newport Beach where he lived and I was renting a room.

"Thomas, you're going to prison," C. T. repeated. "One last night of fun won't hurt you."

I knew we weren't talking about girls. We were talking about drugs, heroin and cocaine. Yeah, there'd be girls in Santa Ana. There always were – coke whores we called them, hanging out, willing to do anything for a few lines or a hit of crack. The main attraction, though, was drugs.

For a moment what Carrot Top was saying didn't sound too bad. I'd be spending some time behind bars with plenty of time to get sober again. What would be the harm of one final blast? But I knew what the harm would be: failure. I'd have failed at staying sober. I would establish a pattern of failure, just like C. T. had, getting sober just long enough for the body to recover, then getting fouled up again until the body and mind failed, a depraved seesaw life of treatment and relapses, with each relapse falling deeper into hell until recovery wasn't possible.

The sign for our turnoff loomed ahead. Beside it, another sign flashed: Santa Ana, Keep Straight Ahead.

"C'mon, Thomas. Go straight," C. T. begged.

But which way was straight? Carrot Top's straight, which was anything but a straight life, or the left cutoff that led at an angle toward a straight life? I looked at C. T. and saw his fingernails dug into knees, haunted eyes searching the distance toward the lights of Santa Ana. If it had been me back when I was using drugs I would have grabbed the driver and forced the wheel to stay straight. I'd have done anything to get those drugs.

"Thomas, no one will ever know," C. T. whined. "You can say you've been sober for seven months and I won't say nothing."

But I would know. I could feel my grip tighten on the wheel. I tried to pull left but the wheel didn't want to turn. We were headed straight to Santa Ana. Straight to hell. I prayed silently. Someone else might have laughed hearing this 240-pound former linebacker asking for strength to overcome the siren call of a scrawny little accountant. My prayers were answered. I felt a great weight lift from my hands and I was able to turn the car to the left.

C. T. relaxed then. The haunted look quickly faded from his face and he resumed fiddling with the radio knobs. He asked if I wanted him to take care of my car while I was in prison.

"You'll sell it for a fix," I replied.

"You're right, Thomas," he said. "I'm not going to make it. Not with you off in prison."

"You'll make it, C. T. Just keep going to those meetings."

I don't know if you can imagine having a devil on one shoulder and an angel on the other. Let's just say that I had this recovery concept, this hope, that anything was possible for me if I stayed sober. The alternative was that nothing was possible if I got high.

That was one of the solid moments in which I made a decision to remain among the sober. A good friend, very ill with his disease, thought that I needed a last hurrah. I was going to throw away my seven clean months for one night of sick, psychotic behavior with him. A couple of things were wrong with that.

First, he would know that I was a colossal liar. Second, he'd never believe me again. That would not be a surprise since for the past 20 years I've had people say to me, "I don't believe anybody could stay sober 20 years...you've done something." And the fact is that I haven't had a drink or a drug since November of 1983 and that is why my life works.

Tom's life didn't work out as well.

Tom did my taxes from 1986 until the mid-1990s. I filed tax forms while I was in prison. Never went a year without doing that to show what a responsible fellow I was. On the line where it says to state income, I entered a zero.

After I was released from prison, Tom had sort of gotten back to accounting. He kept relapsing and claiming he was clean. I'd fly to southern California and go see him with my box of receipts like most Americans do for their taxes and invariably, during my visit to Laguna Beach where his office was located, I'd stare at Tom and say, "You look fouled up. What are you on? Pills or what? What's that crap in the corner of your mouth, Tom?"

Well, he would go ballistic, cursing and denying. He thought the louder he got the more convinced I'd be that he was straight. He wasn't, but in spite of that he was still my friend.

And I knew my friend. I used to tell him, I'm the same guy who gave you mouth-to-mouth. I'm the same guy who saw a cyst on your arm because the needle went in crooked. I'm the same guy who was with you when you drank a pint of vodka while we were in rehab. I'm the same guy you asked to go to Santa Ana and get loaded.

Yet at the same time, Tom attended all these rehab meetings. He was working with newcomers and helping others. He was a great talker and speaker, and people loved to hear from Tom. But he was backsliding all the time.

I got a phone call from Tom early in May around 1995. He said, "Hey, I need $1,500." I said, "Okay, I'll send you a check," and he said, "I'll pay you after I do all these tax returns." So I wrote a check and put it in the mail.

He never received the check. It was in the mail when his body was discovered. Turns out that I had talked to Tom two days before he died.

Tom's wife called with the news. She said, "We found Tom dead in a hotel room down in Santa Ana." An accidental overdose killed him. A speedball, the combination of cocaine and heroin injected intravenously, was the fatal recipe. I asked his wife what exactly happened.

She told me a long complicated story. It began when Tom told her that a guy he was working with was located in a hotel room in Santa Ana. Tom said he needed to make a call on this guy. As a recovering alcoholic he needed to help the man, counsel him and get him in treatment. But that story turned out to be a cover for him to find a room and shoot dope. Yet all the while, every two or three hours, Tom called his wife.

"Yeah, I'm still sitting here with him," he told her. "He's in bad shape and I'm trying to get him to go to a 24-hour club. I'm working with him and I'll be home later, honey." Click.

The maid found Tom. He was long dead. He had a cyst on his arm from where the needle had gone in wrong. I'd seen the same kind of knot on him 10 years earlier.

I loved him but I didn't go to Tom's funeral, memorial or wake. I was hurt but I wasn't disappointed. He betrayed himself, not me. But I couldn't go in good conscience and say a good word about it. It was about me honoring my feelings. In spite of the tough time he had with his addiction, he was still my teacher. He taught me all the way to the grave.

Tom may have saved my life at his expense. I say that because I learned front and center, eyeball to eyeball, from him. I stared addiction in the face and knew what it was. Addiction is a cold-blooded bastard.

When I reflect on that day and replay the little voice in my head, the voice that agreed with Carrot Top – hey, man, go to Santa Ana-I realize how cunning this disease of drug addiction and alcoholism can be and how it's always searching for a way to reassert control. No wonder I failed when I first sought treatment. No wonder so many of us addicts fail in recovery.

We need to learn from our mistakes so that we don't fail the next time. Better yet, learn about the pitfalls ahead of time from other recovering addicts. That was what I did. I finally took the cotton out of my ears and listened. I was no longer acting the part of the big-shot Dallas Cowboy, thinking, "What can that little ass-wipe drunk teach me?"

I realized I had done it my way too long, and I had failed, and that it was time to listen to someone smarter than me. Who? Why, anybody. At that point in my life when I hit bottom, anyone would have been smarter than me. My cat was smarter. Roger Staubach was smarter. They were both smarter than me because they weren't drinking and drugging their lives away.

Once I started listening, I heard simple things that made sense. Such as, "You can't get drunk if you don't take that first drink." Well, duh. It's easier to think, "I'll just have one, maybe two drinks, then go right home." How many of us end up waking up the next morning in some strange city with empty wallets, realizing we've missed our child's birthday party or failed to take our wife to that play she wanted to see?

My little voice was working overtime that night in the desert. Go to Santa Ana, Thomas. You're going to jail in the morning, anyway. Most of my recovering friends tell me they have a little voice that is always trying to get them into trouble. Maybe you know someone with a little voice. Or maybe you've got a voice like mine telling you it's okay to take that drink because you're sad, or that it's okay because you're happy, or that you need to drink because you're alone, or because you're at a party. Maybe your little voice told you it's okay to drink because you're going to prison in the morning.

Well, maybe not that. Not yet, anyway. But it will. You keep drinking and drugging and someday your little voice is going to say, pack your toothbrush, Sweet Cakes. We're off to prison in the morning.

"Redundant. I repeat myself often in this story because everything I am and do are about being clean and in recovery. This is what I do. Every step, every choice and decision is connected to recovery. Redundancy is a habit and it works in my life." TH

CHAPTER THREE

NUDGE FROM THE JUDGE

Being arrested charged and sent to prison was my main intervention. There was no spiritual awakening or a self-conscious choice to clean up my own crack cocaine addiction or behaviors therein.

Frankly I didn't know how to stop. The fact that I couldn't recognize what my problems were... how could I fix them? By the time I hit that granite wall of addiction and consequences I had already been on the run for about two years. I had left my family and friends to seek new companions, fellow addicts and alcoholics. Searching for those who were like me wasn't difficult at all. It's relatively easy to slip into the world of crack addicts and dealers. With football forever gone as a job and my unwillingness to be employed I was clearly free to reside among those just like me. As dangerous as this journey was I was unbelievably comfortable in their mist. I had planned to become an actor or TV personality. On my arrival in California in early 1983 I secured an agent and enrolled into an acting workshop. I actually paid for the class and never showed up for a single session. I was too busy smoking crack. What's interesting about that is the class was closed and the instructor made an exception because I was Hollywood Henderson. Such is the life of a toxic crack addict.

I had left Texas because I owed money to drug dealers and any of the friends that I had left. California was an escape, but as the saying goes where ever you are there you are. There is really nowhere to hide when you are in the midst of a toxic addiction. You really can't work or take care of business so without my knowing I was on my way to a bad place. The addicts' primary goal is to secure his or hers drug of choice and use it as self prescribed. And of course our job, responsibilities and family become second place. Eventually the job and family lose to exclusive addictive behaviors.

The arrest and embarrassment of a sexual assault charge got my attention like nothing else in this drug-addicted adventure I'd been on. This assault was not a pattern. I was 30 years old and had never forced myself on anyone. The world of crack addicts screwed me up. Seeing addicts overdose and die, shootings, being threatened at gun point or having to give a girl mouth to mouth resuscitation after she went unconscious following a hit of crack cocaine didn't daunt me in the least. Seeing women offer themselves sexually just for a little crack was unfortunately normal. This culture was sick.

Facing the Judge and judgement of the court was in part and was my moment of clarity. Of course by then I had been through several treatment programs and halfway houses. Actually, being sent to prison brought my consequences front and center; there were no more excuses or denials about my crack cocaine addiction or alcoholism. I was going to prison. I could no longer rationalize or ignore what would happen if I ever used crack or other drugs. I now knew that bad things were going to happen if I did. With this newfound reality I now had a choice about my future; stay sober and life would get better or get high and go to jail or die. The courts rescued me from self-denial. Those who are in the midst of this same sort of paradox please know that it's not absolutely necessary to get a nudge from a judge. Get treatment and stop the madness.

SAFE IN PRISON

I co-wrote Out Of Control with author Pete Knobler while I was in prison for 28 months. Even though it was a best seller, the story compelling and unbelievable, it probably wasn't the right time for me to write a book. Not while I was angry and struggling with my identity.

I was angry with me, Thomas Henderson. I was angry with me for really screwing up what could have been a great life. So writing Out Of Control, although as an inventory, a way of confessing and sharing my experience, strength and hope with the world, I would write that book differently 20 years later.

The sore tendons of resentment were still flaring then. I stand by everything I wrote in Out Of Control except there were people I talked about and took shots at that I regret. This book is about my thoughts, choices and results as a new man. The new and improved Thomas Henderson. When you shop at the supermarket, get the new and improved product.

Let me say this about the former drunk and drugged-out version of Thomas Henderson. Or better yet, allow me to use Mickey Mantle's words. I saw the dying Mantle, pale and thin, speaking from a wheelchair in a Dallas hospital while waiting for a liver transplant. Reflecting on the alcoholic lifestyle that ruined his health and cut his life short, he said:

"Take a good look. Don't be like me."

I don't think I ever said this but 28 months in prison was one of the greatest things that ever happened to me. You might guess I'd say appearing in three Super Bowls, playing for the Dallas Cowboys or being drafted No.1. Instead it was 28 months that I spent reflecting on my life, choices and mistakes. What occurred to me was, in a metaphorical sense, that I was a bad skater in a professional hockey game.

By that I mean I just flew past the action. I couldn't stop. Just wasn't a good skater. I kept skidding around and busting my rear against the sideboards.

When the judge sentenced me to four years and eight months, my lawyer, Arnie Gold, asked me, "You scared, Thomas?"

"Scared? No. I'm relieved," I said and handed him the keys to my $200 Datsun. "See you in a few years."

I was going to prison, but I was going clean and sober and getting what I needed: time. Time to heal. Time to reflect. Time to find out who I really was and why I had failed, and to change my ways so I wouldn't fail again. Jail wasn't scary compared to the prison that drugs had created for me.

When I tell people that 28 months in prison was one of the best things to happen to me, they look at me like I'm crazy. And I go, "Well, you got it right. I was crazy."

Denial is always the bane of the addicted. I'm okay, man. Things are a little tough right now, that's why I'm drinking. But I can stop any time I want. How many times have we heard someone say that? Prison, though, is a big denial crusher. It's hard to say things are okay when you're sitting in an 8x8 cell looking through metal bars.

So there I sat, confined, another nobody, just a number. No longer Number 56 of the Cowboys but Number 87983-C in the California Men's Colony.

During the first months there I was convinced I'd suffered some type of brain damage because of the paranoia and psychiatric episodes I'd experience on crack cocaine. My thinking was flawed. My memory was short. I couldn't remember a lot of stuff because in the final days of my addiction if I got an ounce of cocaine I could go through it in eight hours.

Those were days you can't recall. Days you didn't know where you were or what you did. You'd wake up and find yourself someplace with no idea how you go there. I was deeply affected physically, emotionally and psychiatrically as a result.

I quickly learned that my fame outside prison meant little within the walls of a penal institute. I also learned about prison justice by witnessing gang attacks and knifings. It dawned on me that if I were going to stay sober, I had to avoid all that.

A big black dude, 6-5, 400 pounds, gave me my orientation lecture in the prison yard. What he said made me realize that prison actually could aid an addict's denial. Prisoners ran the joint, not the guards. Dysfunctional people would be controlling me, creating a dysfunctional environment that addiction thrived in.

"Henderson." Big Sucker said, "this is the way it breaks down. We've got the BGF's, the Black Gorilla Family, we have the Crips, the Bloods, we have the Pyroos...." As he rattled on, listing more than a dozen gangs, my apprehension grew. I was still cocky enough not to be concerned with my safety because I was raised on the streets. I thought I could handle prison life. Pick no fights...kick ass if I had to.

But I was worried about my sobriety. There was no mention of treatment programs, of help for the addicted. What Big Sucker talked about was an intense concentration of insanity. How was I going to stay sane in this place? Not by joining them, that's for sure.

I began to understand the reason these men return to prison over and over again was because they refused to change. Even inside prison they continued gang warfare and smuggled drugs inside their rectums so they could continue using and abusing. They lied, stole, cheated and their lives never got better because they never got better. They continued to do the same things while expecting different results for living an insane life.

There are too many things to name that you can't do in prison. The main one involves freedom. You can't go outside the walls without permission. If you try, they might just shoot your ass so full of holes that what's left gets shipped home in an egg carton. What you have in prison is an overabundance of time.

I spent a lot of time reading. People sent me books. I read hundreds of them. One was titled Zen and the Art of Motorcycle Maintenance sent from Richard Pryor. If you read that you'll read anything, and I damn near did.

I read about spirituality, God, the Bible, recovery books, books on Zen and Buddha. I read soapbox wrappers and how-to instructions on toilet paper. I re-educated my brain. I inserted a lot of stuff to sort out that had never been there before. Prison became a place to exercise my brain because I feared it had been damaged inside and out.

My mind needed new wiring. I had, to some degree, caused mental retardation. There had been something mentally defective about my thinking. I had a big dictionary to look up words I didn't know. I went to college and I could read and I've been smart most of my life. But I had to re-learn.

One book gripped me like no other. That was Lonesome Dove by Larry McMurtry. The rest of the books are a blur compared to what Lonesome Dove did to me. Although a book of fiction it taught me, or let me see clearer, friendship in a form I'd never seen before. As a result of that book I have great friends today.

The part I embraced was the pledge that the C. W. McCall character made to his longtime Texas Ranger buddy, Gus McCrae. McCall promised that he would drag McCrae's body 2,000 miles on horseback from Wyoming for burial alongside a creek in Texas. And by God he did. Even as fiction, I accepted his dedication as a powerful example of friendship. I took something out of that story: That's the kind of friend I want to be and that model of friendship is what I try to practice.

One last thought about Lonesome Dove. I was mad as hell at McMurtry when the book ended. I wanted it to go on and on. Best book I ever read.

Other than the exercise yard, there were two places in prison that I chose to visit on a regular basis and that did more in terms of healing than just get me out of a claustrophobic cell. Someone would call out, "Recovery meeting tonight!" real loud from down the hall, and I'd step out. I would be the only one. Doors would close and I'd have to walk a gauntlet of murderers, armed robbers and deviants. They didn't exactly make fun of me. Nor were they really mean-spirited, either. It was more of a mocking tease in the voices I heard.

Going to that recovery meeting, big shot?

They ain't gonna let your ass out of here just 'cause you're going to that recovery meeting.

You know you're gonna get high.

You know when you get outta here you're gonna smoke some more of that crack.

I used to go to church on Sunday, too. That allowed me to leave my cell and go to a different part of the prison. After being confined it was like going out of town on a picnic. Anyway, I was ordained a Baptist as a child and never had much choice about my religion or politics. It was always, "You're a Baptist and a Democrat."

I do believe in a higher power, but it's nobody's damn business, which is a tough thing to say right next to "higher power." The Gospel of Matthew talks about hypocrites, people out in the streets and synagogues that pray in public and make holier-than-thou pronouncements. The Gospel of Matthew said true piety takes you to a private place to pray. It's Chapter Six. As Casey Stengel would say, you can look it up.

I went to church with Tex Watson, one of those guys who was on drugs and wound up killing people in the Sharon Tate case. He's not the same. Tex led some services, his father-in-law was the chaplain, Tex had married and at the time had three or four kids. He was spouting Jesus Christ as his Savior and Lord. My faith is a private matter. You won't see me on the 700 Club or anywhere else telling people what my faith is. Should anyone wonder, no, I never talked to Tex about the Tate murders.

My guess is there are people who are surprised that I can read anything more complicated than an eye chart. Stereotypes exist that most pro-football players are knuckle-draggers, barely civilized enough to sit in chairs and dumber than a cedar post. So it follows that a street urchin like me from a poor, marginally educated family, grew up with a mind that never developed.

But I tell people all the time that I had the greatest teachers on the planet from the first through the sixth grade. I believe that by the time you're 12 years old, you've put down a foundation, the basics of how you're going to respond to life. Do you have curiosity to pick up the dictionary when you don't know the meaning of a word? I had dictionaries at home. I still do.

Ms. Bannister, my first grade teacher, and Ms. Poole and Ms. Overton who told me to read part of a book and write her a one-page report, taught me comprehension. I think the greatest portion of my education took place by the time I was 12 because I became expert in the basics. I could add, subtract, multiply and divide, and I could spell.

I've always been a good student. I stayed eligible for sports. I went to college for four years and stayed eligible, and that's no easy feat. I've always come off as a street boy because I was a street boy. I was a street boy who threw his books in the alley and went in and shot pool and dice and drank wine behind the store. But when I was through I went back and got my books and showed up in school the next day.

While in prison it occurred to me that if I was going to live and not end my life or go into exile – and where could a guy like me go into exile...Haiti? – I had to face the world with a firm concept: I am not my mistakes; I am who I've become. This would be my motto and mantra, because I was working on low-grade shame with every step I took.

But what could I do for a living?

I thought back to being with the Cowboys. I noticed that after two years with the team that the media relations department wasn't interested in promoting me. I watched the P. R. people talk up Charlie Waters, Cliff Harris, John Fitzgerald and Roger Staubach. Those players were getting interviews and stories on the front page of newspapers. I was being ignored. No one ever came to me and said, "We want you to talk to the head writers of The New York Times."

Thus was born the "Hollywood" Henderson who promoted himself because the Cowboys never got me an interview. I became the Mouth of the South by boasting how good I was ("I am quick. I'm so quick that I'm an illusion") and insulting an opponent ("He only comes in when everyone else is dead)." It wasn't enough to just return an interception for a touchdown. I had to spike the ball over the goal post crossbar.

But now what did I have to promote?

I was in prison. I had pleaded no contest to sexual assault. I was a crack addict. I didn't have any money. I was a convicted sex offender, ex-football player who didn't know what he was going to do. My resume was not looking good.

As I said, I was doing a lot of reading. One day I saw an advertisement in a magazine: "Program Corporation of America. Lectures. Want to book a speaker? Call us."

Well, one of my favorite subjects in college had been speech. I once walked into the classroom to hear my teacher say, "Are you ready, Henderson?" I said, "Ready for what?" The teacher said, "You should be prepared to deliver a 15-minute speech."

I walked to the front of the class, reached into the pocket of my cotton shirt and pulled out a piece of lint. I did 15 minutes on that piece of lint. I told how it got there, what it was made of, why it ended up in my pocket and where it came from. I also did a 10-minute talk on a leaf. I did another 10 minutes on a Coke can. I appeared as an apologist for the can because it was crushed and tried to determine how many times it had been run over.

So from my prison cell in California Men's Colony, I decided I'm going to be a speaker. I'm going to tell people what happened to Thomas Henderson. I'm going to share my story from the podium. So I wrote the manager of PCA a Dear Sir letter that stated my name, said I played for the Dallas Cowboys, I was a Super Bowl winner, articulate, smart and already a speaker. I may have fudged a little bit since I was only speaking to prison groups but hell, I had to sell myself.

From my prison cell on my prison made stationary I wrote the following letter. I was released on October 15, 1986. On October 22, 1986 I was guest speaker at Virginia Tech in Blacksburg, Virginia. You see, you can plan to fail or fail to plan.

Thomas Henderson
C.M.C.C-87983
P.O. Box 8101-7350
San Luis Obispo, California 93409-0001

July 13, 1985

Program Corporation Of America
595 West Hartsdale Avenue,
White Plains, New York 10607

To: Program Corp Of America;

First, let me introduce myself:
My name is Thomas Edward Henderson and I'm a former professional football player.
I played for the Dallas Cowboy'from 1975 til November of 1979.My nickname was"Hollywood;"
I was the first professional football player to admit that I was a drug addict. Since that time I've been in three different drug hospitals and rehabilitation programs.You might say I've been a journeyman in this area.
My last stop was at the Care Unit Of Orange,California under the care of Dr. Joseph Pursch.
I entered that hospital demoralized,depressed,and charged with a cocaine party related sex crime charge; You might say I had hit that bottomless pit of degradation and-shame. It took all that has happened in my life to clear my head long enough to understand life on life's terms. From this experience I had to have a new beginning, and that beginn-ing had to be here in prison. I couldn't start anywhere else.
I had to let go of the past and forget the future.As long as I held on to the past with one hand and grabbed at the future with the other hand, I had nothing with which to grasp today. So I had to begin here,now.

I'm presently serving a sentence of four years & eight months at the California Men's Colony, East in San-Luis Obispo,California. My early release date is October 15, 1986.I've got roughly fifteen months left to serve in prison.

I've been a drug addict and alcoholic for ten years or more and I've suffered grave consequences. I'm not a bad person trying to get good, I was a sick diseased addict who has arrested his illness.

I realize and know today that one day at a time is my only struggle in handling my alcoholism. Alcoholics Anonymous and it's twelve steps are my life line today.

Ive' been in prison for twelve months now and I've been clean and sober for twenty months. I've taken full responsibility for my past wrong and I own those feelings.

Naming,claiming,and dumping my thoughts and experience is my hope and desire. I truly feel optimistic and anxious toward what I can do in the future. My reason for writing your company is because I feel convicted and sentenced for a life term of sharing my experience,strenth,and hope all over this country. Doctors,teachers,heros,parents,preachers, and the police,can talk; Give warning,and advise until they are blue in the face in the area of drug and alcohol abuse without being affective.I feel my message can reach out a touch anyone who listens.

You see, I'm a scrambled egg,and hopefully through my sharing I might educate communities and individuals that they can remain sunny side up and not scramble their lives the way I did,my own.

My ability to articulate and deliver my story is not only educational, it has feelings and depth. I lost everything,including my dignity due to my addiction.I played in three Super Bowls and was a role model to thousands maybe millions during my career. I owe a lot of people an explanation about my behavior and what happened .

People need to know what could have been going on in the mind of a gifted athlete who loses everything including his freedom for the sake of getting high. They need to hear it from someone like me because I'm willing to tell all even when it hurts.

I'm not responsible for my desease but I am responsible for my recovery.

Alcoholism and drug addiction awareness are the most talk about subjects in america today.

I'm truly the model example of a pitiful and incomprensible cretin. I can't take back anything that has happened in my life but I can share my experience,strength,and hope.

Hopefully it might possibly help some " one person".It took several years of denial,pain,suffering,and this ugly case to bring me to my knees. It takes what it takes.

I'd be greateful and honered if your company would consider me as a client. I've suffered the hardship even to imprisonment as a criminal,but my words and desires are not imprisoned.

I'm sober today and that's freedom enough for now. The many honors,trophy,and applauds were wonderful,but I wouldn't trade my <u>sobriety</u> for any of them.

Your company has plenty of time to do a feasibility and marketing study to see if anyone might pay to hear the Thomas Hollywood Henderson story.

I pray that after your company carefully considers me as a client,that you'll be convinced of my conviction and committment to sobriety.

Thanks for your time and consideration on my proposal and request. I'd appreciate a response from a company representative in the very near future.

A real drug addict and alcoholic.

Thomas Henderson

homas Hollywood Henderson

I began moving away from depression and shame. The year before I left prison I began thinking about direction and what I wanted to do. I wasn't going to be defined by my past. You weren't going to find me under a bridge like many athletes, when reality has them so fouled up they can't take the next step. I decided to take my raggedy ass out and try to make something of myself.

I played football for the first half of my life with all my heart. I hated the structure and discipline of the Cowboys. Hated Jim Myers, one of Tom Landry's assistants. Hated Landry for never complimenting me. I hated studying and trying to understand Landry's unique Flex defense. I rebelled against a coordinated scheme that was opposite in every way from the 5-2, sic-'em style I played in college.

But beneath my resentment, I now see there were residual benefits from being coached to play football at its highest level. They sound like clichés to most people since the lessons are as basic as the pre-game coin flip. Like, if you get blocked, don't stay blocked. Get up and pursue. Prepare well. Give maximum effort. Never quit. That was the attitude I adopted. I never backed down as a football player.

I decided the second half of my life would be devoted to telling my story. I don't know where the optimism came from or how I was going to do it but lo and behold, the manager of the lecture company wrote me back. He located some information on me and I marketed myself so well that I wound up in their catalogue of available speakers.

I prepared to leave prison with some fixed opinions about our judicial system that I learned the hard way. When I was introduced to the possibility of going to prison I pleaded no contest, which is basically a plea bargain. I didn't realize how rampant that decision is in criminal justice.

The two worst places for an inmate to find himself is a city or county jail. After being sentenced to prison I was sent to the Long Beach city jail for five days and then to the Los Angeles County jail for two weeks – weeks that were worse than the next 28 months. It was like Matt Dillon and Festus in Gunsmoke. You know, bread and water, beans and bologna on the menu. No newspaper. No television. It's just sitting on concrete and visiting with other pitiful people. After five days in city jail I went to county jail, which was a little better but still no different than being an animal in the zoo. You get a caged feeling from small cells...rows of metal bars...Plexiglas...inability to see anyone left of right or in front of you.

This is where pay phones in the hallway charge $6 per minute to make a collect call to your family. Most folks don't find that out until they've talked to someone for 30 or 40 minutes. Then they get the bill and go, "What the hell!"

I'm sure there are people who think, well, if you're in jail there shouldn't be any recreation. It ought to be punishment, hard labor and breaking rocks. But you must remember that most of the same citizens you lock up you eventually let go. They are back in society with resentment and anger and no hope.

I stayed by myself in prison. I didn't understand what I was experiencing or witnessing until long after I'd done my time. The conclusion I reached was that the American justice system isn't fair to all people. That's no revelation, but bear with me.

Everyone has an opinion on what prison is and what it isn't. What we need to remember is there are two million people locked up in American prisons. We're spending something like $40 billion a year to house, feed and clothe them with very little rehabilitation. I hate the term rehabilitate because it assumes there was a time when you were functional. So rehabilitate you to what, to make you a better criminal? Rehabilitate you to be a better street hood, be more uneducated? So is it fair? I'm not sure I'm talking about fair. I'm talking about reasonable.

I was in prison for sexual misconduct, but it was clear from my record and treatments I'd been through before I got to prison that I was a severe crack addict. Not once in my 28 months, not even during classification, was this mentioned. Classification is a process where the system determines whether you are a minimum or maximum custody candidate. I sat there thinking, oh, my God, what the hell happened to me?

The process itself is impersonal and dehumanizing. You have no identity. You're a package that the conveyor belt has dumped in front of an official behind a desk. This official had my file open in front of him. He never called my name. The only reference he made of me as a person was to say, "Subject played in the National Football League."

We release 600-700,000 inmates every year. And of course we commit 600-700,000 people a year. With those numbers of commitments and recidivism I think the system is broke. I believe there are people who should never get out of prison. I think society should protect itself. You shouldn't have sexual predators working around children. I also believe that with the $40 billion we are paying for incarceration a lot of those dollars should go toward rehabilitation, job skill training, counseling and therapy.

Instead, $40 billion in American tax dollars is spent to incarcerate 2 million a year and release 700,000 people a year into society who are not ready. They are burdened with criminal records. Employers do background checks on people released from prison. If you lie on your application you're done. I say we're missing a great opportunity to turn these inmates around.

Punishment has its place, but punishment can't always be the overriding factor, because if it is, the prison population will double in the next 10 years. We'll have four million in prison, the budget will go to $80 billion and the recidivism rate will be uncontrollable. Prison overcrowding will lead to just letting people out for lack of space.

Make no mistake. There are predators, murderers and mean and violent people in the world. Let's keep them locked up. But there are cases involving petty thieves, non-violent and non-victim crimes where federal guidelines can lock up an offender for 40-50 years just for possession of a little bag of crack. Whereas a high-powered drug dealer can spend $300,000 to $500,000 on an attorney and get probation for possessing 17 kilos of cocaine.

People with resources can even wait to hire the best attorney for their particular charge. But when you are a person of color or if you're white and don't have money, you are at the mercy of a horrific system.

If you're lucky enough to afford bail while awaiting trial, you are indeed fortunate. I'm guessing now but willing to estimate that 70 to 80 percent of all people in prison today are there because of plea bargains. Of course, they're also there because of being guilty of what they did. But while awaiting trial, lodged in a city or county jail, it's close to unbearable living conditions for a human being.

One reason people plea bargain is poor representation, no money for counsel or to bail out. So you're living day by day in a county or city jail and it's the worst incarceration under the sun. It's a Catch 22 situation: If you can afford to make bail, the court usually won't appoint you an attorney because obviously if you can bail out you can afford a lawyer. The only alternative is to stay in jail because you can't bail out. So you stay to qualify for a public defender. Public defenders, God bless them, do some fine work. Guessing again I'd say eight of their 10 clients are convinced or made to understand that if you don't take this plea bargain deal you'll remain in jail another nine to 14 months and then if there's a jury trial and you lose, you'll get 15 to 30 years. But the public defender says he's talked to the prosecutor and if you take a five-to-10-year sentence right now he can cut a deal.

Those we call recidivists, men who've been there before, understand that living conditions in state prison compared to city or county jail is the difference between Motel 6 and the Ritz Carlton. So tens of thousands of people fill our prisons every year and we as taxpayers pay $20-$30,000 annually per inmate for those convicted of non-violent crimes such as possession, parole violations and the like. If everyone had a Johnny Cochran, F. Lee Bailey or a Roy Black to represent him on some of these minor cases our prisons wouldn't be so full.

If I have to stay in city or county jail for the next 14 months and you offer me a five-year deal where I can get out in three with good behavior, I'm going to take it. Because more than anything else, more than going to mama's house for Sunday dinner, I want the hell out of here and prison is a better place to be than county jail.

In prison you can walk around the yard. You can lift weights, listen to music, read newspapers and magazines. You can watch TV, have visitors, go to a vending machine with a roll of quarters and feel like you're dining at Ruth's Chris Steak House. You're fed and clothed better. You can play basketball, softball and football, exercise and jog. You have a job in prison. They pay you 25 or 30 cents an hour in California.

In Texas it's a chain gang where they have you chopping cotton, pulling corn and doing hard labor. But even with the boss on horseback toting a high-powered rifle, and with his horse spitting on the back of your neck in a Texas prison industry field, it's better than county jail.

48

CHUCK DENMARK
(Friend, retired from Ford Motor Company)

Between the time Thomas left an alcohol recovery hospital in Orange County and went to jail, he needed a car. I helped get him a used Datsun to drive. It was so well used, the price was about $200 and we may have over-paid at that.

Thomas didn't drive it. He wore it. He and the car were like two wrecks going down the road. I also got him a bumper sticker that said: ""My Rolls Royce Is Up My Nose." He was humiliated to no end.

I met Thomas when he was a patient in the Comprehensive Care Unit. I'd been through there myself for alcohol dependence years before when it had a different name. I gave monthly talks there, Thomas took a shine to me and I began taking him to men's meetings. We hit it off and became like soul friends.

We've had a lot of fun with that over the years, him being black, me being white and calling each other "Dad" and "Son." I have a big picture of Thomas in my office that he'd signed, "To Dad." It drove people nuts. Then me being a southern boy from Savannah, Georgia, really blew their mind.

Referring to Thomas, someone once said to me, "You know he's black." I said, "No, I didn't, not until you just told me."

I only see the person. I don't see color. I learned that we are all God's children and he doesn't have any grandkids. That's how I feel. That's what I was taught a long time ago.

What I first saw in Thomas was an ego so big you could sub-divide it. It was a challenge to smash that ego so it could save his life. I could see the good in him. He was a big guy with a big heart.

I felt like everyone was after him for his notoriety. I was after him to try to help him get sober. I'd been around a lot of people like him, movie stars and celebrities. I just tried to get him to right meetings to see if he could get off on the right steps.

I sensed from the start that Thomas was genuine. He talked a lot about his mother. Anyone who talks about his mom raising him has to have good qualities. Soon after we met, he began referring to me as a "sponsor." I tell people, I'll be your friend because you can always fire a sponsor. But you can't fire a friend.

49

I was most fearful for his safety while he was incarcerated. He had damage to his neck and I was always uneasy that somebody would try to prove a point and put him in a wheelchair the rest of his life. He confided in me that that was a concern to him because he was a celebrity and a guy often tried to make a name for him self that way. Fortunately, because of his personality, Thomas was able to be friends with people and slide right through that danger.

When he left for prison I gave him one piece of advice: Don't let the time use you. You use the time.

That's what he did. He read a lot and didn't let time get to him. He did it one day at a time.

I retired to Dana Point in Orange County and drove 100 miles almost every month to see Thomas when he was an inmate at San Luis Obispo. I paid some of his bills and when he needed stuff I'd send him a box.

But hell, there's as much to drink and drug in a prison as on the streets. Just because he was locked up didn't keep him from doing something he wanted to do. However, I think I saw total surrender in Thomas when he went to prison. That's why I didn't have any problem being his friend.

His story is, he saw my Lincoln Town Car and my Rolex watch and wanted what I had. I suppose he was impressed because I was a corporate businessman. He thought everyone in alcohol or drug rehab had to come from off the street.

I see the same qualities in Thomas today as I did when we first met almost 20 years ago. He's chipped away that garbage we pick up in our drinking. I look at these steps as if we have a chisel and hammer. And that we're like a big blob of clay, granite or marble an artist is working with.

Artists see what is supposed to be. They don't add anything. They remove. They chip away until the person who used to be before all this happened to him now reappears. He's not only back, but he's better than ever.

Thomas has done well in that area. He's been a very giving person, and that's what you have to do. I believe that Thomas truly from his heart wanted to give back, and he has. Thomas didn't owe me anything to start with. He's paid back society. He pays back the fellowship every day that he stays sober and helps someone else. I think he does that every day.

Chapter Four

IN AND OUT OF LOVE

I was luckier than most convicts were. Not only did I have a good woman waiting for me on the outside. I had a job when I left prison at 10:00 a.m. on October 15, 1986. Because of my fame in football and as a flaming failure – there was demand for me to make speaking engagements.

The woman was Diane, my second wife. We were married while I was an inmate, in October of 1985. Prison weddings are non-traditional. No one throws rice at the departing newly weds because they aren't going anywhere. Our honeymoon was spent standing in front of a vending machine with a roll of quarters, cooing to each other.

"Darling, you want chips?"

"Sweetheart, how about a Snickers?"

"My dear, would you care for LifeSavers."

I met my wife in a drug clinic. As both of us used to say, we were together in Drunk School. That's probably not a great place to forge an emotional or loving relationship although we did end up married successfully for five years.

I wouldn't recommend that when you're in a psychiatric and addicted community sitting in a room with eight or ten people in a recovery or therapy session, and facilitators are talking about addiction and recovery and honesty, and half the room is on anti-depressants and the other half in detox, you look at someone of the opposite sex and think, there she is! That's the one!"

That is actually another form of insanity. It's the worst. I don't mind saying that Diane and I were successful, but I'll grant you that 99.9 percent of people who meet like that aren't. Getting involved in a relationship is a good way to distract your self from yourself.

Every therapist, counselor, sponsor and mentor I had early in recovery was upset with me about the marriage. They said, "You are nuts. How are you going to handle a relationship? You don't even have a relationship with yourself. The only qualification you have on being successful in a relationship is as a stalker."

Alcoholic and drug addict patients don't always follow instructions they are given. I'm guilty of not following that initial instruction from sponsors and friends. They told me, "All you need to do is take care of what is right in front of you. What is right in front of you is crack addiction. In front of you are serious failures in your choices and life. If you're distracted from the primary purpose of what you're trying to accomplish here, there's a high probability that you will not be successful."

I always remembered that. Fast-forward 15-16 years. I win the Texas Lottery and recall those words again. I'm in a better place mentally, socially and spiritually that I gave myself advice: Thomas Henderson, don't make any major financial decisions for 365 days. Well, it's been almost five years and I still haven't made a major financial decision. Twenty years ago my natural impulse would have been to spend extravagantly, buy a motor vehicle company or something like that.

Anyway, I was expecting the October 15 release, and had a $3,000 speaking date on October 22 in Blacksburg, Virginia, at Virginia Tech. I was scheduled to address the student body and athletic department. I worked in the prison commander's office and had access to a computer, so I wrote a complete speech in bold type and put it in a folder.

Soon as I was released I talked to my probation officer to get permission to travel. He couldn't believe I had a speaking engagement. Most ex-convict, alcoholics and drug addicts don't. I showed up at Blacksburg and to my surprise drew a crowd of 2,000 in an auditorium with a podium and microphone. I read my speech for the next 75 minutes and got a standing ovation. After all, it was a pretty good speech. They loved me in Blacksburg.

My second speaking date was for $4,000 on October 29 in Kona, Hawaii. Keep in mind that the Program Corporation took 30 percent of my fee for serving as the booking agent. So that $3,000 turned into $2,100 and the $4,000 into $2,800.

"Honey, you're going with me," I told Diane. I bought her a ticket and we flew to Hawaii. I was to speak to a community group in Kona. My host was a big Hawaiian guy with a construction company and private helicopter. I figured out later this trip was more about him being a Dallas Cowboys fan than about me making a speech.

The night of the speech I wanted Diane to stay in the hotel. The host picked me up and drove to the community center. Ten minutes before the program started I didn't see more than 10 cars out front. I walked into the room and there sat five people. I was introduced to a hollow round of applause. I mean, how much applause can five people muster?

I'll tell you what was important about that scene. On about the third or fourth page I realized my speech wasn't relevant. In about a week something about me was different. I took my 75-minute speech, walked across the room to a trash can, threw it in the trash, moved back to the podium and talked for 45 minutes about where I was right at that moment.

That's been my style ever since. I'm an improvisational speaker. I speak from my heart and my experience. I speak of where I am right then. I may talk about the flight, what that was like, or what's right or wrong with my kids.

By 1987, we were living in Costa Mesa, California. I was doing maybe 20 lectures a year at several thousand a pop. I'd broken my neck playing football so I had some money from Workers Compensation and NFL Disability, and I was married. I was so married that I was hanging out with married couples, going to see in-laws every other weekend and life was going pretty well.

I was successful with parole. I was tested constantly. I continued to see Dr. Pursch, my psychiatrist, seeking his counseling and staying close to him. I was also searching from a marketing point of view. This was for livelihood, not image or ego. It was to make a living in life, something I had never really contemplated. I thought I would play football forever. I thought I'd be associated somehow with football forever.

The dilemma for every athlete who plays eight or ten years is what to do after the uniform comes off. I looked back at Roger Staubach when he was running around selling real estate in Austin and Dallas during the '75-'76-'77 off seasons. I thought something was wrong with him. I thought, "Why are you doing this? Don't you know we're the Dallas Cowboys?"

Of course, Staubach now owns a billion-dollar commercial real estate company. I never expected to be anything but a football player, and hadn't really planned beyond that. I was as surprised as everyone else to be drafted by the Cowboys. I was up at Langston kicking ass, taking names, busting lips and chins and knocking the snot out of people's noses 'cause it was a fun thing to do. Who would have thought I'd get paid for it?

Anyway, a television station taped one of my talks and it ended up in the hands of someone in New York. That led to an invitation to Long Island to meet George Benedict, who'd started a drug and alcohol treatment center in Westhampton. He asked me to give a speech at the center and paid my fee, which was all I expected. But he liked the way I laid it out. The patients identified with me and what I'd been through, the honest and passionate way I came clean: "I went to prison for sexual battery. I went to prison for sexual assault. Here's my story."

So they hired me. I made $50,000 to come to New York once a month to talk to the patient population. This made me curious, and I started to look around. I saw there was Hazelton...Scripps...all these treatment centers in the country. If this one doesn't pan out, I thought, then I'll work for another one.

This experience started the process of me helping friends. I had a wealthy friend in North Dallas, a guy with millions. I used to go to his house and snort cocaine on his bar. We had the same conversation every day. The conversation never changed. We'd get stuck in a cocaine haze and repeat ourselves talking about the same thing. It was like a time warp.

I went to see him again because I liked him. One day I was at his bar talking to him and he turned up stoned on drugs. I told him, "I'm not coming back over here. I don't like being around you when you're like that." He went ballistic. With profane curses deleted, he said, "How dare you! You of all people come to my house and start judging me!"

So I didn't talk to him for a couple of months. But I affected him to the point that he came to the treatment center in Westhampton. I affected him so much that now he's a drug and alcohol counselor.

Not all of my interventions had a happy ending. I worked with an athlete who competed at the highest level of his specialty because Dr. Pursch also had him as a client. He had a candy problem. I got a call from him after he lost a world title event. He needed to talk. One reason was he had an $8,000 phone bill. Remember those X-rated sex phones? They cost

$300 an hour. This guy had talked on the line to some married couple. They invited him over. He went to their house and had intercourse with the wife. All from phone calls!

I called Dr. Pursch for advice. He said, why not take him to a sex addicts meeting? I found one in Orange County and arranged to meet this guy. He hadn't shown up when the meeting started so I went in and sat down. People were going around the room saying, "Hi, my name is blah, blah and I'm a sex addict. The rotation got to me, and I said, "I'm Thomas. I'm a sex addict." When you're in a closed meeting like that you have to identify with the topic.

For the next 90 minutes I listened to stories about masturbation, incest survivors, perverted activities, peeping, peep shows, triple-X porn movies and "I-can't-help-myself." The only requirement for membership to a meeting like this is the desire to quit. If I ever had a moment of clarity it came to me after listening to what these people were doing and thinking and having urges to continue doing. I realized I didn't have any of their symptoms. So although I was there for a client, it ended up being good for me. Part of my low-grade shame went away.

I try to find humor in every experience. This session was no exception. The gentleman sitting next to me talked about how he masturbated to orgasm five, six, seven times a day. Every day. "Today," he said proudly, "I've only done it twice."

The meeting ended. We stood and recited The Lord's Prayer. Then this gentleman turned and extended his hand for a so-long handshake. When the thought crossed my mind about what he'd been doing with that hand, I smiled and said, "How about just a hug."

And what happened to the athlete I tried to help? His life never worked out.

I worked in and around Southern California from '86 to '89 and in New York in '87. I was approached by a company to film my post-prison story and sell it to drug rehab centers. They put me in front of a camera in a Dallas hotel and let me go without a script. I spoke for more than an hour and from that they produced a 45-minute film titled Second Half. The film made several hundred thousand dollars, of which I received a nice percentage.

Doing films appealed to me. I could tell my recovery story and help others. Films had commercial potential. And, let's be honest, I have never been camera-shy. I wanted to do more.

I wanted to go to a prison and film. I had more to say. But the executive running the company said, "We already have the Thomas Henderson story. There is no more Thomas Henderson to tell." I thought there was, and from his refusing to do another picture with me was born the Thomas Henderson Film Company. I've made six more films since, and they are shown today in almost every prison, drug and alcohol rehab center in the country.

The most memorable review I received occurred on the streets of New York. One day I'm walking on Fifth Avenue and about a half-block away I see a big ugly guy coming my way. I can tell he stinks. No teeth, intimidating, dreadlocks like a mop. He's panhandling and scaring the hell out of people. He doesn't scare me because I'm not afraid of any human being. But I was poised and alert, anyway, and in a defensive frame of mind.

His eyes meet mine. I think I'm going to have to knock the snot out of him if he comes over and messes with me. The distance between us closes. We get 20 feet apart, then 10 and five. I'm trying to pass him. We're still looking at each other.

He raises a gnarly finger at me and exclaims:

"I know you!"

My ego says, yeah, he knows me. I'm Hollywood Henderson, Dallas Cowboys. Not quite because what he says is:

"Hey, I was in prison and saw your film!"

There you had it. I'm famous in prison.

Exposure from the first film enhanced my speaking requests. So did publication of Out of Control, which hit the bookstores in the late 80s. Others in the rehab community saw the work I was doing and because I had a film in circulation I was sort of moving in on the competition. This Thomas Henderson cat is telling it like it is without sugar coating. He's letting alcoholics and drug addicts know the crap that he went through and endured unnecessarily.

The work was coming from my gut. Because on a daily basis I was showing up sober, waking up sober, going to sleep sober and traveling sober, I was living sober. That's where the work was coming from. I knew intuitively that if I stayed the course things would get better. My life was good but I was still ashamed. I once was completely caught up in, "What do you think of me?" until I heard a speaker say something profound. He said, "What you think of me ain't none of my business. What I think of me is important."

When I heard that it gave me a little more freedom. From walking out of prison with a barometer of 100 on the shame meter, it slowly started receding into the 40s and 30s.

I had dedicated Out of Control to Diane. Her father went to Tuskegee and was one of those famous World War II pilots. What a character. He must have had every board game in the world and he was expert in all of them. I never won a game. "Hi, how are you?" he'd say, "come on, let's play...." Off I'd go for another whipping.

There came a time in '89 when I'd made enough money that I said to my wife, "We need to get a home." We started looking at real estate in Orange County and a fixer-upper came up priced at $300,000. That summer I went to Austin to take my daughter to see her mother. I rode around and saw nice homes for $100,000 that in California would cost a half-million. I couldn't wait to tell Diane the good news: "We're going to Texas!"

My wife was also a recovering cocaine addict who I met in a treatment center. She was sober, though, and we were doing this together. She was my support system. I loved this woman. I was 35 or so, my wife 28 and I wanted to have children with her.

I said, look, we have a couple of hundred grand in the bank and no bad spending habits. I bought myself a used Volvo, rather than a Cadillac, Jaguar or Mercedes. I was being financially responsible, so I said we're going to Texas because I can buy us a nice home there. She always wanted to go back to college. She had a high school diploma and was computer literate. I'd bought her a computer. I told her she could enroll at The University of Texas and I'd work and take care of us.

But she said, "I'm not leaving my family to go to Texas with you." I'm not sure she meant it like that but that's the way I heard: "I don't want to have your children and I'm not leaving my family to go to Texas with you."

By now I'd been hired by Bill O'Donnell to become a member of the staff at Sierra Tucson. One of my requirements was to attend family week at the facility in Arizona, so I told Diane I had a job to do and would be back in a few days. I was supposed to act as an observer. But I wound up bawling like a patient. Bill, I blubbered, my wife said she didn't want to have my children and she didn't want to move to Texas with me, and I don't want to be married to her anymore.

"Why don't you tell her?" he said.

"I can't."

"Why not?"

"Because it would hurt her."

"So you're going to honor her feelings but not yours? Is that what you're saying?"

This conversation took place on the second day of my assignment. By the fifth day I had been transformed into honoring my feelings from then on. I went home, took Diane to a restaurant and told her I didn't want to be married to her any longer. We paid the check and went home. We were both emotional. After both of us stopped crying she said, "I'm not giving up my parents..." and so on.

For reasons not based on cheating or abuse or anything except that she didn't want to have my children and didn't want to live in Texas with me, I made the decision to get a divorce. Whether right or wrong, it was an important decision therapeutically. I can even say she and I should never have married. We started dating in a mental institution, we consummated our relationship in a mental institution during rehab, and we got married in prison.

By April of 1990 I was working for a second drug rehab center, my NFL disability had kicked in and I was doing fine financially. That's when I moved to Austin and bought a home.

BILL O'DONNELL
(Co-founder, Sierra Tucson)

People asked me if I had concerns about Thomas representing Sierra Tucson because of events in his background. My answer was that the whole nature of addictions is the mistakes we make. It is more important what a person is doing today.

I certainly know one of the slogans we live by is, 'there but for the grace of God go I,' and that applies to me. I developed my own cocaine addiction and alcoholism back in the 1970s and 80s and had gone through treatment. One of my goals in sobriety and in my understanding of what spirituality is all about was to try to be open hearted and non judgmental. Obviously we live in the real world and as a businessman you must use a degree of caution in forming relationships.

Yet it became clear to me that anyone who spent time with the Thomas I met would understand his ownership of responsibility and the idea that he had paid his debt. More importantly, the spirit and usefulness that he brought to our interaction. People in marketing and the business office did raise the question of whether to hire him. It was only important to me what Thomas was doing then.

I knew of Thomas as a great football player and had read his book, Out Of Control. My sister called me about him. She'd introduced herself to Thomas when he was playing golf at La Quinta, California. Thomas had heard of Sierra Tucson, the treatment center I founded with a partner. We talked on the phone, decided to meet and Thomas subsequently did some talks and marketing functions for Sierra Tucson for the next five to six years.

Our relationship grew into a close friendship. Early in the 1990s he took my three sons, Billy, Bryan and Christian, who were 12, 10 and 8, to a football game in Los Angeles where they met John Elway. Thomas is a man with a big heart, an engaging, genuine person. We've taken many trips, played golf and done family things together. He's one of my truest and best friends and I love him to death.

Thomas is a rags-to-riches story in terms of his sports history, his life and in the sense that he came from the background that he did and had the experience of going from Langston to the Dallas Cowboys. All that's been chronicled about what happened with the influence of money, fame, overnight success and great athletic ability. So what sort of person is he now?

I can say that Thomas is colorblind when it comes to people. I always felt he was way beyond the serious issues of race in our country and in all of us because of how we were raised. He's a genuine human being. As big as his heart is, his ego is as big as that sports hero he became. When you get to know him, the real Thomas Henderson, the man of recovery and the man who wants to reach out and help people, it's all wrapped up in one. He has a concern for people and extreme loyalty to friendships. What he's given back to his community is amazing. He's a shining star in many ways.

Despite all that trouble in his past, the fact that he's kept friendships with the Roger Staubachs of the world and people who might shy away or worry about his behavior rubbing off on them or their image, also says a lot about Thomas.

He has shared a steadfast belief in a life of recovery with so many different populations, not just with the people of Sierra Tucson and family members, but through all the work he's done in the prison network.

It takes lots of courage, strength and steadfastness to first get into recovery, admit your weaknesses and addictions, then to take action to do something about them. It so happened that I celebrated 20 years of recovery on July 1 and November 8 is Thomas's date. We've been sober about the same amount of time. I believe the unequivocal miracle of recovery begins with a spiritual awakening that allows us to make the choice of sobriety in the middle of all those problems, all those things that have dragged your life down.

To be blessed with the spiritual awakening of wanting and choosing to do something about it is the universal God-given...whatever terminology you choose for a higher power in our lives. I think Thomas, myself and anyone in recovery would be remiss if we didn't mention that.

I never played professional football. I did play in high school in Chicago and was captain of the Brown University team in 1971. Some of the self-discipline and push and price you pay in football become an asset when you direct that energy in a positive way. I also believe in the karma that if you truly try to do the right thing and make the right choice and be the best person you can be each day, the universe takes care of you. Which it certainly did for Thomas a few years ago when he won the Texas lottery. My three boys call Thomas from time to time. They have their individual relationships with him and he's never too busy to deal with them. As life would turn out one of my sons is in recovery. He was sober for two years, went back out and relapsed, and is clean and sober again for 18 months. His date now is November 8 and he's so proud that because it's the same date as Thomas.

CHAPTER FIVE

THE RING AND STUFF

Recovery created an atmosphere for me to get some stuff back and some other stuff I never had and needed. I used my Superbowl Championship ring to get out of jail after I got arrested in California. The IRS seized my ring from the bail bondsman and sold it for $13,000 at a public auction in Dallas, Texas in 1984. That was painful and embarrassing. Because I'd never pawned or sold my ring it never had a financial value for me. I earned that ring being on a team that won a Superbowl. I vowed to never pay money to recover it. In 1998 a friend invited me to dinner in Dallas and during dessert she gave me my ring back. 'Shocked", I asked her why and her response was "you deserve to be wearing this ring. It's yours. You earned it." She had contacted the Briscoe family and bought my ring back from them.

That's just one of the wonderful things I've got back by staying clean. I've received so many blessings as a recovering man and father; too many to recount. The simple daily decision to stay clean has provided me all the stuff I ever thought I wanted. I'm blessed. I got my family, kids, grandkids and self respect back. By staying clean I've habilitated my life.

My world is small but I care about my country. War hurts my heart. I hope our country creates a new policy in the Middle East and the world and calls it "Operation Even Hand" and treat the whole world and its entire people with respect. Taking sides has created the terror.

I don't think it's any accident that people in the spotlight seem to have a harder time recovering from their addictions. For one it's hard for them to have anonymity and the privacy they need early on. Paradoxically speaking, they're the same as a street drunk or crack addict as far as recov-

61

ery is concerned. The street person feels hopeless and therefore has a tough time finding courage and faith. The celebrity feels powerful and willful and can't surrender. I haven't handed out questionnaires or anything, but from what I've seen a disproportionate number of celebrities seem to get into trouble with drugs and alcohol, and also seem to have a bitch of a time getting sober. Not that it's a stroll through the park for anyone. But when you're in the spotlight all the time, you feel so powerful, so special. You grow very accustomed to preferential treatment. If you're in a jam you get bailed out. Recovery doesn't recognize celebrity. The disease could care less.

I was attending one of my 12-step meetings. I smelled the fresh brewing coffee in the big pot in the back of the room. Cookies and cake were spread out on a table. Rows of folding metal chairs were set up. Signs saying things like "easy does it" and "one day at a time" and the Serenity prayer dotted the walls. I poured myself some coffee and I saw a few of my friends arriving and smiled and said hello. Everything was fine. Then a smelly little thought wafted into my head. Then another one did. Oh, shit. Not now. Not here. It was a Hollywood attack. My thoughts went like this: "You're better than these people in this meeting. You've written a book and been on TV. You won the Superbowl. You're famous. Think about the stir that's going on because you're here. What a charge these people will get out of being at a meeting with Hollywood Henderson." Hollywood was telling me, "You're so cool you should be wearing a crown in this meeting." Hollywood gained his existence from my fears, insecurities and ego. He was a mirage created by a boy who didn't know how to live or feel in reality.

My job in sobriety is to recognize this character defect for what he is. False ego. The truth is I am just a drunk and drug addict trying to stay sober, just like everyone else in that room. The truth is, I must be humble in my recovery. That crown Hollywood wanted to put on was nothing but a bunch of thorns that would bloody his swelled head. I need to be in touch with the wickedness of this disease, like any other alcoholic. I don't need to be walking around thinking, "Hell, isn't it great being out of the woods and well?" This Hollywood stuff may seem like harmless bluster. It is far from that. When that attitude causes me to believe that I am bigger and better and stronger and all-powerful, I am disrespecting this disease. When this happens, Thomas loses. I could relapse.

Robert Briscoe knows what an asshole Hollywood truly was. He was on the receiving end of some of his garbage. Robert Briscoe is a gentleman from West Texas, a place called Levelland. They called it that because it is level. He attended the 1977 Super Bowl in New Orleans with his wife, Robbie. They were big Cowboy fans and they spent a lot of time hanging around the hotel to meet the players. One day during that week, I was passing through the lobby, loaded, of course. Had my shades on and my feelers out, wondering where the babes were and where the cocaine was, too.

The Briscoes' approached me. They were shy, kind and courteous. "Excuse me, Mr. Henderson," Robert Briscoe said, "Do you think we could have your autograph and take a picture with you? We're big Cowboy fans." I stared at them from behind the shades. Everybody wants a piece of you during Super Bowl week. It gets old, but most guys deal with it all right, tolerate the requests, try to be decent about it, but not me. "Don't be bothering me," I said, "I've got to get somewhere." "But it will only take..." Bob started to say. "I said I gotta go!" and I kept walking. Had no time for them. Had no use for them. I was Hollywood. I wish I could tell you this was an isolated incident. I can't. It's the art of pumping yourself up at the expense of others. It's ugly, and Hollywood was a master at it.

Justice was served some years later. When the IRS started seizing my possessions, one of the items they auctioned was my world championship ring from Super Bowl XII. The IRS got possession of my ring because I used it to post my bond when I was arrested in 1983. While I was in prison the IRS had a public auction on my ring. Al Krutilek, my accountant, went to the auction. My ring sold for around $12,000. The buyer was Robert Briscoe.

I had a real hard time for a while about my ring being auctioned. I still do. I'd worked my ass off for it and it was a symbol of the football ultimate. World champion. It was mine. I felt wronged that the IRS would sell my trophy just for publicity. They do that shit all over our country and I still don't agree. Why didn't they sell my plaques, trophies, jerseys, jockstraps, helmet and everything else, too? But I had to remind myself that I have no business playing the victim. I didn't do what I was supposed to do. Now I was paying for it. Had to put it in the right pile.

I didn't know Robert Briscoe then. I had no idea I had blown him off years earlier in New Orleans. I wrote him a letter and he wrote back. He told me about the lobby incident. I made amends to him in my next letter. We talked on the phone a few times while I was in jail. We talked about the ring because I didn't like him or anyone else having it. A year after I was released, I got a phone call. It was Robert Briscoe. "I'd like to invite you here to Levelland," he said. "You could talk to some of our local kids about staying away from drugs and alcohol." I said I'd like to do that.

I flew into Lubbock, about 50 miles from Levelland. Robert and Robbie met me at the airport. He wore a pair of over starched, too long, faded Wrangler jeans and ostrich skin boots, a western shirt with the snap buttons, and a white cowboy hat. You could tell he was a good 'old boy. Big new pick-up truck with a fuzz buster, the whole West Texas oil man look. He drove fast. I liked him immediately. Intuitively I trusted him. He had made all the arrangements. I would be making a little tour of the schools in the area, elementary through high school. Speaking and sharing were still pretty new to me at this point. I was plenty nervous. I said a prayer for clarity and for God to say to these kids through me what they needed to hear. "God, let me be real," I prayed. He delivered. He always does. I had no clue about talking to the younger kids, the six and seven year olds.

Here I was, Mr. Guttermouth, a guy who grew up thinking 'mother' was half a word, talking to these sweet, innocent faces with the squeaky voices that all sound the same. I talked about their parents and we connected. They understood drinking and drugging because their moms, dads, uncles, aunts, cousins and neighbors were doing it. I was real. And I wasn't vulgar. I told the truth. Told them my story, in gory enough detail so they knew I wasn't messing around. I let those kids know how drugs and alcohol kicked my butt.

"I didn't think it would ever happen to me. I was a Dallas Cowboy. I was a big, strong guy. Well, it did happen to me and it can happen to you, too. Choose to be sober. Sobriety is an option." The kids, hundreds of them, stood and clapped when I was done. I felt good. My visit and sharing in Levelland, Texas is one I'll always remember. Robert Briscoe and I were on our way back to the airport. His pick-up was flying over the flat two-lane blacktop. The West Texas earth is red dust clay. When the wind blows hard, the air, trees, horizon, everything looks and gets clay red, including your Afro. This was one of those red days.

We were almost there when Robert turned to me. He smiled. Everything was deep red behind him and passing fast. He said, "You were really good with those kids and teenagers today. You're doing some fine work carrying that message you have. And I'm gonna tell you something, Thomas. I was going to give that ring to my grandchildren one day. That was my intention. But you stay clean and sober, keep doing what you're doing, and I'm going to give that ring back to you." He didn't say when, but he said it. A miracle was happening in my recovery. I think we both knew. God was there. "Thanks for saying that," I said. I looked out at the redness of the west Texas dust and smiled.

As I cruise the road of recovery, I think, "Is this the direction I really want to go? What will be my destination? Am I going to like it there?" I like it here, now, today – a lot. Sobriety is about having control, where there was once none. This awareness comes with recovery. It comes gradually as your mind clears and you start seeing misinformation for what it is.

About four years into my sobriety, I gave up smoking cigarettes. It was one of the hardest things I've ever done. The nicotine craving was relentless and I was addicted. If you're smoking, you're addicted to nicotine. When I accepted I was indeed addicted, I was ready and capable of giving it up, but I thought the cravings would never quit. Seemed like everywhere I went everything I did had an association with smoking. Cup of coffee? Needed a butt. At meetings? Needed a butt. I needed a butt constantly. It was hell. Addiction is hell. I did tough it out and haven't had a cigarette since August 8, 1988. The next time I found myself being judgmental with somebody who was having trouble staying away from alcohol or drugs, I would immediately think of the hell my nicotine withdrawal put me through. Detox, cravings and addiction are part of this vicious disease that us addicts and alcoholics survive. It's hell sometimes.

CHAPTER SIX

GOD AND ME

I was baptized a Christian when I was seven years old in 1960 and I thought they were trying to drown me. The only other time that I was born again was when I found sobriety. That was my rebirth in the strictest sense. I was starting over, learning how to live. Organized religion has never done it for me. As a child, I felt the whole deal was predicated on guilt and fear. If you don't go to Sunday school, if you don't believe in this or that, if you don't pray in the right way and have your knees bent at the proper God-fearing angle, you were going to burn in hell.

It felt joyless, like a burden, like the preachers were there to cram me full of as many do's and don'ts as they could. My young head spun at all the sins I had to avoid. I didn't do too well at avoiding them. I loved God, but the message I got was "Sorry, that doesn't cut it." I had to love Him the way they said. I had to follow steps A-Q if God was going to love me back. Confusing strings were attached. They felt like big fat ropes.

Today, I have a close relationship with God, as I understand Him, which is better than as someone else understands Him or Her. My spiritual faith has played an enormous part in my recovery from drugs, alcohol, sex and dysfunctional living. My God is totally loving, forgiving and has a great sense of humor. The do's and don'ts are gone. Intuitively we know right from wrong. It's funny how that works. The bond is uplifting, energizing. It is based on faith and love, not guilt, fear or damnation, and it has given me gifts in sobriety that I didn't know existed. Spirituality isn't a subject a lot of people associate with sobriety. My sobriety wouldn't be in existence without it.

A friend and I were beginning a round of golf. We were at the first tee when two guys asked if they could join us. They were refined, well-dressed men with southern accents. They were in their late sixties. They seemed nice. We said sure. Everything was going fine until about the fourth hole. One of them asked me, "Do you know Jesus?" "Not personally," I replied, "But I do have a relationship with God, as I understand Him." "That's not enough," he said, "You have to know Jesus. You have to follow His Teachings in the Bible." I told him I had read "The Sermon on the Mount" and I believe in everything Jesus did and said. He wouldn't let up. I didn't want to get into this with him. Hollywood and Wildman wanted his ass. Thomas was in control though. I just wanted to play golf. I explained that I was very fulfilled spiritually and tried to end it there.

"Hey, that was a nice fairway wood you hit," I said. "You must follow the word of the Bible," he said. His friend was chiming in now, too. I had mentioned to them that I was recovering and my work was writing and lecturing. They already knew who Thomas Henderson was. They continued their drive to save me and became increasingly adamant, wouldn't let it rest. I got the sense I had to convert before we hit the back nine or something bad would happen. Mr. Self-Righteous hit a two iron from the middle of the fairway and sent it to the fringe of the green. He chipped from there. The ball bounced and ran right up toward the cup, maybe a foot away. He looked at me and smiled. "That's from being a Christian and reading the Bible," he said.

I was in a sand trap next to the green. My ball was buried. The shot was impossible. I pulled out my sand wedge, set myself, dug in, and swung through the ball. I hit it perfectly. Sand sprayed. The ball floated upward. It kicked onto the green and rolled to a rest five inches from the cup. My turn to smile.

"That's from believing in God, as I understand Him," I said. Spiritual fitness is like physical fitness. You don't just acquire a deep faith anymore than you acquire bulging biceps. You put in the effort and humility and reap the reward. The rewards are great, but they are gradual.

I was in prison when it first struck me that something profound was going on with me. One year before I had been a dead end addict. If you had asked me then, I would have said, "Sure, I believe in God." But right then alcohol and cocaine were more important. My sense of God was absent. Chemicals were my god. Hollywood was god. I would convince myself that I didn't need anyone or anything, so everybody just get the hell out of my way and let me be.

My will had a vice-grip on my life, and a lot of other people's, too. I was doing everything my way. I knew best. I knew all. Nobody really knew me. Nobody knew the hell I was living. They never would. I didn't know how to share my pain. The rest of the world was connected and vital and I was alone and dying. Human power can only go so far. Behind the defiance and willfulness and grandiosity, of course, were Grand Canyon sized voids. The voids were what I was truly terrorized by. I felt hollow, tortured, and the pain was too much and the chemicals were the best medication I knew.

I was fleeing from God, fleeing from awesome fear. I had done all these terrible things. I had lied to Him, promised Him a bunch of times I would quit using if only He would let me get picked up by another team or let me catch a financial break. God was just somebody else to manipulate. Get a blessing and get out. I figured He was pissed off in a big way, figured He'd seen enough. With everything I'd done, I was pretty sure I'd have me a front row seat on the express train to hell.

What happened to me in prison is difficult to explain or describe. It wasn't a spiritual awakening in the sense that most people think of. No brilliant cosmic light gleamed in my eye. I didn't hear a chorus of angels or the voice of God saying, "Thomas, wake up." But it was damn powerful just the same.

Early on I heard recovering people talk about the importance of believing in a Power greater than yourself. I wasn't exactly sure why it was important then, or what it had to do with getting sober. But everyone I met told me that this faith worked for them, worked wonders in easing the compulsion that had trashed their lives. I was game. I believed this God deal was working in their lives. It was the look in their eyes when they talked about their Higher Power.

My faith at the beginning was really nothing more than a belief that life could be better with a faith in God. I was willing to believe that. More than anything else in my life, I wanted that to be true. For years I thought I had the answers to all my questions. Wrong again. What I had tried had not worked at all. I saw all these healthy people with good lives every time I walked into a meeting. Yeah, I was ready to believe there was another way. Without a belief that there was something greater that could help retrieve me from the human scrap pile, I don't think I would have made it this far. Without faith, what would have been the point? Why not just finish the job altogether until my incoherence passed on into death?

I believe that this God, as I understand Him, was always there with me. He never left. I was the one who left. Even as the disease was devouring me, God was that one, soft, gentle voice inside saying, "I'm here for you. You have a place. You are worthy if you can just let yourself believe." I had drowned that voice out for so long. Now, I was trying with all I had to listen. I simply had to be willing to open my heart and soul, let go of my desperate obsession to call all the shots. I had to humble myself to God. I couldn't do it alone anymore. I needed God's help.

God, as I understand Him, was a freedom of faith for me. Whatever it is for you is fine with me, too. God, as you understand Him, is none of my business. So, please, stay out of my God business. Thank you very much. God might be nature. It might be love. It might be intelligence, the idea that there is a Divine order that confers sense to the world and makes everything fit together.

This sometimes bugs a lot of people who are new to any faith in God at all, I know. They don't want to be getting into God stuff. They don't want God in the picture at all, in any form or fashion, whether because they are atheists or agnostics or simply because they think it's irrelevant. They just don't get the connection between getting sober and believing in a Higher Power. So I say; if you believe you don't believe, at least you have a belief system. Just do yourself one little favor and don't fight it right now. Save your energy for getting sober. God will find you. It worked for me and it has worked for a few million others, but you don't even have to believe it will work for you right now. Yet.

I believe that without a Higher Power I would probably be insane, homeless or dead. I'm not going to tell you that it's rock-solid certain that without a spiritual life you can't recover from drug and alcohol addiction. That's not my place. It just makes my life and recovery a miracle every day.

The beauty of faith is that you can begin right where you are. Wherever you begin from is great. Even if you go in thinking, "Well, I don't really believe all this stuff, but I'll pretend I do," that's good enough. Go ahead and think, "These people are a bunch of religious lunatics, but I'll play along." Fake it until you make it. That's fine, too. What faith you choose is your business.

Recovery isn't a contest to see who's most spiritual. The key is simple willingness. It's amazing what mere willingness, all by itself, can accomplish. Faith coupled with my strong desire to be sober has been one of my greatest allies. Going to meetings and gatherings with other alcoholics and addicts has been an incredible and constant source of support for me. It reminds me that I'm not alone. It keeps me in touch with the solutions. It also helps me dump my guilt and shame because it's a gentle place to share my feelings, and because I know the people around me know what I'm experiencing.

And, on top of that, it keeps me in touch with my faith in God, as I understand Him, which lets me surrender in a very healthy way. My faith brings me humility. It is a way of admitting I cannot do it myself, a way of saying, "This is bigger and more powerful than I am." I am not alone. I cannot do it alone. I cried for help. I cried and prayed and at the weakest, most humbling moment of my entire life, I knew God heard me. God was the difference. He was there and I knew it.

In my faith, the voids I felt are gone. The misery is healed. I don't know precisely how or why it happened, and I don't think sitting here all day thinking about it would help me find the answer. This is a matter of spirit. Reasons don't apply.

I'll never forget the day I was sentenced to prison. I was before the judge in the courtroom with my lawyer. It was time for sentencing. He stepped up to the bench and sat down and rapped his gavel. The judge began to read about my term. This would be concurrent that would be consecutive and so on. I stood there surrendered totally. I listened and it was as though his voice was coming from down the hall. I was in another place, a wonderful place. God gave me a moment of inner peace. By all rights, this should have been the darkest day of my life. There was no fear or anger. I wasn't fighting it. It was okay. I had this spiritual feeling because at that moment I knew my Higher Power had picked me up and carried me. I wasn't touching ground at all. A few minutes later, I was in jail. I never felt freer in my life.

I trust in God and in His plan for me. I trust the process of living and of sobriety and it lets me live with a comfort and a grace I have never known. Now I believe that even when there are conflicts and reverses and things aren't proceeding the way I want them to, I can deal with it and things will be okay. I know I have nothing to fear. I feel loved so I am able to love. I feel connected. I know I am part of a wonderful, larger wholeness.

With a spiritual life, it makes you accountable for your actions. I have a Higher Power that I must answer to and that relationship is above all else in my life. Because I feel His Presence inside me, I feel good about what I do. I don't always succeed, but when I don't, I admit it and correct it as soon as I can. The difference is that now I know how to behave and treat others. What a difference that is.

I do all I can, work as hard as I can, to live the best life I can, and that's enough. With the presence of God, the process of life is a joy and a blessing. It unfolds each day and it is exciting and enriching. That is why I'm more grateful than words could ever express. I'm sober and my will is totally broken. God willing, it will forever stay broken.

I was heading from Texas to California a couple of years ago, driving a blood red 1965 Chevy pick-up truck that I'd just bought. I was trucking my way across the Arizona desert. The road was hot, flat and endless. It was a late mid June day, but still very hot. I was driving alone. The sun was about to set. I pulled over, turned off the engine and got out of the truck. I got out a blanket and threw it over the hood of the hot truck to protect my butt. I sat on the hood in the middle of the desert and just looked. Rich sand went on for miles, stretching silently as far as I could see. Everything was magnificent. The sun was huge and orange. The sky was flaming with pinks and reds. Wisps of clouds were lit up. Everything glowed. I gazed into the sun, felt the intense glow on my face. The colors peeked and danced, lighting the whole horizon. The clouds drifted and everything was gentle. I didn't move. I closed my eyes and I could almost feel my breath leaving me. I kept gazing and feeling the stillness and soon the colors were fading and only an orange sliver of sun remained. A soft wind blew.

Nightfall was coming faster now. I took a last look and got back in my truck and headed back onto the road. I knew this was something that had never happened to me before. God was there. I could feel Him. I rolled on over the miles and soon the night was black, but the glow stayed with me. I'm not alone.

"With God's help and doing my part, I am quite different and so is my story." TH

CHAPTER SEVEN

WORKING ON MY RECOVERY

Recovery rules how I live my life.

A black guy named Tony with a big, fat-ass belly sat in the chair in the middle of the circle. He is from Chicago. He reminded me of my father. That's why he was there. It was April 1989, and I was in Arizona at Sierra-Tucson. I was there to do a quality of life workshop. This workshop is a weeklong group session designed to work on feelings, issues and family of origin stuff. I was there to work and grow.

I don't have this recovery stuff all figured out and I don't expect that I ever will. The real constant in my life since November 8, 1983 is that I'm clean and sober and I've changed a bunch. I hope neither of these two things change. Growth is a blessing. The way I see it, there are two choices for living: you can grow and change or you can stay the same. The world is constantly changing. People move and they get new jobs and new ideas and meet new people. Seasons change. New living things are born and others pass away. If I'm not willing to participate in change, I am going to miss all of God's great opportunities.

My recovery is always changing, too. One month the issue is food. The next month it is relationships and sometimes resentments. Issues do come up. New feelings come up, too. I need to stay current and willing.

I can't treat recovery as a past tense deal because I've got some sober years now. When this shit comes up, I don't hold my breath and wish it away. I tell myself that I've got some work to do here.

The stuff I was working on in Sierra-Tucson had to do with issues surrounding my mother and father. Even with all the work I'd done in my recovery, I still had this misery deep inside about them. I hated my father

73

and had issues with my mother. This was stuff I hadn't dealt with, feelings that I needed to experience and let go of. It was some of the hardest work and letting go I've ever done.

I was a typical American male in that I was damn good at stuffing my feelings. Men aren't supposed to fool with those things. Feelings are messy, shameful and embarrassing. Bury them and run. Don't acknowledge your feelings. When men hurt, they hurt just like anyone else with human emotions.

Boys are a society of feeling stuffers. Boys aren't supposed to cry. Big boys definitely aren't supposed to cry and that goes double for big boys who play football, who are supposed to be the epitome of roughness and toughness.

I learned in my recovery that it is okay for me to cry and I learned it was extremely important for me to know what I was feeling while this process of sobriety was going on. But I was still having a brutal time with this misery in my gut about my parents, especially my father. I still had to unload it. That day with Tony in the chair, starring as my father, I gave back the shit I'd been carrying around my entire life. I've heard said that a boy who is not fathered as a child can become a lethal weapon.

Okay, here we go. I had lived with this shame my whole life. This shame and hurt came from being abandoned by my father. There were two counselors and eight other people in the room that day. They were there to work on their own stuff, too. We sat in a circle with Tony in the middle. I moved to the center and faced him. I closed my eyes and envisioned my father. I sat with my feelings and then it all came up and out. I had prepared a tough love list for him.

When I began my list with him, tears welled in my eyes and I trembled with emotion. "You left me," I cried. "I'm hurt and I'm angry because you never came to be in my life when I was a child. You abandoned me. I was a mistake. I was a bastard. You left me alone and fatherless. You came back when I became a Dallas Cowboy. You're not my father. You're an asshole! I am not a mistake. I am not going to live with this shame anymore." I gave the shame back to my father that day. It wasn't mine.

This was my core stuff. I spilled every drop of the deepest hurt inside me. When it is inside, it is powerful. When I let it out and let it go it is powerless. This emotional release was growth for me.

There was nobody in the group who looked like my mother so I used my imagination. They placed an empty chair in the middle of the circle. The facilitator asked me to close my eyes and bring Violet Faye Henderson in the room. I imagined her getting into a cab at the airport and riding out to Sierra Tucson and paying the guy and walking in the front entrance. I saw her limping into the room. She was wearing a bright print dress and she had her hair red and a confused, unsettled look about her. What is this place? What am I doing here? That's what her expression said.

I saw her park herself in the assigned chair. She sat kind of sideways and smoothed out her dress. She looked stiff and uncomfortable. There were no hellos. I started right in. "When you whipped me, I felt afraid and angry," I said. "When you hurt me, I wanted to hurt you back. When you would whip me, mamma, I would never cry in front of you, but I would run down the street and cry there all by myself in the presence of God. I would ask God why He would let you do this to me. Why does she feel the need to hurt me and make me cry?" I didn't know then what I know now. She had been whipped that way herself. We pass on what we get.

"YOU HURT ME!!! YOU BEAT A HELPLESS LITTLE BOY AND I'M ANGRY AT YOU!!!!"

The feelings came up hard and fast. I got in touch with the child inside me, the child who felt the terror and rage of a parent hitting him hard, over and over, always for no good reason at all. Stop hitting me. Stop hitting me!

It's no revelation to me that my mother physically abused me or that my father bolted before I was born. Even though I've written about these things and known them for years, somehow I never truly, fully faced the feelings, never really sat with them and felt them and then let them go, until this particular occasion.

I felt what I imagine was innocent guilt, as a child after my mamma would whip me. I didn't know anything different. I didn't know something was wrong with her and not me. I thought it had to be me. She was my mamma. I figured I was no good. Why else would she hit me?

My imagined mother stayed in that chair for a half-hour that day and I poured out years of feelings. Just as I had with my stand-in father, I gave all that shame, guilt, anger, hurt and crap back to her and him.

I saw more clearly than ever before the intimate connection between the childhood I experienced and the adult I became. Love, sharing, affection, understanding, nurturing – all that was foreign to me. I saw where my fear of abandonment came from. I realized that as soon as my mother stopped whipping me, I started whipping myself with drugs, alcohol and whatever else I could abuse myself with. The feelings of abuse were familiar and I hung out there because that was all I really knew.

The process was painful, yes sir. But what questions it answered and growth it brought me. What peace it has given me in my overall recovery.

I went to Sierra-Tucson thinking I was exclusively an alcoholic and addict. I stayed five days and found out I also was an adult child of alcoholics, survivor of sexual abuse, co-dependent and a guy who needed to continue counseling and therapy. One week and my program resume exploded.

One of the most important issues that came up was coming to grips with how I had been affected by other people's drinking. Co-dependency is a disorder that is also getting treated in centers like Sierra-Tucson, right along with other addictions. I had spent virtually my entire life surrounded by practicing alcoholics. I always wanted to take care of them. I adopted a sick attitude and a clear dysfunctional lifestyle because of my impression and perception of the alcoholics I grew up with.

I needed to acknowledge this stuff. I saw how much I needed other people's approval. For so long, I had thought so little of myself that I had learned to look elsewhere for a sense of being okay. I also saw how my instinct was to take care of others and take care of them obsessively. I felt best when I knew someone needed me. I saw an unhealthy urge to control people, places and things.

I think because I had gone through so many years feeling like I didn't matter that focusing on another person's life gave me a chance to feel that I did matter. My happiness was sometimes contingent on what someone did or didn't do. I felt, on my own, that I wasn't good enough. Happy was only a word. Personally, I was only happy when someone else was. Growing up, about the only time I felt worth anything was when I was taking care of my younger brothers and sisters. There were four of them. When my parents were drinking and out on the town, I was the one who had to get them fed and dressed and tuck them in bed. I was their surrogate parent. I was stepping forward and fixing things and I was important. I liked feeling important. I grew up, but the need didn't go away.

I came to see that I had never met an alcoholic I didn't want to fix. This was before my recovery and during my recovery. There's nothing wrong with giving support to someone, of course, but I realized that I wasn't doing it selflessly. I wanted credit for it.

What one has to be careful of is claiming success in someone else's sobriety. If you want credit for his or her sobriety, you must claim their relapses, too. Take full credit. The trouble is, you can't fix another alcoholic. You can't live someone's recovery for him or her. You can help and be supporting, sure, but fix, no.

One of my big co-dependent episodes came in my marriage to Diane. I wanted to be the big deal there, too, the husband hero. If she had a big bill to pay or had done some overspending, I would always end up paying it instead of letting her be responsible. This happened more times than I like to admit. I would pay for and rescue her from her spending wreckage. I did it to glorify myself, be the big guy, and be her hero. It made me feel important. When I don't feel important in a relationship, I get out of that relationship. When I'd give her large sums of money to pay her bills, I expected major returns for my savior efforts, ticker tape parades, banquet, trophies and plaques. I wanted to be in control. I would stick my nose in her business and I'd make demands. Whenever I didn't feel like I was properly respected, acknowledged or appreciated, I'd get angry as hell at her. "I take care of everything, I pay my bills, your bills, and this is the thanks I get."

I had these self-esteem needs and didn't know how to fulfill them. In my marriage to Diane I was turning the focus toward her to fulfill them; and, again, by depending on someone else to validate me, I was sick in co-dependency. My co-dependency with Diane created all sorts of complications, including divorce. God, I'm glad I'm aware of this sort of behavior today. This is why therapy, recovery and treatment are so important in our world today. I learned how to live as a result of my crisis. These days I work constantly on never looking for personal validation elsewhere. The only kind that really counts comes from within and it's free.

This co-dependent stuff can be a vicious cycle, especially if you don't know you have it. Most co-dependents live with or are involved with an alcoholic or addict. It's as simple as that. My bottom line with my personal co-dependency is "I got tired of doing what I was doing and getting what I was getting."

I believe everyone should have someone they can be honest with. I mean really honest. If you don't have someone like that, find one. Before you can get honest with someone else though, you must first be honest with yourself. I have more than enough close friends, confidants and spiritual advisors today. They listen to my stuff and care about me unconditionally and are there for me, just as I am there for them.

I have men in my life today that I can comfortably give the keys to my house to. That's trust and that's a miracle for me. I once heard intimacy defined as me letting you see me be me. They see me being me all the time and they've witnessed the incredible changes going on in my life. It's nice to have witnesses.

Diane and I decided to divorce after almost four years of marriage. I called my friend, Jimmy Daniels, in Dallas and I was crying and I said, "Why isn't this working? What's wrong with me?" Diane is beautiful, inside and out, and she's a wonderful friend. I was certain when she was my lover and my wife that this relationship would last a lifetime. It hadn't turned out that way, and I wanted out of the marriage. For a year and a half, I pretended that everything was fine, nothing wrong. I was afraid, didn't want to look at it. I wanted the issues to mend themselves or just go away. When you don't honor or acknowledge your feelings, nothing ever changes except the date. I was in a love and relationship denial. It's like there was an elephant in my living room. His trunk was bashing into everything and there were piles of shit all over the rug, but I kept on looking away, saying, "Elephant? What elephant?"

Diane and I had grown apart. We had grown out of our intimacy. We tried to mend things, grow back together, but it didn't work and it was time for me to accept that the passion, love and commitment I had felt were not going to be recaptured. I was afraid to acknowledge or admit that. If my marriage didn't work, I was sure people would say, "There he goes again. Same old crap. He can't stay in a relationship. She's a real nice gal, but he's Hollywood and he ain't no good."

People pleasing creeps into my shit all the time. But I couldn't stay in this relationship just so other people would think better of me. That wouldn't have been fair to Diane or to me. That would have been bullshit, just a bunch of people pleasing. I've learned that people pleasing doesn't really please people.

Even amid my divorce and during my recovery, I experienced growth. I did the best I could. I wasn't hasty or impatient. I didn't just up and leave when the difficulties began. I didn't blame her or shame her and I didn't play the victim. I didn't try to force a solution and I didn't do anything stupid. I gave it time and my best effort. I shared my feelings with friends and tried to sort out my pain and loss. Even though the marriage ultimately failed, I can feel good about what I did and didn't do, and about the support I got from people who were there for me and are still there. I honored my feelings through it all. I never knew how to do that before. This calm behavior for me would have been unthinkable a few years ago. Alcoholics always amaze me, especially sober ones.

When I was early in recovery, I had a fear that I wasn't allowed to fail anymore. My recovery had to be perfect. Now I understand this is an imperfect process. Making mistakes isn't any fun, but it's okay. Shit happens. I'm not going to get kicked out of my recovery or program. Instead of dwelling on my mistakes and stewing over them, which is what I used to do, I try to use them as a vehicle of growth.

Being willing to change has brought optimism into my life that I've never known before. I have a sense that my life is manageable. I can work things out. Recovery can be hard and it's taken me places I'd never been, but I can do it because I'm not afraid to look at myself and not afraid to grow and change. I don't have a tidy, one remedy answer, but that's okay, too, because I'm not mopping the floor here, I'm rebuilding a life.

I truly grew when I faced all that heavy family-of-origin stuff in Sierra-Tucson and I grow every day when I look for my defects and try to make myself a better person. I still have wants in my life – my own jet, a winter home in Aspen, inheriting a few million from a total stranger – but all my needs are being met today. What more can a man ask for? I have a relationship with God and I have a sober life and wonderful friends and a job that lets me earn my living by talking about the work and joys of recovery.

Through it all, relapse was never an option for me. I believe relapse is a process, just like sobriety. Relapse is not inevitable though, it's a decision, just like sobriety is a decision. I've continued to choose sobriety. Every single day I wake up and I make a decision. I decide that the most important thing for me to do today is not to use alcohol or any other drugs. This has to be my focus or nothing else works. You see, I know that my life as it is today is definitely because I'm sober. My sobriety has to come first and it does.

Sobriety isn't that big a deal to some people – mostly to those who don't have it. There have been times when I've told people I was sober and they reacted like I was giving them the weather report. My life in sobriety has reached a comfortable zone. I believe I'm gonna make it. Life is good and I participate in it. With God and a program of recovering people doing it just like me, I just keep showing up and suiting up for the process and growth.

Through it all, what has always kept me close to this program is my new and committed faith in God. I like the results I'm getting out of this lifestyle. If I didn't like the results, I'd have to change and try something else. I've never had anything this good, and nobody can take it away from me, except me. Sobriety is the best thing I've ever had.

The results are spread all over my new life. Today, I have credit and credibility. I'm honest and straightforward. I share and I receive. I used to feel like a fraud and a mistake and I had a constant gnawing deep inside that ate away at me for decades. Now, I am at peace and I believe I am worthy and I believe I am doing good works. Today, I'm an open book and I'm approachable and comfortable. What you see is what you get. It's as real as I know. I'm not afraid of what you think of me or what you think you know about me. I'm a different man than I was in Out of Control or the beginning of this book, for that matter. Life is an adventure ever changing. Life is exciting in sobriety.

I used to live with misery and hurt. Today, I live with peace and fulfillment. My existence used to be a tragedy. Football star ruins life loses everything, goes to jail, and blows everything. That was the story. Today, the story is a miracle with profound successes due to my change and sobriety. That's what I was promised, and the promises were kept. I know a new freedom and a new happiness. If I can stay sober and change my life, anyone can.

I believe that recovery is for anybody who wants it. I don't care how lost or down trodden you may feel or how much you've thrown away or how long you've been using. You know where I've come back from. Lows can't get much lower, physically or emotionally.

This is as real as a heartbeat. Sobriety works. You can have it, too. If you want to be sober, if you want what I have and what millions of recovering people have, you, too, can have it. There is one requirement for anyone who attends a 12-step meeting, which is that you have the desire to stop drinking, using, or eating bad stuff, or whatever it is. You don't have to be a slave to your addiction and pain anymore. You don't have to be sick anymore. Your life can turn around. Mine did. Get yourself into a treatment program right now. Not tomorrow.

I never used to enjoy the process of living or success. I just wanted to get there and get further. I wanted to be done with whatever I was doing. It was hard and joyless. Everything was urgent and instant. I was hell-bent on being a success and being an all-pro linebacker and making big money, getting way ahead. When I accomplished all this, I was ready to do more. It's okay to want to excel. But it's damn sad when nothing you do is ever enough and you don't let yourself feel good about what you've done. That's how I was. Nothing was enough. I just kept pushing, pressing on, never stopped to say, "Hey, look at the distance I've covered." Never told myself, "You are a success, Thomas."

Today, the urgency is gone. I still want to do well and still want to be a success, but now I've redefined what that means. Today, success is staying sober and living right, having a sound spiritual life, and doing the best I can with whatever I'm doing. Today, that's enough. In sobriety and for the first time in my life, I savor my days. I don't just enjoy the process. I embrace it. This is my life. This is the only time I have. Right now. This second. Where I am and what I'm doing is plenty. I'm just going along and I'm growing and I've gotten myself a nice little pace. I don't race anymore. I live.

When shit happens, I stick with the solutions I've talked about in these pages. I try to keep things simple. I work on changing what I can. I make amends when I am wrong. I feel like I can deal with whatever comes up, even something as painful as death or divorce. I accept that pain is going to be part of the living package. We get through it. We move on. We don't get high. I've learned that there is not one thing I can't handle one day at a time.

God gave me several talents. One of them I use today as part of my livelihood is being a public speaker. I lecture all over the U.S.A. to all sorts of groups – recovering groups, drug rehabs, conferences, symposiums, companies, schools, colleges, NFL and community organizations. I love what I do so I do it good.

I was talking to a group of kids not long ago and I was hearing these words come out of my mouth about all the miracles and results I've gotten in sobriety. I stepped outside myself for a moment. I was part of the audience just for an instant. I got goose bumps all over, chills raced through me, an incredible, happy shiver. I had such momentary clarity. This was a miracle. This was me I was talking about, the has-been, and the bum. I had come far. I had accomplished much.

All these young, vulnerable faces were looking up at me and they were rapt. Maybe some of them would be spared the pain and suffering I lived with for so long because I was sharing with them the pain, being real honest with them about alcohol and drugs. I do not give mixed messages. My message is clear – drugs and alcohol screwed up my life and it can screw up yours, too. I also hammered home my theme – sobriety is an option. I say this to young and old. Some of us never knew we had a choice or option.

I hope my sharing all over the country will help the educational aspect of our national campaign against drug and alcohol abuse. Maybe some of them will make choices and decisions that would let them lead good, healthy, sober lives. I stood there before them knowing my message was clear. They weren't stupid. They knew after listening to me that clearly a relationship with alcohol and other drugs is a liability.

My recovery is a private party, a celebration of one that I share with everyone I meet. I am Thomas Henderson and I am a sober man. Nothing I ever do will make me prouder.

FRIENDS, ENABLERS AND CO-DEPENDENTS

No matter how you look at it, drugs and alcohol are a liability. Pour a little on a marriage, a family, a job or country and it will cause shit to happen. The delusion has to do with our society portraying alcohol as an asset. Alcohol is a drug, you know? It has no asset value at all.

If you got out a pad and pen and tallied up the pros and cons, it would be a joke. In my using prime, I would have said, well, it helps me unwind. It makes it easier for me to have fun. It makes my problems easier to copy with, and don't forget the sex. Sex, drugs and alcohol were like ice cream, hot fudge with a cherry on top.

The cons? Where do I start? It killed my brain cells, injured my liver. It did nothing for my problems but make them worse, no matter what I thought. It bankrupted me. It destroyed my relationships, destroyed my career, and wrecked my credibility. Fun? The hell totally outweighed any glint of fun I ever had on alcohol or drugs.

No cocaine addict or alcoholic I ever met looked back and said, "Yeah, well, I've been drinking and smoking crack for five years now and it's been a super great time. Wouldn't change a thing." There was the perception of fun and folly with alcohol and drugs, but what follows is degradation and dysfunctional addiction. There is no future with alcohol or drug abuse.

Thomas Henderson has a purpose today. I believe that purpose is to carry the message of sobriety and hope to all the hopeless that are addicted. I think the most important thing I do, every day, right after keeping myself clean and sober, is doing what I can to help others find their sobriety too. Passing it on is my joy job. I just have to keep reminding myself that I can't do any force-feeding with this deal.

If I want sobriety for the person I'm trying to help more than he or she wants it, it's not going anywhere. This is a sure way to become co-dependent with an alcoholic or addict; make their recovery your mission. People have to want to participate in their own recovery. I could pound my fist and shout and make Louis Farrakhan look like a PTA speaker, and it wouldn't make any difference if the ears on the other end weren't open.

I don't try to drag everybody who I think has a problem into treatment or a 12-step program. If I did, my immediate family would be the first casualties. I don't stand outside nightclubs and recruit folks for treatment. But I'm not going to look away either, not if I work my program. If I love and care about you, I'll just wait until denial relaxes and pain is present. Then I'll tell you I love you and want you to seek help for your problem.

A lot of family members and friends are terrified. They don't know what to do and they don't want to face the truth, so they plant their heads in the sand and hope the whole mess will blow away. It never blows away. People die or go insane.

The whole time I was destroying myself during my Cowboy days, nobody ever said one word about my drug abuse or alcoholism. I'm not saying I would have listened. Chances are I wouldn't have. Chances are I would have blown them off or gone into my Wildman mode and given them an earful of my denial. I'm sure as hell not blaming what happened to me on their silence. All I'm saying is that getting it out in the open is the best thing you can do if you're concerned about a friend or family member's abuse of alcohol, drugs, food, sex, etc.

I gave a lecture to the Denver Broncos about this in the spring of 1989. Dan Reeves asked me to speak to the team about alcohol and drug abuse. John Elway was there. So were Tony Dorsett, Steve Watson, Rulon Jones and the rest of the team. Their eyes were on me and they were glazed over. They looked like high school kids on the last day of school. They wanted to be gone, some place else. They had heard it all before.

I don't get thrown very easily when I'm speaking, but I got in front of these guys and I saw the collective blankness and I was thinking, "Damn, this here's gonna be the toughest gig I've ever done." Their faces said, "Okay, try and make us laugh. Educate us. Just try. Come on, Hollywood." Dan Reeves was there and so was my former teammate, Charlie Waters. He was coaching there. He knew I'd deliver. There was no room for preaching, platitudes or lukewarm warnings. I knew I had to be real. They demanded it.

I had a pretty good idea that every one of them had the same attitude I had whenever I heard Charlie Jackson give his law and fear speech or his NFL wandering anti-drug minstrels. "I don't need this. I don't need you. I'm an athlete. I'm big. I'm bulletproof. I'm strong and rich. Ain't no way alcohol or drugs will ever get the better of me." There's no denial like an athlete's denial.

I told them my story and I urged them to take a hard look at themselves and their relationship with alcohol or drugs. Injecting humor ever so often causes any audience to listen a little closer. After ten minutes, I had them in the palm of my hand.

Mostly what I got into that day was what to do if you think a teammate has a drug or alcohol problem. I told them that a hell of a lot of pain and suffering can be avoided if the people who love and care about each other could learn to share and confront a practicing alcoholic or addict in a constructive way. It seems lots of us are on our own and only cover our own ass. I told them I had bullshit shallow friendships before. Hell, I had friends who would steal my dope and help me look for it.

I told the Broncos a story about two friends who went hunting and were walking through the woods. Their guns were unloaded, slung over their shoulders with a lot of other gear. They hopped over a big fallen tree and suddenly they were face to face with a coiled, snarling mountain lion. Immediately, one of the panic-stricken hunters began stripping off his stuff: his rifle, pack, vest, shirt, jeans, canteen, etc, getting light and ready to run for it. As he stood there in his underwear, the other hunter and good friend gave him a puzzled look. "What the hell are you doing?" The other guy responded, "I'm getting light so I can run." The first guy said, "You can't outrun that mountain lion." To which the guy in his underwear replied, "I don't have to. All I need to do is outrun you."

In the NFL and in a lot of places, I suspect most guys are running for it alone. Drug use tends to be more of a solitary thing because of the penalties that go with that behavior these days. The stigma is worse than ever before. A lot of Perrier is ordered instead of shots of tequila. If a guy wants to use, mostly he'll do it by himself or with a college friend or one of his homeboys. If he does it with teammates, usually it will be just one or two of his best friends, as opposed to when I broke into the NFL in mid 1970's. Then, if one guy had pot or coke, all the guys who were into it would come running like flies heading for shit. No more, everyone is paranoid and careful, if that's possible. This causes a covert use of drugs.

My point was that if you care about a guy and you're truly his friend, just be aware of behavior induced by alcohol or drug abuse. It's easy to see. If your eyes see something you don't like, then open your mouth. Do it for all the right reasons. You don't want to see him screw off his family or career or maybe even kill himself. It's also a practical response. If someone is abusing chemicals or drinking too much, you can't count on him come game time on Sunday. Maybe he'll be okay, but maybe he won't. If his mind is muddy or his body is run down, maybe he won't make the block he's supposed to make or cover the guy he's supposed to cover or break the tackle that he usually breaks. You just don't know, and when games can be won and lost by such things, not knowing if a team member is there for you is a scary thought to ponder.

Confronting someone can be a tough and tricky proposition. But to me, if you think he's in trouble and you don't say anything, you're obviously not much of a friend at all. To be quiet is to be an enabler in the sense that you're doing nothing but enabling him to continue heading down the same path of running, denying and abusing. It's a path that only leads to awful places, places I've been. Enablers have the best of intentions and get the worst of results. They want to be supportive and kind. They want to stay in a person's corner when everybody else is running away. They think that maybe what the person needs more than anything else is a friend who will give unconditional support. They do everything they can to ease the user's burden. They'll cover for them. They'll lend them money and bail them out of tight spots.

I had a friend who did everything for me but tuck me in at night. He's a wonderful guy, then and now; loyal, generous, compassionate. But he wanted so badly to help me that he couldn't see that the best thing would have been to pull the plug on me and not take care of all my needs. I used him terribly. I stayed with him for several months. He gave me shelter, food, money and made everything real easy for me. My drug abuse only got worse. I had no reality check. I was addicted and on a free ride, all day long, because he took care of all my responsibilities. Beautiful intentions. Horrible results.

Another one of my enablers was a doctor. I went to him because I was having trouble sleeping – trouble because I was doing cocaine all through the night. Cocaine causes some serious insomnia. I said, "Doc, I've got to have something to get some rest and I also have some real bad pain." I walked out of there with prescriptions for a hundred Quaaludes and a hundred percodan. I flew through both of them and went back. "Gee, Doc, they really helped me. Gotta have more." "No problem," he said. And so it went. He knew what was going on. WE partied together. He might as well have written on the label, 'Abuse as directed'. I bet Elvis Presley had a friend and doctor just like mine.

I had a lot of enablers. I clung to them when I was using because I needed them desperately. Back then, I thought they were my salvation. I never had to worry about the consequences of my drinking and drugging. They enabled me to keep going. A lot of alcoholics and addicted people die because their friends and loved ones prevent them from being accountable for their own actions.

The one guy on the Cowboys who never enabled me was my best friend Too Tall Jones. He tough-loved the hell out of me without ever knowing what tough love meant. Earlier in my career, before I got too heavily into drugs, he and I had investments together and we exchanged money openly and freely. But once he saw me out of control, he cut me off. I'd say, "Too Tall, listen man, I'm really in a bind and I need $5,000 to pay some bills. Can you float me a loan for a few days?" This was early 1982. His face would be like a stone. "No," he said, "I'm on a budget." I tried other angles. No luck. I pleaded. I tried to con him. Made up stories, real good ones, about what I needed the money for. My mamma's sick. My baby's sick. My basement is full of asbestos. But it was always, "No, I'm on a budget." Nothing worked. I could con anybody and everybody. I could talk a hungry cat off a fish truck. But I couldn't con Too Tall Jones. It ticked me off. I always hated losing. "You know what, you're a cheap son of a bitch and I can't believe you are turning me down like this. I need help, man, and all you do is tell me about your fucking budget. Well, fuck you and your budget." I didn't take it any further. He was too big to intimidate.

Too Tall never got into it with me, never made any accusations, never said, "I ain't lending you money because it's gonna go right up your nose, like all your other money did." He just said no, as the saying goes. At the time, I would have told you he was an asshole, heartless, tightwad. Today, I know Too Tall was perfectly right. I owe Too Tall Jones a lot of thanks. I had to make amends to him for some of the things I'd written in anger about him, too. Right then, he was a better friend to me than all those people who were tripping over themselves to rescue me were.

Most chemically dependent persons don't want to be confronted. They run and hide from reality. We must help the addicted. We may be the best and last chance a friend or family member has. Hard as it may be, angry as they may get, it's the greatest kindness you can offer somebody whose life is going down the toilet.

I've learned the best approach is simple, direct and non-judgmental, saying something like, 'I'm concerned about you," or "I'm worried about you," and taking it from there. They'll surrender or say, "What do you mean?" Then I might say "You don't look so good," or "I'm worried because I've noticed you're drinking more than you used to," or "I hear you're doing cocaine and it scares the hell out of me because that shit can kill you. I don't want you to die." In a non-threatening way, we let them know we know the party is over even if they don't. Or just put it plainly: You look like shit and you're going to die.

Urge them to talk to someone about their problems: their doctor, an employer, assistance professional, their pastor or clergyman, whoever they feel safe and comfortable with. If they are unemployed or homeless, suggest the free self-help 12-step programs. That's where everyone who recovers ends up anyway. That's where I still go. It works.

There's no guarantee they are going to take your suggestions. All you can do is try. You have planted a seed. The goal is to create a well-meaning upheaval in their life. Denial being what it is some forms of upheaval or crisis is usually what it takes for an alcoholic or addict to start getting a more accurate picture of things. It took a big-time crisis and a cold, hard and dark bottom to get my full attention and cooperation.

I believe another way to force a crisis is with a mandatory drug testing program. I hated drug testing. I tested twice a week for two years while on parole. Drug testing stinks, but I'm all for it. This is a huge contradiction, I know, but I believe testing can save lives, families and careers. That's a pretty damn powerful bottom line.

Drug abuse has gotten out of hand. The problem is an emergency. Emergency measures are called for. A lot of folks aren't listening. A lot of folks can't hear. This shit kills. The threat of testing may stop some human beings from ever getting started, and for folks who are already in trouble, it may force a crisis that will make their chances for recovery that much better. It makes people stop and think. It sets up a detour that can't be averted, and that just might save a person's life who is hurtling headlong down a road of ruin – just like the road I once traveled.

There was no testing when I played professional football. If there had been, they probably would have had me pissing in that cup five times a day, based on my behavior, and I probably would have been the first player banned for life. But getting my ass kicked out of the NFL might have been the best thing that ever happened to me. If I'd had the crisis of a lost career forced on me, I might have bottomed out five years before I eventually did. It might have saved others and me a lot of pain. Testing can save individuals and families a bunch of excessive misery.

Drug testing is no panacea for America's drug and alcohol problem. I know that. Testing doesn't mean that people are going to stop abusing themselves by early tomorrow afternoon. It doesn't mean alcoholics and addicts will end their denial or that lights will go on in scores of NFL heads and players, coaches, or owners will come forward, raise their hands and say, "'Scuse me, which way to the rehab?" Denial will be around as long as addiction is. Maybe testing wouldn't have done shit for me. Maybe I would've just felt angry and victimized. But maybe it would have done something, and in this life and death matter we've got to reach out for every 'maybe' we have. No, testing is no cure-all, but I think it's an effective deterrent, and an effective deterrent can save lives. That's the greatest cause there is.

I'll test for anyone, anytime, anywhere. Proving I'm sober doesn't do anything but make me feel good. Rumors and lies don't bother me. I know there are some so-called recovering athletes who talk about drug and alcohol recovery and education and aren't even totally sober themselves. This is dangerous and folks had better be careful about who they have speak on this delicate subject. Some people might ask, "Doesn't asking someone to test mean you don't trust them?" Trust has nothing to do with it. Trust means nothing to someone who's using and who is in denial.

I knew a guy who was working for a halfway house and foundation of which I was a Board member. One of the requirements to work there was to be sober. That is if you were a recovering person. There were people who worked there who drank normally — whatever normal is. He was tested one day and it turned out positive for marijuana. They didn't fire him on the spot, which was a mistake because of existing rules and regulations. He got a warning only because they perceived his value higher than it truly was. They compromised their whole program, staff and existence on this guy. He failed them. Practicing alcoholics and addicts always fail if they don't stay sober. He tested positive again a few weeks later. When confronted, he was indignant, self righteous and angry. This time they fired him. He was later arrested and charged with armed robbery, obviously to support his addiction. He's now serving ten years in prison.

My biggest concern about testing isn't trampling the rights of the individual so much as what is done for the individual if he comes up positive. Not nearly enough is done for them right now, not in the NFL anyway. The NFL does a terrific job of policing its players, but a lot less than terrific when it comes to caring for them. They treat the offense, but not the athlete and his family. The NFL has thirty-two drug and alcohol programs including a thirty-third in the Commissioner's office. No wonder it is a doomed program. I don't believe the intentions are evil.

A player who tests positive is in an acute place. His life is in crisis. He doesn't need to be further alienated or humiliated or ostracized because he's done a fine job of all three by himself. This could be anyone, for that matter. This is a sick person, someone whose body and mind and emotions are under foreign management, no matter what he's using. Like any other patient, the better and more prompt the care, the better are the chances this person can get well.

Drug abuse is a highly emotional subject in our society. When a famous athlete gets arrested for drunk driving, it goes away pretty quick because drinking is all right in our society. When the same famous guy turns into an infamous drug abuser and his life suddenly becomes a headline, a natural reaction is to be judgmental, angry and disappointed. We hear about Stanley Wilson or Steve Howe or Hollywood Henderson and we want to scream at them, "How could you have done this? How could you have let us and the children down" It's real easy to simply scold the guy, to reduce the whole thing to a basic lack of willpower. This habit and compulsion is a disease.

People who get to the point of abusing drugs and alcohol are sick people, not bums without morals or intestinal fortitude. I don't think any of us set out to be addicted. If you did . . . I want to meet you. Feeling disappointed when someone we love or look up becomes a drug abuser is an entirely natural response. Just know that if this person gets treatment, they will be better than you have ever known them to be. If they stay sober.

I felt good when I finished talking to the Broncos. Maybe they had heard some of it before, but never from where I'd come from. I saw them nodding their heads and a few of them asked questions. By the end, I believe I'd gotten through to some of them. One talk isn't going to make a team free of drug and alcohol problems. I believe they heard me and I know they listened. I think they got a pretty good idea of how to talk to a guy who is screwing up his life. One day I'd like to speak to every NFL team.

I never stopped and thought about what I was doing when I was using. I had that early perception and took off from there, grabbing whatever chemicals I could get my hands on. Nobody knew what to say or do. They were as clueless as I was.

The point I really wanted to impress on the Bronco players is that if you see a guy who is abusing alcohol and drugs and you care about him, a few well-chosen words might do a world of good. Basic caring goes a long way. The words might make a difference coming from a friend. You can put into focus that his drinking and drugging are a liability to him, to his family and his team. When someone you love, trust or admire says something like that to you, it can really shake you up.

I told the Bronco players, "Let's not stop reaching out to human beings who are caught up in using and abusing alcohol and drugs. They didn't, as I didn't, intend to end up addicted."

JOHN FREDERICK
(Film Maker)

Thomas will tell you that I took a big gamble on making his first film in 1988 since he had been out of jail only one year and clean and sober for about five years. He was right in one respect because I wound up re-financing my house to complete the project.

But I never felt like I was taking a chance on Thomas himself. Sure, I was aware of his substance abuse situation. That was my situation as well, but I beat him to getting clean. I've now been sober for 32 years.

When I met Thomas, I don't know if nobility is the right word, but there was something about him. I knew what had happened to him. I looked at him and thought that this guy has gone down as far as he could but it hasn't beaten him. Underneath, I could see the goodness in him. I felt like I was talking to a guy who was genuine.

I met Thomas through Dr. Joe Pursch. Thomas went into treatment with Pursch, who worked with him free for a long period of time. I talked to Pursch about three times a week, and all I heard was success and the great things that were going on. Thomas in the meantime had been sent to the Men's Colony in San Luis Opisbo. Your man Thomas isn't doing so well, I mentioned to Pursch.

"No," he replied with what I thought was a great comeback, "Thomas is doing very well. He's just in jail."

A few years later Pursch brokered an introduction to Thomas. I was aware that Thomas was still OK. Pursch filled me in on what was going on. So I asked him a specific question about patient recovery that I knew he seldom answered.

"I know you don't give a 'yes' or 'no' but what do you think about Thomas?"

"As you know, you cannot predict human behavior. But if I was to bet on it, I'd say he is going to make it," Pursch said. That was rare. I never heard Pursch say that about anyone else.

Thomas negotiated his contract with my son Randy to my detriment. He's a good businessman. Randy was in his 20s, running the company and maybe felt intimidated. Thomas got 25 percent of the gross, which is about three or four times what you normally pay someone who'd never done a film.

We made the picture titled, "Second Half." This one had real budget problems after we filmed in Dallas and the sound turned out to be no good.

The thing cost $80,000, about $30-40,000 over our projection. I did a re-finance on my house to finish it and had that picture been a failure... I'm looking at receipts for his picture that cost $80,000 and it's made $800,000. That was one of his first big paydays. I showed him how to do it and that was enough. From then on he figured if he did it himself, he could get 75 percent.

I want to tell some things I learned about Thomas. He never lied to me. He's always been up front about what he's thinking. He could be a master manipulator for all I know but if there was ever a problem he was willing to talk about it and deal with it. He's just a straight shooter. We've never had a cross word and never had to talk about money.

I don't think of Thomas as being black. It's as if he's above race. He doesn't think about black or white.

The substance of his message works for blacks, whites and Hispanics. It works for young and old people. He just has that aura about him. And look what he did with money from the lottery. He didn't go nuts with it. He bought a used Mercedes and a pretty low budget condo in Florida. He didn't go bananas and run off to Las Vegas.

I always thought even with all his trouble Thomas was a lucky guy. I thought that before he won the lottery. One of my favorite quotes is from Napoleon. Someone asked him what quality he most desired from his general. Did he want his general audacious, courageous, brave?

"I want him lucky," Napoleon said.

Thomas was lucky to be alive. He's lucky to have met Dr. Pursch. He's lucky to have been a Cowboy. There is goodness and talent there, too, but lots of luck. I always like to ride with guys who are lucky.

Before we made the movie, I was aware of the charges against him. So I asked, Thomas, did you do that?

"No, I didn't," he said, "but I did so much that I got away with that it all evens out in the end."

CHAPTER EIGHT

MARATHON MAN

In 1989, when my wife Diane and I separated, I was working for Sierra Tucson, one of the premier drug, alcohol and behavioral clinics in America. I had a job there because I was a good speaker——a great speaker, if I do say so myself. For a salary of about $55,000, I was traveling from Costa Mesa, California, to Tucson once a month to lecture patients.

On many of those Thursday nights, I would walk into a room and see stage and screen stars and famous athletes sitting in the audience. I'd walk in and do my thing. Patients knew I was a convicted felon and that part of the charge against me had been sexual misconduct. They also knew cocaine addiction and alcoholism can cause behavior that is against the law.

So I wasn't harshly judged because of my history of addiction. My relationship with Sierra Tucson and the expanding success of my lectures helped earn credibility. I'd gained enough respect so that one night a patient asked if I would try to help him. My talk about recovery and how you do this and stay with that made sense to him.

He was HIV positive, and a billionaire.

I agreed to work with him and we spent time on the phone. I did my best to share my experiences and how I had stayed sober. He listened but didn't hear. His life had become a habitual relapse. He also had sexual problems. He once told me he would go to bathhouses in San Francisco, leave the front door cracked, and take on all comers. Whoever knocked on the door. It was because of this behavior he'd become HIV positive.

He was angry about having the disease. I counseled him and told him that HIV positive was simply the consequence for the irresponsible

94

behavior that he'd engaged in and still hadn't stopped. I didn't give up on him, but it was apparent I wasn't making a lot of progress in keeping him straight.

His wife eventually called and asked if I would do the family a favor. Her husband was a billionaire but his estate wasn't in order. The family needed to get him clean and keep him away from his activities for three or four months so that lawyers and trust accountants could put his financial affairs in order. She said they didn't know how much longer he would live. He's going to Scientology, he's talking to Buddha, there's a Zen man trying to work with him, and he's not any better. Would I come and live with him for an extended period of time?

I didn't want to do that. It was beyond my expertise to baby sit. I'd been successful as an interventionist. I'd planned interventions with families. But I'd never been involved in something like that so I decided I'd give her an extravagant price and she'd tell me to go to hell.

I talked to her as if it were a business deal. It never occurred to me to charge for sharing my recovery with anyone. But in order for me to move in and ride around and stay with him on a daily basis for months, it was going to cost him.

"How much would you charge for five months?" she asked. I said I'd call her back. I thought about it and knew I didn't want to do it. So to keep from doing it, I called back and submitted a ridiculous figure. Damned if she didn't agree.

So I moved to Beverly Hills with this gentleman, who was very smart and engaging, and clearly a tough businessman. He was 65 years old, a crack addict and sexually indiscriminate. Although I had a lot of parties in my life and I'd been involved with orgies and other stuff, I didn't identify with his sexual lifestyle.

I did my best to keep him from going to the main source of his behavior, which were drugs. During my experience over the years I've seen how these side behaviors can be triggered by addiction to alcohol and drugs. People only went on these binges, these hunts and sexual escapades-straight or gay – when they were full of the drug of their choice.

And sometimes, in the process of trying to get sober, they missed that behavior. They missed what they did on drugs. Some would revert to what they did on drugs while they were off the stuff. This got them back on drugs because it's a different feeling without drugs or alcohol.

I lived an interesting life traveling with this man on his business trips late in '89 and early 1990. We often flew from Los Angeles to Carmel, where he had a house and a membership in the Pebble Beach Tennis Club. I played Pebble Beach Golf Links 15-20 times on his tab while he was doing deals, ran into Clint Eastwood once and generally had a helluva great time.

He did sneak off on me once. He went out and didn't come home on time. I had a contract that stipulated I could have him take a urine test at any time. I saw him that morning and told him, I think you got high last night. He denied it.

"I need a test," I said.

"Sure, come on, let's go," he agreed.

We drove a half-hour to a clinic. We parked five blocks away. He said, "I don't know why we're doing this. I don't know why you don't trust me. I've done well."

We went upstairs. We signed in. He entered a room and gave a sample of urine. I witnessed the sample because there were folks who brought a little bottle of clean urine with them and try to substitute it for what they know was a dirty specimen. We finished and headed down the elevator. We were well into spending an hour on this trip.

We didn't have to waste our time. If he'd just admitted it to me, hell, we could have gone from there. We could've engaged about it. Why do you think you relapsed? What does that feel like? What can we do from now on so you won't have that episode again?

It could've been a learning experience. Hell, I wasn't going to abandon him. I told him I was going to leave him but I didn't mean it. Anyway, when he got on the elevator, he looked at me and said, "Okay, I'm dirty."

You know I'm an ex-NFL linebacker. What I really wanted to do at that moment was give him a forearm to his teeny head. But you can't do that to a 65-year old man who is 5' 3".

My mission was to keep him from disappearing for weeks at a time. We shared hundreds of breakfasts and dinners. We took walks. Although the family paid me, I really became fond of this man. I learned much about cross addictions. This was school to me. I was learning significant lessons about addictions, behavior and consequences through someone else's pain.

I'd been with him for about four months when I started to do some running. I had decided to enter the Los Angeles Marathon, although even today I wonder why. My client-friend would go down to Santa Monica Beach with me. He'd sit in one spot and I'd take off and run. Of course, everybody knows that Tom Landry with his limping, Hopalong Cassidy knee could outrun me in a distance race.

I'd run down the beach two or three miles and walk back. I trained for about two weeks, paid my entry fee to the LA Marathon and was given a number. It was a big deal. My client-friend had a lot of fun with it, as if it was almost through me that he had a life. He encouraged me to complete the distance. I told him I thought I'd do it in about four and a half hours.

Of course, anyone who knows anything about running knows that two miles a days is not the right training regimen for running 26.2 miles. But I did the best I could to prepare until the day of the LA Marathon. Muhammad Ali was the honorary starter, the guy who shot the pistol to start the race. My friend was excited. He was going to be stationed past the halfway point to cheer me on. Then he'd be at the finish line to take me home.

What he didn't know was what those 26.2 miles meant to me. Could I endure? I thought it would be a great opportunity for me to meditate and find out something about myself. Who am I? Would I quit? I will say this about 26.2 miles. It's like going out of town without a car.

They put me up front since I was a celebrity, and we began running the streets of Los Angeles early on a cool morning with a little mist in the air. I'd never run more than six miles in my life and there I was among all these anorexic-looking, bony-legged guys.

I noticed from the start and well into the race that people were passing me. I was about two hours into the run at the 13-mile marker and I still don't know how those first 13 miles were so much fun. It was festive. People lined the streets and cheered. I talked to someone who hadn't quite passed me yet. I was getting water and Gatorade and everything spectators passed out to runners. Then I remembered my client-friend would be meeting me at a certain point. We'd looked on the map and agreed that at mile 18 he'd be there.

Well, after mile 13, my body and shins were on fire. We came to a hill and when I got to the top I didn't think I was going to make it. I had meditated enough to know this was going to be a painful experience in an unfamiliar area. I had been through pain in my life, most of it inside me, but nothing like this.

This race was going to inflict more pain than I had ever endured. This was going to be bigger than leaving Austin to go to Oklahoma to attend Langston and then become a Dallas Cowboy. This pain was different because it was physical. The question was how would I react?

Would I crumble? Would I quit? Would I catch a cab? Just in case, I took a few items with me on the run. I had my driver's license, a credit card and a $100 bill. Was I going to rent or buy a car? Hell, I didn't know what I'd need.

The race wore on and people started to pass me in wheelchairs; fat people, old people, people with one leg were passing me. Now my ego was involved. I was a world class athlete but housewives in aprons were running past me.

Then came a moment I'll never forget. I came over a hill at mile 18 and I could see my client. He was waving a red flag so I'd see him. He was pointing behind me because he knew I was struggling. I wasn't running very fast. I was doing all of 2.3 miles an hour, which is barely putting one leg in front of the other.

"Look behind you!" he hollered. I couldn't understand what he said, but I noticed him pointing behind me. I didn't have enough energy to turn around and look back.

Then all of sudden to my left there appeared a midget with headphones. He couldn't have stood more than 2' 7". He had the biggest ass you've ever seen and he was bowlegged. But he was passing me!

By this time my client was laughing and pleading, "Oh no, don't let a midget pass you." Now my ego was completely shot. Everyone had passed me, including a midget. If I could have caught him I would have kicked his big butt.

I moved slower and slower. Approaching the 20-mile marker it was run 10 steps and walk 80 steps. But I was dug into the idea of not quitting. The marathon was a challenge to the core of me, Thomas Henderson. I had no business entering the race. I had no business attempting to run

26.2 miles. This exhausting run had become an exercise in self-discovery. Who was I and what was I made of?

When you have 6.2 more miles to cover, it doesn't look good. You think on the next step that your legs will crumble. You feel a degree of pain you've never known, physically and emotionally. I felt that way at mile 21, 22, 23, 24, 25... When I got to the 25-mile marker I was hanging in there mentally but doubted I had anything left physically. I didn't think I could cover the last 1.2 miles.

So I began having conversations with myself. You've come so far. You must keep moving. You can't give up now. And I did finish. I came in 12,612th out of 17,000 runners. My time was six hours, 12 seconds.

My client-friend? After I left him in March of 1990 he relapsed into his old behaviors. He eventually died of complications from HIV and AIDS. But the family was pleased because he did get his affairs in order.

And me? What was my legacy from completing the LA Marathon? The result was immense pride...and a hemorrhoid.

Chapter Nine

CHANGING THE WAY I FUNCTION

The car was parked and the baggage was checked and I was standing at the gate, happy with myself. Proud of myself. This was a couple of years ago. I'm not sure where I was going or why, I just knew I was doing what I said I'd do, going where I said I'd go. I gave my ticket to the agent and got my boarding pass and I was about to head down the tube to the plane. I smiled, laughed a little, kept walking, saw the stewardess, said hi, smiled again all the way to my seat. I was laughing at me. It was a simple response to a simple pleasure: I was being reliable, being responsible. I made a commitment to go some place and I kept it. I had made the plane. That was all. I'm not going to tell you making a plane is a profound gift of sobriety, but I can say that doing what you say you'll do feels good because it's personal. But for someone who spent years being as reliable as a street corner pimp, it made me feel pretty damn nice.

Today, my word means something. When I was newly sober, my friend, Mike Murray, said to me, "Henderson, just do what you say you're gonna do." It has practically become an obsession. One of the greatest compliments I could hear is if two guys (or gals) were talking and one said to the other, "I'm meeting Henderson at the diner at 1:00." And the other person said, "If he said it, he'll be there." Being credible was one of the toughest battles I had to fight. You've got to prove yourself every day. The truth and your word are the first things to go when addiction sets in.

A couple of my using buddies decided to get help for their cocaine addiction. They had witnessed my recovery. They were both deep into cocaine, one snorted and the other freebased it. Pain and fear had motivated them to seek help. I was set to go. It was no time to dawdle. They could get scared or change their mind. It's amazing what a good nights sleep, a meal and a heavy dose of denial can do. By morning a person will say, "I feel better. Things aren't so bad and I'm fine right now." I do referral and marketing work for a treatment facility in Tucson, Arizona called Sierra-Tucson. It's the best model of treatment on planet Earth. There is no better treatment model or facility anywhere. If you're not treating a patient's family-of-origin issues, inner child, the whole family, sex issues, incest and abuse, you're not providing what works, in my opinion.

One of the guys said to me, 'I'm ready. I'm going in." The other one said, "I'm going as soon as he does." "Great," I said to the first guy. "Let's get your plane ticket and get you into treatment. Let's go. Now!" A blank, uncertain look crossed his face. I've seen it a lot. It's the cold feet look. His particular feet were rigid. I could see it. He said there was stuff he had to take care of first. Errands to run people to talk to. I said I'd take care of the big things for him and let the little shit take care of itself. This was Thursday. "I'll go in on Tuesday," he said I said, "Man, do it today. I know it's hard. I've been there. But it'll be easier in the long run if you just do it. C'mon, man, let's go." He was angry now. He said, "Why can't you be proud that I said I'd go in on Tuesday?" I said, "Because you're an untreated addict and I don't trust you." I told him I knew all about good intentions because I had them, too. My intentions never jived with my actions. I told him his disease and denial wrecks good intentions. "Hey, I promised you," he said, "Now get off my ass. I promised." Tuesday came and went. He never showed. It says less about him than it does about alcoholism, which routinely turns its victims into liars and deceivers and connivers. They made it to treatment 10 days later.

With this disease, the work is telling the truth, not telling a lie. Lies are what we're used to. They come easily. Life becomes a blizzard of misinformation. You'll lie about what you ate for lunch. I always had good reasons for my lies. Telling the truth was too easy. Liars have to have great memories. They have to remember what they told whom.

Now I accept and live by a simple truth: if you lie, you are a liar. If you steal, you're a thief. If you tell the truth and do what you say you'll do that's where credibility comes from. I heard someone say one time, "Show up, pay attention and tell the truth." That works everywhere.

A few days before Christmas one year, I was in Miami. I was a Dolphin that season. My daughter was living in Tennessee. Thomesa was two then, just old enough to be excited about the tree, presents, Santa Claus and the whole Christmas thing. Who likes to lie to their child? "I'll be home for Christmas honey. Daddy has some Christmas surprises for you. Daddy loves you very much." Daddy lies. She thought daddy was coming. He wasn't. He couldn't. He was powerless. He was smoking cocaine in a hotel room a thousand miles away. You precious little girl. My little girl. Daddy is sick.

From the moment she was born, I had this beautiful, peaceful sense that I had the best friend I would ever know. She would always love me. I never experienced that kind of love before. I still haven't. I was thinking what a joy it was going to be to share Christmas with her. To see her eyes, to feel her love, her wonder, to hug her, hold her and kiss her. "I love you, Thomesa," I said. I hung up the phone and continued to freebase cocaine. The pipe never let up. I never made it home that Christmas. The binge did not stop for a week. Christmas was spent in isolation, smoking cocaine. I was addicted and not even my daughter, the love of my life, was more important than getting high.

More than 10 years have passed since that broken Christmas promise. I am proud of the father I have become. I feel good about my relationship with Thomesa, and the love I give her unconditionally. I feel proud that she knows her daddy was very sick but has gotten himself better. I'm grateful that my sobriety and recovery allow me to keep my word to my daughter, myself, and everyone else. I do what I say I'm going to do.

Feeling different was nothing new for me. It's been with me my whole life. I felt different from all my sisters and brothers, and I was. My real father had twelve other children. My mamma had five, including me. Let me confuse you. I've got sixteen brothers and sisters, but I'm an only child. I'm the only child by Violet Faye and Billy. I grew up with sisters and brothers with the last name of Rivers. Mine is Henderson. We lived with their father, my step-dad. I was a bastard. I saw my birth certificate for the first time when I was seven or eight years old. It said, 'Thomas Edward Henderson. Time of birth date. Father unknown.' Stamped right on there was the word 'illegitimate'. I remember reading that and asking my mother what it meant. She explained. I remember being a little hurt. I was different. A misfit. I was a mistake. I spent my life feeling like I was on the outside looking in.

Not having a father hurt. There was a void, and it just wouldn't go away. I'd watch other folks with their dad, including former teammates like Randy White and Bob Breunig. Their fathers were part of their lives – spending time together, sharing things, fishing, and just having a relationship. I never had that. I ached for it. My mamma and step-dad did the best they could. They worked and we weren't going hungry, but we were a long way from the right side of the tracks. It wasn't a nurturing, stable environment that I grew up in. It couldn't be because my mother and stepfather were alcoholics. I was a child of alcoholic parents. Did you know alcoholics give their children alcohol? They do. So, I don't know when my first drink was administered.

I love them both and they worked hard and provided for all of us as best they could. I know that. But their alcohol abuse prevented them from being the parents one would hope. Alcohol screws up everything. Even parenthood. Their drinking was the weekend binge variety. Friday night arrived and out would come the whiskey, vodka, and six packs of beer. Living for the weekend. Let the party begin. In order to have fun, you must drink first.

For this little child it was the start of a perception I would carry until the day I got sober: if I was going to have fun, celebrate, if I was really going to be a card-carrying grown up, I damn well better have something to drink in my hand. I believed that with all my heart. And so I grew up and I was sure that if I wanted to dance, I needed to drink. If I wanted to talk to a girl, I needed to drink. You didn't have fun without it.

Now I know I wasn't alone with this perception. It is practically built into our culture and the brewers and distillers reinforce it at every turn. They're no idiots. They play on it with all the seductive force their advertising agencies can summon. You turn on the television or open a magazine and the images bombard you: pretty people, healthy people, living the good life with their designated beverage in tow. Or a dog, a real dog, an ugly dog, being the life of the party, being the party animal, being pawed over by gorgeous young women, three of them. When this dog has three women with him, it's about how to drink education. When I had three women, it was called a sin. The message is nonstop: alcohol equals fun. By the time a teenager is 18 years old, he or she will have seen 100,000 beer commercials alone. The implicit message, of course, is that drinking is harmless. What a pile of shit that advertisement is. Alcohol kills. It also leads to other drugs.

I wish they would have a sobriety ad for every alcohol ad. One for one. I wish we could see scenes of sober people leading a fun life, getting off on nothing but their own attitudes and resources. Or how about some real-life alcohol scenes? That'd be good. Maybe one could show a drunk driver who didn't know when to say when. Feeling good, being happy, meandering down the road, and then ramming head on into a family of four. Hey, pal, this vehicular family slaughter is for you. Tastes great – less filling – you're dead – no kidding. Or maybe we could see a college beer blast, where everyone's exploding with enjoyment before a few folks explode too much and start puking their pretzels and hot dogs up.

Let's see the whole picture. Sure, show the fun and frolic. Some folks can do this. Alcoholics can't. But also show the cigarette smoke and the fights and the smelly armpits and the puke breath and the blackouts – and the deaths. I'm no prohibitionist. I respect people's right to drink. I just think the information out there is grossly one-sided. Even our role models – from the White House to skid row, drinking alcohol is social and fun. There's a major distortion going on and a lot of work needs to be done to correct it. I was once invited to a "say no to drugs" cocktail party.

My business and pleasure now is lecturing and sharing about alcohol and drug addiction plus recovery. I'm out there on the front lines, so to speak. Week after week, in town after town, I'm talking to people about their attitudes and perceptions. The more I do it, the more I'm convinced alcohol is the number one problem in this country. Cocaine is evil, vicious stuff. Crack is, too. Both will romance and lure you into their unforgiving clutches and wreck your life. You already know how they kicked my smart-ass, and that I'm damn lucky to be alive to talk about it. But alcohol has an insidiousness all its own, and it stems precisely from our perceptions, and that lie is foisted on us by the people who sell it.

I've been sober awhile now, and I can still watch a commercial on TV and see that rich, golden brew pouring into a frosty mug, and be tempted. It looks attractive and harmless. I'll see the pretty people and all their pals and I'll be thinking, "That looks like fun." Fun. Taps right into my perceptions. The message is powerful. That's why they run those ads.

I'm not surprised that people end up alcoholics. I'm surprised when they don't. Alcohol is everywhere in this country. If they're not selling it at this corner, drive to the next. It is widely considered to be no big deal. Getting drunk is something to joke about the next day. Everybody laughs and tells his or her 'drunkalogues', makes fun of the guy who can't hold his liquor, and recount all the stupid things they did the night before. Hey, wasn't that funny when you kicked the dog or the next guy pissed in the flowers? And so the next generation of alcoholics, our kids, get the same message I got back in Austin, Texas: give me some of that stuff. No big deal. It's only alcohol. Over and over, I've spoken with kids and been stunned and saddened by how often I hear, "I'll never have a problem with alcohol. I just won't let it happen." It's the nature of this beast that nobody thinks it will happen to him or her. One teenager told me, "I'm kind of afraid of cocaine because I know you can get addicted. You can't get addicted to alcohol." The 'say no to drugs' campaign conveniently left out alcohol. It's just the way it is in America. Wake up everybody!

Some progress has been made on the subject of alcohol abuse, but it's a battle that's only just beginning. The prevailing attitude remains that the only true alcoholics are the guys with the two raincoats under the bridge. Everybody else is safe because, well, it just won't happen to me. Bullshit! It can happen to you. It happened to me.

Alcohol caused violence in my family and my childhood. My mamma and step-dad would fight when they got drunk. He would beat her. She would beat him. One night the fight was more intense than usual and seemed to never stop. It was the worst night of my childhood. Mamma shot daddy. I saw him staggering. He had just beaten her. He went out to the car. He was still plenty drunk. I didn't know what he was doing, maybe getting a bottle or something. He started back toward the house. I thought, "Oh, no. He's going to start hitting her again." This kind of fighting between them had been going on as long as I could remember.

My mamma had bought him a .22 rifle for Christmas. As he weave back toward the house she went and got the gun. She stood there in the doorway and opened a latch and slipped in the bullets. She snapped it shut. This is not normal shit. This was not a normal home. She stepped onto the porch, the rifle clutched across her body. I moved out there with her. My sisters and brothers were asleep. He was near the house now, a few feet from the steps leading to the porch. Mamma was crying and I hurt for her. Her eyes were swollen and she reeked of alcohol. "Get the hell away from this house!" she screamed. "Get your ass out of here. You ain't gonna hit me no more." He kept coming. He was trudging up the stairs. I was between them, to the side, against the railing, each a few feet away from me. My mamma pointed the gun at him. She was angry, hurt and ready. She said, "Don't take another step, mother fucker. Don't take another step!"

He kept coming and she cursed him and warned him again and still he came on. Then I heard the gunshot and saw the fire fly from the barrel of the rifle and saw my step-dad stagger down the steps and fall. I was shocked, numb, afraid and stuck to the wall like paint. My mouth was dry and my heart made my shirt move. It was beating like a thousand drums. My mamma had just shot my step-dad, right on the same porch where I was conceived twelve years earlier. This was a powerful moment in my dysfunctional family and life. Perceptions.

He survived the wound and moved back in when he was released from the hospital. My mamma was put on probation because daddy didn't file charges. There would be many more Saturday night parties. This was my first lesson on relationships. This was my theater on how a husband treats his wife. I was well trained wrongly. Violence wasn't only acceptable, it was expected. No wonder I hit my first wife.

My mamma never shot me, but I believe she would have. I feared her for years after that. She whipped me though. I believe it's assault if you whip a child. I was whipped and beat most of my childhood. I never deserved to be beaten or whipped violently. It is a violent act, you know? My questions to God when I would get whipped were why does mamma want to hurt me so? Doesn't she know this hurts inside, too? Does she know this breaks my heart? I was terrified. The hurt had no place to go. She wanted me to cry, but I never would. I was defiant. If it was going to deprive her of some satisfaction, well, good. Damnit, you ain't getting one teardrop out of me. When she would finally stop hitting me, I would run out of the house and keep running, and go down the street or somewhere. I would find a safe place to feel. I was safe. I was beyond my mamma's reach. And I would cry. I would cry until I was hoarse, asking God to stop her.

I was ashamed of where I came from, and that shame stayed with me into adulthood. I felt terribly inadequate, like there was some big chunk of me missing. I didn't want anyone to know that. I didn't let anyone know me. I never liked living in the house I grew up in. I always wanted to be in the house down the street - anywhere but where I was. I wanted different parents, their dog, their yard, their car and their love. I intuitively knew there was a better life. I felt I had to protect my shame. The fear went to my core. If I was opened up and exposed to the world, everybody would know the truth, know that I was just a little misfit bastard who grew up with parents who hit and shot each other. If I let somebody get close, my cover would be blown. Why do we feel the need to cover? Deep down, I felt worthless. I just didn't want you to know.

So there were all kinds of secrets that I felt I had to keep, and just as many reasons why I felt like an imposter. I had to pretend everything was fine. I had to escape from where I came from and from who I was. The more I got a sampling of drugs and alcohol, the more the voice inside was saying, and "Reality ain't so bad when I'm high." Right up until I got sober, my deepest, most powerful instinct was that I was a big phony nothing. Forget being a Dallas Cowboy and a Pro Bowler or a Super Bowl player. That was window dressing, fluff. This was the naked, brutal truth. I was defective.

There's a lot of research going on about alcoholism these days. Doctors, psychologists, treatment centers and scientists are trying to figure out exactly what makes somebody an alcoholic. Trying to sort out the mystery of the disease, why two people can drink the same amount of alcohol in the same way over the same span of time and one can become an alcoholic and the other does not.

Alcoholism runs in families; that much is fact. It sure as hell runs all over my family. What's trying to be sorted out is exactly why this is so. Is it something in the genes, an inherited trait, just like the color of your hair or the shape of your kneecaps? The trait is an allergy to alcohol, a physiological condition that makes you more vulnerable to the drug or alcohol. Or is it the nature of the human environment here on planet Earth. Is it life in the alcoholic household that makes the disease run on for generation after generation? Is it fear and turmoil and insecurity that make a fragile young person seek to escape from all the dysfunctional bullshit?

I believe all this stuff factors in. I believe I was born with a predisposition that made me more affected by and vulnerable to alcohol than someone else was. I think I was an alcoholic waiting to happen, even when I was making gurgling noises and muddying my diapers. But I also think my perceptions took this built-in condition and ran with it, far and fast, and that the horribly low self esteem I had – the secret keeping, the misfit feeling – are in the mix, too.

Drugs and alcohol produce euphoria, at least at first. They numb pain, physical and emotional. They whisk you away from problems, soothe the deep hurt that comes with feeling that you don't fit in or that you're just no good, period. These wounds are damn slow to heal. Try a little of this – presto! Everything has a much nicer spin to it. It's better than anything you've ever known. They don't call it getting high for nothing.

Alcoholism feasts on low self-esteem the way a buzzard feasts on a carcass. It won't stop until there's nothing left. When I first got sober and slowly started to lessen the void I felt inside, I started to loosen the god awful grip of my cravings. I didn't have to escape anymore. I didn't have to pretend. I was accepting that I was okay just the way I was. I started to see all the baggage I'd been carrying around my whole life and stuff I could learn to let go of. I had an undying willingness and desire to grow, to get sober, to get behind this diseased, dysfunctional bullshit.

I wasn't a misfit bastard. Life wasn't a game where everybody else was on one team and I was on the other. The hell with that uncle who said I wouldn't amount to any good. The hell with him. In sobriety, I found out he had his head up his own judgmental ass.

I had weaknesses and defects like anybody else, and I had a terrible disease and I did some terrible things, but I could and would do something about it. I started to believe that. I started to believe I could feel better. What a revelation. For the first time in my life, I believed I mattered. The world was a place where I was welcome. I wasn't alone. I didn't have to be outside looking in anymore.

These were all beautiful things to believe, and I was beginning to truly believe them. Learning how to live takes trial and error. A better way was in focus. I had to develop self-esteem before I could truly recover from drugs, alcohol and a dysfunctional up bringing. That's why my credibility was so important. If I was going to feel good about myself, I needed to believe myself. Then others would believe me too. No more con games or lies or half-truths. No more manipulative, self-serving behavior. Enough with the bullshit. I didn't want my life to be a lie anymore. I didn't want to be a fraud anymore. I need my word to mean something. I needed to kick the dishonesty the hell out of my life. I had to be able to look at myself and feel comfortable, know I was credible – from the inside out. This process is an inside job.

Now my word is good. Apart from sobriety itself, nothing means more to me. Indeed, my sobriety would not be possible without personal credibility. I feel the need to tell you where I've been so you can appreciate where I am and what is possible for you, too, in sobriety.

CHAPTER TEN

AUSTIN

Mid-July 1989 I was on a flight between New York City and Austin, Texas. I was not traveling alone. My daughter, Thomesa, and I were on our way to visit Violet Faye, her grandma and my mamma.

Since I've been sober, my child spends the summer months with me. This summer had been rough on me because I had her all by myself. Me. Daddy. Responsible for her. Diane and I were separated and divorcing. Parenthood is a full time job and then some. I will never minimize a woman when she says she's a full time mother. It's a job.

Thomesa had to travel with me because I couldn't just leave her with friends. New York City was our first stop. I had been invited to speak to about. 1,500 recovering cocaine addicts at their annual convention at the Grand Hyatt Hotel. The other half of my dysfunctional family lives in New York City. Thomesa and I spent some of our time visiting aunts, cousins and other relatives. Thomesa was reintroduced to her grandfather (DNA donor), Billy. He had seen her when she was a baby. She was now ten and her own person already. I support her right to individuality. Just like her dad, she had no emotions or affections for him. Introducing Billy to Thomesa as her grandfather was uncomfortable. I watched her reaction to my introduction and I could see her feeling my sarcasm. Her intuitive insight impressed me.

While there we were invited to my Aunt Gwen's apartment for a family gathering. The night before I had met another sister for the first time in my life. Her name is Dianna. I saw my features in her face. Billy hadn't seen her since she was a tiny baby. She was now in her early thirties. This was an incredible day in the life of the dysfunctional family.

Mine. Billy seemed nervous as we all waited for the arrival of his long-abandoned daughter. What a dad. Apartment living in New York to me is like project living. I don't like it. My Aunt Gwen lives in a building of red bricks, green hallways and creepy elevators. Aunt Gwen is married with one child. Her apartment is a small two-bedroom concrete section of a building. Billy, Uncle Chuck, brother Duane and myself were playing pinochle and waiting for Dianna to arrive. Thomesa played and visited with Gwen and Chuck's child, Christi, our little cousin.

Everyone was waiting to see Dianna. I had been told that Dianna knew of me during my NFL days but didn't want to meet me or any other member of this family. I understood and supported that boundary and decision. I wish I had done it. Hell, I wish I had never met my father now that I knew the story.

We sat there as if we were in a high stake poker game. We were all uncomfortable and uneasy. When the knock on the door came, we were all nervous about how to act. When she entered the apartment, there was an awkward silence. It seemed to last ten seconds or so. I broke the silence with my expert sarcasm, "Billy, this is your daughter, Dianna. Dianna, this is your father, Billy." I looked at Billy. He didn't know what to do. He's never quite known what to do. I would have asked for a hug if I were he. He didn't know that that was an option. Their relationship will always be strained because through a family source I was told that Billy tried to get some cash for the twins when the adoption and custody issues were being dealt with. Dianna knew about the barter request by her dad. Wow!

Billy has twelve children or so. I'm still the oldest so far. He didn't raise any of them that I know of.

That afternoon was shallow and non-emotional. This was an average day with my Aunt Gwen and my family on the East Coast. Duane Bell and Uncle Phelan Gore are the only adults in my family that I have come to love and respect so far. Thomesa and I took the subway from the Bronx back to midtown Manhattan. It was fun. I don't think I'll ever go back to the Bronx.

The lecture went well at the Grand Hyatt. God really shared hope and healing of recovery through me that night. After finishing my business in New York, Thomesa and I flew to Austin to visit mamma and my other dysfunctional family system. We hung out in Austin for a week or so vacationing and visiting. Visits are good because there is no pressure for commitment. People are nice to visitors, even if they don't really care for you. We had a nice time and Austin felt different. I was still living in Costa Mesa, California, so Thomesa and I boarded a plane in late July heading to my apartment in Orange County.

About an hour into our flight I said to Thomesa, "I'm moving back home to Austin." Who said that was my instant reaction. I had sworn in public that I would never live there again. Never say never. I was committed to going home instantly. I didn't have a reason for going home - yet.

The truth is, I needed to move somewhere. I had begun to feel like a visitor and stranger in California. The divorce and all had taken away my surrogate family. After saying it to Thomesa, I started planning to move. It took nine months. I'm not compulsive anymore. In my old behavior, I would have been moved to Austin by the end of the week. Pack and go.

Austin is where my childhood pain lived. Working exclusively as an author, lecturer and marketing person in the drug and alcohol field, my schedule was full to year-end. I also had to entertain and be father to my daughter until the end of August.

By April 15, 1990, I had completed all my contract commitments and was ready to go home. On April 23, 1990, I arrived in Austin. It had been twenty years since I had lived there. I was coming home a success. I wasn't looking for or expecting anything. What freedom. I didn't even need a job. All I wanted to do was live there. I had engaged the services of a real estate agent months in advance and had purchased a condominium. I was a homeowner when I arrived home. Being a homeowner at this stage of my life is a miracle and gift of sobriety.

I'm an adult child of alcoholic parents (ACOA) from the East Side where I was raised, too. Drug addiction and street alcoholism is alive and well here. Everyone knows me or knows of me in my community. They all know I'm sober, too. What a reputation. God sent me to Austin for two reasons so far: CB and mamma. Now I understand. There's more for me to do here. More will be revealed.

GOING HOME

Near my 37th birthday in 1990, after I'd been out of jail for four years, I decided to go home. I could have moved to Tucson or New York City. Dallas was an option. But I sensed that there were already too many ex-Cowboys in Dallas.

I didn't want to go to Dallas. I hadn't made amends to Dallas. I hadn't written that Dear Dallas letter. There were some things about Dallas that I was not prepared to face in 1990.

Going home seemed to feel right. It had been 20 years since I'd gotten out of the same bed where my two little brothers and I slept three-deep. I'd gone out into life and moved to Oklahoma. I finished high school. Gone to college. I'd been a Dallas Cowboy. I'd been a San Francisco 49er. I'd been a Houston Oiler. I'd been a Miami Dolphin. I'd broken my neck. I'd been arrested. I'd been to prison.

Now I was clean and sober. So I had a lot of baggage good and bad. I had some money. I had a career. I thought it was okay to go home under the right circumstances and pretenses. If going home meant being defeated, jobless, looking for help and support, I couldn't have done it.

Yet the drive from Costa Mesa, California, to Austin, Texas, was full of fear and apprehension. What was I going to do in Austin? My mother was there. My family was there. They were all poor. How would I be accepted in my hometown?

What I found is that you can go home. Those who know you and grew up with you, who pulled and prayed for you even if you'd made mistakes, they always have a place in their heart for the prodigal.

I bought a condominium on the west side of town, which was opposite from the part of Austin where I grew up. The price on this small two-story place was $84,000. I qualified for a mortgage because I had a job. I got a mortgage because I had credit. I'd never messed up my credit. I'd had a wrangle with the IRS and liens against me. But as far as Sears & Roebuck, Master Charge, VISA and those people I never screwed anyone out of any money. I never had charge-offs.

Coming home, I wasn't looking for anyone in particular. One motivation for moving to Austin was business. California was too expensive. I couldn't afford to buy a house there. For what I was trying to accomplish, all I needed from a city was an airport. My lecture series was going well. I was working for drug rehab centers, referring patients and doing interventions with families. I didn't have any idea how significant this move would be to my development as a man and a father.

Keep in mind that when I moved back to Austin I was about seven years clean and sober. I was still trying to find my feet, still looking over my shoulder. I sensed there were those who'd see me or meet me and think I wanted something from them. Still worse, that they would only remember the bad things I'd done.

Some of the most awkward reunions happened when I'd meet people I knew in the first and second grade that didn't look remotely familiar. A few got very angry with me for not remembering them. Most of my reunions were pleasant but there were those that weren't when someone said, "What's my name?" with a challenging look in their eye. My answer later for not remembering became, "Well, you know, I was on drugs for a while."

I understood for the rest of my life there would be people who won't believe that a man can really change. Forgiveness is supposed to be a given for Christians. But there also has to be longevity. There has to be proof; evidence of change. I of all people understood that. I would rather understand than be understood. If I go through my life needing to be understood it sets me up for a lot of hurt feelings, frustration and even relapse.

When I say relapse I mean that if I don't take care of myself physiologically and socially, I won't have the mental capacity to stop myself from saying, to hell with it, and go get a bag of crack.

Instinct as much as any emotion drew me back to Austin. In the process of my recovery I remember being told that eventually you will intuitively know how to handle situations that used to baffle you.

With that thought in mind, I quietly slipped back into town, bought some furniture and saw my mother, who was working as a maid, almost every day. I figured that before you can help anyone else you have to help yourself. For a long time all my mother wanted from me was bingo money. I could handle that.

I wasn't in a position then to set her up where she didn't have to work anymore. I was trying to take care of Thomas Henderson. If I took care of me, then it was possible I could support her in the future. It was good to be back in Austin but there was a downside. The alcoholism and drug addiction that had always infested my old neighborhood was more evident now that I was sober. I learned in treatment that addiction is a disease-a progressive, terminal disease. East Austin had it bad.

I drank as a kid because it was something you were going to do when you grew up. That's the way it was in the America I knew. When I went into treatment one of the first subjects we discussed was dysfunctional families. I said, "Well, damn, listen to this story about my family!"

I was 12 years old and standing on the front porch. My mother had a black eye. She had a .22 rifle in her hand. My stepfather was staggering around the yard. She said to him, "If you don't leave this house I'm going to shoot you." He didn't leave and she shot him. What was even more remarkable was that six months after he got out of the hospital my stepfather moved back in.

I made a decision that day. I made a rule that I will never break. That was, if a woman ever shoots me, I'm leaving never to return.

Although untreated alcoholism is often fatal, treated alcoholism is 100 percent curable. The remedy is easy. Just stop drinking. But to get an addict to the point where it's easier to stop than to continue is the real trick. No sooner than I hit town than I had a trick on my hands: toothless C. B. Banks Jr.

I knew C. B. as a lifelong drunk and drug addict. He was also one of my best friends from way back. When I was with the Cowboys and made a trip to Austin, C. B. would find me. Not that I was trying to hide. C. B. was a pillar of Austin's active using and abusing community, and that was my favorite community back then.

"Hey, brother, you got a ten for old C. B.?" he'd greet me, and big shot that I was, I'd give him a twenty. He'd disappear into one of Austin's many back alleys to shoot heroin or cocaine, maybe speedball them both, drink wine, Robitussin syrup or whatever he got his hands on. Here I thought I was being his friend.

Once I got sober, I wouldn't give him money anymore.

"Don't chump me, brother," he'd say in disgust.

Something about my appearance interested him, though, and he started asking more and more questions about my sober life. Then it hit me. If

I could get C. B. sober, and if Mamma saw what sobriety did for him, maybe she would be willing to give up booze.

Mamma knew what years of boozing had done to C. B. She'd watched him grow up. She'd seen him in the early days, a colorful character wearing purple crushed velvet and big floppy hats, a Cheshire cat grin on his face. Now he wore whatever rags he was given and slept in the back of an abandoned Plymouth. And his mouth! Whew, it was raggedy.

A year before I returned to Austin, I was visiting and of course, C. B. found me. I checked his pitiful state. He was a bone-thin 120 pounds, had no teeth and smelled like a broken sewer line.

"You know I've been off that junk for six years now. When are you going to stop that stuff?" I said.

"When you come home," he replied.

A year later I moved to Austin, went to see my mother, and C. B. showed up. Half kidding, because I didn't think it would lead to anything, I reminded him of his pledge.

"I'm home. I'm here to stay."

"Alright, I'm going to quit," C. B. replied.

"Okay, when?"

"Right now."

"You're going to quit shooting heroin, drinking wine and syrup?"

"Yeah."

I decided to start my C. B. makeover by fixing that raggedy mouth of his. I had a friend who owned a dental lab and with help from him and a sympathetic dentist, we got C. B. a new set of choppers. He was so proud of those teeth he strutted around east Austin like he was once more a flashy young man, a looker under his big floppy hat. But he wound up scaring the hell out of people by running up to them to show them his teeth and snapping them together like castanets...chomp, chomp, chomp.

I was mildly surprised when C. B. showed up on the doorstep of my new west Austin condo, drunk as a tree full of owls, and missing his teeth.

"Where're your teeth, C. B.?" I greeted him.

He shook his head. "Don't know man," he said, and began to cry. "Look brother, I need your help. I just can't go on no more."

One thing I learned in treatment was that you couldn't make a drunk get better until he's ready to get better. But when a drunk asks for your help, when he admits he can't do it on his own and that he's powerless over alcohol, he's taken that first mighty step. I knew if I could help him now he had a good chance to make it.

"Get your ass in here, C. B.," I said, and forgot about the teeth. I knew enough about drunks to know his teeth could be anywhere. They could be riding around the ocean in the mouth of a porpoise, for all I knew. "Listen, I'll help you C. B. but only if you promise to stop drinking and using."

"Whatever you say, Thomas."

I took C. B. in. We didn't have to move his stuff because he didn't have anything, not even his teeth. My condo was still unfurnished but I'd stocked up on soap, shampoo and towels at the drug store. All I had left from California was a TV, blankets, pillows and a recliner so we sort of camped out on the floor of the living room. A '65 pickup truck was my only other possession. Remember the old saying that in a divorce, they get the gold mine and you get the shaft? I came to Austin with the shaft.

I didn't have clothes for C. B. to wear so I gave him a pair of boxer shorts and a T-shirt. I pointed him upstairs to the shower with specific instructions: "You know you haven't washed your ass in about 15 or 20 years so be sure to use that whole bar of soap and keep lathering until it's gone."

The honest to God truth is that the first thing I did at home was to help an alcoholic-which is who I had become, who I am and who I will remain the rest of my life. C. B. came downstairs, clean and happy, we ordered pizza and just started hanging out and laughing. At the same time, we understood that two alcoholics lying around on practically a bare floor was a pretty sad scene.

Still, everyone is more likely to be successful with a tough decision having to do with drugs and alcohol if he plans it in advance. This wasn't a spontaneous idea for C. B. He had months of forethought: if Thomas comes home, I'll quit. I didn't come home just so he could quit. My decision was separate from his.

We woke up the next morning and had a good-buddy chat. Then the atmosphere changed. I'd never been around a wet alcoholic; that is, someone seized by delirium and tremors. But suddenly they got to C. B. He began registering 100 for a drink on the crave meter. He'd been off the

stuff for 24 hours and he was in trouble with sweats and shakes.
I was lying on a pillow on the floor and I heard him getting up. My left eye opened and I saw him walking toward the stairs to go to the bathroom. He didn't know I was watching. There was a sway and stumble in his walk. He got to the stairs and I saw something I'd never seen before. I saw he couldn't negotiate the first step.

He grabbed the banisters on each side with his hands. I saw him try to lift the left foot to the step but it wouldn't go. I saw him shift weight to the left foot and try to raise the right one, but it wouldn't go. I saw him put both feet on the floor in confusion.

"Are you all right?" I asked.

"No, man, I'm sick," came a weak reply.

I called a doctor whom I understood dealt with alcoholics and drug addicts. I told him about my friend. Understand that I'd only been back in Austin for 36 hours. Fortunately, the doctor had heard of my work with substance abuse so he had some respect for what I did and bent backwards to help. He said to bring C. B. to his office. There the doctor checked vital signs and confirmed that this is a case of serious withdrawal.

The doctor had enough influence at a detox clinic to get C. B. admitted immediately as direct referral from a physician. Without that type of referral, even if you walk in off the street bleeding from the nose and losing it from the other end, the detox center will say, sorry, we won't have another bed for two weeks. C. B.'s bed would be ready for him to check in at 4 p.m. that day. I looked at my watch and it was 10:15 a.m. What was I going to do with him until then? The doctor didn't have any medications on hand at that moment.

"See if you can get some alcohol in him on the way over," the doctor said. "He'll be easier for the staff to deal with that way."

I drove to the liquor store where we had to wait until 11 a.m. when it opens. I went inside and get a bottle of Silver Satin, the wine of the wino trade. Now I'd watched C. B. struggle all morning with the shakes but soon as his hand fit around the bottle, his moves became as delicate as a surgeon. He twisted the paper bag to a tight wrap below the cap. He gently twisted open the cap. It was like slow motion, and two minutes passed before he got the cap off. He put the bottle to his mouth and took about a tablespoon sip. The cap went back on the bottle as slowly as he'd taken it off.

I peeked at him while driving to the park. Three or four minutes later, he repeated the same deliberate routine. Twist cap off...sip...cap on. The process irritated me because it took so much time and he was barely wetting his lips.

"Why the hell don't you drink it?"

I got the professional wino answer in return. "I can't drink it too fast. It will make me sick," C. B. said.

What I was doing at that moment went against everything I believed in. I bought a bottle for an alcoholic to drink although it was with the instruction of a doctor. I was still uncomfortable. I thought if this had been me, how would I drink it? I'd probably have emptied a fifth of wine in about four drinks but I wasn't a wino. Winos know how to drink their bottles.

C. B. didn't drink more than one-fourth of that wine before he checked into the detox center five hours later. That was April of 1990. C. B. Banks Jr. hasn't taken another drink of alcohol since that date.

I visited C. B. often during his treatment. He was detoxed over a 10-day period and then stayed five weeks more. One day, lying in bed, he snapped to attention and said, "Dang, now I remember what I did with my teeth."

"Well, what?"

"I was drunk and about to pass out, and I worried that someone would steal them."

"Steal false teeth?"

I'd known a lot of sick people but I didn't know one person on earth who would steal false teeth. C. B. did, apparently.

"Sure. Got a little gold tooth in them. Someone could sell that."

He went on to explain how he took his teeth, wrapped them in toilet paper and then put that in a paper bag. Standing near an abandoned one-story building, he threw the bag with his teeth on the roof. "Bet they're still there," he sighed and settled back on a pillow.

Passing on one's sobriety to a friend or family member, or even to a stranger, is one of the greatest accomplishments in recovery. It's an indication that you are succeeding because to be able to pass something on, you have to have a grip on it yourself. If you don't, as any quarterback knows you'll fumble or get picked off.

That's one reason why recovery programs always tell you to find someone with solid sobriety as a mentor. Otherwise it becomes a game of intramural football, each player struggling to pick up the other guy's fumble, the ball getting kicked all over the field until it gets lost in the mud. Eventually the players say, "This sucks," they give up and go home.

After C. B. was released from treatment he returned to the abandoned building and climbed to the roof to search for his package. He reported to me that he found a lot of weird stuff up there, but not his teeth. "Some nigger saw me throw them up there and got 'em," he complained.

"Don't worry, C. B.," I said. "We'll get you some more teeth."

Thomas and childhood friend C.B. Banks

C. B. BANKS
(Childhood Friend)

Thomas and I were together in elementary and junior high school until he went to live in Oklahoma. When he came back to Austin to visit he told all of the guys that he was going to play football for this college. It didn't seem real, him playing football and not at the pool hall with us.

Some of us kept getting high and drinking and stuff like that, but Thomas sort of slacked up and got serious in school. We didn't know anything about that, and then we looked up the Cowboys drafted him. That was a real shocker since we couldn't keep up with him in college because we didn't know where Langston was on the map. You had to go to some major college for folks to keep up with it, but not Langston. Nobody knew where Langston was until Thomas came out of the draft. That was a knockout. I believe it shocked the whole city of Austin.

Drinking and drugging was a way of life in Austin, Texas. You don't start by drinking a bottle of beer by yourself. You may steal two out of a six-pack every now and then. But the thing was, five and six-year olds sipped beer every so often. When you got nine or 10 and old enough to have money, you would buy beer. Then when you got to be 12, you really drink every day if you can get the money. You can't buy it, but you can have other people buy it for you. I think that is how we got caught up with it.

Being in a dysfunctional family and having an alcoholic for a father was my reason. My daddy drank every day. He went to work every day, but he was drunk every day. The only day I remember that he didn't have any whisky was because he was so sick he couldn't stand up. My mother didn't drink a drop, but he made up for it. I thought it was okay for me to get a job and drink, and that is what I did. I drank every day just like my daddy. The only difference is, I became an alcoholic and wouldn't work, and he was an alcoholic who did work. I was one of those guys who drank all day and drugged all night, whichever one came first didn't make any difference. Thomas kept coming back to Austin and telling me about treatment. I was messing with cocaine and stuff like that. I'd say, "Yeah, right," because I didn't believe him. He came back again and told me about treatment, because I was still drinking and messing with cocaine and sleeping in my car. He said, "I'm going to move back down here, C. B.," and I said, "Okay, you move back and I'll go to treatment and get sober." I didn't think he was going to do it.

Sure enough he came back and bought a townhouse. He invited me to stay with him; he didn't even have any furniture on the floor. I stayed with him until I went to treatment. I kept my end of it. You know I got a job, after being 10 years without a job. I got a job at a car wash. Then Thomas helped me get a job with Ann Richards, the state treasurer at the time. Believe it or not, me, alcoholic, dope fiend, whatever you want to call it, drove the money truck for the state of Texas.

Would you believe it? I started liking sobriety. Thomas started taking me to meetings, and to meet people. He started helping me out of my addiction. I think with his help I hung in there because at that time if people had known I was on the premises they would have called the law. Thomas helped me get credit. He co-signed a car for me. He co-signed a loan for me. I paid my loan off and I paid my car off. I started getting credit cards in the mail.

My life really turned around with his help. He came back and showed me what it was like to reach out and let you know there is another way. But that's not the whole story. This guy has not only helped me. He's reached out and gotten about 20-30 of us.

Little by little, he showed us the difference between using and being sober. Lots of us have jobs and homes and got our credibility back. We have families. Thomas has made an impact on so many lives down here, including the kids. That is what it's really about, to be in a position of influence for the sake of other people.

He didn't have to come back here and let me know there was such a thing as treatment. I didn't know what treatment was. I was 30-something years old. I had not dealt with it. I wasn't trying to find it. Thomas helped guys like me and Lee Arthur and Jugger Red and a host of other brothers to find churches to meet in. He opened doors in east Austin on how and where to get help on treatment and things like that. He made opportunities for lots of addicts who didn't know there was help for addiction other than being locked up in jail.

I got sober April 25, 1990, so that's 13 years and I haven't had a glass of champagne. I've been married since 1992 and have three kids. Of course, I didn't get married until I was sober. If I wasn't sober, where were we all going to sleep...the back seat of a car?

I've had my own janitorial service since 1996. That's why I stopped working for the state. When Ann Richards became governor I worked for her for four years. She liked me pretty good so she let me be her personal messenger. It was an honor to work for her. That was one of the best parts of my life.

Thomas had much to do with saving my life and I'm so happy and grateful to him for that. And it's just not me. Like I said, it's at least 20 other guys I know of that he touched in a positive way. He hates to see someone suffer if they really don't have to, I will tell the world.

CHAPTER ELEVEN

COCAINE

The ache of craving is intense. The joy of recovery makes all of the pain worth it.

It comes from the south in pounds and kilos. I was introduced to cocaine by a friend who said I was his hero. Numbing at the taste and white as a swan, its sometimes yellow, some toot it, some smoke it and some others shoot it up their arm. Its powerful stuff that runs its course so you first time users had better beware because it only gets worse. When I first started to use cocaine I thought I had found paradise. I later found it to be hell and almost lost my very life while freebasing, smoking crack, tooting, eating it and partying day and night. I was staying on the streets late 'oh what a flight'. I'd sometimes drive my car while smoking a crack pipe. When paranoia set in I couldn't leave my house. I thought the swat team surrounded me, police and vice. Cocaine was a way of life for most folks I knew. There was a time when I felt that if you did not do crack or toot there was very little we could do. I was a very sick man and I am going to share what it was like for me to you.

Obviously I had a death wish because I couldn't seem to get enough. I'd toot and hit that crack pipe and get rush after rush until it felt like my heart and brain would burst. One night a fellow addict took a big hit off the crack pipe and I thought he had lost his life. He had an epileptic attack and flopped like a fish on a deck. After he settled down I asked him 'Show me how I can get a hit that would make me flop like that." I know today and it's a sickening fact that the only good crack hit is an epileptic or heart attack.

The power of cocaine is as boggling as trivia pursuit girls sleep with ugly guys just to get some toot. Those who sniff the stuff can't tell cut up cocaine from pure. But a crack addict will rock it up, smoke it and know for sure. It doesn't matter whether to toot it, shoot it, eat it or smoke it. Cocaine will surely destroy each and every aspect of your life. I was once a superstar in the NFL. I'm now a fallen star in a prison cell. Cocaine will ruin a life and career, it will remove your husband or wife, kids, parents, friends, reputation, jobs, money, vision from the eyes, food from the table, furniture from the house, cars from the driveway and turn an honest person into a thief. As a remover of things cocaine has no equal. Cocaine will get you broke, hooked, helpless and homeless. The insanity is sordid and we get way, way low down. We find ourselves on kitchen and restroom floors with a flashlight thinking we dropped some rocks on the ground. We begin to tweak, checking out everyone and staring near or around our feet. We also accuse every one of stealing a rock or trying to beat. I even owned a minor's cap with a flashlight attached to make sure none of my crack was lost like that. The partying is over but we don't understand why we can't get that first feeling back again. It's over but we are the last to know. All is ruined around us but we want to go and go.

A man or a woman will do anything you ask, just to hit a rock on a crack pipe and will beg for the last. If like me you have lost control of the things you thought you were in control of, then you must awaken, surrender, pray and admit defeat. Divorce it if you want to live free again. If you don't you will realize and understand that it won't ever be good again. Once paranoia sets in it will be that way until the very end. Stop now and join a 12-step group where everyone there is determined to stay off the toot. The miracle of recovery comes to those who seek it. That's why it's important to find a therapeutic group and take your seat. I found recovery and serenity by sharing with crack addicts just like me.

It won't be easy and you've got to fight with all your might, cause crack cocaine will stay in your mind for the rest of your life. It won't be easy so take it slow time and determination will heal your nose and body that were hurt by the snow. One day at a time is the only way to go.

California Departments of Corrections
California Men's Colony 5/11/85
Thomas Henderson

GWEN MURRAY
(Friend)

You cannot please a mother more than to be kind to her children. Thomas has done that twice for me and those experiences ring dear.

I met him in 1979 through Mike, my husband now, although I was married to someone else at the time. We lived in Dallas and were Cowboys fans. Mike was a bachelor and friends with Thomas, who lived up the street from me even though I'd never met him. He was quite the hero around town.

Mike asked Thomas to stop by and say hello to my son Kelly, who was 12 and a football player in junior high. On an evening when Kelly and a friend were getting ready to go to a bar mitzvah, there was a knock on the door. I was behind Kelly and before I rounded the corner I heard him say: "Oh, gosh. Oh, god."

Kelly just stood there with Thomas at the door. Then I heard Thomas ask Kelly, "Can I come in?" Kelly had been too dumbfounded to speak.

Thomas came in, and I stayed in the background and listened. He didn't come by as a favor to Mike to say "Hi," sign an autograph and leave. Thomas stayed for more than an hour and I think the only reason he left was because it was getting close to bathtub time for Kelly.

I overheard them having the most wonderful conversation. Thomas asked Kelly if he knew what a bar mitzvah was all about. Kelly didn't, so Thomas sat there and explained about the young man becoming a man. It was a meaningful conversation.

I wasn't aware that Thomas used drugs. I wasn't on the inside circle so I had no reservations about him talking to Kelly. We just knew he was very flamboyant. He certainly displayed kindness above and beyond the call. How many times had he been asked to drop by, say hello and give an autograph? Staying so long and sitting there with a 12-year old boy was such a kindness.

We all have moments when we rise to the occasion, but unfortunately they get fewer and far between. But that good person is always there even when you are under sedation by your drug of choice. These moments of wonderful functioning are hard for people to understand. How can you be so kind on one hand and be a druggie on the other?

That's why I say the emergence of Thomas Henderson was not a study in what he became, because I think he was always that way in terms of *basic goodness. You can take a sane person and put him under anesthesia and he becomes completely different. That's basically where we all were. I hope that includes Mike and me.*

Thomas was always a kind and caring person. Those parts of his nature were just anesthetized during the years he wasn't sober.

That was my first and only real sighting of Thomas for several years. I subsequently divorced. I am a recovering alcoholic and my marriage went the way of most alcoholic marriages. Mike and I had been friends since we attended SMU. We wound up retiring to cabins on the Red River, north of Bonham, began dating and eventually married.

My husband and I have been sober for 10 years now while Thomas is going on 20. I lost a son during an alcoholic-related accident 10 years ago last June. We called Thomas, and he was heartbroken for us. Mike and I got sober as a direct result of that accident.

Mike and I went back to junior college and wrestled with what we were going to do since we both had our counseling license. We ended up with a volunteer program for clients who are members of the First Methodist Church in Bonham, and other people in need in the county.

Many people we work with are older, and remember Thomas as a hero back there with the golden Cowboys. They have a graduation before going back into society after being in a rehab program. Thomas volunteered to speak at one of those graduations. He drove all the way from Austin and gave away a bunch of his books. They still talk about it. I remember him being here as a random act of kindness.

Now for the second time Thomas influenced a member of my family. After her brother died, my daughter, Wendy, really lost it. Her alcohol use became a lot heavier.

Mike and I left with friends one day for Indiana to buy antiques. Wendy hit bottom while we were gone. She was in a relationship with another drug user and reached the point of realizing, "This is not me. This is a terrible way to live." We were out of town, so she called Thomas. Wendy got him on his cell phone and I'll never forget, he was sowing grass seeds on that field in Austin.

Thomas was doing public relations for a recovery unit called Father Martin Ashley's up on Chesapeake Bay in Maryland. He told her, "Wendy, I know a wonderful place for you. Shall we call your mom and dad? Should we talk? How do you want to do this?"

She said, Let's work out the details, and then we'll call mom and Mike.

He made phone calls in the next few days and got her a bed in that facility. So when we got back from Indiana, she sat us down and said, "I think I'm an alcoholic. I believe I'm in real trouble. I've been talking to Thomas, and I think we have everything worked out."

Thomas stood in for me, and for that I will never forget him and neither will Wendy. She now has nine years of sobriety, a baby and a sober husband that she brought back from Maryland.

CHAPTER TWELVE

BUILD IT AND THEY WILL PLAY

Although sobriety brought me financial success, and I now lived in a $250,000 condo in west Austin, I still kept in touch with my roots. My mother continued to live on the east side, in the old neighborhood, and on Saturday mornings I would often pay her a visit.

One Saturday morning in 1990, on my way to Mamma's house, I stopped to watch a group of eight-to-10-year old boys play in the East Austin Youth Foundation Football League. At first, it was only nostalgia, a glimpse of my past—young boys playing football as I once had many years before.

But I noticed they weren't playing on a regulation football field. It was actually a baseball field, closer to 80 yards long than the standard 100 yards. Crooked chalk lines marked out of bounds, and it didn't appear as if they'd even got the rectangle right. Parts of the field were covered with mud; there were no goal posts and no scoreboard.

As I leaned against my car and watched, one little boy, running a sweep, broke free from the crowd and headed down the sideline with the ball tucked under his arm, a broad smile on his face. I pressed against the fence and resisted the urge to yell, "Go, Thomas!"

But his glory and my remembered glory were short-lived. The little boy hit a patch of mud and slid head first out of bounds. He was still smiling when he got up, but his smile was smeared with the bright red mud of east Austin. Not only his face but his helmet and uniform was caked with it, and when he tried to spike the ball in celebration of his fine run, the ball didn't bounce up but stuck in the muck where the others children walked up and stared down at it.

I shook my head as I climbed back in my car. I thought to myself, "Why don't the inner city kids of east Austin have a proper ball field?"

I took a detour from my mother's house and drove a quarter mile to my old high school, where Pro Football Hall of Fame cornerback Dick "Night Train" Lane and I had played football as kids. I wanted to see for myself why these boys weren't playing there. What I found was that the Anderson High School campus had been turned into Austin Community College, and the football stadium no longer existed. This historic field had been torn down 20 years ago during integration and become an asphalt parking lot. The fields surrounding it were fenced off and overgrown with scattered trees, weeds and grass. I walked to the gate and held the rusted padlock in my hand, wondering what the key might be to opening that gate and bringing the old Yellow Jacket Field of my youth back to life.

I knew what the key would be. It was money, of course. I knew people with money, ball players and coaches who I had once abused. But I'd worked hard the past 10 years. I'd stayed sober and made amends where I could. Had I done enough, though? Had I earned their trust?

I drove to Momma's, ran into the house and shouted:

"Guess what, Momma? I'm gonna build a ball field!"

I plopped down on the sofa and began taking an inventory. I had become good at taking inventories during my recovery program, constantly listing all my faults and all my assets. Now I was running through my head the names of people who could help with a football field. There was Too Tall Jones, Tom Landry, Drew Pearson, Roger Staubach, Jerry Jones, Troy Aikman and Nate Newton. I only needed a few to support me and then others would come.

Anyway, by now I had made a connection. Why should those kids play football under those conditions when, with a little work, that parking lot over there could be a football field? I went to my office to figure out whom to call to turn this parking lot over to me. I contacted the Austin Independent School District and inquired about old Anderson High School. If I restore the stadium, would you let me have it for a while? I hired a lawyer and got a 30-year free lease on the property.

Then I went downtown to meet with AISD officials and told them what I planned to do: add a scoreboard, goal posts, bleachers, a football field and sprinkler system. They all laughed. They were looking at me like, "I don't know guys, he may be back on that junk."

They gave me the keys to the gate and I went over there by myself. The weeds hadn't been cut in 12-14 years. That's how long it takes grass to become trees. I had approximately six acres to work on. I also had $40,000 in donated money to work with, and this is how I got it.

I had played many rounds of golf with Darrell Royal, the great former head football coach at The University of Texas, and I'd gotten invited to events and met many movers and shakers in Austin. One day late in 1990, I walked into the 19th hole at Barton Creek and Darrell said he wanted to talk to me. I had joined Barton Creek Country Club in 1990.

"Thomas," he said, "I sponsor this golf tournament and I need to figure out what to do with the proceeds. I want to turn it into a fundraiser. What do you think about doing the tournament as a fundraiser guaranteeing about $500,000 to the East Austin community? I'd like you to be involved in it."

I said I thought that was a great idea. So it was Darrell Royal involving me in a philanthropic cause for east Austin that gave me my start in charity. I didn't know what charity was before. I'd heard the word. As a Dallas Cowboy I'd show up and sign footballs and give autographs. But I never wrote a check in my life to charity; not to the March of Dimes, Goodwill, Salvation Army or to kids. Royal introduced me to the concept of charity.

We had a successful tournament. I understood that if proceeds were going to charity, Thomas Henderson needed to apply for 501c3 non-profit status. I formed a six-person board, registered with the IRS and founded the East Side Youth Services and Street Outreach (ESYSSO) with me as chairman. Meanwhile, proceeds from the tournament went to the Austin Community Foundation, which takes applications for grants from organizations in the needy part of town.

I applied for $40,000. Because I was one of the founding members of the event I received a check for that amount. My vice chair was a woman who I was led to believe could help me decide how to disburse this money. I won't use this person's name to save her more embarrassment because of what happened after we deposited the money in an east Austin bank.

She had asked how many signatures I would have on the bank account and recommended two: hers and mine. I agreed. The bank called a few days later and reported that the woman who signed on my account wasn't legally clear to do that. She had some theft by check charges in Houston against her, plus other things. An interesting board meeting took place the next day when I repeated what the bank told me. She got this look that said, "You found me out." And out she went.

Back at the stadium site, I was looking at a 100-yard wide and 150-yard long asphalt parking lot that had to be removed. I had to start cutting weeds. With the $40,000 we got dumpsters and began clearing weeds. When I inquired about asphalt removal, all the environmental issues, dumping issues and fees were about to use up all the money.

What to do? Then a farmer I knew in Georgetown, about 30 miles north of Austin, contacted me. He said he needed to fill a deep ravine to build a dam.

"I have about 50 truck loads of asphalt," I told him.

"If you get it here, I can use it," he said.

I'd met a guy on the golf course who owned a trucking company. He said the normal cost was $50 per load but his drivers knew what I was trying to do so they'd charge $20 per load. I knew an African American gentleman named James Harper in east Austin who can pick up a dime with a backhoe. He joined the project. So one afternoon I had about 20 trucks lined up outside the field and by the time we got the last truck loaded here comes an empty one back from Georgetown. Before you knew it the asphalt was gone.

Next day a city official showed up at the field and asked what happened to the asphalt.

"The damnedest thing happened," I said. "I got here today and it had vanished. I have no idea what happened to it."

I got dirt donated and a sprinkler company to donate much of the labor to install the system. Harper worked for minimum wage with his heavy equipment. I got companies to give me a scoreboard. Jones, Newton and Aikman donated money for the bleachers.

I never sought reward or accolades. It was almost like something that I was told to do. Something I felt compelled to do. Charity has helped strengthen my character. Giving has built the foundation under me. Building that stadium is the greatest thing I've ever done in my life.

I got the sheriff's department to send me inmates from the Del Valle jail to help lay sod. I'd get 40 three-piece chicken plates from Church's to feed them. The inmates loved it because all they got to eat in jail was bologna and bread. The first day I had about 20 guys. The second day they came back with two busloads after everyone heard about the chicken. I inspired the inmate population with Church's three-piece.

I'd bought 419 Tifway, the same grass you find on golf fairways, for the field. So by the beginning of football season in 1992 the kids of east Austin not only had goal posts, scoreboards and bleachers, but a soft field and full-sized football stadium to play their games. And no more mud.

Later, I decided to put a track around the field. Royal got me going with that first contribution. I spent the $40,000 and about $25,000 of my own money to get that stadium over the top. Then it became personal. I wasn't going to start something without finishing it. I wasn't going to let money, or lack of it, stop me.

I'd gotten angry that children in the community I grew up in didn't have an adequate football stadium to play in and the parents didn't have a place to sit. I remember as a child that my folks were working all the time. They never had time or took time to watch me play sports. I saw other parents doing that and I always felt bad no one from my family came to see me.

Some of my heroes today don't know they're my new heroes. They're coaches who volunteer to work with eight and nine-year-olds in football. Most of them hadn't been great players. But they get out there on Thursday nights and work with these kids year in and year out. When I first saw a guy that I knew was a fourth-string backup now coaching and heard him screaming at the kids to do this and do that, I thought, he couldn't even play the game. So why is he hollering at the kids?

Then I thought, you know what, Thomas? He's a lot better person than you because he's doing what he can for kids. If there weren't volunteers like these guys what would happen to so many children in America?

After I built the stadium, I heard a rumor. A guy who didn't know he was talking to a friend of mine said, "Henderson stole my idea." The poor guy probably could have built the stadium if he'd had Darrell Royal give him 40 grand and he could rally 60 trucks to haul asphalt and negotiate with a sprinkler company to install a system. Yeah, I think he would have done it but he never moved a finger to get started. I just happened to be given the opportunity.

When I later fasted for seven days to raise money to build a track around the field, the local guru track coach surveyed it with the same envy and said, "That Henderson, he stole my idea." So what do you do?

Here's what I learned from the experience of meeting Darrell Royal, getting my first $40,000 and eventually becoming a community leader in Austin. You do not become a community leader because you say you are. You become a leader in your community by what you do, what you volunteer for and the service you provide. Then people recognize you. You're not ordained in that role.

CHAPTER THIRTEEN

PRIDE AND PREJUDICE

Building that football stadium, my field of dreams if you will, brought children, alumni and elderly citizens' back to the site of Anderson High School. The 60-70-80 year- olds were overwhelmed that I'd returned life to old Yellow Jacket Stadium. They walk it. They jog on it. They pick up trash on their own.

Many of them had watched me during the summer months of '91 and '92, digging out sewers that made me stink. It was me, not the city or county or state, not the contractors or crews that were hired, with nobody's dollars or energy but my own, that got it built. An audience kept track of my progress from long range. People pulled up on the hill overlooking the site and thought, "I wonder what he's doing down there today?" I saw them but they wouldn't come in the gate.

By volunteerism and concern for the youth of the community the status of a leader was bestowed on me. The entrenched leaders of east Austin began inviting me to attend certain meetings. I didn't go to these meetings to apply for leadership of the African American community, or to try to be a leader. I just went because I was invited.

I was anointed a leader because I had fund raising abilities for causes, which is a tremendous trust. Initially people give you the benefit of the doubt about donating to a fund-raiser, but later on it has to be trust. They need to see results with the money. I've seen fund-raising done by other athletes and, without being critical of anyone in particular, I know how they take 20 to 40 percent off the top for themselves. I've never taken a dime. Actually, it's cost me personally about $20-30,000 a year to make sure what I'm doing trickles down to the kids. And that started years before I won the lottery.

Mention of leadership brings me to a lady named Dorothy Turner. She is a legend in Austin, a civil rights activist with a strident, give-no-quarter voice and attitude. She's the 21st century version of Harriet Tubman, with a more radical slant. She's fought for women's rights, gay rights and black rights. She's a relentless figure at city council meetings, raising all kinds of hell about issues.

Dorothy called me one day and said, "Hey, Thomas, I'm doing an event coming up and I need $500." I said, okay. I liked her, and donating to certain causes had been part of my role in the community. There was money in the Eastside Youth Services and Street Outreach account. The outreach part was for small organizations that needed a hand. I don't give money to executive directors or for payrolls. But I do give for special projects, like buying a bus or uniforms or kick balls for a youth team. I've helped hundreds of organizations in the community this way for less than $1,000 per event.

So I gave Dorothy $500. Two weeks passed and I was at home watching TV. I am a habitual watcher of news and cable access in my community because there's some interesting stuff on it. All of a sudden I saw on my local cable television the "Anti-July 4th Celebration," sponsored by Thomas Henderson!

No matter what you may think about Thomas Henderson, I'm an American. I'm a patriot. I love this country. I love the 4th of July just like I love Juneteenth.

I was furious. And just because I'm sober doesn't mean I've lost my swearing vocabulary. I called Dorothy and shouted: "God damn, why the fuck didn't you tell me what this was all about? I wouldn't have given you $500 for an anti-July 4th celebration!!"

She started laughing at me.

"Boy, don't you know what I do?" she said. She started ranting and raving and saying things like, I'm not thinking about these god damn white folks and this god damn flag and blah, blah...

"Damnit Dorothy" I said, "Don't ever use me to protest against the United States of America. Just because I'm black hasn't stopped me from doing anything in my life. I've never been a victim of racism. Any racism that affected me was emotional. It wasn't based on fact."

My exposure to racism goes back 50 years. I was right on the cusp between those who didn't necessarily feel it or experience it – and those who did. I never saw my step father or mother called 'nigger.' I never saw anyone called "nigger" when I was young. I never saw them embarrassed as a result of it. I have never been called that name. Well, just one time at a bar when I was a Dallas Cowboy. I knocked the bastard out.

Let me qualify this. If I had been raised in Montgomery, Alabama, Mississippi, Louisiana or some southern state, I was at the right age to see it, feel it, smell it and feel powerless as a result. And watch my parents feel embarrassed as a result of it. We didn't have television when I was growing up. When we heard things about Martin Luther King, it was as though it was from a different world.

Here's an example of how oblivious I was to racism. We'd go downtown to a movie when I was 10 or 11 years old. I remember the theater as a very nice place where we went upstairs to sit. No one told me that was the only place I could sit in the theater, though it was. I just thought it was a nice spot to watch the movie.

I was probably a year or so younger when I started working at the Balcones Country Club in Austin. Dunie Riley got me a job working in the locker room with him on Saturdays and Sundays. He was the locker room attendant, and other blacks wearing white jackets worked the dining room. I was making 20 or 25 cents for cleaning off spikes and shining shoes. There was a beautiful swimming pool outside the dining room, and on Sundays families would show up after church. Their kids would order sandwiches, Cokes and French fries and then get in the pool.

After working there a couple of months, I didn't tell Dunie, but one day I packed a bathing suit. I put it on under my clothes. It was mid-day in July, I was done with my shoes and I was hot. I decided to go for a swim. I threw my little pants and shirt in the locker, grabbed a towel, went out and got on the diving board and dived in.

When I surfaced, white folks were running everywhere! The pool was rapidly emptying. When I swam to the edge, I saw Dunie with a look on his face that said, boy, get out of that water. "I just went swimming," I told him with an innocent smile. The blessing of that incident was that he never told me why I couldn't swim in that pool. No one did. All the other black men and women were too embarrassed to say anything. No one told me, "You're just a little nigger..."

I know when the hired help went home they laughed and cracked up about it. But they didn't scar me emotionally for the rest of my life. Does that make sense?

I can relate to the fact that Frederick Douglas, Martin Luther King, Malcolm X and many others saw, felt, heard and smelled the venomous nature of racism. I happen to be somebody who at 50 barely missed it. My mother tells me of times when there were signs around town that said, Colored, but I wasn't old enough to read then. You can't experience racism by osmosis. I think it's stealing to try to own someone else's rage, degradation and shame as the result of their experience with racism when you've never had that feeling. I can try to understand it. I can agree that it did happen. But I can't experience it second hand.

I know I'm a rare case. When I became a Dallas Cowboy, that's why guys like Jethro Pugh and Cornell Green sometimes looked at me like, "Fool, do you know who you're talking to?" They knew things I didn't know. They had experienced things that I hadn't seen. So when I joined the team I was a breath of fresh air.

Bob Hayes told me that on many occasions he would go home and all the veterans would call each other and say they were scared for me; they knew the power of the white man. "But we laughed and laughed about it," Hayes said.

* * * *

Through the 1990s I worked for Sierra Tucson as a consultant and also spent a year with Father Martin Ashley in Havre de Grace, Maryland. I was now a member of the profession that literally had saved and changed my life. It was a wonderful feeling to be working in that area, because if not for treatment and therapy I'm not sure my life would have gotten better.

While in Austin I was making money to live on and invest, well over six figures lecturing and another plus-six figures consulting. People came to me. I spoke to mothers and fathers, girlfriends and boyfriends, fiancés, uncles and aunts of drug addicts and alcoholics who were trying to find relief. People didn't seek me out because I was once an NFL linebacker. They knew me as a recovering drug addict and alcoholic.

I've never had what most people would describe as a real job since I left the Cowboys. I've worked without a net ever since. I've been an entrepreneur. By blessing and choice, I decided that it was not a good idea for me to work for anybody. I remember a guy who wanted to hire me. He was going to pay $5,000 a month with benefits, travel expenses and so on. All I thought about while he was making a presentation was a silent warning to the man: "Do you know who you're talking to? If you hire me, I'd probably take over your company."

I didn't have the DNA of a subordinate. That's probably the reason I was not a successful Dallas Cowboy. I've been a free-wheeling, independent guy my whole life. I need freedom to go in whatever direction life beckons.

Frankly, I have this gift or instinct for business. When I got to Austin in 1990 one of my first business moves was to buy real estate. I'd appear at the courthouse on the first Tuesday of each month to buy properties that were foreclosed or that people hadn't paid taxes. Before you knew it I owned 15 properties: condos, commercial buildings and houses. As modestly as I can put it, I was damn proud of myself.

I remember one moment of clarity when it dawned on me that I was in the real estate business. I was showing off, riding a friend around town saying you know I own that, I own this and I got three of those. I was bragging that Thomas Henderson was doing well in real estate.

"How many tenants do you have?" my friend asked. His question threw me off balance.

"What do you mean...tenants?" I said. That's when it occurred to me that I was playing a bad game of Monopoly. I owned all these properties, I was paying taxes on them, the values were rising but I didn't have any tenants. Then I recalled why I didn't have tenants.

I had leased a house to an acquaintance who moved in and gave me a deposit plus the first month's rent. After that, they wouldn't pay me. They got two or three months behind. I always felt like they thought I didn't need the money. I did the only thing I knew to do to get them out of the house. I had to think about it but I finally said, okay, I think this will work.

I went to the house one day at noon when everyone was gone and removed the back door. That was a big surprise to the tenants when they got home. The first thing they did was call me, the person they hadn't paid. They wanted me to put another door on. I said, well, you haven't paid me, so scrimp around because it's an emergency and you can't leave the house without a back door. So they replaced the door.

Two days later I went back and took that door off.

That's why I don't lease property anymore. It's too hard to get paid. But for those of you who are having tenant problems, taking the back door off really works well to get rid of them.

CARL PAUL
(Golf company founder)

Years ago, I started a company called Golfsmith International in my spare time from the basement of a home in Manhattan. The business took off and expanded into a golf academy that we moved to Austin in the mid-1990s. That's were I met Thomas.

One day a pro at the academy told me about the swing on someone named Thomas.

"Thomas who?" I said.

"Thomas 'Hollywood' Henderson, the football player, is here. I thought you knew that."

I didn't have any pre-formed conclusions about Thomas. I was vaguely aware that he played football for Dallas and had problems with Tom Landry and had gone to prison. I just knew what everyone else did from reading the papers.

Here's the point about Thomas at the academy. Many celebrities came through the school and we made arrangements for most of them at no charge. It was good for customers to see various football coaches, basketball players and so forth at the school. In the case of Thomas, he didn't call and ask for anything. He had celebrity status around Austin, but he paid full price and went about his business of learning to play golf better.

He could have called and said, how about so and so, and we'd have loved to had him out there. But he didn't. He found out about the program, paid $700, and took lessons. That always stuck with me that he didn't take advantage of the situation even when it wasn't taking an advantage since we'd loved to have him, anyway.

We weren't best friends or anything like that. He'd come around to say hello and we played some golf together. We'd talk and go to lunch every couple of weeks at some place like Luby's Cafeteria. One day he came to me and said, "You're going to think I'm crazy, but I'm starting a line of apparel that has to do with golf."

Later, he said he received a Federal trademark on the name Sandbagging Dog. He said everybody called him a sandbagger, so he'd trademarked a logo with a Snoopy looking character named Sandbagging Dog. He asked if I'd take a couple of shirts and put them in my store to see if they'd sell.

We took a dozen or so of Sandbagging Dog golf shirts and lo and behold, they sold. So we expanded the deal and made a contractual arrangement where we'd sell them on a percentage basis. We put them in a catalogue that went out to 30 million golfers and did substantial sales. Lots of people thought it was humorous and the brand sold amazing well for the first year or two before it trickled off.

Thomas has a bright, agile mind. I hesitate to say he's a marketing genius, but look how he went on a hunger strike and raised funds for a track in east Austin. He got the city behind him and all the media to cover it.

After I knew him a little better, Thomas gave me a peek at his inner self. Maybe I'd remarked about what a good job he'd done with his life by straightening out and holding the values he does today. Whatever I said made him reply with these thoughts:

"Carl, people think I've really straightened my life out, that I'm clean and sober and just this really nice guy without any faults. I try to be but you know what? I'm a kid raised on the streets of east Austin around things that take place in a poverty area. I went to college and didn't get a brilliant education, but I've cleaned up my act. However, that guy still lurking inside is the same as the one raised on the streets in east Austin."

What Thomas meant is that he wrestles every day with that guy inside to stay straight. Some people think what he's done is easy, it's all over and he's just a wonderful guy. But he wasn't raised like most of us. I didn't get into details, but I read his first book and anyone who has can just imagine what he goes through.

We got together for lunch another time after he saw a TV clip about a couple of black fellows who were starting a bar-b-q shop. So we drove to northwest Austin to this hole in the wall place. These fellows bought it cheap, put up a sign and began turning out quality food. Thomas had two reasons for going out there. One was terrific bar-b-q. The other was to see if they needed any money to expand their business. I thought that was a neat gesture.

We have a retail golf store in Austin with a deli cafeteria in one corner. Thomas and I finished eating there one day and were walking back across the putting green. Out of the clear blue a man about 50 years old cornered Thomas.

"Hi, do you mind if I tell you an ethnic joke?" he said.

"Can I tell you a joke first?" Thomas said, looking down at the stranger.

"Well, okay."

142

"Do you know what's black and blue and floating down the river?"
"No, I don't."
"The last guy who tried to tell me an ethnic joke," Thomas said, and walked off into another part of the building.

GOLF

The game of golf is a relationship that I'm glad I got at ease with. Golf has taught me as much about life and myself as recovery from alcoholism and crack addiction has. Call this activity or hobby what you like but it's become essential to the balance of my life.

Golf is about the balls, the clubs, the wind, the rain, the sun, the leaves, the course, companionship, par, bogey, double bogey, handicap, respect, honest, integrity, behavior, being a gentleman, truth and a learning curve that never ends. I'm being taught life by a game. I can play 18 holes of golf with a person and tell you much about their character and values. I've learned a lot about my own too.

When I'm not working I play golf. Today when I travel I carry my golf clubs. Never know when you can get a game on the road. I'm currently an 11 handicap. My best round is a 76. I've played some of the best courses in the world. My one golf wish is to one-day play at Augusta.

I have something to do for the rest of my life as long as I have a game and can get to the course. This gives me something to look forward to forever. Before golf life in part was depression and isolation. Now I have this game and many friends to play with. Golf has created a balance that was much needed.

Thank you golf for being a part of my life. I needed you.

NAT MOORE
(Former Dolphins teammate)

I had mixed emotions when Thomas landed with the Miami Dolphins. You knew you were getting a guy with talent if he could stay straight. You also realized that if Thomas would have done the things he needed to do with that talent, there's no way in the world Dallas would have let him go.

I say this based on my first impression of watching him run back a kickoff for a touchdown as a rookie with the Cowboys. Like everyone else in the league, I wanted to know who in the hell was this big kid who could run like that? I think it was the following year that I had a chance to play against him in a preseason game.

Ever since, I've told him that my most famous memory of him was beating him for a touchdown in that game. He claims it wasn't him but Mike Hegman who had the coverage on me. That's the way it's supposed to be-amnesia when you get beat and great recall when you beat someone.

One of the conditions for coach Don Shula to take a chance on him was that Thomas had to go through rehab. He asked me at times to drop him off at a south Miami rehab center and the sad part was that even then I knew he wasn't serious about straightening up. You hoped for the team's sake he could make it through and not screw himself up any worse. Somehow, he still looked good during training camp until he fractured a bone in his neck.

Some negative signs were already evident to me. Thomas sometimes disappeared in the evening after curfew. One of the times he asked me to take him to the rehab center he said to stop at a convenience store. He went in and came out with a six-pack of beer.

"Whoa, Thomas," I said, "aren't you going to the rehab center?"

"Nat, I don't have a problem with alcohol. As a matter of fact, it gives me a big kick to go in there and watch the alcoholics squirm when they smell alcohol on my breath," he laughed.

That alone showed he wasn't serious about cleaning himself up. You knew he was a great football player and hoped his love of the game would eventually win out. But I wouldn't have given a 20 percent chance that it would happen because he was making fun of his problem. I had a brother who failed over and over with an addiction. Now he has about seven years of clean time. I understand it's a disease and difficult to control. It's a testimony to Thomas that he had the strength to whip his.

The difference between the person I knew in Miami and the Thomas I know now is 180 degrees. We've become extremely close over the past seven to 10 years. He bought a place close to Miami, so we've played golf together a lot. I'd say this about the Thomas of today. He's a model citizen, a stand-up guy who still enjoys life but has found other ways of doing it without including drugs and alcohol. He's a guy who can go places where everyone else is drinking and not drink.

I don't know how many people he's helped, people with goals and dreams who if he doesn't help them have no chance. He was helping them out long before he won the lottery. Most guys would say, you know, I've got mine, so I don't need to be involved. I'm not saying this about him because he's a friend. It's what I honestly believe. Good things happen to good people. Just look at the rewards he's reaping for working hard to beat his demons.

Thomas used to tell jokes in the locker room when he was in Miami about how he couldn't pay his taxes and the IRS was after him. Someone asked what happened to the money from the 7-Up commercial he did. Thomas said he snorted it all up. He was always happy go lucky.

I was closer to Mercury Morris than Thomas. I played with Mercury. I watched his transformation after he went to prison and came out and became a dynamic speaker in the fight against drug and alcohol abuse. Yet I've been more impressed with the way Thomas handled himself after prison than Mercury, and Mercury has done a superb job. But to me, Mercury at times still lives in the 70s. You know life goes on.

That's the difference in someone like Thomas. Life has gone on for him. The days with the Cowboys were fantastic and fun, but it also was a bad time in his life and he's been able to walk away and forget all that. With Mercury, the biggest thing in his career was Miami's perfect season. Players from that team pride themselves for going 17-0 and they should.

When it's time to be recognized for something like a perfect season, that's great. But you are not what you used to be anymore. You are only what you make of yourself today. I'm impressed with what Thomas has made of himself.

Chapter Fourteen

THE FAST

The football stadium had been a big hit in the community but I sensed something about it was still incomplete. Word of mouth made me realize what was missing.

I heard that The University of Texas wouldn't allow summer track programs to practice over there. Nor would the Austin Independent School District unlock gates at other facilities to let the kids in summer track programs have a place to run. It occurred to me that kids in East Austin needed to have the same kind of facilities as other kids in most neighborhoods in the city. What was missing was a running track.

No one lobbied me to do something about it. I just heard there was a need. I remembered that I had really never given anybody any money in terms of charity. I'd never given any time per se to charity. I was always nice. Even as a Cowboy I'd tried to be considerate and helpful to those with handicaps. I've always had a compassionate nature. But I'd really never done anything for anybody except myself.

The football stadium was one thing. This track was another. I got on the phone and called a company that specializes in installing tracks. I had no idea what a project like that would cost. I started learning words like polyurethane, tar, drainage ditches, elevations, surveys and topography. It was an education.

They finally presented me with a cost figure: $300,000.

It was in my bones now. The film company was doing well. I had several employees. We were selling films. I was doing lectures. I was into real estate. I was fine.

And then I hired Ricky. Ricky Walker was a homosexual who looked like Diana Ross and all the Supremes. I'd met Ricky at a recovery meeting.

I'm not homophobic. I had a good time talking to Ricky, so I hired him. The building where my office is located also houses the Texas Public Employee Association, which is by all accounts, filled with ultra-conservative types.

Ricky would come to work looking like Diana Ross almost every day. Except on a bad day, he looked like Harriet Tubman. My friends and even the people who leased me the office started to wonder, "What is Thomas thinking?"

What's hard to make people understand is that everyone deserves a chance. And Ricky, although he looked like Diana Ross and all the Supremes, was a recovering drug addict whom I happened to like. I made no judgment about his sexual orientation or the way he dressed. He had worked for MCI, which meant he was good on the phone and I needed people to make cold calls. So I hired him and he worked for me for about a year.

People kept saying, "Why do you have that thing working for you?" I'd say, Ricky passed the first test with me and that was that he's a recovering alcoholic and drug addict. Lots of folks had given me chances, and I felt like I needed to give him a shot.

Anyway, it came to me that I needed to raise this money. I'd never tried to raise $300,000 all at once. I have no idea where the impulse to do it by fasting came from. I called my staff together and told them, "Get me a tent. Get me a sleeping bag. Get everything together, take it to the field and put it near one of the goal posts."

Within a day we had a tent, a sleeping bag and a chair. I told them to get me a five-gallon water bottle. I got a knife and cut a hole in the top big enough so you could put your hand inside.

Then I called a press conference at Eastside Field. One television station showed up. I said, "I want the citizens of this town to know that I'm not going to eat and I'm not going home until I raise $300,000 to build a track for the youth of our city." The reaction was, he's got to be kidding, but the story made the news that evening.

I slept that night on the ground in my sleeping bag. I made a fasting concoction of water, molasses, lemon juice and cayenne pepper. Where'd I get that recipe? Somebody told me it was the thing to drink while fasting.

Next morning, all the radio and TV stations came out. They were skeptical, but they kept coming. It became a daily ritual for the press to check me out. By the third day, people were coming from everywhere to make donations.

One of the most memorable contributions was from a homeless guy who gave me the nastiest-looking $1 bill I've ever seen. It was grimy, crumpled and crusted. He said, "You'll do better with this dollar than I will." He gave me all he had when he came in and put that dollar in the bottle. He'd walked from all the way downtown, which is about three miles, to give me a dollar.

White grandmothers brought their white granddaughters to give me a check for $100. Kids came by and gave me change. Organizations donated $500 and $1,000. By the fourth day I probably had raised $50-60,000 and I was thinking, "At this rate I'm about to catch Gandhi on this fasting business." Either Gandhi or Jesus, but then I remembered Jesus went 40 days.

Because by now one part of me was thinking, Thomas Henderson, you have bitten off more than you can chew. You're in big trouble. When are you going to whimper your ass out of here and say, sorry everyone, but on the doctor's advice I've been told to go home?

But the part of Thomas Henderson that's been successful in life, the determined Thomas Henderson, the linebacker, said something else. Whatever it takes. And it took a lot.

My mother came over. She was crying. She said, you have to stop this and go home. I said no Mamma, I've got to do it. Don't worry, I'll be fine. None of it made an impression of her. When she said, "You need to stop. This is dangerous," I told her she had to leave, and she did.

Mamma went home and called my doctor. My doctor came over on the fifth day and he said, "What is going on? You can't do this." So I said to my doctor, "Tell you what. If I get sick here, take me to the hospital. Put me on IV liquid only until the money is raised. You understand?"

He agreed.

People came and went. Some came to spy on me at night to see if I was still there and not sneak eating. Oh, and the gangs. One gang in particular parked up on a hill at night from about 3 a.m. to daybreak with a boom-boom box, the bass and sound of hip-hop music playing. When I waved to them in the morning they said, hey, we were just watching you, making sure nobody would bother you.

On the afternoon of Day Five I was asked to attend a board meeting at St. David's Hospital. I had my staff come get me because I wanted witnesses present at all times to prove I wasn't going to Denny's or Luby's to eat something. So I showed up with an escort.

Before St. David's had been bought by a public company, the auxiliary volunteers raised money every year and donated a piece of equipment to the hospital. They'd have $200,000 and would buy some micro-biotic laser something to enhance the hospital's ability to take care of the sick. Now that it had become a public company, they had to find other ways to give money to health causes.

I got to the door of this meeting smelling like I just played the Washington Redskins five times and hadn't showered. I was malodorous. No Right Guard or left guard. This lady walked up and I noticed right away she's caught a whiff of me. Her eyes watered.

"Mr. Henderson," she said, "the auxiliary board has $60,000 to give away. They are trying to give that to six organizations, so if anyone asks you how much money you are requesting for your track, I strongly suggest that you say $10,000."

I thanked her and went in. I was introduced to the board. The chairman was a woman who looked more than 80 years old, but she was still sharp. I looked around the room and everyone reminded me of food. I started to tell the story of why I was fasting. I said I couldn't personally afford to give my foundation $300,000. But I thought if I sacrificed myself, sacrificed food and shelter, and did it unselfishly for someone else, I could get it done. Not for me. Not for Thomas Henderson's gain, but to build something for the kids in the community.

I said I'd never done anything like this. I said, how do you sit around and go, "Hey, I'm not going to eat until somebody gives me $300,000? Where does that come from?" I told them I had no idea and began to cry. I started weeping in front of everyone.

"I'm going to be out there until I get the money," I told the board. "At this point I'm up around $150,000 and that's good. But my promise was that I would stay until I had $300,000 so I've got a ways to go. I thank you for calling me over. I appreciate the opportunity to make a presentation but you remind me of food, I'm hungry and I want to get back to the field so I can continue to fast for the kids of east Austin."

As I got up to leave the lady in charge motioned me to stop. " M r . Henderson," she said, "how much money do you want from us?"

You could hear a pin fall in that room. The woman who greeted me had already prepped me for this moment. But I disobeyed her advice. I looked at her, looked around at every board member and with tears streaming down my face I said, "Just give me whatever you want." And I walked out.

I went back to the field and probably raised another $10-15,000. Accountants and brokers were bringing me $2,000, $5,000 and $10,000. The dollars and half dollars were still coming in.

The next morning was Day Six and I saw about 10 people walking toward me. I recognized that they're from the board. One gentleman had an envelope in his hand and, he walked up under the tent. I greeted and thanked him for coming by. He said, we just came to tell you that the board voted unanimously and we're giving you the entire $60,000.

The other significant event of that day came later when the UT track club and other athletes came to the field. Remember Beverly Kearney, the track coach who was in that bad car wreck? Beverly brought over her track team. There were basketball players and just some girls from UT in the bunch. They brought me several hundred dollars in $1 bills and coins.

They were all standing under the tent when I saw a girl take a brown paper bag and drop it through the hole in my plastic 5-gallon jug. I thought maybe there were some dollar bills in it.

The group got ready to leave and said all the typical things. We're proud of you. Can't believe you're doing this. This is great, amazing...etc. As they were walking off the young lady who put the brown paper bag in the bottle whispered in my ear. "I put a cheeseburger in there for you," she said.

Oh, no. "Hey, everybody come back in here!" I shouted. I called about 30 people back into the tent.

I said, "I'm not criticizing this young lady, but she put a cheeseburger in the bottle. She meant no harm. But I want all of you to know and I want her to know that what I'm doing is real. What I'm doing is difficult, but I'm willing to suffer through it. Don't ask me where the motivation came from. Don't even ask me how the hell I came up with this idea or why."

I started crying again. I don't know if I was crying because I was hungry or that this was a powerful moment. I told the girl to remove the cheeseburger. If nothing else, I think that left an impression with the group they'll never forget.

By the time I got the $60,000, I was probably up to around $240,000. It was Day Six and yes, the field had restrooms but I didn't have to go often. Trust me, I was doing pretty well physically. But I knew it was about to become difficult.

My recovery from drugs and alcohol was helping. Cowboys training camps at Thousand Oaks were helping. Self-discipline from the marathon in Los Angeles was kicking in. I had several wells to draw from. If there's dysfunction in your life, whether it's food, drugs, alcohol, sex or whatever, I hope there's a well you can go to and draw strength. I did that so, by God, I can do this. I was able to draw from some tough activities and situations in life for strength.

And I prayed. You know that I'm not a very religious guy. But I prayed to God, as I understand Him, and I don't need anybody to try to figure out what that means. All I asked was to help me through this. Just help me, be there with me, and I'm going to do this.

Around 11:30 a.m. on the sixth day I had about $270,000. I was close enough to call it a victory. I was close enough to even claim I had all the money. I was close enough that I could write a personal check for $30,000 and do the deal. But something spiritual inside me said to do 24 more hours. I was sitting there sweating, hungry and hot.

Gigi, one of my employees, came over and said, "Why don't we just shut it down?" I said no, I'm going to do 24 more hours.

That became the most painfully difficult 24 hours of my life. Pain centered in my head. I didn't hallucinate, but I wanted to go home. I wanted a shower. I wanted food. I wanted to be out of there in the worst way. I felt the pain of hunger for the first time. It was more painful than the marathon. It was more painful than prison. Those 24 hours were mentally, physically and spiritually the most painful I've ever endured. But before noon the next day I had all the money.

Best I remember, a $1,000 check about 10 a.m. did it. But then I had to fulfill my 24-hour pledge because I'd told myself I'd do it. Finally, I had two hours to go, and they were simply awful. My fast ended at noon on the seventh day.

I'd been making deposits across the street in a store that had a safe in the floor. We took the bottle over there, got all the money and went to the bank. Every bit of it, penny for penny, dime for dime, dollars, tens, fives, twenties and hundreds, was counted to $300,000. To be honest, the final total came to around $298,000 because I miscounted somewhere.

We made the deposit into Eastside Youth Services and Street Outreach. As I did every year I sent out a compilation report of spending and contributions to all my donors. I sent out about 1,000 notices. Here is how much we have. Here is how much we spent. Here is what we spent it on and how much we have left. I did that every year. You know why? Because Ronald Reagan once said, "Trust but verify."

My first meal consisted of pea soup, two French rolls and a cup of fruit. I got it from a place next to the bank and ate while we were counting money. And oh, man, did I take a shower! It was one of those showers where if you don't use the whole bar of soap, you ain't through.

Volunteering for service in your community works. If you're out there for yourself, it's a different arena. If you're there for a cause, then your effort is pure. I'd never heard of anybody fasting to do anything like I did. Not that I will ever try it again. That's a once in a lifetime experience.

That ranked among the accomplishments I'm most proud of. Whether it's a place to play basketball, hockey, soccer, tennis or football, whatever it is, go back to your community, whether it's affluent or poor, and build something. Build something so that the next generation and those who follow have better opportunities.

The magic of doing that is how good you feel doing it, even when it gets hard. Because I've said this before and I'll say it again. If it were easy, everyone would do it.

BUILDING THE TRACK

By mid to late October I realized two factors involved in actually building the track. First, I had enough money to get started. Second, which I never considered, was that 20 to 30 percent of the almost $300,000 could be mine.

I'd gotten into the non-profit charity business or whatever you want to call it because non-profit is my strict definition of charity. Before and since I've known others to raise money for certain causes who use that nasty phrase in their promotions – " proceeds go to charity." What it fails to mention is that the final figure is what's left after subtracting expenses, kickbacks or to pay volunteers or the staff. You can make up any reason, or dip into the till without a reason.

I had no desire to rake off the top for personal gain. It occurred to me that this was a time for Thomas Henderson to do the right thing when no one was looking. I felt a huge responsibility with this $300,000 to do what I pledged to do. So early in 1998 I again called my friend and contractor James Harper, who'd been a blessing in helping build the stadium with his heavy equipment – backhoes, graders and water trucks.

"James, you saved me tens of thousands of dollars building the football field," I said. "Now I need you to save me money on building the track." He agreed, and we got started.

I contacted the people who'd given me plans for the track. They came to the site, and as contractors will often do, they started telling me, if we find this it will cost you more. Or if we find that, we will have to increase our fee. This went on until I said I'd call when I needed them to lay the track surface and paint it, put the runways in the high jump and long jump areas. Until then, I decided, "Hell, I'll be the contractor."

Those people didn't do inside and outside boundaries of the track or the drainage system, anyway. I knew early on that they were going to eat up that $300,000 and charge me another $300,000 if they could.

Luck has always played a part in my life. This time luck appeared over the hill at nearby Austin Community College, where the Hensel Phelps Company was doing construction. I went over and found the job foreman. I told him I was putting in a track and sure needed some help. He said he'd keep me in mind.

153

Meantime, we had begun by removing the asphalt. Surveyors figured the curvature of the track, the angles and slant and the drainage. I got a shovel in one hand and a pick in the other and started to dig and contour the ground. It broke my heart when we dug a hole six feet deep across the 50-yard line of my beautiful field, but that had to be done for purposes of drainage.

My field didn't have stadium lights. The lights we had were of poor quality. But I have big ears. I hear things. I heard that Austin Energy was putting lights in parks around town and also were installing a set of stadium lights in a playground or school outside the city limits. I went to see these folks and told them we needed lights over in east Austin for minority kids. Our old raggedy-ass pine telephone pole lights barely cast a shadow. Help me out, I said. They said, we're not sure we can do it with the budget as is.

This is too bad, I said, because your refusal will cause me to appear before the city council and complain loud and long about how you are putting lights outside the city but won't add us to your list. They said, no, don't do it, let's see if we can work it out. Lo and behold, I wound up with about a $400,000 set of lights installed without charge by the city.

The track project was far bigger than I imagined. I didn't have the expertise, but I had the tenacity. I also had a shovel in my hand and was there every day trying to figure out all the complex details. It was like learning Tom Landry's flex defense. Stay with it long enough and the picture clears.

One worry vanished. City building inspectors stopped coming out. One of their duties is to red tag a project and stop construction when some permit is out of order. I suppose the word downtown was not to bother red-tagging us, because they knew I'd just toss it. I give many thanks to the city of Austin for letting me do the track without a lot of hassles.

Before long I had the Hensel Phelps people over the hill involved. They know how to line up curves and boundaries. I guess most people aren't aware of the type of work necessary to lay a track. The assumption is, you just outline a flat surface around an oval and you're done. That's not the way it's done. I started to ask for expert advice from the Hensel Phelps crew.

They knew the surveyors and they knew how to do concrete work necessary for the base, and so they began. The odd thing about them agreeing to work with me was the lack of a signed contract. They never talked about cost. There were times when not all of them were busy at the Austin Community College site, so the boss would send crews to help with whatever I was doing.

Harper was invaluable. The biggest job after we got the dirt and curves in was to smooth and pack the surface. It's like laying a highway with a huge roller. Everyone has seen cartoons of these machines that roll over an object and mash it into a pancake. To compact the track you roll it over and over. Harper would use a tractor to smooth the dirt and it was my job to even it out and pack it down.

I went around that 400-meter track again and again. I probably spent 80 to 90 hours going around in a circle on this giant piece of equipment I rented. The machine has a button you can push that causes it to vibrate as it rolls. Spend 10 hours vibrating and you get off still shaking. That feeling reminded me of one of my reactions on crack cocaine – an uncontrollable shaking of the head.

An important moment arrived when Hensel Phelps showed up with an invoice for the work it had done. We were almost done now. The track, sewer, drainage and lights were in. The bottom-line total on the invoice was $90,000, and I only had about $100,000 left to pay for equipment, dirt and concrete. I went home, knowing that was going to cut me short.

I wrote a letter to the president of Hensel Phelps. I'll have to paraphrase what I wrote but it went something like this:

Dear Sir: I appreciate all that Hensel Phelps has done in assisting me to construct this track. Without the expertise of your crews and cooperation of your administration this project could not have happened. I received your invoice and acknowledge that I owe the stated sum. However, if I pay you, my foundation will be broke.

I thought this project would cost $300,000. As you very well know, in real money and sweat equity the total was closer to $800,000 to complete. I would appreciate it if Hensel Phelps would make a contribution to Eastside Youth Services and Street Outreach for the total amount.

Thank you for your time.

155

About a week later I got a response. Hensel Phelps said, okay, they'd do it. I think I know why they were so generous. It was because I was out there in the middle of a hot summer, dirty and stinky, digging holes, riding the tractor and paying attention. They saw me working. They understood it wasn't about Thomas Henderson. It was about kids in east Austin. They made a gift based on what they saw me doing rather than how well I begged.

We completed a beautiful track by the fall of 1998. All the starting lines and handoff lanes were painted. We had a pole vault pit, a long jump pit and space for shot put, high jump and javelin throw. Kids and adults had a place to play and exercise. Building the stadium and then the track reminded me that Thomas Henderson's ticket out of the ghetto, his ticket to education and to the Dallas Cowboys, was sports. If that track helps just one kid make good, it will all have been worth the effort. I really hope it helps more than one because that was my aim.

Most of my friends had either passed away, were in prisons or hanging around the same street corners where I left them in 1968. They had been murdered, killed in accidents or in Viet Nam. Some were even my heroes who I thought were great athletes. Early on I remember how people looked up to athletes.

I was a juvenile delinquent although not really that bad. My stepfather and mother worked for minimum wage or less. We had five kids living in a two-room house. I thought that getting involved in sports would be more fun than shining shoes, working at the golf course and hustling soda water bottles for a deposit. Maybe there were kids like I used to be who liked sports and all they needed was a place to play.

Anyway, we had a huge grand opening with the thanks and blessing of the city. I put on a 10K run with a first prize of $1,000. It made a big impression around town.

Remember that one of the first comments after I built the field was from a guy who said I stole his idea. The track guru in east Austin also made a similarly bogus claim that I swiped his plan to put in a track. I want to keep stealing ideas from sideliners, people on the side, because I don't know what I'm going to do next, but I'm pretty sure it's going to be something I build and leave for generations to come. The best sort of charity work for me is to build. When foundations ask me for money that may go into the black hole of executive directors and pension plans, I prefer a piece of equipment, a bed, computer, pens, pencils and paper. Something real, that you can point to and say, I built this.

I can't tell you how many Pop Warner and football teams use the field, how many senior citizens walk it or how many track programs practice there. Many Saturday mornings I get up and drive over, pull up and stop on top of a hill and look down. I look at the lights. I look at the track. I look at the field, the goal post and bleachers, the scoreboard and long jump pit. Then I look at the kids who are playing in the middle of the field, teams in the corner getting ready for their time to play, parents over at the snack bar. I see kids at the high jump pit tearing up the equipment. I smile and think – this is good. If I never do anything else as long as I live, I did something that made me feel good.

The complex at Eastside Field at Yellow Jacket Stadium was now complete. That's how I named the place. The Yellow Jackets had been Anderson High School's nickname for 70 years. My ego didn't demand that this would be Hollywood Henderson Stadium. That would have spoiled it for me and frankly, my name on it seemed out of place to me.

I am the chairman of my board and trust me I am the boss. I could have named it anything. I don't need to name anything after me. My grandson was an exception, but I couldn't even get him named after me. Best I could do was squeeze in as the middle name, Carl Thomas. My daughter named him after his father.

JIMMY DANIELS
(Friend)

We were getting ready to play golf, singer B. J. Thomas and me, when B. J. said, Thomas Henderson just got out of prison and he's going to join us. We played 18 holes that day and Thomas and I sort of clicked because we came from the same kind of place. Our stories are similar.

Thomas came from deep poverty. I came out of the housing projects in Louisville, Kentucky. My mother raised 10 kids by herself. I quit school when I was 15, got married and ended up going to prison. My wife was murdered while I was in prison so I gave up.

I ended up going to prison three more times for a total of about 11 or 12 years. The first time was for forgery, the second time for burglary and the third time for armed robbery of drug stores. For the fourth, I had four DWls (Driving While Intoxicated) arrests in 22 days. I was drinking two quarts of vodka a day.

So you see why Thomas and I clicked; I've been where Thomas had been and Thomas has been where I've been. We were like soul mates.

Thomas was one of those rare people able to pull it off by staying sober in prison. The number of people who can do that is infinitesimal. I know that if you had money you could get drugs or anything you wanted in prison. I saw that myself, but I stayed out of trouble in prison. I didn't like it there.

I was 39 when I left prison for the last time, got sober at 40 on June 10, 1982, and today I run a full service dental laboratory. I'll tell you how I quit alcohol.

I just fell down in a field one day, all pitiful and pissed off about what had happened to my life. I'd never been a praying guy, although I'd been to church as a little kid. I fell down and started cussing God. I said, why did you do this to me? You made me poor. You killed my wife. You kept me locked up for half my life.

I got up from the field, and two days later I was in recovery. I saw this sign on the wall. It told the story of a set of footprints in the sand and this guy talking to God. He was asking why God wasn't with him in all those dark places. God said, because I was carrying you, there's only one set of footprints.

I started a treatment center after I was sober for five years. I named it the Ethel Daniels Foundation after my deceased wife. But I ran out of money before it was completely furnished. Thomas dropped by and said, "Jimmy, aren't you going to put beds in this house?" I told him, "I ran out of money, so I guess we're going to have to find some beds."

Thomas started laughing. Then he called all over the country, checks started coming in and he paid for the rest of those beds. We sat on the porch of that halfway house and watched 22 beds being moved in. Both of us had tears in our eyes.

Another time, Thomas invited me and some other guys to ski in Aspen, Colorado. I'm not a great skier. We were out on the slopes and l fell down. I was tangled in the skis, lying there with my arms under my head and my leg under my butt. A skier in a gray suit came over, grabbed me by the arms and helped me to stand up.

"Are you okay, son?" he said. Then he raised his goggles.

It was Jimmy Carter! Former president Carter!

"Yes, sir, I'm all right," I told him That's all I could say. I was in shock.

Thomas skied over to me and I stammered, "That's President Jimmy Carter over there. He just helped me up!"

Thomas immediately began to ski toward Carter with me in tow. A group of men stood in a semi-circle around Carter. As we approached unannounced, their hands began dropping inside their ski jackets.

"Hey, Thomas, we better slow down. Those are Secret Service people with him." I cautioned

"No big deal," Thomas said. "The President knows me."

And you know what? He did know Thomas. We sat there and chatted with Carter. He told us how great he felt about what we were doing in the recovery field.

From where I came from, to have Jimmy Carter say that to me, was totally incredible. I came up without having a lot of self-esteem Now I realize that every man has to get up every morning and fight his way through, no matter how popular he is or how big a celebrity he is. That did me a world of good. It let me know that I could do what everybody else could do.

CHAPTER FIFTEEN

RAISING THOMESA (And the birth of Dalis)

My daughter Thomesa was born in March of 1979, and when she was a baby and up until five or six years of age she lived with her mother in different places. Her grandmother in Tennessee eventually took care of Thomesa for both parents since her mother was running around the country and I was in jail. I felt guilty about my daughter living with a grandmother.

I didn't know if I could ever make up for that, but I planned to do my best by teaching her and being patient with her when I got the opportunity. She began spending summers with me in 1987 and each reunion brought us closer to confronting an issue that lay unspoken between us. That is, Thomesa Holly Henderson's father had gone to prison for an alleged assault against a member of her gender.

How would I explain that to my daughter?

My past had not been a problem for Thomesa or me but it was a problem for me to tell her about it in a candid, honest way. That way, if anyone said something to my now impressionable 14-year old girl, she would know the facts and not pay attention to rumors.

Before I told her, I asked for lots of advice. I called mentors and friends like John Lee, Chuck Denmark and Dr. Joe Pursch. I told them I had to have this conversation with her. They agreed and gave me advice.

I sat with Thomesa at our dining room table and shared my story with her. I told her I'd been accused of sexual misconduct. I told her the details. I told her I'd been smoking crack for several years – but more importantly, for four or five days in a row when the incident occurred.

I told her it was an unfortunate situation. I said your father paid his dues for it. I hope this doesn't bring any embarrassment to you. I want you to know that you did nothing wrong and that anything your father did was your father's fault. The only thing I can tell you now is that I'm sober. I am not evil. I've never been an assaulter of women.

I'm not sure how I got it all out. She had questions. One of them was, "What were two teenage girls doing smoking crack with you, anyway?" I was able to say that drugs are insidious. People try them. Some people like them. Some people die as a result from them. Some do drugs for recreation. Honey, teenagers do drugs too. I gave her the best answer I could.

One of the proudest things I can say about myself is that I always took care of child support payments. I'd even paid them from prison. I wrote old friend Richard Pryor a jailhouse letter saying I needed money to pay child support for my daughter. I'd met Pryor at his home in Los Angeles in 1976 when I was dating one of the Pointer Sisters. Richard wrote me a check for $15,000. When I got out of prison I increased the amount of annual payments to Thomesa's mother, who Thomesa lived with in Nashville, Tennessee.

The experience of having Thomesa for the summer was one thing. But I didn't know how I would handle what was about to be thrown in my lap. One day my daughter said she wanted to talk. Her demeanor was a mixture of fear and rejection.

"Daddy," she said, "I have something to ask you."

"Okay, what is it?"

"Come here and sit down." I went to the table and sat.

"I want to live with you but..." she said, and started crying.

"What's wrong?"

She wanted to live with me but her mother would make her feel guilty. Her mother would think she's abandoning her. Her mother would be worried about child support...sob, sob, sob.

"You can live with me," I said, without hesitation. "You will live with me. It's done."

I enjoyed the look in her eyes. I could have done two things at that moment. I could have said, let me talk to your mother. Or I could have said, I can't do that because I'm too busy and can't manage my life with you around. I'm single – what am I going to do with a teenage daughter in my house?

There were a dozen places to go with that conversation. I could have said something wrong and affected her for life. So I made the phone call to her mother and my former wife in Nashville. "Wyetta, this is Thomas. Thomesa wants to live with me. She is fourteen and can make that decision. We have agreed on that decision so she is not coming back."

Oh boy. I was verbally assaulted for about 10 minutes. She screamed, You are stealing my child! You can't do this! I listened and said, look I'm not taking her away. She wants to live here, so we made the decision she will stay with me.

The next morning I was still asleep at 7:35 when my daughter ran into the bedroom and jumped in my bed. She was upset and sobbing, "I'm going back! I've got to go back! She needs me!" I sat up and said, come here and give me a hug. I knew I had to do everything in my power to keep her from leaving.

It was a moment in my life where I had to say 'yes,' to my girl, a moment where I intuitively knew how to handle a situation that in the past would have baffled me. I knew the right thing to do was the say, 'yes,' in spite of the alterations to my lifestyle, my social life, my dating life and travel life. All that was in play but it didn't matter. This was my child.

Her mother had called and made Thomesa feel guilty. Wyetta said she was going to lose child support. She'd lose her house and car. She was going to lose everything. Didn't Thomesa understand what she was doing to her mother?

First thing that morning I went to my office and wrote a check for $6,000-one year of child support payments in advance-and mailed it without calling to say it was on the way. Less than a week later I got a different reaction from Nashville. It was amazing. Now it was okay for Thomesa to stay with me. I'd known what the problem was; the question was whether I was going to let money stand in the way of my daughter's happiness.

It had been a courageous thing for Thomesa to do because I think she knew her mother was going to react that way. She also had to be uncertain how I would react. She'd spent summers with me. But she didn't know me well enough. She couldn't know what her father was going to do at that crucial moment. I'd like to think that I did a good thing.

Thomesa was in the eighth grade when she moved in with me. We lived in west Austin, and I drove her across town to east Austin to the junior high school that I'd attended many years ago. We left the house at 7 a.m. so she'd be at the front door before 7:30. For a couple of years, five days a week, we'd come around a curve and there'd be dew on the grass, a sun-shadowed downtown and flowers in the spring. I'd become pretty senti-mental during recovery so for two years, several hundred times, I would say to her when we turned the corner, "Look, isn't that beautiful?" Or, "Look at that sun...look at those flowers."

Meantime she'd sit there thinking, what a dork.

Another significant memory of raising a teenage daughter was the shock of seeing the mess in her room. One day I walked in to find there were all sorts of clothes under the bed and behind the curtains. I started to go nuts.

"Get your laundry and mine and I don't want you to come out of the garage until it's all done. I want clothes folded and put away. I want your room vacuumed and when you're through with that...meantime I have errands to run," I told her.

I returned home and hit the garage door opener to the condo. A wall of water poured out. A mini Niagara Falls flowed over my feet and into the driveway. I walked into the garage and found that the washing machine had been stuffed with about 100 pounds of clothes. There were blue clothes, red clothes, white clothes and orange and beige clothes, cottons and nylons and some of my slacks all in the same wash load.

I started upstairs to Thomesa's room to horsewhip her. I mean, I was on my way to do great bodily harm. Her room was on the third floor. I crossed the second story mad as hell. But when I got to the third floor landing and stood in front of her door, this voice said, "Hey, big shot. Guess what? You never taught her how to wash."

I opened Thomesa's door and instead of a harangue I asked her a question as gently as I could.

"Honey, did you happen to notice a flood in the garage?"

We went downstairs and swept out the garage. We pulled everything out of the washing machine, which she had broken. It was a Maytag so those things do break, especially when you put 100 pounds of clothes inside one. I called and ordered a new washer, and a repairman had it installed by the next day.

I did know that you put colors together. Whites and darks are separated instead of mixed. So I showed her. If you have a small load, put it right here with a lesser amount of detergent. If it's a medium-size load, you don't have to use the maximum volume of water. If there are mixed colors, don't put bleach in there because bleach will spot clothes. I could have screwed up everything by screaming at her and whipping her butt for breaking a washing machine that I never taught her how to use.

We had house rules. I didn't want to see any boys around the house until she was 16. Boys weren't welcome until then. That was part of the deal. Thomesa got spanked a couple of times for sneaking out and I found out years later she'd taken my car out several times without my knowledge. And I was rough on boys by the time she started dating. Teenagers!

"What do you want with my daughter?"

"Who are you?"

"Where are you taking her?"

"Have her home by 10:30 p.m."

I was fair, and I don't think I embarrassed Thomesa too much. Raising a child taught me patience and tolerance. It taught me a lot about myself and about responsibility. We've always been close enough to share thoughts and feelings. We've had hundreds of conversations about politics and money and people, and about how to handle situations and circumstances.

Thomesa breezed through the 9th, 10th and 11th grades. I think she was a sophomore when I bought a house for her mother and moved Wyetta to Austin. Before that, it was difficult to leave Thomesa behind when I had to travel and do my lectures. I'd have my mother and sister stay in my home with her. I didn't let her stay at the homes of different girl friends or people I didn't know well. I was adequately but not overly protective. However, it occurred to me that if I moved her mother to Austin, and she didn't have any rent, then we could share responsibility of our daughter. It worked perfectly. Thomesa would stay at Wyetta's a couple of days a week, but mostly at my house. So we started sharing and raising her together before she finished high school.

We sent Thomesa to magnet classes in math and science for advanced students. She's extremely bright. In April of 1997, she was 17 and a high school junior. She wasn't supposed to graduate until the next year. When she's a senior we will talk about college, I thought, a subject that hadn't been discussed yet. Naturally, Langston, my alma mater, would be a personal choice. But as her junior year was ending Thomesa floored me when she said:

"Daddy, I'm graduating next week."

"What do you mean, you're graduating? You have another year."

"No, Daddy, I went to the magnet school and took advanced classes. I took the test and I'm graduating."

My daughter finished high school a year early based on intellect and performance. Her news left me proud of the excellent work she had done but confused about the next step. We had a 90-day window to figure out what to do about college. She had a boyfriend and they were hot and heavy. She had her own car.

I was strict about how often she took it out and where she went. Thomesa only told me she hated me about 27 or 28 times. I'd always say, you don't really hate me, all you want is to go out. I never took that stuff personally. I did take her phone once. I made her read and do homework and helped with homework when I could.

I remembered that Thomesa had been in ROTC, and mentioned the Air Force several times as a future option. She talked about what she could learn in the military, especially discipline. I asked if she'd given the Air Force much thought and said I'd like for her to enlist to learn some people and authority skills.

"Dad, here's what I'd like to do," she said. "I want to go to Austin Community College."

"Where are you going to stay?" I asked.

"With you."

"No. Daddy is not going to be part of your dating and social life. That is absolutely not going to happen. If you go to college here in Austin you will get your own apartment and a job. You work it out but you can't live with me and have some sort of social life going on around here. I don't want any part of that."

We decided she would take the test for the Air Force. Of course she passed. She had to go to San Antonio to sign papers and be inducted. I didn't attend. I'd gone with her to the recruiting office where they took Thomesa's picture because she was Thomas Henderson's daughter. Wyetta went with her to San Antonio, and it was from there I received a tearful phone call from my daughter.

"I don't want to go!" she sobbed. "I want to go to ACC. I'll go to Langston. I'll go anywhere. I just don't want to do this. Please, Daddy."

I listened. I let her get it all out. I said, You're upset at the moment. Sign the papers and I'll see you when you get back. I assured her in a calm manner that it would be okay. A short time later she was inducted into the United States Air Force, and it did turn out okay.

After her four-year military tour ended a few years ago, Thomesa returned to Austin after I won the lottery to live and work as my assistant in the film company. We still talk a lot. I speak to my daughter every day. She is not only my child, but my closest ally and friend.

* * * *

Early in 1993 I went to Dallas to hang out with my old Cowboys teammate, Too Tall Jones. I met a woman named Shondon Stoker and we had a brief affair. I was single at the time.

Later she called me to say she was pregnant. She was living with another guy but said she was pregnant by me. Nine months passed and on September 25, 1993, an infant girl was born.

I'm the same guy who paid child support from prison. I love my children. I've never had a court order me to pay child support. Now I didn't know if this child was mine.

For proof we took a DNA test. I went to Dallas, where blood samples were drawn from the baby, the mother and me. A couple of weeks later I got a phone call with the results. I was driving down Guadalupe Street in Austin when the call came from a doctor at the clinic. I was nervous and pulled over to the side of the road. My heart was racing, but I thought whichever way it goes, it's okay. I'm going to take care of my own.

"Is this Thomas Henderson?" said the doctor.

"Yes."

"Can I have your driver's license number?"

"You called my damn number. You think this is someone else?"

"Well, I have to be careful with confidentiality laws."

"I'm not giving you any damn numbers. What are the results?"

Then he came to the point and the way I heard it his words sounded as if they were spoken in slow motion.

"Thomas...Henderson...you...are...the...

(I have to be honest—I didn't want to hear that next word) "...Father by a 99.9 percent certainty." I took a deep breath. I had a question.

"Are you sure that I'm like 99.9 percent the father?"

"Let me put it to you this way," he said. "We're not sure she's the mother but we're certain you're the father."

I called Shondon and said, "How's my baby?" Of course, she wasn't overwhelmed. "Hah, you weren't trying to be the father last month, now all of a sudden you are."

"Well, the test is in and I'm in. What do you want me to do? What can I do? Here's what I'm going to do—send you a monthly check for $500 to start with," I said, and told her I was also mailing a lump-sum check to cover eight or nine months since the baby had been born.

She wanted to name my daughter Octavia. I didn't even know how to spell it. I knew I wasn't going to call her that. I got involved by insisting on naming her Dalis, a slant on Dallas, Texas. I gave her the middle initial of 'T' for Thomas. So her full name is Dalis T. Henderson.

She's 10 years old and a sweet child. She looks like her older sister, Thomesa. Dalis lives with her mother in Dallas but I have a wonderful relationship with her. As for her mother, she still curses me out occasionally.

THOMESA HENDERSON
(Daughter)

Let me explain something. The father I know has never been an alco-holic, drug addict, liar, thief...all the things he experienced I never knew about. That was Hollywood Henderson. I don't know Hollywood.

I never knew Hollywood. I knew my daddy and my dad never did any-thing wrong. I know nothing about it when my mom talks about abuse and drug use, broken noses and broken doors. Or things like pawned Super Bowl rings. I have no clue about things she says and he says about their marriage. I thank my mom for that because she never presented him as a bad person.

I know the supportive father who gave me total love and support beyond financial before he won the lottery. His past was never put in my face when I was a kid. My mom never told me anything, and she was there when it all happened. My grandmother and mom never said anything neg-ative about him. I just knew he wasn't with me. And I knew he was sending me letters. I thought my dad lived out of state.

I remember receiving letters from my father when I was living with my grandmother in Nashville, Tennessee. I still have them. He had someone who was an artist decorate his letters with the newest cartoon character. The whole time he was incarcerated I received letters at least twice a week. I never knew about any divorce or anything that happened between him and my mom. I just knew my dad was sending me stuff every holiday, every birthday, all the time.

My dad finally told me after I grew up that he had a friendship with Richard Pryor. While he was incarcerated he told Richard Pryor he needed money to help his daughter, and Richard Pryor sent $15,000. That is how he paid child support. I went to private school from the first grade through the seventh grade. My dad paid for it while he was in prison. I mean, he wasn't locked up for seven years, I think it was just two years, but he paid for it the whole time. He sent money directly to my grandmother.

I made a decision when I was around 14 that I wanted to live with my dad. The difference was being with my mom who was struggling and had difficulties with her own issues, and us not getting along as a 14-year old ready to be a teenager. I went to my father, and he put braces on my teeth, I went to camps, and he let me drive his car at 13. Dad gave me $500 to put in my purse as a 14-year old. I just took advantage of it and said I wanted to be with my dad.

I started eighth grade at Kealing Junior High in east Austin where he was raised. About two years later, my mom moved to Austin because I was getting out of control when my dad wasn't here. Mom came to put me back in check. I had a little too much freedom and I took advantage of it.

I never tried drugs or alcohol. My dad lectured about that, and he lectured me. There was no sense in even trying them like the average teenager. I went to meetings and speeches involving my dad. Avoiding drugs and alcohol was so drummed into my head I never had to worry about using.

But I was a little frisky and being the average 13-year old with too much freedom I ran around at all times of night. I needed a mom to set guidelines for being a lady. A dad kind of lets you go. My mom needed to be here to help me become a young woman. I was here about two years before mom decided to move here and help out. She came and everything picked right back up. I became the person I was before.

Regardless of the fact my parents were divorced in 1980, my dad always supported my mom financially. When she moved to Austin he got her a house and a car. This was before he won the lottery, and he did it just because I was there.

One time I went too far. I think I was 16 when my dad spanked me for the first time. I had a boy in the house when my dad wasn't there. That was the first time daddy literally put his foot down and said we can't have that. I can never forget that Karl Kani belt. I had the Karl Kani name written all over my legs like a tattoo when he finished.

Something else happened when I was 16 that allowed me to help daddy. My sister was born. She was 10 on September 25. I took responsibility for taking care of her, changing diapers and all that. I got firsthand experience with a baby, which is kind of odd at 16 to be caring for a newborn. She lives in Dallas and would come down for a couple of weeks and visit for Thanksgiving, birthdays and holidays.

At 16, I made the choice to leave high school early. I took extra classes and went to summer school and graduated in three years. I needed to get away from home. Austin is secluded and small. I wanted to do something different, and I was tired of school. I graduated in May of 1996 and enlisted in the Air Force in July.

My dad supported the decision. Since I was 17, I had to have parental consent to enlist, and he signed the papers. I mentioned the Air Force once and he was gung-ho about it in every conversation afterwards. He even

169

drove me all the way to Hampton, Virginia, to report to Langley Air Force Base. He drove the whole time and the trip took 19 hours.

I have a strong relationship with both my parents, but I've always gone to my dad to make a final decision. I value his opinion that much. We don't have what some people would call a normal father and daughter relationship. He will call one day and cuss and the next day it's, "Hi, honey." We are so, so close. We have a private saying between us that everybody else is crazy.

I didn't move to Austin for financial reasons. My dad always gives me my autonomy, such as when I joined the military. He let me do my own thing, but I eventually came back home. I work for my father's business, Thomas Henderson Films, and have a real estate license that I use on the side. I'm divorced and have a 5-year old daughter and 10-month old son. The girl is Taylor Patrice, and Patrice is my mom's middle name. The boy is Carl Thomas. My dad made sure Thomas was in there somewhere.

Langley was my home for the entire four years I spent in the Air Force. Throughout that time my dad would update me with a new car. He would drive it up himself, and then catch a flight back to Austin. I've been daddy's girl for a long time.

CHAPTER SIXTEEN

RESENTMENTS, AMENDS AND INVENTORY

Amends to our family, friends and other victims is a must if we want to truly clean up our side of the street. Saying I'm sorry isn't enough. Prove it.

There are some things I can never change, and I accept that. There are amends I can never make because of the people I will never see again, and I accept that. But for my conscience and my program, I've got to clean up the wreckage of my past. I hope that someday I can make direct amends to those two young ladies I wronged back in 1983.

My house was out of order and full of crap when I got sober – the house being my dysfunctional life. There was hurt, pain, resentment, blame and all kinds of feelings and wreckage and amends to make sense of. A mammoth spring-cleaning is what I was facing when I got sober.

The stuff I had to clean up was the wreckage of my alcohol and drug abusing past. There were the secrets and lies and misdeeds and mistakes that were so much a part of my alcohol and drug abusing life. There were things I desperately wished never happened, but did. There were things I tried to forget, as though they never happened. I tried pushing them into a remote corner of my life but found that I couldn't – not totally. There was guilt, shame, remorse and resentments that would crop up there, too. I kept hoping the mess would go away by itself, that somehow it would disappear without me having to do anything. Guilt and remorse are hell when you don't find solutions or forgiveness.

The questions wouldn't quit: How could I have done this to so and so and that to such and such? Just what kind of scum am I to have let my life come to this? For all the thousands of hours I spent with my drugs, I've probably spent about the same time with guilt and shame, the alcoholics' constant companions. I got out of that funk by doing an inventory and making amends to the people I hurt, including me. In sobriety, I've learned that before I could become the person I wanted to be, I had to deal with the wreckage I caused.

I kept thinking of those words: before I could become the person I wanted to be, I had to look at the person I was. I had to look at where the dirt and garbage was, and also where the unsoiled parts were, parts that I could feel good about as they were. All of my life wasn't bad and horrible. I was directed by my recovering friends to do a serious inventory of my life and share it, sit down and write out an exhaustive coming clean with vigorous honesty with myself. No cheating allowed. Share the good, the bad and the ugly. I spent so many years running and hiding from reality that what I was about to do, at long last, was stop and look at all of me. The flight was over, and so was the self-deception. Here was a hard look at myself as a human being, the pros and cons.

I didn't know what I would find, but I had a pretty good idea it would be awful. I found some things I was genuinely proud about. I came out of a small college (Langston University) and made myself into a Pro Bowl linebacker in the NFL for the Dallas Cowboys. It took hard work and commitment to accomplish that. I felt good that after dropping out of high school as a sophomore, I had the drive and perseverance and smarts to get back in school and cram three years of work into two and graduate with my high school class. I had escaped the cut — my old neighborhood in Austin, Texas. I survived my neighborhood and didn't waste my entire life hanging out on some street corner, like a lot of guys I knew. I went to college. I tried to do stuff for myself.

I was able to feel good about some of the good deeds I had done for others. When I had wealth, I shared it. I gave a lot of money and support to my family members. I bought my mother a house. I gave to charities my time and money. I didn't do it for a big headline in the local press. I did it because it feels good to give especially when it's unconditional. When I pulled this out of my inventory, it felt good.

Other stuff wasn't so nice . . . wasn't so nice at all. I was a victim of sexual abuse with an adult woman when I was ten. The first time was abuse; the second time I was part of it. I was also the victim and perpetrator of physical abuse. I was whipped and abused as a child. When I was a boy I used to ask God to make me big so I could hit her back. I also felt a lot of shame and remorse about the career and fortune I had squandered. I crapped on people. I stole and lied and did a lot of other things in pursuit of chemical happiness.

I felt bad about the people I'd fought and bullied and hurt with my physical power. I once hit a guy in a bar right between his nose and eyes as hard as I could. When I left the bar, he was still unconscious. That was wrong. I was ashamed for the times when I wasn't a father to my child. I was ashamed for all the promises I'd made and broken with God. I was ashamed and hurt that the house I bought for my mother was seized and sold by the IRS. I was ashamed of being an illegitimate bastard.

And so it went with my inventory: some good, more bad and ugly. It got no easier from there. I was only beginning to clean up and amend the life I had lived. I had to admit all this stuff to my Higher Power and another person. I was determined that if I was going to go through this painful sludge, I was going to do it right, rigorously honest, and trust that I would be better for it.

I remember this guy who used to live in Dallas. He now lives in New York. His name is Peter and he's in the rag business. He sells clothes. Awhile back, he got real worried about his cocaine habit, which was reaching 3 grams daily. He knew I was recovering but declined to ask me for help. He's got money and a rich dad, bad ingredients for a sick cocaine addict. He did some digging around and got an appointment to see a big time psychiatrist and addictions specialist in New York. He wanted to know how much trouble he was in. He wanted top-notch professional guidance on what to do. Peter made the trip to New York and made it an expensive long weekend in the Big Apple. He stayed at the Plaza, snorted cocaine all day long and ate at four star restaurants – well he ate as much as he could. Cocaine kills an appetite. He probably spent $4,000 before he was done. On Monday, he had the meeting with the doctor. It lasted an hour and a half. He returned to Dallas. Our mutual friend, Mike Murray, asked him how it had gone. "I snowed him," Peter replied. Mike pressed him for details. "I just told him a bunch of bullshit," Peter said. He'd gone to the psychiatrist with the best of intentions, but honesty was too much to ask. He lied, minimized his use to the doctor, saying he only used about one gram a month. He lied to protect his addiction.

I wasn't going to let that happen to me. I was in search of the truth that would set me free. Now I was going to tell it. I came clean with my Higher Power and now it was time to do the same with another human being. A clergywoman was the human being I would tell all to. I had never seen her or talked to her before in my life. I had no clue about how this was going to go. I imagined what it would be like. I imagined that when I was finished, she would stand up and look at me with a face full of disgust, and say, "I've decided you should be shot."

This stuff was hard enough to admit to myself, much less a stranger, much less a female stranger. Her office was small and sparsely furnished. There were few religious trappings. There was no picture of the Pope on the wall, no crosses or prayers that I could see. She was sitting behind her desk when I walked in. She looked stern. She had pasty skin and dirty blonde hair and she wore a plain white shirt with a long plaid skirt, conservative looking. We sat down and she asked me if I was ready. I took a deep breath. I could feel myself trembling. I had a lot of fear going in, but now it was rising and surging and feeling like it was going to do me in. I stayed put. It's only fear and denial, I thought. It's not going to kill me.

I had written forty pages of inventory and I read it to her, unabridged. It was emotional. Tears rolled as I shared my pain. For an hour the guts and glory of Thomas Edward Henderson got spilled all over that office. By the time I was done and every last bit of ugliness had been exposed, I fixed my glassy eyes on her face. She looked shaken, like she couldn't believe she'd heard all this. She looked like she couldn't hear anymore. That was good because I had nothing else to say. I think my sex life while in the NFL was the part that got her. I looked at her and I was quiet now. For me, it was a moment of profound silence. All had been revealed. There were no more secrets. I had done it. I'd done what they told me I needed to do and I felt relieved by it.

She did not order me to be shot. When I said goodbye and thanked her and walked out of there, I felt good, light and proud. I had unloaded some family and life baggage and set myself free.

The clean up process is about self-forgiveness and knowing, in spite of myself, I had done the very best I could. It's about facing up to all your stuff, freeing yourself to get beyond it. The torment stops. Self-esteem comes and you start building on it.

There was nothing to flee from any longer. My mind was quieted. I told myself, "You don't have to pretend anymore. You don't have to deceive." Everything was out. I could let it go. I was forgiving myself. I could start over, and the possibilities were neat to think about.

The forgiveness allowed me to break the vicious, self-destructive cycle of my alcoholism and cocaine addiction. More than anything else, what the house cleaning did was flush away so much of what my disease was hanging onto. Letting go of shit is a must. As I cleaned up, I got past my regrets and wrong doings. I stopped being the victim. I saw Hollywood and Wildman for what they are. I admitted every single screw-up I could remember, backed off nothing, and washed away years of pain in the process. I wasn't going to self-destruct anymore. I hoped.

Not only did I become able to forgive myself, I also became able to forgive others and free myself of other emotional rubble I'd been toting around for my entire adult life. I spent years being a walking warehouse of resentment. A resentment is like pissing in your own pants: others can see it and you feel it. I could hold grudges with the best of them. I prided myself on my long memory. If you screwed me in 1982, I still had it in my mental catalog and you would get yours some day. Never did I realize what all this activity was doing to me. As more was revealed to me, I recognized that holding onto resentments was a way of playing the victim and that the longer the resentment endured, the more I could claim to be jerked around. The disease loves this kind of shit, of course. It kept me bitter and pissed off about something all the time.

This was crap I needed to let go. I used the Serenity prayer constantly. What did it say about my self-respect if I was ready to get all out of sorts over somebody saying in 1979 that Jack Ham of the Pittsburgh Steelers was a better linebacker than me? He wasn't, of course. And don't even think it. One question, if you doubt me could he cover Terry Metcal man to-man out of the backfield? Case closed. I could do that and did that. I was a real and whole linebacker. But what did this say about my prospects for long-term sobriety? Not much.

And so I started putting the broom to my resentments. Two of my biggest ones, and my two oldest, were about my real father and my mother – my father for leaving me and skipping town and my mother for hitting me when I was a child. I let go and forgave them. It was time to move on. It wasn't much of a choice, for somebody who was hell-bent on getting better. So I felt my feelings about it. I didn't stuff them. And then I let it go. I couldn't change what had happened. They didn't sit around when I was an infant and try to figure out ways to screw up my life. It was time to move on.

I broke my neck on the field in a preseason game with the Miami Dolphins in August 1981. I never played again. I had a career-ending injury. The vertebrae broken was C-l, and a doctor told me that a fraction of an inch in one direction or another and I would have either been dead or ended up paralyzed. This was the start of a long-running resentment toward the Dolphins and the NFL.

In 1982, under the collective bargaining agreement, a player is entitled to a one-time benefit of $37,500 if he suffers an injury that keeps him out of a football season. This ended my career. I wanted and deserved the benefit, felt that then and feel the same way now. The Dolphins and its battery of NFL lawyers who work their ass off all over the league to screw injured and disabled players fought me tooth and nail. They said I didn't pursue my rehabilitation. They said I went against doctors' orders, which is true. I got a second opinion and liked that opinion better. I went with it. The case went on for six years. They spent a lot of time and money to deny me my benefits.

There were meetings, letters, hearings, depositions, the whole legal works, and it came down to an arbitrator and basically the question of which he believed. He said he put a lot more stock in the character of the Dolphins' doctor than in an ex-convict crack addict alcoholic. "No benefits," he ruled. He was wrong and I forgive him. The NFL had done a great job of making this an issue of character rather than a case of injury.

The NFL was also giving me hell over an entirely different benefit called total and permanent disability. This is for someone who suffers a particular football injury that prevents him from playing football or any other job. The benefits pay $4,000 per month if the injury is football related and $890.00 if it was non-football related. Guess which one I got.

Through fighting them and not giving up, I got $890.00 per month for life, reduced by 25% because I took an early retirement benefit in 1983. So I actually got $667.50 per month and a few increases over the years. When I won the lottery they cut me off again. I broke my neck on the field but the NFL's attorney convinced the arbitrator that I had had a bar fight and that my injury was an accumulation of injuries. I won a small victory but was a victim of my own wreckage. I needed to know who was at fault here. I was.

This was right off to the 'can't change' pile. I believe my life is too worthwhile to ruin it with resentments that can't change anything. I was ready to let the piss on my leg dry off.

After taking stock of myself and doing my confessional with the clergywoman, I had another task to do: making amends for my wrongs wherever possible. It wasn't enough merely to look at myself and to divulge what I found. To really scrub my conscience clean, my program suggested whenever possible I locate my victims and let them know I was wrong and be willing to make amends. I wasn't merely saying I was sorry. To me that's too easy. I think 'sorry' gives you permission to do whatever you did again. Wrong means the behavior was unacceptable and won't be repeated.

I also wanted to make restitution wherever possible. Where I conned a guy out of money, I aimed to make financial amends. Where I abused somebody, I wanted to let him or her know I was way out of line. Who were my victims? Hell, who wasn't? I made amends far and wide. Some people I visited in person, some by phone, and others by letter.

Most people were willing to forgive me, and even seemed grateful that I had the courage to do this. I made amends to Mike Murray, whom I'd borrowed money from and never paid back. I'd made threats to him when I was desperate for drug money, and I squared that, too. I also made amends to Tom Landry. I had seen him at the Cowboy's training camp in Thousand Oaks, California. We spent a few moments talking. Light stuff. He chided me about putting on some weight. For some reason it didn't really hit me until later what I needed to do. I was driving home with a friend and I thought about my relationship with Tom and the crap and hate I had laid on him. I fought his authority because it never occurred to me to be afraid of him. I mouthed off and acted outrageously and got high in meetings and God knows what else. I told my friend, "I've got to write Tom a letter." And I did – a long letter of amends. I explained, as best I could, why I acted the way I did. I let him know that what I suffered from was far deeper than too much cocaine. I was hard on him in my first book Out of Control, and I wanted to let

177

him know that it was much more a reflection on me than on him. As I wrote that book, I climbed back into my old life and my old characters, characters who were only too happy to make Tom Landry look bad. I asked him to forgive me for any embarrassment I had caused him. I also told him I admired him because I really do respect him now.

I had resented and envied Tom Landry. He had so many of the things in life that I wanted, things that I have found now in sobriety. He had credibility and respect. He had a loving family life and a deep Christian faith. As I was falling apart, seeing a man who had so much together made me mad as hell.

I didn't write this letter so Tom would like me. I wasn't looking for a job. I was looking for peace of mind and I found it. I wrote the letter for me so I could heal the wrongs I perpetrated against the man, the good man. I didn't need a return letter from him.

I saw him at the last Dallas Cowboys reunion a year before he was fired and I asked if he had received my letter. He started to apologize for not answering and I stopped him. I told him all I needed to know was that he had received it. For the purpose of my program and recovery, that was what was most important to me.

My amends to my first wife were the toughest of all. To try and make amends for physical abuse seems short of the mark. You do your best and share how you feel and hope for forgiveness. The amends enabled me to forgive myself, which is of utmost importance. My first wife was one of the people I victimized the most. I had lied to her and broken promises to her and had been unfaithful in our relationship and marriage. Worst of all, I had hit her and that was wrong. I had a lot to say and I said it, all of it. I expressed every regret I had and said I was wrong for everything I could think of and then some. She said, "What's this bullshit? Who are you conning?" I tried to convince her that I was sincere. She said, "You're full of shit and I know it." I tried again and she said, "Nice try, but I ain't buying." I totally humbled myself to her, coming to her with only honest intentions to make amends and she was not accepting it. It bothered me a lot at first. I had one choice here: deal with it and get past it.

I told myself that I couldn't control the way other people react. You can't get her to say, "Oh, Thomas, I'm so glad you made amends for kicking my ass all those years," and then expect her to offer milk and cookies. This was heavy stuff. I put this woman through hell. I couldn't change or manipulate the way she felt. I had to remember what my recovering friends had shared – that you're not always going to get the desired response. Some people have a harder time forgiving. Sometimes they may have things going on in their lives making it impossible for them to really hear you. In my ex-wife's case, I think I'd lied and deceived her so much that she thought this was just another one of my raps, thought I'd just mess her over once again if she trusted me. Sometimes, people never forgive or forget. That's their problem. We must move on. She didn't know the new me I was becoming.

I knew I was coming from an honorable place, even if I never had been that way with her before. That was enough. I had made amends in my heart. It didn't take away the wrongs and the horrors I caused in her life, but it was all I could do at the time. The more I thought about it, the more I was able to accept that I had no power to coerce a happy ending for her. So I needed to focus on the positive. I had the strength and courage to let her know I was wrong.

Sometimes, I would make amends without planning on it. I would bump into people and realize I needed to clean up an issue with them and the amends would flow. It was the nicest way for it to happen sometimes, an unexpected chance to get real right now. No rehearsal. That's how it was with Dwight Douglas (D.D.) Lewis, longtime linebacker for the Cowboys and my longtime enemy. D.D. Lewis and I were the Farrakhan and Falwell of the Dallas Cowboys. Opposites don't attract. The only thing we had in common was our hate for one another. Many a practice would end with us jawing at each other in the shower, a hair away from going at it. I thought he was a racist and he probably thought the same about me. I didn't like where he was from (Mississippi) or the way he looked or the fact that he didn't go off and play for the World Football League when that league was after him. His absence would have gotten me a lot more playing time at the start of my Cowboy career... I think.

He thought I was an arrogant, hotdog jerk who showed no respect to anybody. He savored every chance he had to slap me down. When the Cowboys fired me in 1979, he went on television and said I deserved it and that I was disruptive and that he was glad to see me gone.

In March 1987, I was speaking at a drug rehabilitation center in Dallas on recovery and after care. I was waiting in a back room area beforehand. It was a cozy room with a soft, round couch and nice plants by the window. I was praying that God would give me a message to deliver. After my prayer and meditation, I looked around and saw a reflection in the mirror. It was the smiling face of D.D. Lewis. This look said one of two things; I'm gonna kill you or I'm glad to see you. He had heard I was going to be speaking. "Tommy Wayne," he said. Tommy Wayne was one of my college nicknames. "Tommy Wayne will do anything," he always said. "Dwight Douglas Lewis," I replied. I was wondering what the hell this was about. He was not on my amends list. I still hated him. He edged closer to me. He started to talk. "Thomas, I did a lot of things and said a lot of things over the years to you, and I feel bad about it. I'm sorry I was always cutting you down. I'm sorry I went on television and said that shit when you were released." He talked 'til he was through. I listened. He talked about how he fueled the animosity between us and how he was wrong to rag on me. He was staring straight into me all the while.

My eyes were on high beams, bugged out in disbelief. I wasn't really hearing this, was I? Was this really happening? D.D. Lewis poured his heart out. Finally he was done. His eyes were moist. Mine were, too. "I got some amends to make, too," I said. "Forgive me for making the racial slurs and wanting to fight you and for saying the things I said to hurt you." I told him I was wrong for baiting him and going out of my way to be belligerent. By the time I was done, we hugged. A thick, hostile wall that had built up over twelve years melted away in five minutes, and it was one of the most profound moments of my sobriety and life. It was one of the miracles one experiences if he or she works for it.

I wiped my eyes and pulled myself together and went out and gave my talk to three hundred people. D.D. Lewis was one of them. I shared with those people the miracle that had just occurred. I told them that I felt just a little more healed. But that day, because of the gift of what had happened with D.D., I focused a little bit more on cleaning house.

It's hard as hell, I told them. No work you ever do will make you feel any better, I told them. I explained why, for me, the cleaning process was so critical, how it allowed me to stop years of self-destructive behavior. I'm clean now, and not just from drugs and alcohol. I'm clean because all that garbage has been dealt with. I've taken stock of myself, faced all the wreckage, bared my soul, and have made amends as best I can to those I had hurt. Running into D.D. Lewis took care of just one more pile of garbage.

When I lay my head on my pillow to sleep these days, I know I've done the best I can and I'm comfortable in my own skin and bed. Therefore, I sleep and no guilt movies come on in my head. I think about my day, my life and, most of the time, I feel right. Stuff still comes up, of course. I make mistakes and I need to make amends. The process of my life is nowhere near perfect, but it's an honest process, and I feel great about that. I feel healthy and liberated. I'm on a constant lookout for my defects and shortcomings. I don't want to keep any more secrets. A covert life or program is as dangerous as drugs and alcohol themselves The only direct amends I haven't been able to do is the two young ladies I terrorized in California. I am willing for the rest of my life. I was wrong.

Today, I am in a great place. Today, I am clean and, most of the time I'm happy, joyous and free. I put all I have into it. It is a process that I love and embrace because it has brought me a life I never thought I could live. For all this, I am too grateful to express.

RANDY WHITE
(Former Cowboys Teammate)

I think Thomas always had a little resentment toward me because I was drafted lA (in 1975) and he was drafted 1 B. I think that always stuck in his mind even though I had no control over it. I don t understand his reasoning but he always carried a chip on his shoulder about it and probably still does to this day.

That never affected me because Thomas one-on-one was likeable, funny and entertaining. He could get away with saying things to me that if someone else said it, I would have nailed him. But he had the kind of personality to get away with it.

I had a locker near him and he'd always say, "Randy White, I'm going to kick your ass." I can remember his saying that about 50 times. I always told him, "Thomas, I'll be sitting here every day and if you ever want to quit talking and do something, let me know." That was a common conversation between us.

I used to be amazed watching Henderson play linebacker. He never worked out, never lifted a weight. He was just physically gifted; jumped like a gazelle. He could go stride for stride with Tony Dorsett in a 40-yard sprint with pads on as good as anybody.

I've always said Thomas Henderson was one of the greatest pure athletes I ever saw. His problem was lack of discipline. You could never tell where he was going on the field or what he was going to do. He could make great plays but he just didn't work real well within the frame of our flex defense, which was a disciplined type defense.

That was the thing about Thomas. On the other hand, he could make big plays and make things happen that no one else could. How many linebackers do you ever see return a kickoff with a reverse handoff and run 70 yards for a touchdown? And be running away from everybody on the field?

If Thomas could have stayed free from injury, learned to discipline him self and play within the network of the defense, he could have been as good as any linebacker ever played the game. He could have been a Lawrence Taylor-type player. One of those impact players that when he walks on the field you need to account for him because if you don't, he'll turn the tide of the game. He will make plays to beat you. Thomas had that type of ability.

As far as off the field, I never traveled to the same places or the same route that Thomas did. He had a locker two down from me and I never *knew he was using drugs. I wasn't aware he was going to the bathroom to snort cocaine or that he had cocaine in a vial on the sideline during Super Bowl XIII. I was surprised when I read that in his book.*

We had a confrontation after he left the Cowboys and came back to the locker room one day. I think he was with Miami at the time. I was going to shake his hand and say hello. I did one of my karate moves where I slap hand and punch toward the face, but I actually never land a punch. I stopped short.

When I did, he threw a left and whacked me on the side of my head. When he did it, it pissed me off. I grabbed him by the hair and smashed his face down into the floor. I could have drilled him but I didn't. I let him up.

He came back at me and I grabbed him and stuffed him in a locker. I'd been listening to all this crap about he wanted to kick my ass. I knew in the back of my mind there hasn't been a day gone by that Thomas Henderson was going to do anything to me. So I stuffed him in the locker, a bunch of people came over, and basically that was it.

I'll be honest. I didn't like some of the comments he later made about me in his book. I was too dumb or this and that. It bothered me at first. But I don't have it in me to hammer back at him for what he wrote because it didn't make any difference in my life whatsoever. I knew where he was (prison) at the time he wrote that book.

Like I said, he always had that underlying jealousy and that was the only thing he could do to take a jab at me. I don't know if that was his intention. It's not something I think about. Someone gave me the book not too long ago and I read again and just laughed.

As for the Super Bowl where he wound up on the cover of Newsweek for saying Terry Bradshaw couldn't spell "cat" if you gave him the 'c' and the 'a'... that was another of Thomas's most intelligent moves. I was thinking, how could a guy say that? If that were me, I'd be embarrassed enough to stick my head in sand. He had no effect on my game or anything else, but I was embarrassed for him anyway.

I know I said he was an idiot, and it was stuff like that made me say it. Talk about digging yourself into a hole. I don't care how good you are, you don't make those type comments. At least not the way I was brought up and the way I was coached. You don't make those comments before a Super Bowl game, tiddlywinks or anything else.

You respect your opponent. If you do anything, give them compliments before you play. You don't tell them you're going to kick their butt. Just tell them how good they are and then you go and kick their butts.

That always worked better for me. Thomas didn't see it that way. But then, my picture wasn't on the cover of Newsweek magazine either.

There are penalties for making bad choices, but something touched Thomas to open his eyes so he could see the light and know it was time to go in a different direction. He went through all those experiences and survived them. What he's doing today is a credit to him. He can talk to people about what drugs can do to your life and have an impact because he's been there. Done that. Bad choices don't make someone a bad person.

Aside from all the mouth and all his antics, Thomas is a still a good person to this day. I always thought he was a good person back then. I never thought he was a bad person. I always liked him even when I had my little confrontation with him. I never really disliked Thomas. I just though he was a pure idiot, but a good idiot if that makes any sense.

******

RANDY WHITE AMENDS

I said some things about Randy White in my first book Out of Control that I regret. He didn't deserve my comments. I often wish that I'd been more like him. He was a gifted athlete who worked and played hard. Now I know why Coach Landry loved him. I've always respected Randy White. Like myself I never saw him back down. He was awesome. Out of all the players I ever played with he was the most fearless. It was an honor and pleasure to line up with him for five years. I made a mistake when I slapped him upside his head in 1981. He manhandled me but he didn't hit me. Thanks, Randy.

Now that I think back I never had a chance in that fight. Here you have one of the strongest men in the history of the NFL and me on crack. The fight wasn't fair. Randy White is and has always been a standup guy. If I was in an alley fight and could have just one person to choose to be at my back it would be Randy White. This amends is a long time coming. I was wrong to talk bad about him and paid for slapping him.

He is in the Hall of Fame because there is not a better football player anywhere.

AMENDS

When I first returned to Austin in 1990, I had an occasion for a one-on-one conversation with my mother. At the time she wasn't sure if I was sober or what sober meant or what the hell was going on with me in this recovery process. So I sat her down one day.

"Mamma, I need to apologize about losing your house because I failed to pay my taxes," I said. "I got into a bad tax situation and your house was taken from you and you were put out while I was in prison. I need to make amends."

But I made a mistake. I wanted her to forgive me on the spot and say it's okay for the mistake I'd made seven years ago. When you're making amends the response is not your decision. The point is to make a proper amend. The other person may tell you to kiss off. You are not responsible for the response as long as you made amends from your heart.

"Will you forgive me for that?" I asked her. As I said, that was a huge mistake. She responded and I deserved her comeback.

"I'll think about it," she said.

Her response gave me great pause and I reflected on it for a long time. I talked to my sponsor in California and he said I wasn't supposed to ask her to forgive me. I was just supposed to do my part.

I've thought of another way my mother could have reacted. She might have raged at me and said, "You lost my house, you embarrassed me, my kids and I had no place to go and you want me to forgive you?" Instead she calmly said, "I'll think about it."

* * * *

(Thomas Henderson wrote this open letter of apology and confession to the city of Dallas. It was published in the Dallas Morning News on January 7, 1997).

This is a letter I have wanted to write to you for over 13 years. The truth shall make me free. Abraham Lincoln once said, "When I do good, I feel good. When I do bad, I feel bad. That is my religion." That is not my religion, but it is exactly how I feel. I did good and bad as a Cowboy and a Dallas citizen. Here goes:

A little more than 13 years ago, I was hopelessly addicted to crack cocaine and the lifestyle. I had arrived in Dallas eight years before as a 21-year old, wide-eyed, big mouth rookie from Langston University as the Cowboys' No. 1 draft choice. There was a problem. I did not know how to live.

I had a covert life in the fast lane of stardom, cocaine and sex. I made a name for myself early with a 97-yard reverse for a touchdown. I ran right in front of our bench and coach Tom Landry that day. I impressed him. I was getting an equal reputation on the cocaine and sex scenes in Dallas. I became addicted to the fast lane-and did not refrain from it.

Looking back now, I realize I was always on my way to prison. Before Coach Landry fired me on Monday before Thanksgiving, 1979, John Wooten of the Cowboys told me the team knew of my cocaine use and underworld friends. As I walked to my car, I had this overwhelming feeling of powerlessness. I knew there was nothing I could possibly do about my cocaine use. I was addicted. I couldn't live without it. My friends and associates were none of their business. I loved these characters.

Without giving all the ugly details of the volumes, times, places and behaviors having to do with cocaine, let's just say I went paranoiac nuts smoking crack. At many points along the way, I wanted to quit but didn't know how. I was a crack addict before crack addiction hit the national scene. It got weird, to say the least. An out-of-body experience would best describe the insanity I witnessed. It is me physically doing these paranoiac gymnastics and the inner me was a spectator. The paranoia became real, and I could not tell if something was real or imaginary.

That got scary.

While this was going on, I was still trying to be a football player, husband, father and celebrity. At some point, I intuitively knew something real bad was going to happen. I just hoped I wasn't there when it did.

After escaping an arrest for possession of more than an ounce of cocaine and a series of mishaps, I moved to Long Beach, Calif., to pursue an acting career. My starring role as a crack addict would not allow me to audition for other parts.

On November 2, 1983, I was arrested and charged with one count of sexual assault and two counts of false imprisonment. I had been smoking crack with two young women in my apartment. I received a sexual favor from one of them for letting them smoke crack with me. Sex for crack. That is the way it was.

With that said, I admit I was wrong. The other woman had been in a car accident and was recovering in a wheelchair from a back injury. She smoked crack with us as well, but I never had sex with her nor was I ever accused or charged with having sex with her. It never happened.

I am sure that when you read or heard about this incident in your paper, on television or on the radio, you probably thought I had. This has haunted me for 13 years. What happened was wrong, let me make no mistake about it-I just wanted to clarify this fact.

When I read the papers and all the coverage, I surely thought you thought I had sexually assaulted someone in a wheelchair. It did not happen.

I was 30 when this went down. In my arrogant cocaine mind, I did not think I had done anything wrong. This could be defined as a moral deficiency. I damn sure had that. I was above the law in my ex-Cowboy mind.

When a celebrity is accused of a crime or immoral act, it is reported by the press and thus, people presume guilt. In essence, by the time a lie or allegation gets halfway around the world, the truth is just getting up to catch up. The recent Michael Irvin situation is a case and point.

After that night in Long Beach, I was arrested and charged. When someone is arrested and accused, the district attorney, police and lawyers are usually the only one stating the case...and then there is the truth.
The accused, under orders from the attorney, never publicly defends himself. Well, I am going to change that. The truth is better than anything I can come up with.

After I was arrested, I was interviewed by a detective and confidentially told him exactly what happened in my apartment that night, just to clear the deal up so I could go home. He informed me that the truth, as I told it, was a felony. At 30, even while smoking crack, I still was the responsible adult that night.

Over the years I have never defended, rationalized or spoken publicly about that night until now. Why now? For closure and my own esteem, I had to share this with you.

Going through my life with people thinking I had assaulted someone in a wheelchair was painful. I had to tell you the truth or I would suffer in my own conscience. Whether you choose to believe me is none of my business.

It has taken all of these 13 years to find the courage to confess, apologize and set the record straight. It is still shameful and painful to discuss. That night does not define me.

There is no window to go to get my reputation back. Hell, I wouldn't want my old reputation back anyway. In my life I have done some things I regret. This case was one of them. This tragedy that shamed me, my children, family, friends, fans and Dallas, Texas, devastated me. I had to explain this to my teenage daughter. I wanted to commit suicide on many, many occasions.

What you thought of me haunted me. What I think of me is the deal now.

Luckily, I found the answers to my troubles...stay sober and see what happens. This simple decision has saved and changed my life. Since I have been clean and sober, I have made better moral and social choices for myself. While in prison in California, I felt rescued rather then punished. I needed that time to really change.

Thomas Henderson is not the same guy he was 13 years ago or 20 years ago. I am self-confident, emotional and dedicated to the cause and lifestyle of sober living. I have never been a humble man. False humility is a con. I have never tried to come off like that. Never will.

Family, friends and acquaintances who know me today will tell you Willie Nelson described me, in part, in the song, "Momma's Don't Let Your Babies Grow Up To Be Cowboys." The verse says: Them that don't know won't like him, and them that do sometimes won't know how to take him.

I can live with that. I was a proud man long before I had troubles. By osmosis, I inherited some of the values and principles of Tom Landry. I respect that man today. In a weird way, all the troubles have been worth it. How else would I be who I am today if I had not been who I was?

A simple faith and a sober-living decision has given me the opportunity to build a new life based on the principles of sobriety, honest and hard work. I am not perfect, and that is not the point. I still have plenty of fun and I live an open life. I have confessed my wrongs, stayed the course and helped others as part of my walk to freedom.

I read a writing that described success as winning the appreciation of honest critics and enduring the betrayal of false friends. I have done some of that. Got some to go. A sin or mistake should not define a man his whole life. Just like all the great games I played as a Cowboy does not make me a great guy. Many former Cowboys who made mistakes would set the record straight if given a chance. None of us are all bad. Forgiveness and understanding comes with confession.

I know some of you felt badly for me. Others were rightfully angry and disgusted. I was disgusted, too. The amends I offer are to go on in my life and never shame you or my family again. That is a road I will trudge to a happy destiny, hopefully. Forgive me even if you do not love me anymore.

I close with this: We all make mistakes. Admitting my mistakes to you was a must for my sanity, recovery and future. To anyone suffering from alcoholism, drug addiction, I say this: If Thomas Henderson can get sober and stay sober, anyone can. If you have made serious mistakes in your life, you can change the outcome over time. If you work for change, you will get the results you want.

This chapter of amends to Dallas is now closed. God, thank you for letting me laugh and smile again...but please, God, don't ever let me forget that I cried.

* * * *

It's 1989, I'm in California laying around in boxer shorts on a lazy Saturday, football season is about to start and even if I don't play anymore I'm hungry for the game. I turn the TV to the Hall of Fame Game in Canton, Ohio, although I know it's nothing more than a intra squad scrimmage.

They show clips of Hall of Fame inductions and I'm wondering why Drew Pearson isn't getting in. I wonder why Rayfield Wright and Chuck Howley aren't in. Why Too Tall Jones and Harvey Martin aren't, either. Then I wonder why all these Pittsburgh Steelers are going through the door.

I reflect about playing in that same game with the Cowboys. It was nice to go to Canton. We went inside the Hall of Fame, walking around and looking at the busts of famous players. I saw our 1977 Super Bowl XII championship team picture there. As I walked through I thought, well, I'm in here. I don't have a bust but I'm in the Hall.

Now I'm watching the inductions and Terry Bradshaw is one of the inductees. He asked a friend of mine, sportscaster Verne Lundquist, to introduce him. He didn't ask a receiver like Lynn Swann or his coach, Chuck Noll, to do the honor. I thought that was odd. Bradshaw got up and gave his talk about coming out of Louisiana Tech to quarterback the Pittsburgh Steelers. I'm half-listening when all of a sudden he referred to me without calling my name. He said something to the effect of, "That fool down in Dallas who said I was dumb."

I didn't expect to hear that. At that moment I knew what I'd said about Bradshaw before we played the Steelers in Super Bowl XIII – that he couldn't spell 'cat' if you gave him the 'c' and the 'a' – had cut him deep. I believe it was Gil Brandt, the Cowboys head scout, who had brought that kind of information to my attention. Sort of joking around, Brandt said, you know Bradshaw couldn't go to LSU because he couldn't pass the SAT. So I made up he couldn't spell 'cat' based on that.

That was nothing new for me. It had been a part of my brash persona for years. I'd said after a Thanksgiving Day game that the Washington Redskins were turkeys and if you didn't believe it look at all the feathers on the field after we whipped their asses. When we beat the Denver Broncos and their Orange Crush defense I took a can of orange crush soda and bit into it. I said the Los Angeles Rams didn't have any class.

It was my brand of theater. All the stuff I ever did or said was theater, self-promotion and antagonizing the opponent. I didn't start doing it with the Cowboys. I was doing stuff like that in college.

I'd get on the opponent's bus at Langston and talk crazy to the whole team. I'd see a team bus pulling up on campus and run to meet it like I was giving directions. I'd knock on the door and the driver would let me on board. Then I'd say: "Welcome to Langston. The stadium is straight ahead and we are going to kick your ass today. By the way, I'm Thomas Henderson, Number 91."

But what Bradshaw said made me bolt upright. There he is, standing on a podium getting the most wonderful award of a lifetime, and he mentions the incident. So my remark still bothered him after all these years. I decided I was going to make amends to that man some day.

Only recently on several television programs, Bradshaw talked about suffering from depression as far back as when he was with the Steelers and then during his marriages. He's had some hard times. Depression is no joke. Bradshaw said he'd been on anti-depressant medication for years. I never knew that, so it played no part in my decision to make amends to a person I'd hurt. My decision was based on the way I'd changed my life.

So I waited. I didn't seek him out. I didn't call Fox Television where he works. I didn't go to Pittsburgh looking for him. I was willing to make amends when I could.

As life and karma would have it, I get a phone call late in 1995 from Fox Television. Fox was doing the Super Bowl – Steelers against the Cowboys in Arizona. The producers said they were filming a pre game show and wanted to send Bradshaw to Austin to interview me. More times than not, I've said no to an interview.

I turned down "The Oprah Winfrey Show" because they were featuring several former athletes who'd had drug, alcohol and legal problems. I turned down Geraldo Rivera for the same reason. I didn't want to have a two-minute sound bite to try to describe what happened after they trotted out a litany of charges and mentioned prison.

I told Oprah Winfrey and her people that when they treated me like Elizabeth Taylor and Michael Jackson and others who rated the whole show so we could talk about my past, present and future, I'd do their show. But I wasn't going on with Mercury Morris and whoever else and have my life reduced to 'Cliff Notes'.

When Fox called I knew it was an opportunity to make amends to Bradshaw. So they set it up. I was standing at East Side Field in Austin when in walked the camera crew and Terry. He and I shook hands. I gave him a tour of the stadium. I showed him the bleachers, how we put the lights in, where I slept outside to build the track. I showed him where Dick (Night Train) Lane, maybe the greatest NFL cornerback ever, played. I pointed out the field house I remodeled and restrooms we installed.

We were standing in the middle of the field when I told Terry I needed to talk to him privately. The camera crew backed off and I took Terry by the hand and looked him square in the eye.

"I need to make amends to you," I said as I shook his hand. "I want to apologize for suggesting that you were dumb, stupid and ignorant. What I did during that Super Bowl was nonsense, something I'd been doing all my life. I've been an antagonistic guy. Since I saw you during the Hall of Fame induction I've wanted to let you know I was wrong to do that and I'm sorry if it affected you the way I think it did."

"That's all right," Terry said.

"No, Terry," I said, "this is as much for me as you. I need to do this. Will you accept my amends?"

"Yes," he replied.

I'm not sure Bradshaw understood the sincerity of what I was doing. He didn't know that it had been 15 years in the oven.

You can't predict the response when you say you're sorry or that you are wrong. I think saying you're wrong is better. It's a blanket confession with no loophole. We've all heard the words, I'm sorry. I think saying you're sorry is the weakest form of apology because it's a reusable apology. You can be sorry again tomorrow.

* * * *

Darrell Royal called to say we had an opportunity to get the Celebrity Golf Tour to play in our tournament, with guys like Michael Jordan, Dan Marino and John Elway. We would use this celebrity event as a fundraiser where people would pay to play with Jordan and the others.

Darrell asked me to come out to Barton Creek Country Club and meet a guy named Jim somebody who was in charge of the tour. He wanted me to take Jim to east Austin and show him what our charity had done. So I did.

This tour had a bogus rule, in my estimation. You had to be a 10-handicap or better to compete. I told this Jim fellow, look, I'm a member of Barton Creek, a co-founder of the charity, this is my hometown, I've played in three Super Bowls and I want to play in the tournament. I'll embarrass myself but that's fine. I won't be competitive but I don't mind and frankly, there are people in this town who will pay $2,000 to play with me.

Jim said, No, I couldn't play. It's a rule. You have to be competitive. You have to have a 10 or better handicap.

I went to Darrell. Royal is still God in Austin for coaching Texas to national championships in 1963-'69-'70. Whatever Darrell wants... I appealed to him. He said, Well, Jim is in charge of this operation and I have nothing to do with it.

The tournament went on. I didn't play. And I was quietly furious about it. A week or so later I was watching television. They were showing another celebrity event somewhere in the country. Charles Barkley, the former NBA star with the Phoenix Suns, shot 130. There were guys shooting 110, 114 and they obviously weren't 10 handicaps. I got angry again. But I had no one to take it out on because the circus had left town. Next time I saw Darrell at the club I went off on him.

"You know, y'all dissed me."

"What do you mean?" he said.

"I should have played in that damn tournament. It's a bunch of crap that you said you didn't have anything to do with it and had no power over it."

We went at it back and forth. Darrell didn't back down and neither did I. We had a shouting match in the locker room over my feelings being hurt and the fact that I felt he didn't defend or help me. Our relationship remained strained for some time thereafter.

As a recovering alcoholic and drug addict, ex-offender and ex-convict, I have to figure out a way to make amends when I am wrong. I finally realized that I was wrong to have that fight with Royal. I wound up making amends to him twice.

The first time, I went to him and said, "Darrell, I was wrong to come at you like that." He said, "Fine...fine." but I sensed that he really wasn't really accepting my amends at that time.

About 90 days later I walked into the club locker room again and made amends that touched him. I said something to the effect that, Darrell, I know I've made amends to you but listen and let me tell you how wrong I was. And I went down the list about this Jim guy and how I thought what happened had to do with my past and so on. Darrell looked at me and said, "I believe you now." Except for that slight glitch in our relationship, Darrell and his wife Edith and I have been good friends for a long time.

It was out of my fear and shame of being slighted that I took it out on him. Darrell Royal is a legend and a good man. He grew up in a time of racism and prejudice but refused to allow those qualities to take root in his soul. He has black, Hispanic and good old' boy friends. I like and respect Darrell Royal immensely.

Amends – I've made my share. And every one has made me a better person.

"In spite of my recovery I still feel bad about the victims of my addictive behaviors. I don't think I'll ever recover from feeling bad about that." TH

SYDNEY
(A friend, not her real name)

My story with Thomas began when I was driving down a highway wishing I could stop putting poison in my body that was killing me. I had already been in the Betty Ford Center and just gotten out of Sierra Tucson, another country club style rehab for the rich and infamous. They're great if you're ready for those things.

I was driving, drinking beer, popping pills, doing a line, and feeling like crap. I was feeling so guilty. I had two little girls, ages 13 and six. I loved them and I was spinning out of control. I wanted to be a better example. I wanted to be a better mother.

For some hazy reason, I knew there was a cassette tape in my glove compartment. When I was at Sierra Tucson, I bought a cassette from this guy, Thomas "Hollywood" Henderson. I threw it in my car, and it had been there for 11 months. I didn't know the guy, but had heard of him. He was 10 years older than me.

It occurred to me while I was completely high and drunk and everything else to plug in that cassette. The title was Learning How To Live. Something about his story spoke to me. He was telling of where he'd been and what it was like and what it was like now and he was okay with that. He was okay with where he had been. His acceptance of himself and approval of his journey and the way he was laughing about things...his story was so extreme I thought to myself, if this guy can do it, so can I. I listened to that tape for more information to make contact and found a phone number.

I picked my cell phone and dialed the number in Austin. I thought I'd get a recording or an office secretary. This voice on the other end said, "This is Thomas."

"I've been listening to one of your tapes. I like it and want to know where I can get another one."

"Who are you?"

"My name is Sydney."

"No, who are you?

"My name is Sydney and I am a drug addict."

"Yes."

I knew then I was dealing with someone I had to be level with. I felt like I'd made a spiritual contact. He said, "Tell me what is going on with you." I told him exactly what I was doing, and he was probably the first person I'd been completely honest with.

"I'm flying down the highway with a six pack of beer and a bottle full of pills and a head full of cocaine," I said. "I've been listening to your tape and want to hear more about how you did what you did because I don't want to do this anymore."

I flew to Austin the next day and Thomas met me. He arranged for me to go to a place in Rochester, New York, where they dried me out for seven days. Then I flew back to Austin for three weeks and went to at least three meetings a day. My father was dying of cancer and I wanted to be sober before he passed away.

My dad died three months later. Thomas was there for me and I don't know how I would have made it if it weren't for him. Or later when a dispute arose over my father's estate. Today my dad is paying my bills and my children's college education from the grave because Thomas kept telling me to get my money. I would call and he'd say, "No, that's not right. Ask your attorney about..." I did and the attorney would go, "Oh, yeah," It was if Thomas was directing this man through me.

He even bought me a car after a driver without insurance totaled my vehicle. I paid him back after my lawsuit was settled.

Sometimes I'm hyper and get angry about things. I'll call Thomas and say, "You know that ex-husband of mine...blah, blah...my mom blah, blah...and I can't believe blah, blah...I'm so mad..."

Right in the middle of one of my tantrums Thomas will start going, "Row, row, row your boat." I thought the man had lost his damn mind. I said, "What are you doing?" He sang it to me again real slow.

"I used to do that when I called my mother or grandmother and they would start singing me that song," Thomas said. "If you listen to the words it's telling you to paddle your own canoe, not anyone else's. Paddle it gently, not like a bull in a china closet. 'Merrily, merrily, life is but a dream.' It's just so simple."

He knew if he raised his voice I wouldn't hear him. Singing that song gently is how I heard him. Sometimes when I get in that frame of mind I sing that song to myself and laugh.

Drugs and alcohol are quite a way behind me now. I've learned that they were the symptoms of my deeper dysfunction – not knowing how to live life. Thomas helped me help myself. That was something no one taught me before. He taught me to take care of myself. I'm 41, and that was probably the greatest gift I ever received.

Chapter Seventeen

THE CANDIDATE

My daughter Thomesa was in the Air Force, married and pregnant in 1998, which wasn't the plan. At least it wasn't my plan. I was happy, confused and grateful anyway. The gratitude had to do with being alive and having a relationship with my daughter, who I raised as a single parent for five years.

I was proud of her, but that wasn't what I would have wanted for her, married and with a baby already on the way at 19. But those are things you can't plan for other people. On July 9, 1998, Thomesa gave birth to a girl, Taylor Patrice, and I took a trip to Norfolk, Virginia, to see her. The sight knocked me over.

Taylor was the second extension of the Thomas Henderson family. Then I realized I was a grandfather at 45.

Meanwhile some odd things were happening within my family in Austin. My mother had long been the matriarch; my stepfather was sort of passive in his role as father. My mother was bold, profane and confrontational, and everyone brought family problems to her feet whether she could solve them or not. All of a sudden, my mother began to defer family problems to me.

Domestic violence, gossip, what we were going to do about this or that, those kind of things, wound up with me. There was no vote, election or campaign. I didn't choose the role. But I got it anyway.

I was working in prisons and rehab centers around the country, and hustling real estate. I was selling films to rehabs and prisons. I saw myself as an entrepreneur, grandfather and patriarch, carving my path in life.

The same thing happened when I wound up anointed as a community leader but accepted it with the wrong perspective. There's no vote or election when you're given a leadership role. It was bestowed because of the works I'd done in the community, so I got invited to meetings and to make decisions on various issues.

Because I was a businessman and marketing guy, I started to take it seriously. I had a lapse in judgment. I decided to become a candidate for election to the city council.

The Austin city council had seven members; the mayor plus representatives from Place 1 through 6. Place 6 was the east Austin seat and, like the others, its member was elected at large rather than only by voters in the district he represented. Willie Lewis was the Place 6 incumbent, and our community felt that he'd been put in office by the west side of town. No one in east Austin wanted him in office.

Everybody bitched and moaned, which is what they do best in my hometown. But few took any action. I called a meeting with Veana Clay and Gigi Edwards, who worked in my office. I told Gigi to find out if, as a convicted felon, was I eligible to run for public office.

My motive to become a member of the city council was to be of service. It wasn't an ego trip. I felt I could get things done in the district I represented. I'd get it done the same way I built that football stadium for the youth of our community. I was willing to step out, work without a net and say, here's what I'm going to do and if y'all want to help me, fine. If you don't, I'll get it done anyway.

Gigi reported that she'd checked with the clerk's office and I was clear to run. I made the announcement. Then a childhood friend named Danny Thomas jumped up on the same day and said he was running, too.

I didn't think he could beat me. People liked what I did in the community and knew I'd represent them well. I'm an environmentalist. The very people who had put Lewis in office were the environmental community, and I've been donating money to them ever since I arrived in Austin.

I felt comfortable and confident I could win that seat, even against an incumbent. Weeks passed and my name made the news. Then I heard from the Secretary of State of Texas that a convicted felon couldn't run for public office! Gigi didn't check with the right sources. I was livid. I felt backed into a corner, in my prison cell, thinking damn, I don't need this. I was in tormented hell.

I already had campaign letters printed. I had Henderson For City Council envelopes printed. I was embarrassed. People were talking about me all over town. I go to the cleaners, the grocery store, to lunch or dinner and all I heard was, "Aw, man. I was going to vote for you...I'm sorry you can't run...We wanted to beat that guy in office...." Yeah, thank you, thank you.

When I'd told Robert Spellings, one of my best friends, that I was going to run for city council, his response was: "Have you lost your mind!" Then, when it made news that I couldn't run because I had a felony on my record, he called and left a message on my answering machine.

"Tommy Wayne," said his recorded voice, using my college nickname, "Walls rise up to protect the pure at heart."

Those words actually made me feel good. Robert was really saying, Thomas, for a moment you were a damn fool to get into the public arena with politics. No matter what your cause, no matter how right you thought you were, it was just a bad idea.

He was right. Most of my lapses in judgment occur when I only consult Thomas Henderson. When I don't call my mentors, friends and support group-all the people I trust. When I don't run it by the board. One of the things I have to remember as a partially sane human being is that I must continue to rely on friends, people who mentor and sponsor me. I do it more times than not about decisions concerning my children and finances. And it works.

There is one person I hate to call. He's also a recovering alcoholic, and he won't cut me any slack. I'll call him, it doesn't have to be anything extremely serious, and say I'm ticked off about something. Here is what happens. His comeback every time is, "Where were you dishonest and selfish?" He nails me, forces me to examine what part I played in the scenario. You really don't want to, you'd rather not, but it helps.

That is the therapeutic nature of being a recovering alcoholic and drug addict. It's not just about quitting drinking and drugs. It's about living your life in a rigorously honest fashion. It's about developing integrity where there was none. It's about telling the truth when you used to not know how to do that. It's about experiencing your feelings, your pain and your fear. All of it helps lead to a functional life.

Unexpected things pop up in the middle of a functional life all the time. It's like spam that appears from nowhere on the Internet. You're going along, searching for something and an unexpected sight pops up on the screen. What is this? I didn't ask for that.

So I couldn't run for city council, but Danny Thomas had declared for the Place 6 seat. Thomas was two years ahead of me in high school, a police officer for more than 20 years, a religious guy and someone I'd known my whole life. I went to see him and told him if this helps, I'll endorse you because we have to figure out a way to get Lewis out of there.

In Austin, the maximum amount of money you can give a city council candidate is $100. That ordinance passed some years ago. If you are on a policeman's salary and can only get $100 from each donor, it's difficult to beat an incumbent. My advantage was that I was willing to spend $50,000 of my own money through radio, TV and newspaper advertising to kick Willie's ass. I didn't feel $50,000 worth of generosity toward Danny at that moment, but I had a building in east Austin he could use as campaign headquarters.

Lewis had been put in office because people in west Austin hated Eric Mitchell, the previous city councilman for Place 6. Mitchell said some things about gays. He imploded on the spot. It was a shame – the guy had as much potential to become a U. S. congressman or state senator as any black man I'd seen. But he became sort of radical and "Farrakhan-ish." He made a huge mistake by calling someone a faggot. In a liberal town like Austin with a large community of homosexuals, it killed him.

The black community was passive about the issue. It probably happens in every major city in the United States when you try to get out the black vote. People sit at home and go, "It's a little hot today...It's raining...It doesn't make any difference...I didn't like him either..." The black community was satisfied with Eric Mitchell even though everyone may not have agreed with his militant style.

Lewis beat Mitchell, and now I was hell-bent on getting Lewis out of office. I went on morning radio shows and pumped up Danny. It was a delicate walk. I was trying to tell west Austin, where I play a lot of golf and where most people know me, if they wanted Lewis they could have him, but east Austin didn't want him as our representative. Furthermore, if you liked him that much, run him in Place 5, 4, 3, 2 or 1. Run him somewhere else except Place 6.

I wasn't out of line voicing what the east Austin community wanted. Lewis was a buffoon. He held grudges, and he wouldn't see or meet with people. Just said to hell with them. He wasn't a good politician.

And right in the middle of the campaign I won the Texas lottery. After we went through the process of getting the money for eight or nine days, I called Gigi again. I'm the kind of guy that if I'm mad at you or you fouled up, I'm going to tell you about it. I don't want wait 20 years and then say, "Oh, by the way, I remember when you...." I get it off my chest and move on. That way I don't walk around with lasting resentments.

So I told Gigi that she had screwed up and embarrassed me, that she hadn't checked out my election eligibility far enough – but that I still loved her. I also needed Gigi to research how I could legally support Thomas beyond a $100 donation. She found that I had to avoid coordinating anything with his campaign. Anything I did had to be independent of Danny.

I wrote a half-page column in the Austin Chronicle, the independent weekly, stating my support of Danny Thomas. I bought half-page advertisements in two other periodicals. I bought political time on television and got 100 people to show up at Eastside Field to film a commercial on his behalf. Those commercials ran for several days before the election. I spent about $30,000.

There's a local political operative named Alfred Stanley who works mostly for the Democratic Party, a guy I've known for 15 years. I spoke to him about Danny Thomas but he said, they were supporting Willie Lewis because, frankly, lots of people voted for him when he beat Eric Mitchell. I told Alfred we didn't want him. But I couldn't change his mind. He was honest about it. I liked the fact that we could have a sensible difference of opinion and he stood by his man.

Then came the thunderbolt. I knew I was vulnerable to criticism by being involved in the political arena. But I was still shocked by the source when it arrived. A week before the election, someone asked Willie Lewis what he thought about Thomas Henderson spending money on Danny Thomas' campaign.

"Well," Lewis said, "if he wanted to spend some of that money he should give it to that victim he assaulted out in California."

That hit way below the belt. He lost the election right there because I had done enough unselfish good in Austin and gone about my business in a responsible way. Nor had I ever said anything mean about Lewis. Even Stanley called and said he was sorry about that remark and would now support Danny Thomas because Lewis had crossed the line.

When the day of election dawned, there was a third candidate in the race. We didn't pay much attention to him. A candidate needed to win 50 percent of the vote, otherwise there's a runoff. I stayed at home that night to watch election returns. We were ahead early and stayed that way.

When the numbers settled, Danny Thomas had a magic number. It's a number attached to Thomas Henderson, a number that comes up all the time in my life. It means something to me when I see it. Danny Thomas won with 56 percent of the vote-my uniform number as a Dallas Cowboy.

I need to add a personal postscript to the election. I can say with rigorous honesty that I did not campaign against Willie Lewis because of what happened in 1984. I was motivated to elect the best candidate to represent east Austin. But I did reflect months later that this was the same guy who bought my mother's house in '84 and kicked her out so he could have the rental property, and then wouldn't sell it back to me.

Then I thought, yeah, but I was the one who didn't pay taxes on the house. I was the one who didn't answer those letters from the IRS. I was the guy who got into one of those oil deals to avoid paying taxes. All of that was my fault, not Willie Lewis'.

Still, I admit a bit of satisfaction. Personally, I'm glad we beat him. And as Paul Harvey would say, now you know the rest of the story.

GEORGE BENEDICT
(Founder, Sea Fields Alcoholic-Drug Treatment Centers)

I was watching television one day and I saw this dynamic speaker, a phenomenal man presenting himself as a recovering addict. I am a speaker myself, and I recognize someone who's exceptional.

I had my assistant try to find him. She called all over the place and finally in California we located this fellow, Thomas Henderson. I had no idea who he was except that he played football. I am not a sports fan so I didn't know too much about him.

It wouldn't have made any difference to me if I'd known everything about his addiction. I liked what he had to say about recovery. Yesterday is history. Tomorrow is a mystery. Today is the gift. That's why we call it The Present.

I called Henderson, and while we were having a conversation he asked me, "Why were you watching that TV show? Are you a brother?"

"No, I'm not a 'brother,'" I said.

"Then why were you watching a show named, 'Positively Black?'"

I said, "I don't care if you're purple. I'm interested in what you have to say."

That made him laugh, and we got together. He came to New York. I thought he could be an asset to do some outreach work for us as a speaker. I could listen to the man talk forever. So we stayed together for a year or two, and then he left to do something else. He started doing his own tapes. I've known Thomas for 15 years now. He's one of the finest gentlemen I've had the pleasure of meeting in my 27 years of recovery. He has learned through his process of recovery how to give, expecting nothing in return.

I love him. He tells everyone I'm his stepfather. The only difference is that he's black and I'm white. My wife is Italian. Her first name is Annette and he calls her 'Nettie'. When she would answer his phone calls, she would immediately say, "Yes, Thomas," and he'd say, "How the hell did you know it's me?" Then she'd say, "Ain't too many black guys calling this house."

I don't take inventory on who's going to make it and stay sober. There once was a man who was given 20-1 odds that I couldn't stay sober for six months. He lost $7,000. He didn't pay me. He paid a lot of other people. I stayed sober and he got drunk. I've been sober for 27 years. He was sober before me but went back out there again. So you don't know.

I had a notorious reputation then, strictly from alcohol. My nickname was Magilla. There was an old cartoon character named Magilla Gorilla. I was a gorilla. I used to hurt people. I was fast with my hands. I could pick them up and take 'em down. I had a terrible reputation but now I'm a little old man.

Anyway, the last trip I made with Thomas was about a year ago when he asked me to go to Danbury, Connecticut, to speak at a women's federal penitentiary. These women had seen his film. They wrote to him day after day begging him to come to their graduation ceremony. He came all the way from Texas at his own expense.

But in order to fake them out so they wouldn't know he was coming, he asked me to go as the featured speaker. My name was on the program. I took the stage and said, "I have a gift for you. It's my good friend, Thomas Henderson."

Well, he came bopping out and the women in the audience went absolutely nuts. It was so emotional to watch the reaction of those women. Their faces lit up. I was thinking of Danbury as I'm telling this story and my eyes filled with tears.

Chapter Eighteen

DEATH ROW

Gigi Bryant and I had been friends for 10 years and I had never known or if I did know I didn't pay any attention to the fact that her brother was in prison. I'd met her mother and three children. They would come to my mother's house to eat turkey and dressing on Thanksgiving and Christmas, and still do. Nothing else about her family registered with me.

Gigi and I became close as brother and sister. I hired her to consult with me on building the track and football field, my personal business and charities around Austin. She talked to me about personal things, her hopes and dreams. Gigi worked for me so long that people in Austin thought there was something romantic going on between us. We never crossed that line even though she's a very attractive woman. I have an intuitive rule about business relationships and it's that you can't have sexual relations going on in the office. So we were just good friends.

Gigi came to me one day and said, "Thomas, my brother's execution date is coming up. I'd like you to go with me to be with him as a witness."

"Hell, I didn't know you had a brother on death row!" I said. That was my first reaction. My second was, I don't want to go! So I said, "Give me his name and I'll write to him."

"He has only a few months to live and he's writing poems and songs. He asked me for a couple hundred dollars so he could get a typewriter, paper, some stamps and envelopes. He wants to mail these things to friends and family," Gigi said.

I told her I'd do that for her. I grabbed a piece of paper in my office because I was thinking inside that I wanted to avoid going to this execution. I'd do something for him and her without having to go. So I sent him $200

205

and a note: "Hi, I'm good friends with your sister. Here's money to get your typewriter and what you need. I'll talk to you later." That went out to him about six or seven months before the execution date.

I got a note from him thanking me for the typewriter. He said it was such a big help because his family didn't have any money. Gigi was supporting three children and couldn't do much for him. So $200 was a lot to him at that time in a life that was growing short for a guy convicted of murder.

About a week before the execution in March of 1999, Gigi came to my office and I told her, "Listen, honey, I'll do anything for you but I don't want to go. I don't want to do this."

"But you promised. You told me you'd go with me," she said, looking me straight in the eye.

She reminded me that I said I'd do it even when I didn't remember making that pledge. I was tied up in "I don't want to" for an obvious reason. Why would I want to see a man strapped to a gurney and killed? I don't get any satisfaction out of that. It's hard enough for me to go to a funeral, but an execution? That's extraordinary. It's nothing I ever wanted to sign up for. If they called me once a year and said, hey, want to come down and watch an execution, I'd say hell no.

I asked Gigi to give me 24 hours to make up my mind. I called a lawyer in Houston and told him about it. I called my sponsor and another mentor and many friends. They kept coming back at me with, "You told her you'd go...You don't have any choice...You have to go."

One friend in Houston said he wanted to go. Ask her if I can be there, he told me. I thought it was a good idea. Gigi was going to be in a hysterical, mourning state, and maybe I could have company to ease the strain.

"OK, Gigi, I'm going," I told her. "And an attorney friend of mine in Houston wants to go with us."

"No!" she shouted. That stopped me in my tracks. I would understand her resistance later.

"Thomas, it's not a circus," she explained. "This is serious. Anyone who wants to go – I don't want them there."

We drove to the state prison in Huntsville on the appointed day in separate cars. Gigi had asked me if I wanted to have lunch with her brother. I said absolutely not. I couldn't have lunch with a condemned man. It was too much for me. I just couldn't do it. Thank God she understood.

Gigi arrived about 10:00 a.m. and went to lunch. The execution was set for 6:00 p.m. I got there about 3 p.m. Those coming to Huntsville on behalf of the condemned are taken to small family quarters. They have another similar place about a half-mile away for the victim's family, so that these people never see each other. You never make eye contact. You don't look over and say, Oh, there goes the family of the man who murdered.... Those groups don't intermingle.

There were only three or four in our room, which was outside the prison and across the street. Me, Gigi, some cousin and the chaplain were all that came. I wasn't talking to anyone. I found myself in this community center-type facility that had pictures on the wall of people who had been executed over many years.

You walk down the line of pictures as if you're in a hall of fame. The faces of this guy and that girl and this guy stare at you from 8X10 photographs. Some are signed by the condemned. I found the wall sickening but fascinating. You look into the eyes of people who were condemned to death by the courts and whose executions were carried out by the state of Texas.

There were footnotes beneath each picture along with the date of execution. The notes were sort of a celebration of who they were, that they'd found Christ, that sort of thing. I felt a gallery of the condemned was creepy, but I was still transfixed into reading every little word about them under their photographs. It was surreal. And in the back of my mind, I thought, "there but for the grace of God go I."

From about 3:00 to 5:45 that afternoon I drank coffee. Donuts and orange juice were available. You're just waiting. These hours often are spent waiting to see if the Supreme Court or the governor is going to stay the execution. No one is sure. I wasn't hoping one way or another because I wasn't emotionally attached. I was there to support a friend.

Because my name is sometimes recognized, the media director asked if I wanted to make a statement to the press. I said absolutely not. They respected my wishes, but I did make the local papers in Austin because Gigi mentioned that I'd been there to support her. Otherwise, it was a rare day that found Thomas Henderson mute.

An official came for us around 5:45 p.m. As we walked across the street, it was like an out-of-body experience for me. I was behind the walls in Huntsville. I've spoken to inmates there several times. Matter of fact, by 1999 I had probably spoken in every prison in the state of Texas about my program, "Sobriety Is An Option," so going behind the walls was no big deal to me.

I had lived behind some walls myself. I had a sense of prison, of guards and cells and walking. Convicts don't walk down the center of the hall. When you go to the infirmary or anywhere, you stay close to the wall. It's a security measure. They don't want the place to look like Times Square. So as I walked I recognized the subtle currents of fear, anxiety, loneliness and anger that are imperceptible to the normal citizen's antenna. I was familiar with the atmosphere and environment with one exception: I'd never attended an execution.

We went through security. You give them your driver's license. You're checked through a metal detector. You empty your pockets. Now we're in another little room. I'm looking at Gigi. This is her moment to see her brother strapped on a gurney and put to death for a crime he committed many, many years ago. This is traumatic for her. I have no emotional attachment to the victim, the state of Texas or the executioners. I'm already numb from the experience.

Officials enter and tell us what is going to happen. They say the curtain will open. They say, James (not his real name) will already be lying on the gurney. His arms, legs and chest will be strapped down. He will have IV's connected to his veins by the time you see him. You will see a sort of operating table. The victim's relatives will be in another room. There will be no contact with them.

Then we start to walk down this long corridor. I'm about to witness an execution and again I'm thinking, "there but for the grace of God go I." How many times in my life on crack cocaine could I have killed someone? I'm experiencing a gratitude attack. It's an affirmation that being sober and sane and being a father and doing what I'm doing now is a lot better than being a crack addict, ex-football player and a pitiful example of a man. This recovery and sobriety is a good thing you did, Thomas, because you could be a dead man walking right now.

The corridor seems to go on forever. We pass through three or four doors. We finally reach the viewing chamber, they unlock it and we enter. The room could be a holding cell or just a hole. People in prison know what The Hole is. It's just a small place. This room front to back was about 8X8, with a Plexiglas window behind a closed curtain.

Gigi walks to the window to stand in the left corner. I take a position directly behind her. I'm 6' 3," she's about 5' 6", so I can look right over the top of her head. There's dead silence in the room. No talk. No eye contact. Everyone is standing and looking at the drawn curtain. No one is saying, "How are you?" or "How have you been?" It's as serious a moment as I've experienced in my life.

Ten minutes that seem like two hours pass before the curtain opens. I have never seen Gigi's brother before, didn't even know his name. She tells me later that when I was running the streets of Austin in 1968 and 1969 as a teenager her brother was 10 or 11 and already moving in bad company. When the curtain opens I look at an African American man about 38 years old. He's wearing white prison pants, white prison shirt, tennis shoes that are untied and pulled apart as if he grabbed them at the last minute. They don't look like his tennis shoes, just something to cover his feet. A microphone dangles from a cord above his head.

He looked at his sister, apologized to her and said he was sorry. He looked at me and said, "Hollywood, thanks for what you did for me and for the hope." I didn't expect that. Now all of a sudden I am emotionally attached, because some of the last words of a condemned man have been spoken to me. He looked at the victims' family and said:

"I didn't kill your daughter. That's all I have to say."

He laid his head down on the gurney, turned and looked at Gigi and me. His eyes were on her but I'm feeling his eyes because I'm standing right behind Gigi. I don't know when the drugs were released. He made a cough or two as if clearing his throat. He never moved an eyelash. There was no twitching. No movement. Only his eyes stayed fixed on Gigi. And he was dead.

Gigi fainted. I caught her as she was falling. She began to sob a deep, sorrowful and devastating cry. I let her gently fall to the floor. I sat on the floor, put my arms around her, and just let her cry. She got her cry out, the curtain was closed, and it was over.

But it wasn't over for me. The shock of what I'd seen made a searing impression. I'll never forget it. My mouth was wide open, but I couldn't make a sound. Words still fail when I reflect on what I saw. I can't find the right ones to describe the impact on my soul.

I got Gigi up and we left the death chamber, walked that long corridor again, out of prison and across the street to the room for the family of the condemned. Now I didn't know what to do. Do I jump in my car, run and cry? I'm there for her so I think, Thomas, this isn't about you, it's about Gigi, so see that she's okay. She regained composure and went about the final details. She made arrangements to take possession of her brother's body and have it cremated. She had to get working on that.

"Is there anything I can do? If there isn't, can I leave?" I said. I was done. Mentally whipped. My mind was reeling. Gigi told me it was okay to go. Leaving prison, we saw anti-death penalty people who protested the execution. They were respectful. No shouts.

As for the victim's family, I wonder how much pleasure they found in seeing that man executed. But I guess if you're a cold-blooded killer convicted of a cold-blooded crime the family gets something out of it. What, I don't know. A sense of justice or closure, I guess.

Even after watching an execution I'm uncertain where I stand on the death penalty. Except to say that if one of my kids or grandkids were murdered I'd damn sure want whoever was guilty to be executed.

I got in my car and pulled out on the highway back toward Austin. As I drove those 180 miles I'm not sure my mouth was open like a dead carp on a creek bank, but I think it might have been. I am sure if you passed me and looked over you saw a man in shock. A man with glazed eyeballs and his mouth open as if trying to say, "Oh, my God, what did I just see?"

PETER KNOBLER
(Co-author, Out Of Control)

Once we decided to do the book, I had to prove myself to Thomas and he had to prove himself to me. That took all of about 30 seconds. By then he was clean and sober for a year, so he was out from under his old habits. But he was in jail.

You can't talk to Thomas for more than five minute without knowing this is a guy with a great heart and a great sense of humor. He told me stories about that side of the tracks in Austin when he hung out at Greasy Dick's Bar-B-Q and as a little kid running around the pool hall. He told me stories that I had absolutely no cultural touch with. It was amazing, exotic stuff.

I had no contact with poor black culture on the wrong side of the tracks in Austin. I'm a New York, middle class Jewish guy. I knew athletes. I'd done a book with Kareem Abdul-Jabbar. But this was a total eye opener. It changed my outlook and the way you look at people.

I didn't know much about Thomas before I started talking to him. I knew him from his pro football career. I'd seen him on the sidelines and always kind of liked him. I was watching TV the day he waved his little towel in Washington, and the Cowboys were losing. I always liked his spirit and thought he was funny. I didn't have any idea of his family situation. I barely knew where he went to college.

Thomas was in an inmate in Chino, and he'd call every Tuesday collect from prison because that's the way you've got to do it. We spent hours on the phone, and it occurred to me that he was having a great time telling his story.

After what he had done, he was lucky to be alive. The other parts of what he'd done...the characters he had hung with...the people he had known...the good and bad things he had done...it was an amazing story. It occurred to me that on each of these Tuesdays, by telling his story, he was basically getting himself out of prison. While we were talking, he wasn't in jail. He was doing what he did, reliving the event.

I didn't want a story like, I went to school and I came home. I'd say, what did you see on the way to school? Who was there? How did you get there? Who was hanging out front? What does the building look like? Who were your teachers? I wanted intensive detail.

Thomas had command of all that. Because he was in prison, he was happy to spend lots of time talking about high school, college, football and locker room stuff. We gave everyone everything they wanted to know about

Thomas Henderson from his public personality, then what they had no idea about, which was his family life and how he got to be such an out of control guy and put himself back together.

He told me a story about how he was standing on the steps of his house between his mother and stepfather when she shot him. He could see the flash out of the barrel of the gun. Who do I know who had seen his mother shoot his father? No one.

He took me into the depths of when he was doing freebase, completely out of control and totally unreliable. He would lie and cheat and do anything he had to because he was a pipe addict. But the guy who was talking to me was none of that. He was very clear about that and pleased with himself.

Thomas used to say, "Just do what you say you're going to do." This was a guy who never did what he said he was going to do. All of a sudden, a year into being clean and sober, he was doing that. I thought that was one of the most genuine, good-hearted ways to live: Just do what you say you're going to do.

He has lived his life that way, and that's the kind of guy he really is. I think it's hard to say whether he was that way growing up. He clearly got away from it. I think he always had a good heart. He always cared about people and was good-natured, mixed with a little con. Once he hit the depths and came back, he's been a remarkable guy for his honesty and forth rightfulness.

I love him to death. He still does what he says he's going to do. He's an honorable and upright guy in ways he never thought he'd be. He continues to surprise himself. He's been very gracious and generous to my son who's 14.

My son is a rock 'n roll guitar player. Thomas went out of his way to introduce him to Jimmy Vaughn. There was my son in the presence of Jimmy Vaughn. That was along the lines of me sitting on a couch with Willie Mays.

Doing something for others without thinking of getting a return is so different from the way he was brought up, the way he had to struggle and con to get himself where he wanted to go. A sense of selfishness is not natural to him. He's learned that, and I like that about him.

Thomas calls when he comes to town. I see him every once in a while. I'm happy to see him every time that I do. I don't see him enough.

CHAPTER NINETEEN

A $28 MILLION SORE THROAT

March 22 is my mother's birthday. On March 22, 2000, I played golf at Barton Creeks Lakeside Golf Course and won $200 in side bets. I think I shot 79 with a 17-handicap, and I was sick, too. When I say I think I shot 79, it's from memory.

I know I won $200, and I know I was sick. The money was in my shirt pocket, and I had a sore throat that was getting worse. Since I wasn't using a doctor then, I called my dentist on the way home from the golf course.

"Do me a favor," I said, "I feel lousy. I've got a sore throat, headache and maybe the damn flu. I need some antibiotics and cough medicine. Can you call in a prescription for me at this drugstore near by home?"

"Dentists usually don't write prescriptions, but I'll try," he said, so I headed for Nau's Enfield Drug.

My order was ready when I arrived. Something like 10 tiny antibiotic pills and a little bitty dose of cough syrup cost $87 and change. A rip-off. No wonder people need a prescription drug program from the government.

I reached for my billfold to pay. No wallet. I'd left it in the truck. Then I remembered $200 in my shirt pocket. I paid for the prescriptions, which left me with $12 and change and another $100. That last $100 prompted a sudden thought.

"Hey, how much is the lottery?" I asked the guy behind the counter. He said $28 million. That was enough for me to keep betting on a private hunch.

I'd played lotteries in California and Texas for at least 13 years. From 1987 to 2000, I guess I put $5-7,000 a year into lotteries. Believe it or not, I always was certain I would win. I was so convinced about winning a lottery that even if the jackpot were only $4,000,000, I'd sit down with paper and pencil and write the names of everyone I was going to give money to. As if it was going to happen tomorrow morning. I must have done that 100 times. My motto is: if you don't play you can't win.

"OK," I told the clerk, "give me $100 worth of quick picks."

The clerk punched the computer. The machine rolled out four or five tickets and then quit. Shut down. Bam! It stuck on the spot.

"Tape got jammed," he mumbled.

Now I was doubly frazzled. My throat hurt. I've been screwed on the price of a prescription. I wanted to go home to take this expensive medicine. Meantime, the clerk couldn't get his freaking machine to function.

The clerk opened the computer, wrestled with the tape, and finally got the thing re-programmed. He closed the damn machine, dialed it into working order and gave me the rest of my tickets. I walked out cussing pharmaceutical companies for gouging the public, the government for not doing anything about it, computers and drug store clerks.

I took the tickets and flipped them on the front seat of my truck. They weren't high security items. I went home, took two antibiotics, drank the bottle of cough syrup, and began to feel better. So I went to dinner that night, valet-parked my truck at a restaurant and was there until 11 p.m. Tickets on the passenger front seat.

Next day, Thursday, I played golf again at Lakeside. My cell phone rung as we were finishing. My daughter, Thomesa, who was then stationed in the Air Force at Langley in Virginia, had called. Her mother and my first ex-wife, Wyetta, who lived in Austin, joined us on an extension. Ever so often we'd wind up in a three-way conversation.

"How ya'll doing'?" I said. "I've just finished playing golf. Let me get in the truck and we'll talk."

I threw my clubs in, slammed the door and took off toward Highway 71. Then I heard Wyetta say: "Hey, you know that drugstore close to where you live? Niles or Naw's or however you pronounce it?"

"Yeah," I said.

"Whoever won the lottery bought their tickets there."

"Well, I bought $100 worth yesterday when I got my medicine."

"You did?"

"They're right here on the front seat of the truck."

By this time, I had turned onto Highway 71, a 70-mile-an-hour speedway. I was rolling like a big eight-wheeler when I picked up a stack of about 20 tickets.

"What are the numbers?' I asked Wyetta.

"I'm not going to tell you the numbers," she shot back. "Are you serious? You got tickets?"

"Swear I do. I went there to get medicine yesterday and bought 'em."

"You got any that start with a five?'

Numbers on quick picks appear in sequence, the lowest first and so on to higher numbers. Yeah, here's one with five, I said. It's five, 13. No good, said Wyetta.

Here's another one that starts with five, I said. It was about the sixth ticket I handled.

"Next is eight," Wyetta said.

"Yes."

"Seventeen"

"Yes."

"Thirty five."

"Yes."

"Thirty eight."

"Yes."

"Forty one."

I have heard Wyetta use expressive language many times. She was in top form on this occasion. Her exact words were:

"You lying mother fucker! You've got a newspaper or something there!"

No, I said, I'm still driving. Don't play with me. Here are the numbers in front of me: 5, 8, 17, 35, 38, 41. Are those the winning numbers?

Yes, she said.

How many winners?

One, she said.

"That be me!" I whooped.

I won the Texas Lotto jackpot worth $28 million on paper but much less in reality. The state whips your ass for taking cash option instead of stringing out payments for 25 years. Taxes eat up more. I wound up with less than half of the advertised amount: $10.43 million.

Hell, they got me again a year later. I had to write a check to the Internal Revenue Service for $1.7 million. Let me tell you what would have happened

if that had been my last $1.7 million. It would have been ""Hello, Mexico!'"
That's how a $28 million jackpot shrank to $8.7 million.

Hey, I'm not mad. I still had enough money to last me the rest of my
life if I didn't listen to every con artist, deal maker and I'm-going-to-
make-you-rich hustler that came along. I'm a guy who'd already lost one
fortune. I swore I wouldn't lose the second.

Back during that dizzy moment of discovery that I'd won, my truck
was wobbling all over Highway 71. I was following my friend Dick Janicki
to his house for dinner. I got him to pull over and stop by honking my
horn and flashing my lights.

"Dick, I've won the lottery!" I shouted.

"What?' he said, because he couldn't hear with cars flashing past us
like bullets. "Let me see that ticket. Give me those numbers."

Dick got back in his car and called his secretary. He told her to check
the newspaper and call the lottery commission. He was hell-bent on veri-
fying that I'd won.

When we got to his house, Dick's wife prepared one of my favorite
meals: pasta with prawns and scallops in a cream sauce, salad and bread.
I walked in still processing the fact that I was holding a ticket worth $28
million and two friends had invited me to dinner when what I really
wanted to do was go lease the Titanic.

Weird feelings struck me as dinner was being prepared. First came a
strange sense of unbelievable happiness. I don't know how you feel if you
win $100,000 playing blackjack. I know that winning $28 million is an
indescribably strange sensation.

The next wave took me in an opposite direction. Deep stress replaced
euphoria. The middle of my body locked up from my Adam's apple to my
pelvis. It was as if somebody took a piece of iron and stuck it inside.

I became overwhelmed, a feeling I never had before. I even felt a little
fear. I have no idea where the fear came from. Looking back, I think the
question in my soul was, "Okay, Mr. First Round Draft Choice of the
Dallas Cowboys, how are you gonna handle this one?"

So there I sat at the table with my favorite food and my favorite
friends, we've gotten this huge news and we're sharing the excitement of
the day. I took the big spoon and the big fork and filled my plate with
prawns and pasta from a beautifully prepared meal. I buttered a piece of

French bread and...

I couldn't take a bite. Raised the fork to my mouth, but my mouth wouldn't open.

I was starving. I hadn't eaten all day. It would be 11 o'clock that night before I went to a 7-11, bought a sausage and egg biscuit, white donuts and a pint of milk. That would be my meal of the day and the only reason I ate at all was I had to put some nourishment in my body.

Talk about food for thought. Odds on winning any lottery are many millions-to-one. My chances of winning $28 million were even longer when I reconstruct how I came to possess the jackpot ticket. And how there was a chance to have lost that ticket twice and never been the wiser.

Talk about eerie coincidence. First, I had to be sick. Without a sore throat, I wouldn't have needed prescriptions and gone to the drugstore. If I hadn't gone to the drugstore, I wouldn't have bought $100 worth of quick picks. You might say that in rare cases, good health can be a handicap.

So I retract bitching about the high price of antibiotic pills and cough syrup. I bought $87 worth of cold medicine and wound up with a multi-million-dollar cure.

Next, the machine that dispenses lottery tickets had to jam. Remember that it spit out a half-dozen or so tickets and then locked. It felt like an hour but that computer was actually down for about three minutes. But that was long enough because meantime, all over Texas, computers at thousands of other sites were churning out tickets.

That meant the sequence on quick picks changed by the millisecond. It figures that the winning combination had been programmed for distribution at whatever site was dialed in at that precise instant. My ticket could have shown up in Port Arthur, El Paso or Texarkana. Anywhere.

If the computer at Nau's didn't jam, 5-8-17-35-38-41 would've rotated and popped out somewhere else. The reason I believe this is because the winner was among the first batch I received after the machine re-activated. A three-minute delay meant the difference between 100 worthless quick picks and the jackpot.

Finally, I had a scary thought recalling what I'd done with the tickets. Just flipped them on the front seat of my truck. They lay unguarded that Wednesday night when I valet parked at a restaurant, unaware of how the lottery turned out.

So I didn't know the attendant was driving away with $28 million within arm's reach. I shudder at the thought that anyone could've glanced into my truck and said, look here, free lottery tickets. Then scooped up the entire bunch.

I was vulnerable to theft again on Thursday when I valet-parked to play golf and a lot of people except me knew the winning ticket had been bought in Austin. Do attendants lock vehicles when they park? I think they do. Then again, it probably depends on which goober is behind the wheel.

Yet the luckiest thing about me winning the lottery was this: there wasn't a man on the planet better prepared to handle it. Had I won it 20 years earlier, I'd have been dead early. If I'd had this money while active in my alcoholism and addiction, there would have been police, helicopters, dogs, DEA, sheriff, local police and the coroner at my residence.

Now I faced the question of what to do with the money.

I have rich friends and rich former teammates. One of the first calls I made was to Roger Staubach and he gave me the best advice I've gotten from anyone short of Warren Buffett.

"Roger,'" I said, "you have a lot of money. Where's the safest place to invest money?" Roger recommended Triple AAA municipal bonds. That sounded good to me.

By the next day I was getting 940,000 letters and phone calls from people who wanted to help me invest, donate or give them money. A friend of mine-I'll call him Robert – called to say he had a money handler I should meet. I invited this guy to my office.

All he had to do was walk in and shut up and he would have cinched the account. But he comes in, sits down and starts pulling out a chart where some guy had $25,000 and now it's worth $1.7 million. He goes on and on like I'm a damn dummy.

"By the way," I said, "I spoke to my friend Staubach and he thought Triple AAA municipal bonds were a sound investment. Do you think we should put about $5 million there?"

"Why would you want to do that?" the guy said. He acted like that was the worst idea he ever heard.

Is it a myth or an assumption that some people think football players lack intelligence? My reaction to this guy was that he thought he was smart and I was stupid, and this was never going to work. But I was very nice. I didn't confront him, he left and I wrote him a Dear John letter that I'd decided to go in another direction.

I did put my money in Triple AAA municipal bonds when they were 5.5 to 6 percent. Now they're down to 2, 3, and 4 percent if you extend them out 20 years. I locked in around $5 million that returns about $250,000 a year tax-free. I knew I'd done the right thing when I told my mother.

Now, my mother has never had much more than dimes in her pocket. She never had $1,000 in a savings account. So when I told her, "Mom, I put my money in something that makes $250,000 a year," she erased any doubt I might have had. You know what she said?

She said, "That sounds good to me."

My next thought was to spread some of this money to relatives and friends. One difference between Thomas Henderson now and Thomas Henderson of years ago is that I'm not afraid to say I don't know. So I asked people who were smarter than me about stuff I didn't know and was told by tax accountants that the legal limit of a gift was $10,000.

I gave every member of my immediate family and some extremely close associates and friends $10,000 apiece, to the tune of about $600,000. I sent a note went with the checks that read: "Don't ask me for no more money."

I also settled business deals. I owed Staubach. He had loaned me $55,000 on a real estate deal in Austin that didn't work out so well. I wrote him a check for $65,000, gave him a little interest on his money. I wrote $50,000 checks to a couple of other partners who'd helped me in the past.

Several days later and before I collected the millions, I returned to Nau's and sought the clerk who'd sold me the winning ticket. I asked him to step outside to where I had parked in front of a dry cleaners store. I wrote him a personal check on the hood of my car for $10,000. A 40-ish man, he was floored and said, "Thank you so much. I'm going back to college."

Then, in every interview I did as a lottery winner, someone suddenly sitting on top of a pile of money, I repeated a message to anyone who'd ever met, heard or even seen a picture of me and thought I was a soft touch.

"No new friends need apply," I kept saying. Of course, they did, and I'll you tell later about the most extreme requests for donations.

What I'll relate next will sound spooky and hard to believe, but I'm convinced that something I did one month earlier was related to winning the lottery. And maybe that incident was also tied to building a million-dollar stadium at my old high school and later fasting for seven days to raise funds for a track around it.

I'm not superstitious. I don't believe in the supernatural or a boogey man. I believe in God in a personal way that is nobody else's damn business. I'm long past believing in stuff like the Tooth Fairy because if she ever came to my house when I was a kid, it wasn't safe.

What I did wasn't motivated for personal or monetary gain. I didn't need either. I was already successful in real estate, the film business and on the lecture circuit. I had a substantial amount of property and money.

I don't want this to sound like a religious experience. But I will say there are people with a connection to God called to preach or do different things. I've been inspired on occasion by voices or messages in my conscious or sub conscious. The ideas for the six films I made that are shown in prisons all over the country came to me that way.

I was driving to San Antonio one day, the cover on the sunroof back, enjoying the scenery and just thinking. I like to meditate when I'm driving. I heard a strong suggestion that I should do a film on Learning How To Live. Two months later I was shooting that movie in a small theater in Austin.

It occurred to me later that I hadn't talked to kids yet. I thought I should do a film at a school with kids and emphasize that sobriety is an option. And I did it.

Then this voice came to me and said, What about inmates after they leave prison? You need to make a film called, Getting Out, Taking the First Right Step. It's your responsibility to try to effect recidivism in our nation's prisons. Again this voice said I should stress another theme to the prison population called, Do The Right Thing When No One Is Looking.

Maybe I was just talking to myself rather than reacting to some higher power. Who knows? I don't. But the same experience happened one month before I won the lottery.

In February I went to visit a pastor friend of mine at his church. There was a guy with him. I'm nosy, and I'm only dropping in to shoot the breeze with the preacher. So I asked the guy what he does.

"I sell wholesale busses," he said, and told me he was there to try to sell one to the preacher for the church to use.

"Don't say. Tell me about that business. I never heard of anybody who goes around and wholesales school busses. How'd you get involved in that?" I asked.

We talked and talked until I said, ""Well, how much do you want for your bus?" He said he was asking $2,200 and invited me to examine the vehicle parked out back. I'm no mechanic but we still had to play the boy games, the little growling about, "Hey, check that spark plug." Yeah, it's ok.

"See if that horn blows." Yeah, it works. "How's that left blinker?" It's on. "Put the headlights on." They're fine. "High beam?" Looks ok. "Mash the brakes." They check out. "Put the emergency brake on." No problem. "Raise the hood...now what kind of carburetor is this?"

Then came the moment when I thought the preacher needed to talk to the salesman about price. So I went to the front of the church and backed out. Then as clear as a bell I heard a voice say:

"Go back and pay the man for half of that bus."

I had absolutely no idea where that voice came from. It wasn't a charity day. I didn't wake up that morning and say I was going to go around town writing checks. I ignored what I heard, put my truck in drive and pulled to the edge of the street. That's when the voice said again:

"Go back and pay for half of that bus."

I did what I was told. I obeyed my sense of duty, charity or philanthropy at a moment when I was not in a giving mood. However you want to look at it I feel I was blessed 30 days later with a gift.

Look, I know millions of people have done kinder and more generous deeds than me and never been noticed, much less rewarded. I mean, if doing good works were the key to winning lotteries, someone like Mother Teresa would've won 'em all. I don't understand that experience to this day. So I made a right turn instead of a left to go home. I drove behind the church and called the preacher.

"What are you doing?" he said.

"I'm writing a check for $1,150, half the price of the bus."

"You don't have to do that," he said.

221

"Yes I do," I said. "I heard somebody tell me to do it. Twice."

* * * *

Many folks have heard I've won the lottery more than once. I'll be at dinner or somewhere and someone will say, "Man, you won that lottery twice." I say, well, sort of. The first lottery I won was on November 8, 1983, when through the help of God, friends, therapists and a psychiatrist I made the decision to be sober. That was the greatest gift, the greatest win, bigger than the Super Bowl.

Once I went to Abilene to speak on a slow night in west Texas. Yet 2,000 people showed up on a Tuesday night in the downtown civic center. I opened by saying, "Boy, must not be nothing to do in Abilene." The sponsors gave me a ring with diamonds and embroidered on it were the words Sober Bowl (November 8, 1983) inscribed around the perimeter.

Lots of times when I do speeches people ask about the ring. I say, It's from the Sober Bowl. Do you know anything about that? So the first and most important lottery that I won was my recovery, my sobriety, my serenity and the change in my life. I'm only a soldier, one of millions of people in the recovery community of our country. But I do want to share how I do, what I do and why I do it.

Albert Einstein said that nothing happens until something moves. I want to tell you that I've made some moves in my life. Here are the actions I've taken to keep what I have over the past 20 years. It's a list of 12 things that I do daily that have given me the life I have today.

1 – I don't use alcohol or drugs. On a daily basis as a recovering crack addict and alcoholic that is the first waking decision I make. Then I go 24 hours and keep that commitment. I've been doing that since November 8, 1983.

2 – I do my best to act and remain sane. It is clear that in the past I was insane. I didn't know how to live. I became involved with chemicals and went more insane.

3 – I ask God to help me help myself every day.

4 – I look at my past honestly and learn from my mistakes. I don't have to repeat past behaviors if I choose not to. That falls into the category of where I stress that regrets are avoidable. I just don't do anything that I'm going to regret.

5 – I admit my wrongs and I'm committed not to repeat them.

6 – I keep my ego in check as best I can.

7 – I prefer to understand rather than be understood.

8 – I maintain an honest willingness to make amends and atone for my past as a work in progress when I meet people I may have harmed. For instance, not too long ago, I ran into Frank Parra from Parra Chevrolet in Dallas. I 'd been given a courtesy Corvette from him and I wrecked the man's car. I scattered fiberglass all over I-35 in Dallas and left the car for him to pick up. When I met Parra years later he reminded me of who he was and I said, "Mr. Parra, I've got to make amends to you for that car." To which he said, "Oh, don't worry about it Hollywood. I just filed a claim on your insurance."

9 – When the opportunity presents itself, I clear wreckage from my past. That means when I have those clandestine moments of meeting people that I affected one way or another, I am always willing to say, "I was wrong. I am sorry. How can I make it right?"

10 – I stay current in the reality of my life and the work I must do to stay clean and sober. This means that I continue to be fully aware of who I am. I am a drug addict. I am an alcoholic. I was dysfunctional. This is who I am. When I stand before the world or anyone it is on the tip of my tongue to say, hey, I'm a recovering drug addict and alcoholic. There is nowhere that I go to sleep that I'm not a recovering alcoholic and drug addict. There is no place that I wake up that I'm not a recovering addict and alcoholic. There is no party, no adventure and no boy's night out that I'm not a recovering alcoholic and drug addict. I am what I am everywhere that I am.

11 – I do personal and world prayer daily.

12 – I maintain an absolute willingness to help other alcoholics and drug addicts find his or her sobriety. That is a mandate. The commitment for the rest of my days is that I'm open and willing to help another human being find recovery.

* * * *

Since 1975 I have probably bought my mother 10 cars and here it was 2000 and she needed another upgrade. After I won the lottery I went to her house and told her, "I want to get you a really nice car, a 1998 or 1999 model. Something clean with low mileage."

I glanced at her and saw that she had tears in her eyes.

"What's wrong?" I said. Mamma looked like she was 10 years old and standing at the door while Santa Claus left with all the presents.

"I'm 63 years old and I've never had a new car," she whimpered.

Oh, my. She just closed the deal. I said, "You'll have one tomorrow." So I bought her a brand new 2000 Lincoln Town Car.

LOTTERY MONEY

I've given money, homes, cars, loans, groceries, scholarships, sponsorships and many material things to family, friends and strangers. What I've come to realize is that money, property or things don't make people happy or fix them. You think you've done a great thing and you come to understand that money and material things don't really make people happy. They invariably want more. I even had one recipient that I bought furniture for an apartment, a truck, gas, working equipment and got him a job. In the end he asked me for more and when I listed for him all I had done he said, "You did what you wanted to do not what I wanted you to do." He didn't want to work. He wanted to hang out with me.

Accepting a lot of money is easy. Handling and managing a lot of money is difficult, false profits everywhere. I see now how a few bad and or impulsive decisions could've had me bankrupt by now. Winning the lottery has been an extreme exercise of restraint.

If you ever win the lottery call me as a consultant. I'm worth my weight in gold on how to handle family, friends, lawyers and thieves.

Thomas Henderson

MARK POWELL
(Financial advisor)

I had parked my car in downtown Austin when the cell phone rang at 6:35 a.m. I'm certain of the time because I was on my way to teach a Bible study class to a group of men, and I was already late. The meeting was supposed to have started five minutes earlier.

I was literally getting out of the car, had my hand on the door handle when the call came. It was Thomas. I thought he was in trouble.

"Mark!" he said, "I won the lottery!"

"Well, that's good news, Thomas," I replied.

"I think I want you to manage part of it."

"I'm honored and flattered."

"I think I want you to manage one million bucks of it."

"I'm very honored that you would think of me and I look forward to visiting with you, but I'm late for a Bible study right now."

I hung up and went about my business. When I returned to my office, Thomas had called again. He was holding on the phone when I walked in the door.

"I've been thinking," he said, "and I think I want you to manage two million dollars."

"Golly, I'm honored, Thomas. That's great" I told him. "We'll get together when you're ready and talk about it."

An hour later he called a third time.

"Mark," he said, "everybody and his uncle has got somebody for me to talk to about this. Now I want you to have all of it."

"Out of curiosity, why me?" I asked.

"Because you're a good friend and then because you're the only financial advisor I know who goes to Bible study."

I gave Thomas two pieces of advice about how to handle the money. The first was, don't make any major decisions for one year. The second was, the name of the game has changed. You are not in the get-rich business anymore. You are in the stay-rich business. So we are going to manage accordingly, and put about 90 percent of your money in Triple AAA municipal bonds.

That's what we did at the peak of the market in 2000 when people everywhere were putting their money in stocks because stocks were going to 50,000 on the Dow. From where we got in, the NASDAQ went down 75 percent.

225

The first thing Thomas did was to settle a few debts. He wanted to make sure he settled with everyone. He did that. He had a list.

Next he got a fistful of $10,000 checks. He gave me a long list of people that he wanted to have them, including his second grade teacher. He had the best time for the next week or so going around and passing out money. Everyone who had been important in his life received a check.

Thomas was smarter than we gave him credit. He's a smart guy to begin with, but in this incident he was much wiser than we all realized. I think he figured if he acted aggressively and gave everyone money first, they wouldn't come asking for it. I don't know if this was his strategy, but the way he handle it impressed me.

Now he has a nice bond portfolio that pays him a handsome monthly income. He doesn't have to worry about it and he's sleeping well at night. He took a few dollars in mad money, but has done nothing in grandiose style. He bought a small, modest condo in Florida and a golf club member-ship. Nothing extravagant. He also bought a home in his old east Austin neighborhood. He's not on the west side where anyone else would be. He's been wise, careful and subdued with money. He gradually invested a little in stocks, but that's his own doing. Nothing huge, he just likes to tinker with it. He knows how valuable those bonds are. He can enjoy the rest of his life if he keeps doing what he's doing. Thomas understands that.

What impressed me most about Thomas when he came back to town was that he was thinking beyond himself. He was thinking more about oth-ers than himself. Having gone through what he did, it would have been easy to be bitter and have a chip on his shoulder. He didn't.

He had processed the experience and moved on. He had an insatiable desire to do good works. He was constantly doing things for people; some we heard about, some we didn't. One thing he worked hard at doing was to produce films to show to the prison population. I invested in those with some others.

It wasn't a big financial investment, but it was a great investment in what Thomas was trying to do. The return was that Thomas got to tell his story and maybe people would be positively impacted by it. I'm sure they were.

People ask me if I was shocked or surprised that Thomas won the lot-tery. I say, no. I've learned never to expect anything but the unexpected from Thomas.

NEWFOUND FRIENDS

The foremost temptation I had to resist as a lottery winner was found in these words: Give me $2 million and I'll turn it into $20 million. You know the seven deadly sins? Greed is one of them. If someone can successfully tap into your greed, he'll rob you blind.

People all over the country win Power Ball and lotteries, like a police officer in Austin who won a $50-60 million lottery jackpot. I did my best to contact him. I could have recommended advisors who would have helped him manage that much money.

Things like where to invest. How you might handle it within the family. Sources to explain the tax consequences. And to beware of newfound friends.

I don't care if it's $50, $60 or $10 million, there's a strong chance that an unsophisticated citizen listening to the wrong people at the wrong time will be broke shortly thereafter. I see clearly, only three years later, how I could have been flat broke.

One way would have been to fall for a con from overseas. I got an e-mail from a person who elaborately explained that he was the son of a king in some empire in Africa. He had $100 million, the king was dead and he was the prince. He had $100 million in a Nigerian bank but he couldn't withdraw and transfer it because he needed a bank account and somebody to accept the money for him.

He needed about $100,000 to get the proper documents. The e-mail said that for $100,000 he would give me 50 percent of his $100 million. All I had to do was send him my bank information and check for $100,000 so he could get the kingdom to release his money to my bank.

I sat there for about 12 seconds and thought, "This is a great deal. I give this guy $100,000 and he transfers $100 million into my account. What could go wrong with that?"

Then I remembered those simple words you've heard in the investment world: If it sounds too good to be true, then it is. You have to believe it and avoid getting so comatose from greed that you say to yourself, damn right, I'm gonna go for it.

* * * *

The most shocking plea for money came from one of my college coaches at Langston. I answered the phone and he said:

"I owe $50,000 on my Lexus, $212,000 on my home, owe $31,000 on my Range Rover, and I owe $80,000 on furniture and college loans for one of my kids. I need you to loan me $500,000. Pay off all my debts and I'll just pay you back whenever I can."

My reaction was as serious as his nerve to ask me to donate half a million to haul his ass out of this ditch he'd dug. I said to him, "I'm not going to do that. Why would I want to own your house?"

He and I had never had any financial dealings in the past. I don't remember ever getting $1 from him at Langston to buy a cheeseburger. He started to get mad anyway.

I'd already given a lot of money to family and close friends in $10,000 checks. So while he went on talking, I was reminded that I kind of liked him and I thought to myself, "All right, I'll probably give him $10,000, too."

Except that he kept talking, sort of berating me, and at one point he even said something like, "All I did for you...." Which in truth was only his job and the way I played had little to do with technical instruction from a coach. Everything I did was based on talent and instinct.

I'd convinced myself by then that I wasn't going to give him 500 grand. He wound up with nothing because near the end of the conversation he said these words: "Well, how much are you going to give me?"

He blew $10,000 right there. He never knew about the $10,000 and he blew it because now it was as if he was entitled to it. He doesn't know to this day what he missed. He won't know until he reads this book.

* * * *

Not long thereafter, I received a weird visitor in my office. She looked to be mid-80s, small and frail, and in danger of passing away from terminal wrinkles. She was oddly dressed in a full white gown. She wore a veil, referred to a God I'd never heard of before, and could talk in tongues at the touch of my hand.

I'd never seen her before I won the lottery. So when she walked in I shook her hand and said, ""Nice to meet you."

Soon as our hands touched she went, ""HAAAJAAAA!!!" She snapped like she was hit by a spasm. Then she began talking in tongues. That threw me off a little while.

The first thing she wanted to do was pray. I made the mistake of giving her my hand to hold while she bowed her head and began to jabber. Well...39 minutes later she still had my hand in a death grip and my secretary was sitting out there cracking up.

There I was, respectful, courteous, a gentleman, but really feeling like I was being abused. Her prayer finally ended and she got to the point. "God told me that you wanted to give me $1 million," she revealed.

Oh really? I'd already had some sort of mystical experience with the $1,100 I donated for that used school bus at a church. Now the ante had gone way up. She told me why she needed it. She had a home for wayward children and blah, blah, blah, and the lights were about to be cut off and blah, blah, blah. So I said, hold on a second.

I closed my eyes in front of her. If she was going to play the God trick, I was going to go with it. I kept my eyes closed and then slowly opened them with an expression that indicated I'd had a vision.

Then I said: "He told me to give you $1,000."

A month later I discovered that she was blind when I gave her a $50 bill. She was still asking for one million but that day I busted it down to fifty. What did I give you, I asked. I wasn't making fun. I didn't know she couldn't see.

"A twenty?" she said.

She was the most aggressive of all the people seeking me for money. Whenever she'd called, my staff would mess with me and say, oh, he's here, come on over. Not until the day she took off my shoe, kissed my feet and went into a spasm of talking in tongues did the staff realize they were making fun of her. I never was, even though she was relentless about wanting the one million.

I probably wound up giving her about $2,000 total. I gave her a $1,000 check to pay utilities for the home and some groceries. She came one day with an electric bill that I wrote a check to cover. I gave her $100 bills on four or five occasions, but I kept letting her know she wasn't going to get one million. I must have explained that to her 30 times, but she kept after me.

I made two adjustments to deal with this woman. I never let her get hold of my hands again and I kept my feet on the floor when she was around. If I didn't, she'd grab my hands and wrist or feet, start kissing them and hollering, "HAAAAJAAAA!!!"

The second thing I did was to stop going to my office. I didn't do it simply to avoid her. I just ceased going to the office. That way when someone asked me what I'm doing these days, I could spring my new line on him. I'd say, I'm not doing a damn thing and I don't start that until after lunch.

* * * *

I have a younger half-brother who is another of my DNA donor's victims. To clarify, we have different mothers but the same father.

Years ago on the East Coast, he was defending another brother and murdered a guy by shooting him. He was given a 30-year prison sentence. I got a phone call from the family asking if they could give him my address and I said, sure. So I heard from him before I won the lottery. He was just saying hello, he's in prison and it's awful.

Hey, you're singing to the choir. Turn around, I think to myself. Of all people, I know the tough psychological and social concept of being incarcerated. Anyway, he said his family was screwed up and nobody supported him. His mother didn't send him anything and our daddy wasn't ever going to do anything for us. He never had and never will. He needs some zuzus and wam-wams, which in prison talk means things like Kool-Aid, Snickers bars, tuna fish, crackers, sardines, toothpaste, soap and razors.

I sent him a check for a couple of hundred dollars. He was grateful and said he'd write from time to time. He'd been so good about not asking for money on a monthly basis that I sent him another $300. Then after I won the lottery and he became aware of it I got this long letter that said:

Dear Thomas:

You know I committed this murder but I want to appeal my conviction. I want to hire an attorney in New York and work on this appeal.

I'd never written to him before other than short notes that said, hope everything is okay, see you later. I decided then to write a letter and it went like this:

Dear Baby Brother:
I understand the predicament you are in now. You shot a man in the
head from close range and you took his life. Now you are living the conse-
quences of that action. Whereas I am willing to continue to support you
with zuzus and wam-wams and stationary and stamps, I am not willing
to spend tens of thousands of dollars toward your appeal. You are current-
ly suffering the consequences of murder. I don't see what I can do with
money to change the fact that you are in the midst of your own conse-
quences. So if you want to become a jailhouse lawyer, get in the law library
and do your own habeas corpus. You have time to learn how to do this but
I'm not willing to fund it.

We still correspond. His letters are often depressing. Nobody cares for
him. Nobody is behind him. He has no options. About twice a year I sit
down and write him a check for $350, $400 or $450, whatever figure
comes to mind.

His last letter said, "When I write to you I feel like I'm writing to
someone I don't know."

Well, he's right. We are strangers. All we have in common is we're both
victims of the same DNA donor.

* * * *

On the other hand, after I won the lottery I started getting phone
calls from local political players. All of a sudden I was invited to meet
President Bill Clinton, Senator Joseph Lieberman, and told that Vice
President Al Gore was coming to Austin. The Democratic Party got all
over me. I went to several fundraisers and hung around affluent people. I gave $10,000 to Al Gore's whatever fundraiser and another
$5,000 to Lieberman or some committee. Before you know it, through
the year 2000 and into early 2001 I'd given $20-25,000 to the
Democratic Party.

By then I'd met seven or eight U. S. Senators in Austin. I'd met Tom
Daschle, Dick Gephardt, Lieberman, Gore and Clinton. I'd escorted Eddie
Bernice Johnson, the Congresswoman from Dallas, to the White House on
three occasions, including a Christmas party. A long time friend and supporter, she'd taken me there twice before I won the lottery. I met Tony

Blair at the White House. I had pictures taken with President Clinton. And I'd given them my money.

About this time I heard from a guy named Mickey who I met in Las Vegas in 1976. Mickey sold drugs, cocaine and huge amounts of marijuana, and he'd done it for years. I was at his home once and went to the bathroom. His bathtub overflowed with money. There wasn't room for another dollar bill.

"How much is in there?" I asked him.

"About $2 million," he said.

When Mickey got busted in the mid-80s I was sure he was guilty. He got 40 years for conspiracy to deliver. They didn't find any drugs or weapons and there was no violence. Still, it's a bad thing to be a drug dealer. No doubt about that.

But now he was 65 years old and had already spent 18 years in a federal prison. If nothing happened he wouldn't be released until he was 83. He told me all of his co-conspirators were out of prison. They plea-bargained and took lesser sentences. He accepted a trial, everyone testified against him and he got more time than they did. He said he had never hurt anyone, which of course wasn't true because if you sell drugs you hurt someone.

He was guilty of selling dope. I'm not justifying or forgiving that. But how much time is enough time on a conspiracy charge?

I thought, since I've given all this money to the Democratic Party, maybe I can get him a pardon. I started writing letters. I wrote Clinton, Gore, Lieberman and everyone I met around town. I made it clear I wasn't looking for favors, but just wanted to be heard on the possibility that someone would read about this guy and go, yeah, if the President commuted his sentence and gave him an earlier release date that would be as good as a pardon.

I was disappointed by the response from each of the people I gave money to and the political party that I'd supported. I wrote nine specific letters and got back nine Dear Johns. Sorry, I live in another state, I can't interfere, I can't lobby for, and I can't make a phone call to help your friend. I wrote many other letters to President Clinton right before he left office and was compiling a list of pardons. Mickey's name wasn't on that list.

It was disappointing to me because I had a chance to lobby for someone other than myself. I only did it because I thought the guy deserved it. I didn't do it because I wanted a political favor. I believed the guy deserved a break. The feds just gave him too much damn time. It reminded me of when I went to court in 2002 to testify on behalf of a kid charged with possession of crack cocaine and a semi-automatic weapon. The kid was 20 years old and they gave him 210 months in federal prison. Pull out your calculator factor 12 into 210 you get about 17 1/2 years.

There is always a lesson. So what did I learn? Did I learn there is no quid pro quo? Maybe. I'll continue to contribute to the Democratic Party because I'm a Democrat, maybe an independent, a moderate or a liberal. It depends on what day it is. I even like to listen to Rush Limbaugh. He entertains me and makes me think. He also nauseates me.

There obviously is a quid pro quo in politics. President Bush raised about $200 million to run an election campaign. If you don't think that $200 million was part quid pro quo you're out of your damn mind. I just don't know how it works and as a matter of fact don't want to know how it works

I don't like government contracts. I don't like government money. I've never tried to get city government tax abatements and all that. It feels like dirty money to me. I know people who do that for a living and I find it sacrilegious. I think it's dirty money to use county, city, state or federal funds for self-profit. I find that vulgar. I'll always make my money as an entrepreneur and private citizen with borrowed funds or my own funds.

* * * *

Shortly after I won the lottery I was playing in the Eastside Charity golf tournament that Darrell Royal and I started. Golf carts were lined up forever. Willie Nelson and every songwriter, picker and grinner from "Hee Haw" and "The Grand Ole Opry," was there. People like David Allan Coe and Charley Pride. I'm a closet fan of country music now. When I played for the Cowboys I didn't understand a black guy singing country. Later on I would understand.

Anyway, I was walking around meeting people and everyone was saying, "You lucky dude, you won the lottery! I can't believe it." I was shaking hands until my hands were sore, and I was grinning.

As I walked around Jim Bob Moffett grabbed me from behind and said, "Hey, big fella." Moffett is a great friend of Royal's, and played football for him at The University of Texas. He's a multi-multi-millionaire CEO of Freeport Macmaran, a mining company and one of the key sponsors of the Eastside Charity tournament. I think he put up the first $500,000 to give away to the east side community.

"Congratulations on winning the lottery," Moffett said. "You know that money can be a curse."

I looked at him and thought, "What are you trying to do...rain on my parade?

I said that to myself since there were so many other people around us. I popped back and said, "Oh, no. I've already been cursed. This is a blessing."

But as time passed and I was confronted with family, friends, loan requests, silly business ideas and crying, whining, begging, people kissing my feet and wanting money from me, I understood. Now I know what Moffett meant, that it could be a curse because everyone knows you have money. Everyone knows you have the reputation of being charitable.

Then you have to stare. I've had to stare into the eyes of poverty in my own family: drug addiction, unemployment, hard luck, alcoholism, family members and friends who just don't work, don't want to work, aren't going to work. I've had to say, "No," and that was painful. I've had to say, "Yes." and that was painful because I knew I was enabling a family member or friend to stay the way they were. So the curse and the burden of the curse came true. Oh, well!

* * * *

All my newfound friends remind me of the night my first wife and I were lounging by the fire. She had on her fur coat and diamonds. I was stretched out on the floor, playing the big shot and saturated with my celebrity. I looked at her and said, "Honey, if I lost everything and was broke and homeless would you still love me?"

"Love you?" she said. "Oh, I will always love you. But I will miss you."

7

FRED "Birdie" FERRIELL
(Friend)

I didn't start drinking until I was 18 months old. I learned that bit of trivia the first Mother's Day I got out of drug and alcohol rehabilitation. I had called my mother to wish her a happy day and she began to cry, saying that she might have contributed to my becoming an alcoholic. That was the fact she gave me beer to sip when I was young.

I told her I remembered that I must have been five or six years old. She said you were 18 months old, and loved it and couldn't get enough, and we thought it was funny.

I guess the first time I was drunk I was 17 and got arrested. That was my story for the next 35 years or so. I became a daily drinker when I was probably 18 or 19 years old and soon became a binge drinker.

I was in my family's construction business, then went into nightclubs and overseas for jobs, and finally into partnership with a friend in a casino. Over this period I was married and divorced four times to four wonderful people. I put them through tremendous pain the whole time. I later spoke to those I could in every relationship that started and ended with drugs and alcohol because my behavior was the result of it.

Finally, I received a letter from my brother after I had played in a golf tournament with him and his friends. He wrote how embarrassed they were at my behavior. I was vulgar. I was inconsiderate. I was rude and incoherent. They asked me to get help and on that basis I thought I would try.

I flew to a treatment facility and heard a tape that described 16 symptoms of alcoholism. I had 15 for years that I could agree to immediately. The only one that I couldn't was because of my interpretation. So that's 16 out of 16. I finished treatment and got a sponsor.

I met Thomas in Dallas through my sponsor. Thomas was the keynote speaker before about 800 people. I was completely impressed. My sponsor planned to go to a conference where Thomas again was the main speaker and asked me to go with him. At that time Thomas was seven years sober and I was seven months.

We hit it off immediately, and the day of his speech we decided to play golf. He relieved me of a couple of thistles on the golf course. We played the next day and I won them back, and it's been that way ever since.

We stayed in phone contact and began visiting each other regularly. I have a son and daughter. He knows us very well as I do him through our shared interest in 12-step programs. This was how I learned that Thomas was always helping others and never too busy to talk to someone who needed it.

Both of us wound up supporting a treatment center in Dallas. Thomas helped get it started and was working to fund it. They brought in Willie Nelson and B. J. Thomas for concerts to help raise money. We attended one of those concerts and during the intermission Thomas and my son disappeared. I thought they'd gone to the restroom. Fifteen, 20, 30 minutes pass and my wife and I were getting a little concerned. A few minutes after Willie appeared on stage my son came back.

"Where have you been?" I said.

"Dad, Mr. Henderson took me to see B. J. Then we went on Willie's bus and sat there and talked to him. Dad, it was awesome!"

Thomas used to take me to prisons where he spoke. We went to one facility that was pretty scary to me. All the inmates who were planning to hear Thomas were gathered in a holding area. When Thomas got off the elevator the entire group gave him a standing ovation. Here were guys who were pretty tough and they sat there listening like a class of fourth graders. When it was over he signed matchbook covers, pieces of newspaper, anything they brought. He sat around and talked with them an hour or so afterwards. This happened at least a half-dozen times where I went with him.

I live in Florida and he's come down here at least a dozen times to speak at treatment centers, halfway houses and meetings where I go. He met other people I knew who asked him to come to their place to speak. It was incredible how he always had time to do it.

Thomas continuously helps get people into treatment. It seems like every month someone we know or he knows needs help or asks for it and they can't get in a center. He was able to pull enough strings to get them in.

Thomas called me one day and said, "Birdie, I've won the lottery!" I thought he was kidding. I guess a lot of people did until it was all over the news and his telephone began to ring. A few days later, he called and said, "Can I come and stay with you for a while? I'm trying to get away from the telephone because it's driving me nuts."

He came and we sat on the patio where he told me what he had done with some of the lottery money. He said the first thing he did was take care of his brothers, sisters, nephews and everyone in the family. He'd given each a sizeable gift. He told me he'd helped his mom get a new car, a truck for his stepfather, and this and that. When he finished telling me all these things he was actually saying, "Did I do enough? Was this what I should have done?"

I said, "Thomas, it sounds to me that you have done more than enough. I don't know how anyone can say you haven't."

"Okay," he said, "I am through with that. Now what can I do for you?"

I can't tell you how deeply that touched me.

"Thomas," I said, "I appreciate that more than you can ever know, but just being my best friend is more than enough."

Ever since he's still my best friend. I hope that continues for years to come.

HOME AGAIN IN EAST AUSTIN

After I won the lottery real estate agents and brokers advised me to buy a bigger house, naturally thinking only of my personal comfort and not their commission. At the time I lived on the west side of Austin in a beautiful three-story condominium with a private elevator. Most people thought Thomas Henderson was struggling but I was living in a $350,000 condo in an affluent neighborhood called Clarksville.

Shortly after I won the lottery I sold the condominium and moved back to the east Austin community where I grew up. My family didn't believe that I would move back to within a quarter mile of my original house. At times, I didn't believe it either, but it seemed right to complete the circle.

I could live in Trump Plaza on Fifth Avenue in New York or a highrise in Los Angeles, Beverly Hills or Bellaire. I can live anywhere in America. But I think Dorothy said it best in The Wizard of Oz: There is no place like home.

So I moved into an area with prostitution on the streets, crack sales and arrests and drug stings within a half-mile of my house. But because I am a black man who was raised in east Austin I tend to know these people. I know their hopes and dreams.

I'm not a segregationist. I'm not a racist. Never have been and never will be. But as a black man who walked the yards of a penitentiary for 28 months and who ran these streets doing fun felonies as a juvenile delinquent, I am not afraid of my environment. Maybe not being afraid is part of my own mental illness.

I bought a little house for $38,000 on a 50 X 214-foot lot and went to work on it. It was the Thomas Henderson homestead. I built a 1,000-square foot house and furnished it nicely but not elaborately. I have a parking area and a garage apartment to the rear with a gym underneath. I have a 1,000-square-foot swimming pool with a Jacuzzi. I have palm trees and great landscaping and a seven-foot-high fence around the perimeter. I have a gate with my initials on it that opens automatically.

I could have moved to suburbia. I could have bought a $1-2 million house. But why and for whom? After you live in a six-by-eight prison cell you don't need much room.

As I drove around reacquainting myself with friends, neighbors and people I grew up with, I saw the same obvious drug dealers and users. Guys I knew from elementary and junior high school. I knew where they were and what they did. Over the years they figured out that Thomas doesn't do that anymore. I have earned a certain respect from the professional drug community, those guys who are on the street when they're awake.

That used to be one of my bleak jokes: "When am I on the street? Only when I'm awake."

When my addiction was at its worse someone once asked me how often did I get high. I said, "When I'm awake." And frankly I think I was loaded when I was asleep.

So even though I live in a high-crime area, no one has ever bothered me. Everyone knows where I live. I was sitting on my porch one day sorting out my mail. A young gang-banger walked by. He was a Crip, a gang member. His pants were hanging down behind his knees.

"How are you doing, Mr. Henderson?" he said.

That greeting alone was absolute respect from a knucklehead.

"You live here, Mr. Henderson?"

"Yes, I do."

"Man, you keepin' it real, ain't you."

What he meant by keeping it real was that I didn't move to the suburbia. I didn't leave my community. I'd also built a track and football stadium a half-mile from my house. I just...came home. My people would have expected me to flee. They would have expected me to be afraid, and acting Caucasian and getting away from the area. But I've done the opposite. I'm buying lots around my home. I'm even thinking about putting in a sand trap and putting green next door – in the 'hood.

I could live on a mountain in Aspen, but I choose to be a half-mile from my mother. "Keeping it real." is a good line. I'm keeping it real because it keeps me balanced and gives me stability. A lot of times in my life I was pretending to be okay. After recovery and heartache, failure and disappointment, I said I wasn't going to pretend anymore. So by living in a black neighborhood in east Austin, Texas, I'm keeping it real.

But let's say, for imaginations sake, the independent Thomas Henderson needed help. I'd want the comfort of knowing that someone was looking for me.

That reminds me of the story of two guys on a cruise ship. The ship went down at sea. These guys were the only survivors. They floated in the ocean for days and ended up on a deserted island. One guy walked onto the beach, sat under a palm tree and began eating a coconut. He just sat there in the shade.

The other guy went to work. He found leaves and debris and made a big HELP sign on the beach. He ran around looking for flint rocks to start a fire. He went further down the beach and drew HELP – COME GET US in the sand. He finally realized he was doing all this by himself. His buddy was hanging out in the shade eating a coconut.

"Why aren't you helping me?" he said.

"Listen to me carefully," his buddy replied. "I tithe. I make $2 million a year. I give my church $200,000 annually and I've been doing it for years."

"What the hell does that have to with us being on this damn island needing to get home?"

"My preacher will find me. He's on the way."

I hope that in my time of need someone will be on the way to find me.

"The hardest thing about having wealth in the midst of poverty and struggle in your immediate family and friends is their impression of entitlement of use of your assets. What I've learned by trial and error is that saying yes and no about money can be both joyeous and painful." TH

VEANA CLAY
(Former secretary)

I started working for Thomas when I was a junior in college and spent two years as a secretary in his office. On my first day he handed me his autobiography and said I must read the book. It was a requirement for working for him.

I didn't know his history or have any contact with things that had gone on. I didn't consider those things when I went to work for him. To me, he was just a man who owned a business, and I was going to help him out. I read the book, but no, it didn't make me hesitate to take the job. I try very hard not to judge a person and to let them show me, as my mom would say, "what type fruit the tree bears." After working for him, it didn't take long.

Thomas was open about his background. I think once people got to know him, his past became just that. They see he had turned things around and done better at it than most who didn't have those issues in their background.

I got to know Thomas as a person, as a human being, and I saw how giving and loving he was because he provides. He is a provider. When I worked for him, he had people on his payroll that probably shouldn't have been there. He was a philanthropist with a capital "P." That was one of the main things I took away from my experience with him, learning how to give.

He taught me a distinction about how to give. I remember when two elderly ladies came to the office. They were from a church, all dressed in white and asked for money. I'm a soft, heart-on-the-sleeve person. I wanted them to get the money. These women were praying, they were crying, they said they were desperately in need. I don't think Thomas was able to help them that time.

Afterwards, he asked me whether or not I thought he should have given them money. I said, yes.

He gave me a talk about giving. It was about judgment. About having clear decision-making. You have to understand that in giving you can't give everything to everyone. You have to use discriminating factors. And you can't feel bad about it.

That is something I feel I'm going to use quite often if I haven't already. It was little things like that. Every so often I'd go into his office and we'd talk 15 or 20 minutes about life in general. It wasn't anything specific where he sat down and said, "Veana, in life, such and such..."

First of all, it was Thomas just making himself available. And him telling me his experiences, what happened during his day and how he handled it. Mainly, it was just talking and learning from what he was doing. Those talks helped me grow up. They helped me mature in lots of ways.

I would come home and tell my father about some of the advice Thomas had given me. All the ways he'd helped me, helped his family and his extended family, and the entire Austin community. Thomas took risks. He goes the extra mile.

I also learned business sense from Thomas. He was a direct, straightforward communicator. That was something I picked up and it helped me while I finished college and went to law school. I think about it all the time now that I've started interviewing for jobs. Whenever Thomas talked to anyone he said exactly what was on his mind. He kept conversation very simple in that respect.

He has a big, big heart. He's compassionate and understanding, but business-first. He has arranged things in his life to where he can use his business and other great qualities to help people. Thomas was especially aware of the disadvantaged who didn't have the opportunities that he did.

I was studying microbiology before I decided to go to law school. That's when I moved to Chicago and enrolled in the Chicago-Kent College of Law. Thomas won the lottery just before I left and he gave me a token of his appreciation. I graduated from law school two weeks ago and without his help, I couldn't have done it.

I was one of those who received a $10,000 check. He gave it to me during a relaxed atmosphere in the office. He just laid the check on my desk and said, "Here you are, Veana. Use it wisely."

There was no way I could have moved here and started my courses without it. I think highly of Thomas. He has acted paternal toward me.

CHAPTER TWENTY

SUPERBOWLS

I was lucky to play in three Superbowls. Superbowls X, XII, and XIII. The Dallas Cowboys won Superbowl XII and I was on that team.

In 1975 we were just lucky to be there in Superbowl X. Drew Pearson's Hail Mary catch from Roger Staubach got us there. We had twelve rookies on that team nicknamed the dirty dozen. We were not a good team yet and did not have Tony Dorsett. We competed well against the Steelers but clearly were not that good overall.

In 1977 in New Orleans in Superbowl XII we were in my mind the best football team ever. Both offensively and defensively we were over everyone else's head. We won 27 to 10. We would have beaten anybody that day.

In Superbowl XIII against the Steelers we were the better team. When you look back at all the breaks in that game the Steelers got them all. The pass interference against Benny Barnes on Lynn Swan, bad call. Randy White fumbling the ball helped the Steelers. Charlie Waters running into the official against the Franco Harris touchdown trap play benefited the Steelers. Jackie Smith dropping the touchdown passes favored the Steelers. Luck plays a part in any football game. But the Steelers got every break thinkable.

It is a shame that the Steelers seem to get all the Hall of Fame induction's for that period. Players like Drew Pearson, Leroy Jordan, Ray Fieldwright, Ed Too Tall Jones, Harvey Martin, Cliff Harris, Charlie Waters and even Jethro Pugh have been overlooked and passed up because the Steelers won Superbowl XIII. These guys were great players. Some say it was the greatest Superbowl of all time. I agree, but as a participant who was there on the field. The Dallas Cowboys would have won that game nine out of ten times. We were just better.

I started going to Superbowls as a spectator in the early nineties when I began some consulting work for Dan Reeves and the Denver Broncos. Dan had asked me to work with Clarence Day who was having some substance abuse issues. I was able to attend two Superbowls with them of which Denver lost both. On my own I made plans to go to Arizona when the Cowboys and Steelers third match was had in a Superbowl. We finally kicked their ass. The NFL provided me with four tickets on the fitly-yard line at face value. I felt good about how they treated me.

My Superbowl experiences since then have been adventures in reality to say the least. The NFL sponsors a golf tournament and I have been lucky and famous enough to get an invitation to every year. They provide a free hotel room for four days, a party, and a few meals. They do not provide tickets to the game nor do they buy airline tickets. A room for four days in a Superbowl city is a big deal. If you want to go to the game you are on your own. I have always found a way to get at least two tickets to the game. At least twice I have been able to get them from the NFL League Office. There have also been times when they have turned down my request. There is also the gigantic Commissioners party. These tickets are as hard to get as Superbowl seats. When the League Office would not give me two tickets to the Commissioners Party I got mad. They invite thousands of people to this party. Why can't a former Superbowl champion get tickets I wondered. Don't they want former players to be there to help with the atmosphere? I remember in Arizona when I was at the Commissioner party there was a section of the party closed off to the public. There was police and security at its entrance. I wandered over close enough to see it was for NFL owners and executives from the League. I noticed Charlie Jackson. Charlie used to head NFL security when I was a player. I eased close to the entrance so I could say hello to a few of the people I knew. Charlie saw me and shook his finger at me, sort of saying with his finger no, no, no you can't come in here. It still puzzles me that former Superbowl Champs can't get tickets to the game or the Commissioners party. I guess I need to understand rather than be understood.

I attended the Tampa Bay vs. Raiders Superbowl in San Diego most recently. My adopted son, Marcus Wilkins, is a linebacker with the Green

Bay Packers. Every current NFL player gets the option to buy at face value two tickets to the Superbowl. Because of our relationship Marcus gave me his two tickets for that game. The only problem with the tickets is they were not good seats. These tickets were at the very top of the stadium so you'd need binoculars and an oxygen tank to watch the game. I had to find a way to better my seats. My worst fear is to be in the worst seats at a Superbowl wearing my three Superbowl rings and have people sitting around me say something like "you played in three Superbowls, you won a Superbowl, your wearing your Superbowl rings and this is the best seat you could get?" You see my ego cannot handle that conversation. I called a ticket broker and to my girlfriend Linda's surprise I traded my two bad tickets for two good tickets on the 40-yard line. Her shock was that the trade cost me an additional three thousand dollars. I won the lottery and I believe that my pride and good seats were worth $3,000.

The day was perfect and the game was outstanding. Tampa Bay flat kicked the Raiders ass. I did not care who won. I just enjoyed the game. I learned a long time ago that when you go to the Superbowl do not pull for a team. If your team loses you have a bad day. I did that with the Broncos in the nineties and missed the Phil Simms super passing performance. I was so sad at all those completions he made that I could not appreciate what I was actually seeing.

I use to bet on football too. I lost a lot of money one weekend in the early nineties and I quit. Smoking crack and betting on football are on the same page now. Just because I played the game doesn't mean I can pick winners. My impression of the Superbowl as a player and fan is that it is just a game. Take away all the hype and publicity and its just another football game. There is nothing super about it.

BEASLEY REECE
(Former Cowboys teammate)

I didn't believe the stories of personal destruction that I heard about Thomas Henderson and Lawrence Taylor of the New York Giants. It wasn't that I doubted that either could self-destruct. Hell, both of them did, but both came out of it. I just never thought either of my former teammates would fall as far as he fell.

Yet I still didn't believe they would lose. I'm 49 years old and I see life as if there has to be a winner and loser in everything I do. So I could never imagine Thomas being a loser. The same went for L. T. Those personalities were too powerful, their confidence too great, their aura too champion-like.

They were THE alpha male in a group of alpha males. I couldn't imagine those guys not leading the pack again.

I'm like a preacher who preaches the word of Henderson. I still run across people who are skeptical about him. In Philadelphia, where I'm sports director for CBS affiliate KYW and a sideline reporter for CBS Sports, I might see someone and say, "My buddy Hollywood is coming up. You might remember him."

And they'll say, "Oh, yeah, I remember him...." And then say something negative. That's when I jump in and say, "You don't know this guy. He's turned his life around."

I tell people he's clean and sober for, let's say, 17 years and so many months. When I'm around him enough I know the exact date. I say he built a football field for kids in his hometown. He has such a feeling of responsibility for kids in his depressed neighborhood that he lives there. He built a house in the lower income area from where he sprang as a youth.

When he won the lottery I told him to buy one of those $2 million houses in Barton Creek. He listened, but his ultimate decision was that he felt kids who knew him as an example needed to see him in their part of town.

Thomas knows how his life works sober. His life doesn't work drinking and doing drugs. Here's something else about him that truly impressed me. When he was in prison he read books, novels and periodicals and can tell you the total number. I think it was 217.

I was never around Thomas during his cocaine craziness. I spent my rookie year in 1976 with the Cowboys before going to the Giants for the next seven seasons. Thomas had been drafted a year earlier and had a level of confidence about who he was and his abilities that I've never seen in another player. And I played with L. T. and some of the greatest players in the game.

Thomas walked and talked with a swagger. He was brash, cocky, loud and boastful. To him, it was his team. Dallas was his city. Pro football was his playground. That was his attitude, and it was very attractive to me.

I immediately gravitated to Thomas. He was extremely handsome and fit. His body was like something you'd ask an artist to render. He was doing things that no one who played his position had ever done – return kickoffs, cover punts and sprinters split out wide. He had a diversity of athletic gifts that I'd never seen before. I don't think the NFL had, either.

He drove the nicest cars. He wore custom clothes. He took me to the finest clubs in Dallas. It was an incredible time. If he was using drugs then he'll have to tell you because I didn't know it. He might have smoked marijuana now and then. What I remember was beer, women and song. HH

I saw him being one of the most popular athletes in the country. He did a Bob Hope Special. Hope introduced him as "Hollywood." For someone like me, from Waco, Texas, it literally blew my mind to see a guy in such control of his environment.

That was Thomas of 1976, and the start of a friendship that never wavered in my heart, although once I left the Cowboys we didn't stay in touch. I don't think I said two words to Thomas after I left to join the Giants and he went to jail. Then we got back together about 15 years ago.

Thomas is fun to be around. He is totally in control and I can't say that about all the people in my life. I have so much respect for the road he's traveled because in my 49 years of observation, the most difficult thing to do is affect a personal change. I don't care if it's losing weight, stop drinking, quit smoking or doing drugs. To correct a character flaw and affect a personal change in your life seems to be the greatest challenge.

If I had to make a speech on behalf of Thomas I would say you could trust him. You couldn't have a better friend. You could believe what he says. I hear lots of people make speeches. I hear lots of sermons. As time goes on, you realize that people are not what they report themselves to be.

I think I have a tape of every film Thomas made, and I periodically pop one in the VCR for several reasons. Number one, because I read uplifting, motivational stories that tell me how someone got from point A to point B. Number two, is to hear one of the great public speakers in American today. His tapes have been a real inspiration in my life. And my kids have seen every tape Thomas sent me.

NFL REUNION

Somewhere around June of 2000, a few months after I won the lottery, I got a phone call from the National Football League headquarters in New York. I hadn't had any contact with anyone there since 1981 or 1982. That amounted to 19 years of dead silence, and I know why.

I went to prison for sexual assault and I was a drug addict. I wasn't the image the NFL wanted to portray to the public. So there it is. Right there I had to understand rather than be understood. But it was still sad for me not to have had any contact or relationship with the NFL. I've never been mad at the League. I've been mad at me for fouling up the possibilities of a relationship.

After talking with my sponsor at 12-step meetings, I came to understand their view. I had been a wild man who had caused the NFL a lot of image problems. I'd also once tried to extort money from Gil Brandt, head of the Cowboys scouting department, threatening to blow the lid off drug use on the team if I wasn't paid $30,000.

Good thing they never knew what was on my mind before we kicked off against Pittsburgh in Super Bowl X. Here I was from the ghetto, it was my rookie season, and playing for Tom Landry and the Cowboys is fun. The country was 200 years old, so this was the bicentennial Super Bowl and I was captain of the specialty teams. In fact, I ran back the opening kickoff and nearly broke it for a touchdown.

Before that, I was in the middle of the field with the rest of the captains – Terry Bradshaw, Mean Joe Greene and Roger Staubach – for the coin flip. The official had a gold coin with George Washington on it, a beautiful thick piece that had to weigh two or three ounces. I'm from east Austin, so you know what I'm thinking at this moment? I want to steal that coin.

Anyway, my reputation as a model of recovery had grown over many years before the NFL made contact. When he coached the Denver Broncos, Dan Reeves called and asked me to help one of his players stay clean and sober during the playoffs. I agreed and traveled with the team, feeling once again what it was like to be in the game. I did my job; my player stayed out of trouble and played well. Yet I learned that all was not forgotten. The NFL, having seen me on the bench area during a playoff game, told the Broncos they didn't want me to appear on the sidelines at the Super Bowl. I accepted their decision and watched the game from the stands.

I'm convinced the phone call in June of 2000 was related to preseason talks I had given over the past few years to six NFL teams. Head coaches had invited me to speak to their players about how to avoid the temptations that come with NFL celebrity. I was an expert on that subject.

Contact came from a secretary involved with the annual Rookie Symposium, an orientation for all the new draft choices. The rookies learn about what to expect from life as a professional. The NFL even hires people to do skits to simulate domestic violence, interacting with police, and the type of characters the players should avoid. Former players also are invited to share their experiences.

That was why they called me, although I think winning the lottery had a lot to do with it. Not only did I have a story to tell, now I was news. I was told that Mr. Dan Rooney, chairman of the Pittsburgh Steelers, had insisted I be a speaker at the symposium. The Steelers were one of the teams I had addressed, and I guess whatever I said impressed Mr. Rooney. I didn't realize how significant his endorsement was until moments before I went on stage to give my talk.

I flew to San Diego in mid-July of 2000. Of course, there was no fee involved. I didn't even ask about a fee. It was such an honor and privilege I forgot to ask. I have two prices when I do speeches: zero and my fee. I didn't look at the NFL as a charity cause. I went because it was a privilege to get the call.

The set-up was grand, an impressive stage with rookies seated in the audience in big high-backed chairs. Irving Fryar, a former wide receiver who played mostly for New England, was the speaker to follow me-a position I don't wish on anybody. I was backstage mingling with people before I went on when I met Harold Henderson, an NFL executive. He's an African American and to my understanding went to an Ivy League school.

"Hello, how are you, Henderson? Nice to meet you," I said.

I'm not sure how the conversation got around to my invitation. But this man said to me, and I admire people with balls, "You know, if it was left to me you wouldn't be here speaking." He didn't know it, but he was lucky that I was in recovery and can handle judgment and criticism. There was a time when I would have slapped him.

This Harold Henderson walked out on stage and introduced me. There was a brief highlight film of me when I played for the Cowboys. I began my presentation by displaying a board I had brought that had these words: REGRETS ARE AVOIDABLE. That was the title of my talk. I went from domestic violence to drug use to getting caught smoking marijuana, all the things that present you with the choice of an avoidable regret. Getting caught means you can lose your career, money and family.

I got the rookies laughing. I got them thinking. I was on a roll. After 35 minutes my microphone was cut off. I looked to the side and here came Harold Henderson. From the feedback I got later, the rookies were on the edge of their seats. They were involved. They wanted more. No one was looking at his watch. I looked at Henderson, and while I wondered whether there was a technical difficulty he took the mike out of my hand. I guess he told somebody backstage to throw the power back up because when he got the microphone he said, "Mr. Henderson's time is up. The program has to continue on schedule."

The rookies booed the hell out of him. They booed him and gave me a standing ovation that didn't stop for a couple of minutes. Poor Irving Fryar had to follow that.

Mr. Harold Henderson was in control of the NFL Rookie Symposium. The summers of 2001, 2002 and 2003 are gone, and I have not been invited back. I'm satisfied with the feedback from rookies and representatives of NFL teams who met me outside after the program ended. They said my lecture was the best they ever heard on the subject, and they couldn't understand why the guy turned my mike off.

It was still a wonderful experience for me. I just thought it was too bad that personality overrode principle. Based on experience, I'm probably one of the best sources to educate rookies on the dangers they will face on and off the field in the NFL. But I always return to the fact that Harold Henderson doesn't like Thomas Henderson, and that is fine with me. It's none of my business what anyone thinks of me. It's what I think about me that's important.

GRATITUDE

The last time I'd been at Texas Stadium, five years earlier, I was pathetic and loaded on my ass drunk. I was a has-been looking to see if anyone recognized me. If they didn't, I'd stare at them until they did. Done as a football player, damn near done as a human being. Nobody wanted anything to do with me... not even me

Now I was back and that in its entirety was remarkable. But what made it even more wonderful was that the Dallas Cowboys had invited me back. The five years might as well have been fifty for all the change that had gone on inside me. I was a new man with a new view of the world. A sober man. And now I was standing in the tunnel, right at the edge, the great unknown just a few steps away. It was my turn next.

I glimpsed outside. I could see a sliver of Texas sky through the roof of Texas Stadium. This green turf is where I'd run, jumped, hit and flown in the air. I could hear the fans, tens of thousands of them, exploding in bursts of cheers. I looked around at the dark, drafty corridor where we were waiting. Not much of a spot really. But as I stood there pulse racing, it looked pretty damn nice to me. This was hard to believe. But hell, there's a lot of shit in my recovery I didn't believe. No one else believed it either. I was wearing my old jersey, number 56. I was listening to all those folks who used to roar when I knocked Earl Campbell on his ass or when I made an unbelievable interception. I was surrounded by a Who's Who from American's team, and from my own past: Roger Staubach, Drew Pearson, Charlie Waters, Jethro Pugh, Rayfield Wright and a bunch of others. My heart was flip-flopping! Goose bumps were popping! I just kept thinking, "Man, I'm back. I'm finally back."

This was December 1987. It had been fourteen months since I left prison, eight years since Tom Landry called me in and told me I was fired. On that previous visit when I went down to the locker room to see the guys on the team, two security guards stopped me at the door. "You can't go in there," the guard said. I almost punched him and made a scene. "Why not?" The Cowboys were like a family. I was stunned. Can't go in there? "I'm under orders. You're not welcome here." That said it all. As I stood there angry and embarrassed, a couple of my former teammates were permitted to enter. It was pretty clear this policy was for me. Thanks,

Gil Brandt. The Dallas Cowboys didn't want me around. Didn't want me close. Not many people did.

The game I was now being invited back for was a team reunion. They were having them every year. If you'd asked, I would've told you no way would I ever be invited back for anything. Ever. They've got the ring of honor at Texas Stadium with inductees like Staubach, Lily, Howley, etc. I thought the only time they'd ever ask me back would be for my induction into the ring of dishonor. Once, I had been an all-Pro and Super Bowl hero for the Cowboys. I also had been a definite linebacker non-grata. I was a pain in Tom Landry's ass and Tex Schram's ass and the entire organization's ass.

I was brash and I had a big mouth and there wasn't a soul I wouldn't confront. I was a raving alcoholic and cocaine addict. I would say anything to anybody. I set records for profanity every time I opened my mouth. For the longest time, I thought 'mother' was half a word. I would make up my own rules for when I would come and go, what I would and wouldn't do. Damn the Cowboys. Damn the consequences. No surprise I ended up where I did. God help you if you crossed me. I wasn't just full of myself; I was overflowing with pure dysfunctional shit. I was angry and alienated and even though I didn't see it then, I was very sick and out of control.

As time passed, my addictions only got worse. I was under foreign management. I snorted cocaine in team meetings and on the field. Before long, it was the only thing in my life. I lost my job, my wealth, my home, my marriage, and the person I loved most in the world, my daughter, Thomesa. And then, I lost my freedom. Self respect? None available. Self esteem? Not a trace. By the time my drinking and using days were done, I had no home and no hope, and no reason to think this was a pit I would ever climb out of.

I'm glad I found the faith and hope I needed to survive my addictions. Getting sober has taken more courage and faith, more perseverance and commitment than anything I've ever done. With a lot of help and support, I have been able to do it. I'm sober and damn proud of it. My life is simple today because I don't get my needs and wants confused. All my needs are being tended to. My wants are wanting. I travel a lot, because my work these days is lecturing to and sharing with as many people as I can about the wonderment of recovery and change. My life is fulfilled and committed. It has a purpose and it is full of gifts, and one of them was being back at Texas Stadium that day in 1987. I had been bad and I knew it. That's growth.

I was in the tunnel and I was honoring my feelings. I was happy and free. One by one, the former players are being announced: Bob Lilly; Rayfield Wright; D.D. Lewis; Mel Renfro; Each got a long, loud ovation. Now it was my turn. Fear and joy coursed through me in waves. How would people react?

Would I get a standing "boo-vation"? Would they yell crap at me, throw things at me, call me names and tell me to go back to jail or go stick something up my nose? Just how ugly will this be? I couldn't wait. Had to do a little straw poll. I edged toward the field, poked my head out the tunnel just far enough so I could see a few fans. Like sticking your toe in the water to check the temperature. My body tightened.

I took two steps outside and looked up. A whole section started cheering. "Hey, Hollywood!" "Hey, number 56!" I stepped back in. I took a breath, a big one. I was ready. The announcer snapped my attention. The voice boomed through the stadium. I heard: "Ladies and Gentlemen... here he is... he's back... Thomas Hollywood Henderson!" I began walking onto the field through two lines of Cowboys cheerleaders, the wholesome girls of Texas. I could see some people standing. People were cheering. I kept walking, feeling almost numb. They were going nuts. I covered the field to where the other guys were.

I looked up into the stands. They seemed to reach the sky. My ears and heart had never heard or felt it like this. They were cheering, not booing! They were cheering my recovery! And then I lost it. Tears began pouring down my cheeks as gratitude overwhelmed me. The old linebacker was putty.

It was one of the most profound moments in my life. Just to be back. Just to feel this heartfelt acceptance, this warm embrace, after all I'd said and done. I looked up again and a new wave of tears came. "This is beautiful," I said to myself. "This is a gift of sobriety."

The reason this day was possible was because of the programs I had been lucky enough to find and adhere to. I go to 12-step support group meetings regularly. I wouldn't be sober without them. I believe the process of recovery is taken lightly and clearly misunderstood by some. Many don't recognize it as a process at all. I was one of those people who thought a 30-day or 60-day stay at a treatment center would fix all my problems.

My approach to recovery was straightforward: I stop doing cocaine, the trouble ends. You hack your way through withdrawal, rid yourself of the physical cravings, the deal is done and I go on with my life, no muss, no fuss. I had to lose this attitude and approach because my old way of thinking had all but killed me.

In 1981, when I entered my first treatment center for my addictions in Scottsdale, Arizona, I diagnosed my problems myself. I truly believed my only problem was cocaine! I told a doctor that marijuana only gave me the munchies. I went on to explain and minimize my alcohol use.

This is clearly how one develops a hidden agenda early in their recovery or treatment. I believe if you're addicted to any one thing, you're probably addicted to everything, or capable of it.

Recovery is not simple and clear-cut. If only it were that easy. The truth of the matter is that if an asshole stops drinking and does nothing more, all you've got is a sober asshole. In order to become a better human being, one has to work on changing. If you don't, nothing will change except the date. Getting sober is a day-by-day journey, a gradual unfolding of a healthier way of living. You can't be cured of alcoholism or drug addiction. Once you have it, you have it for life. I'm glad I believe that. Many don't and many die.

I'm still an alcoholic, addict, etc. The disease is there, but it's in remission because I'm in constant treatment. Drugs and alcohol kept me screwed up and dysfunctional for a long time. You feel you don't know anything different, so why change. Those of us who abuse drugs, alcohol, food, sex and other substances have something fundamentally wrong with us. The trick and the miracle is to find out what's really wrong. I'd felt defective, ashamed, and abandoned all my life. Plus, I liked dope. So, my ass was out from the beginning. Dope and alcohol worked for me for a while. As fears, doubts, and hurts cruised the corridors of my dysfunctional head, a toot, a smoke, a drink, or a pill would quiet that turmoil within. The turmoil does get quieted. But what a price. What a fucking price! When you have the disease that I have, you get addicted to escape and you can't stop, and even in the face of overwhelming evidence that it's wrecking your life, your now sick body and mind keep craving the chemicals. "Just one more, just one more, just one more." I've lived with this shit, and it's miserable. It's the sickest place I've ever been.

Misery is a mother fucker. I believe misery is the sum total of my feelings if I don't deal with them. Whether it's anger, fear, drug abuse, abandonment, sexual abuse or just feeling less than nothing, these thoughts all bottled up inside an addicted person spell M-I-S-E-R-Y. Today if I see somebody in misery, I respond to it by stressing the fact that he or she does not have to take alcohol and drugs in order to cope. It is the man or woman who needs help. The family of origin, inner child and self-esteem issues are what need work. From there, happiness, joy and freedom are near.

Alcohol is legal and socially sanctioned. Parents who would be mortified if they knew their kid was doing cocaine are the same parents who roll out the keg for the graduation party. Alcohol is advertised and glamorized. It's very easy to take alcohol less seriously than other drugs, but it is where I believe it all begins. I drank alcohol long before I knew cocaine existed. I believe drinking alcohol is a liability and can screw up your life. It damn sure screwed up mine. Our society is uninformed and as long as alcohol and drugs aren't looked at equally, nothing will change except the number of victims.

Sobriety is an option. Exercise your option and choice! Don't fuck up like I did. Learn from my life. "Anything is possible in sobriety. Nothing is possible if you use." Those words were quoted to me by my doctor and friend, Joseph Pursch, in 1983. He also said, "You alone can do it, but you can't do it alone." I've run those words through my head a few million times. They have given me something to hold on to. When things felt totally chaotic and fucked up, they gave me hope.

Alcoholism wants all its victims to believe that there is nothing to hold on to. It wants us to say, "fuck it" and give up right now. Forget the fight. Forget about getting better. Let's get high. The disease lies.

Each day that I'm clean and sober, I am continuing to get better. Because of sobriety, I'm blessed and grateful. God saved and changed my life. Because of this Higher Power and recovery, I was able to experience a sober homecoming at Texas Stadium. My gratitude is boundless.

DREW PEARSON
(Former Cowboys teammate)

Forget for a moment everything you've ever heard about Thomas Hollywood Henderson.

Forget about his being a first round draft choice of the Dallas Cowboys and playing in three Superbowls in his first four years in the league.

Forget that he snorted cocaine on the sideline during Superbowl XIII then became the first NFL player to confess his addiction, seek treatment and return to pro football.

Forget his arrest for one count of sexual assault and two counts of false imprisonment and the two years four months in prison that finally get him to sober up. Even forget that he won a $28 million Texas Lottery jackpot on March 22, 2000. The past tells little about the man he is now.

Meet the new Thomas Henderson: philanthropist, lecturer, and entrepreneur. Alcohol and drug free for over 20 years.

"I know how far out there Thomas was, and if he continued to be out there he wouldn't even be alive today", former Cowboys receiver Drew Pearson said. He's turned his life around and he's using the negatives, the adversity the obstacles he had and he's turning them into positives.

"I had a lot of teammates I was proud to say I played with. There was a time that I wasn't proud of Thomas. Now, without hesitation, I'm proud to say that Thomas Henderson is a friend of mine. He's changed and his recovery is real."

Chapter Twenty One

TREATMENT

Best I can remember John Wooten was the first person to mention the word 'treatment' to me. I had never heard that word until the Cowboys scout talked to me about getting help for my problem in 1980. I'd heard of psychiatric hospitals and knew there was a state mental hospital located in Austin. But to me the people in there were crazy.

I had never connected the dots, that my addiction to crack cocaine and alcohol and the behaviors that evolved from them could be construed as insanity. I remember when I made the connection. It occurred during my introduction to treatment in a psychiatric hospital in Scottsdale, Arizona.

I can't recall the complete scenario of how I got to this clinic. I assume some friends who cared had convinced me to seek help. So there it was 1981, and I found myself in a room with seven or eight people for another round of something called group counseling.

Then I began to pay close attention to the others. One woman was a housewife, and while we sat there she kept pulling up her dress. There was an Eskimo, who'd look at me 30-40 times during the meeting with an I'm-nutty-as-hell grin. Another character was a guy who'd see walking the hall of the clinic turning all the doorknobs. I'm sitting with this group, Mr. Big Shot Thomas Henderson. I'm thinking, These people are crazy. They are nuts. Lunatics. Then the realization hit me: I am a member of the group.

So what are they thinking about me? Here is a black guy who thinks that he's a Dallas Cowboy. So we're all crazy!

The reason I share that experience is important, because I disassociated myself from the process. From within my own insanity I judged the process as inappropriate for me. Therefore I sabotaged my education and learning experience. I judged the other patients and never looked at what I had done and why I was in the group. It took me years to realize that while I was sitting there judging them, they were doing the same to me.

I wasn't a good patient as far as staying clean when I got a pass to the outside. At the same time I was bothered by a deflected nasal septum. I had surgery, and in my drug-addicted mind I was sure my nose was fixed. That gave me a false sense of self-control.

When they released me from Scottsdale, prematurely I might add, a friend who had driven my car from Texas met me. He brought some weed. I fired up a joint of high potency. I took a huge drag, blew it through my new nose and let go an addictive cough. Then I said, "I really feel good. I think this program is going to work."

This was early in 1981. From there until mid-'83 was a nightmare. I was 10 minutes out of treatment when I went into free fall relapse for 2 1/2 years.

I never knew the disease of alcoholism existed. I saw alcoholism and drug addiction in the community where I was raised. I saw it in my house. I saw it on the street. I assumed that was what people did and if they did it too much they just died. I never connected that their lives weren't manageable, that their health was in grave danger and there was anything in life having to do with sobriety.

I assumed with the education I received by observing that when you grew up you drank. It was an adult thing to do. It was what grown people did. I never understood that sobriety was an option. I understood that I was going to drink when I became an adult. When I lecture around the country I remind young people that 21 is the legal age to drink. Then I emphasize that it's also the age when they can choose not to drink.

Treatment in America is basic. There is the psychiatric angle and there are psychiatric clinics. There are methadone clinics. Methadone is a drug dispensed to heroin and opiate addicts to ease their craving. I'm not in favor of giving one drug to get off another drug. I find the concept self-defeating. I say that from my bubble boy pose, never having experienced the agony of heroin addiction. I do believe that detoxification can stabilize, keep you from having seizures or dying, and take you down from addiction over a period of time. But today there are people who've been on methadone maintenance for 20-30 years and show up at a clinic on a daily basis to get their methadone.

To me that's substituting one addiction for another. Other than the toilet I don't have anywhere to go every day to get something. I don't want to be too critical of this medical alternative to heroin addiction. But for me any heroin addict on a methadone program is the same as changing decks on the Titanic. That said, after years of working in the treatment field and seeing all the underlying issues of human beings, it's clear to me that there is mental illness and disorders that require medication. For instance, it's been proven that the chains of depression can be loosened by anti-depressants.

I've suffered momentary depression as opposed to daily, dark, sordid depression. But I've never sought or taken any medication. Depression is a universal human condition and surely affects everyone in various degrees. Happily most of these periods are brief and temporary.

Treatment in America includes expensive programs, not so expensive programs, inexpensive programs and free programs run by the state or county. The best program in my opinion is the 12-step group: Alcoholic Anonymous, Narcotics Anonymous, Cocaine Anonymous, Sex Addicts Anonymous, Overeaters Anonymous and even Emotions Anonymous, which I encountered in Europe. The 12-step approach can be applied to any malady. These groups are anonymous and free, the only requirement for joining is a desire to quit whatever harmful thing you're doing. If you don't have that desire, it won't matter because you won't go there anyway.

Thus the best programs in America and the world cost nothing. It's like church. You participate in a community of individuals who have similar problems with their employer, marriage, parents, finances, boyfriend or girlfriend. You are in company with people who are doing their best to work out problems in their lives using a 12-step approach.

But if you have a serious crack cocaine addiction or alcoholism, there is a time you should go to a hospital or clinic, stay at least 28 days and try to understand why you are there. You have time to sit with addiction, examine it and sort of geographically remove it from your personal map. The bottom line is that when you leave the institution, it's one of these 12-step groups that will help firm your decision to maintain recovery.

I'm not a big fan of the psychological angle of recovery although I do subscribe to the therapy and counseling if someone doesn't want to participate in a 12-step group. In that case they should engage a good counselor or therapist so there is somewhere to go to vent, someone to share their issues and somewhere to work out solutions. There are those who wouldn't feel comfortable in a room with alcoholics, sex addicts, overeaters and cocaine and heroin addicts. If you're sitting in that room and think, "These people are crazy," and don't realize you're in there with them, then I recommend therapy and counseling.

The reason I recommend 12-step groups is because that process single-handily helped me maintain the life I have today. Many friends I've known in recovery, some who went through it with me, others who came behind, have relapsed. Some experts even say relapse is ultimately part of the process. I don't agree because I can envision the disaster of a Thomas Henderson relapse.

I catch a plane to Peru. I get two mules and a wagon. I go to the coca fields with the processors. In other words, I don't see myself buying a little or sneaking to do a little or hiding to do a little or drinking a sip or two over here or there. I'm going to the source and it's over for me. I wouldn't ever be coming back. I'd be right in the middle of the insanity of relapse.

I have dreams of smoking crack but I never seem to get a hit. I'm always being chased. There is drama. I can't find a light to fire up. I can never get the rock on the pipe. I go through dreams where there is cocaine everywhere but I can't get high. Didn't Freud say that you are everything and everyone in your dreams? I guess that over 20 years of sobriety, my recovery is also in my dreams. I can think about drugs, see it and hold it, but I can't use because of the distractions. The wind is blowing...someone is coming.... Many, many years ago I used to get high in my dreams. I can't even do that anymore.

I bought the 12-step approach to recovery hook, line and sinker. It was like finally comprehending the flex defense ("Oh, so that is how the thing works"). I also said to a friend that there must be some luck to this recovery business because a lot of people around me had relapsed.

"Know why you haven't?" he said. "You're afraid of you."

He was right. I was afraid of me because I knew what I would do on drugs. I knew that I wouldn't be around my children. I knew that insanity would take place, because one of the horrible side effects of drugs I did for so many years was severe paranoia. We called it tweaking and geeking on the street.

Geeking is looking out of windows, pulling the shades, peeking in air conditioning ducts, examining electrical plugs, outlets, any holes and any break of light. Geeking is thinking someone is outside and maybe inside, somebody is looking and listening, they're going to get you because constitutionally your spirit knows that you are doing something awful.

Tweaking has more to do with your mouth stopping to work. You know what you want to say but your lips can't form the words. Your tongue and lips can't get together. They are like, "Hey, just forget about it."

A good illustration is a story about an addict and his dog alone in a room. The dog is sitting there. The guy is smoking crack. He starts geeking and tweaking. He runs to the window and looks. The dog goes with him and looks. The guy goes to the door and listens. The dog goes with him and perks its ears. The addict squints through the peephole, he's at the back door and up in the attic. Finally the dog gets tired of following and says, "Hey, damnit, if there was someone out there I would have barked."

Treatment works all the time in one respect. Here's what I mean. A human being exposed to the idea that you know you drink too much and you do too much dope has heard that from family members, employers or friends. You've lost your job, you are homeless, on the street, down and out. So you go through a treatment process where someone says, "Partner, you are a drug addict and alcoholic." That's where your life is now.

If a person goes into treatment and experiences the information that you should refrain from drinking, then you know that sobriety would work a lot better in your life. You may have liver damage and some brain damage and you're extremely paranoid. Treatment may include going through detoxification for seven days to purge all the heroin and opiates you were taking. The process is saying that the only way for you to get better is to stop putting drugs and alcohol in your body. That information has been plugged into you despite the fact that you have other ideas about it.

I want families and friends to hear this clearly. For the rest of an addict's life, if they are sitting somewhere sipping bourbon, a margarita or beer, they will experience guilt with every gulp. If that person is smoking marijuana or crack or back on heroin, there will be guilt with every whiff or injection. I believe that the enjoyment is gone because now you know. You know that what you're doing is absolutely wrong. Therefore, one way that treatment encourages abstinence is through a guilt complex.

Some say relapse is normal behavior. I visited with a medical adviser to the NFL drug program who runs a methadone clinic in New Jersey. He believed that alcoholism, like diabetes, is a relapse condition. That is, relapse was inevitable. I'm not surprised that a doctor who treats heroin addicts and feeds them methadone every day holds an opinion that everyone relapses. But I don't believe that.

I think the causes of relapse are dishonesty, sexual issues, covert behaviors, food, and relationships. Sometime the alcoholic or drug addict thinks, "If I go through 28 days of treatment I should get my life back. I should get my wife back. I should get my money back. I should get all my cars and children back."

That is not reality. Society and even family members have the right to hold that person accountable. It is their right to enforce the consequences that the individual deserves. If you go through life just saying you're sorry without making real amends, and there isn't time and effort and proof that you've changed, I think you have to be held accountable.

Halfway and three-quarter houses help individuals go through the treatment process. If you live in New York and have a serious crack or alcohol problem you can find yourself at an all-men house in south Florida. From there you walk down the street to work at McDonald's or Taco Bell for $6 an hour and give half the money to the house because it's a non-profit operation. Places like this are where addicts can leave their community and go somewhere to sober up. Where they can rethink their lives, wake up in the morning, look at the roof and the guy in the bed next to them and wonder, "How the hell did I get here?"

I have many of those memories from prison. I lay thinking, "How the hell will you work this one out, Thomas?"

I've also worked with people who did not want to be sober. That is a reality that families and friends of addicts must come to terms with. There are people who are constitutionally incapable of changing. They will never stop using. That's a sad thing for me to say but I know it through first hand experience.

There were three guys I worked with over a 10-year period. I did my best to love them and counsel them. I told them to read this and do that and pray like so. Then they'd get drunk and run off. This happened three times. Three-for-three gave me the answer I deserved. My solution was to call the men together.

"Will you let me off the hook?" I said.

"What do you mean?" one asked.

"Will you relieve me from hoping for you, from praying for you, from pulling for you? Will you let me off the hook, because the fact of the matter is you don't want to quit, do you? And you're not going to quit, are you?"

"You're right," they said.

That reminds me of a fellow inmate I knew in prison, when I had about eight months to serve before release. This guy was on my bunk watching me read self-help books. He saw me read 12-step books and knew I attended 12-step meetings in prison. He started asking me questions. He was about 60 years old and became my guinea pig, my first student. I started working on him because he was a short-timer with little time left to do. He was in for crack possession and use so I gave him a plan for when he got out.

We had a couple of months to visit. We talked often, every day. I told him I was seven months sober when I came to prison. Being sober, just that little decision to quit drinking and using drugs, had given me more hope than anything in my life. Like the Cowboys' assistant coach Gene Stallings would say, I had my tit in a wringer when I made that decision. But I told my inmate pal that it was a good thing. And he went yeah, yeah.

I did my best psychiatrist, therapist, counselor/sponsor/mentor deal on him. He got out and left me with five or six months to go on my sentence. But in 90 days he walked through the prison door. I don't know if citizens are aware of how hard it is to get back inside the penitentiary in only 90 days. A return that fast takes extreme determination.

He walked into my dorm and at first I thought, well, he's visiting. But no, they don't allow convicts to visit. And even if he was visiting he couldn't come into the dorm. I was running possibilities through my mind when he approached and said:

"I relapsed. I went back."

I started questioning him. Did you move somewhere else? Did you hang out in the wrong neighborhood? Did you get away from that woman? Did you get away from your mom's house?

No, no, he said. He gave an answer that floored me, that put me in my place. I was trying to find out what was wrong with him and why he didn't understand what I was trying to give him when he told me the reason he was back.

"I don't know nothin' else," he explained.

Those words took the rap out of me for four or five months. When I say rap I mean he took all the talk out of me. I couldn't rebut him. When he said, "I don't know nothin' else," I heard those words to also mean, "I don't want to know anything else." This was long before I understood there were addicts who should release people trying to help them by saying, "I appreciate it. Thank you for caring, but I like getting high and I'm going to keep doing this."

That experience reminds of another guy being released from prison. Only he'd been there 40 years and didn't want to go home.

"I'd rather stay inside," he told the warden.

"You have to go home. You've been released, so you can't stay here," the warden said.

They released him the next morning and put him on a bus to his home. Around midnight the next night one of the tower guards called the watch commander in alarm.

"We've got a man on the fence!"

"Shoot him!" came the order.

"But sir," said the guard, "he's trying to climb in."

FRANK WEIMANN
(Literary agent)

Thomas and I got together in a peculiar way. I was attempting to write a celebrity book of lists and even though I'm not a writer the project didn't dissuade me from carrying on. I heard about Henderson being in prison in California and wrote him a letter thinking he would have some appeal down south.

I hadn't watched football in years and when I did I couldn't stand Dallas and in particular I didn't like Henderson. But he had been popular and I thought I'd include him in my book. I got a return letter where he listed his five favorite sports with a note thanking me for including him. He added this postscript:

"I need a ghost writer for my autobiography."

Well, of course, without the education, training or ability, that was me. I'd moved to New York a few years before and hadn't renewed my driver's license. So I needed a photo ID to get into prison to see Henderson to discuss the book. I went to Times Square and got a fake New York state employee badge, arrived at the prison and literally walked right into the yard.

I may have walked through metal detectors without knowing it, but I wasn't searched at all. That was surprising because it was a pretty tough joint. Tex Watson and other lunatics were in there.

Everything went wrong with the trip. I had a delay out of New York, a 10-hour layover in Denver, my luggage got lost and I ended up taking a bus to the prison. I was good and pissed off by the time I met Henderson in the yard. The first thing he said was, "Hey, you were supposed to be here at 10 a.m." That set me off royally so we wound up straddling a bench glaring at each other. We weren't getting anywhere until I guess ultimately he needed to tell his story so badly that he decided to let me try it.

I worked hard on a proposal and sent it to publishers. The publishers loved his story and hated my writing with very good reason. Thomas said, you did all this work, you represent me and I'll have a friend find a writer. Henderson's friend was Ted Ashley, vice chairman of the board of Warner Communications, a very heavy hitter. He could have been owner of a corner deli for all I knew. I was just a hick from south Jersey. Ted then found a great writer named Peter Knobler.

When an offer came in, Thomas kept his word. I was part of the deal. After the book was published I paid my way on a P. R. tour with Thomas. It was amazing to see how he could grab an audience and have them laughing one second and crying their eyes out the next second.

The reason he and the book were successful was because first of all, he told the truth. Second, he didn't blame anyone but himself. It wasn't like, oh, if it weren't for Aunt Sally or Aunt Mary or my mom or my father I would be a nuclear scientist. Or I never would have snorted coke or had a drink. Thomas made it clear that he was the cause of his problems. I think people responded to him because they were tired of hearing celebrities, athletes and others in the public eye blaming everyone but themselves.

Thomas had a habit of calling me late at night or early in the morning and it used to piss me off. I said, I've told you for almost 20 years not to call early because I have two young kids. Don't call late because my grandmother is 98 and I'm afraid of what the person is calling about.

Sure enough late one night Thomas called, and he was laughing. He won the Texas Lottery and said,. "I'm going to celebrate, but not like I used to. I'm going to the 7-11 for milk and cookies. I appreciate all you've done for me over the years."

I hung up and thought, This is too good to be true. A guy who actually did good things for others was being rewarded in this life for doing something great. I looked at caller ID a couple of hours ago later and it's him again.

"Are you all right, Thomas? Why are you calling so late?"

"I'm calling for one reason," he said. "When I went out tonight I found I had a whole lot of new friends. I'm just calling to say I'm going to stick with my old ones. You and I will be friends 20 years from now. The lottery is not going to change me, or our friendship."

I felt like an ass. I was hollering at this guy for calling late, he was calling to say he would stick with old friends and I'm at the top of my list. Next day at 6 a.m. he called again. This time Thomas said, "I'm sorry I called you late last night. I was just excited and felt like I need to talk to you." Then he hung up.

One month passed and it was time to hear from Thomas again. I'll be damned if he didn't call at 5:30 in the morning. By now the glow had gone off his kind words. I went off on him.

"Whoa," he said, "I want you to know that if you need money at any time for any reason, tell me the amount. Don't tell me if you are going to pay it back. Don't tell me when you're going to pay it back. Just tell me how much money I can give to help you."

Then he hung up. Once again I'm feeling like a jackass because I screamed at him for making the phone call and he was only showing more kindness.

GOOD BYE TO CHRIS

The entry on my journal of 12/27/2001 says: One of my best friends committed suicide today.

Chris was a complex guy I had come to love. He loved Richard Pryor and Robin Harris and hated Republicans. I think depression, alcoholism, financial problems and the election of George W. Bush pushed him over the edge. When my younger brother Allen killed himself in 1984 while I was in prison I cried hard on a pay phone in a long dark hallway. I cried for me that time. On this December day I cried for Chris.

I understand why people kill themselves. I don't see life ever getting that bad for me. Maybe a terminal illness could influence my departure. Anyway, it wasn't the first time Chris had attempted suicide. He'd already driven his truck off a mountain and survived.

I met Chris in Arizona while I was working for Sierra Tucson. He was a lawyer and a Vietnam veteran, and had been on anti-depressant drugs his entire adult life. He was one of the funniest human beings I've ever known. Playing golf with him was an incredible experience, especially in mixed black and white company. Chris would start a Richard Pryor rant with "nigger" this and "nigger" that. The white guys hearing a Caucasian using the "n" word, especially with a black man present, got Little Orphan Annie eyes.

Chris told me stories about his life and experience in Vietnam. About being a trial lawyer in the Tucson area where his depression and mood swings got to the point where he couldn't practice law anymore. For instance, he told me if the judge granted a motion to the other side or failed to give an injured party their proper amount of damages he would wail and cuss the judge. Pretty soon he wasn't allowed in court anymore.

I had so much fun talking to him about world affairs, politics, Democrats and Republicans, that we spoke to each other almost every day for seven or eight years. He would call me "brother man," a phrase that originated with Harris, a black comedian who also died before his time. Harris also had a routine in which a panhandler asks a guy for money, and the guy hits him up side the head and says, "That will hold your monkey ass." My phone would ring, I'd pick it up and a voice would say, "That will hold your monkey ass."

Chris was smarter than anyone I ever met. If I was on the Who Wants To Be A Millionaire? TV show and I was down to the $1 million question, he'd be my lifeline. Chris was brilliant. He used to blow my mind, and I think I'm pretty bright. We'd be talking and come to a word and he'd say, "You know the origin of that word, don't you?" I'd say, "What are you talking about?" and he'd launch into Latin or Greek mythology to explain the word to me.

I got a phone call earlier in 2001 concerning Chris. I was told he'd intentionally driven his truck off a 300-foot mountain near Tucson. He tore his truck all to hell. Chris didn't get a scratch. I tiptoed around that subject, but eventually we talked about it. I made fun of him and we laughed about it. But at heart I was mad at him. I told him, "Hey, you know our deal. If you're going to do something like that, call me. I'll go with you."

Chris struggled with his recovery. He wasn't as successful as I was in staying sober. I think his problem lay with taking anti-depression medication and drinking non-alcoholic beers. The latter hurts many recovering alcoholics, who fool themselves by saying they just like the taste of beer, and then they return to the real stuff. I've seen many relapses by those who want to play-drink. Chris was one of those.

I'd never say anything to him if he drank a non-alcoholic beer. But I wouldn't do it. I don't want a Shirley Temple or a virgin Margarita. Just give me a glass of water.

I'd won the lottery before his first suicide attempt, and so I called Chris and invited him to Austin. The plan was to hang out, play golf and drive to Las Vegas and on to California. I bought a car, a 1996 600 V-12, four-door Mercedes, the car of my dreams. I paid $60,000 for it instead of $140,000. I bought it used and on a discount, one of those decisions with money that I'm proud to have made.

I drove from Austin to near El Paso. We were talking, laughing and listening to music, Chris retelling all his jokes. Because of what he'd tried to do to himself, there was still a serious undertone to our relationship. But I didn't treat him any different. I wasn't trying to hold his hand. Neither was I feeling sorry for him. I was his friend.

We took our first break at a truck stop near El Paso that served awful eggs and bacon. I filled the car with gas and gave him the wheel. I was tired. I needed sleep so I got in on the passenger side and he got in the driver's seat, this guy who not long before had plunged off a mountain. I already knew what I was going to say to him. I had it planned.

Chris got on the highway and accelerated to around 70 mph. That was my cue. I turned to him and said:

"Look, you're not Thelma and I'm not Louise. So don't you drive my damn car off no mountain!"

He laughed for half an hour. Six months later I got the call. Chris had put a gun in his mouth and pulled the trigger. I was so mad at him I didn't go to his funeral. He left me a suicide note that his wife mailed to me. It read:

Brother man, I sure hate to leave you like that but every day I awoke it was getting darker and darker. Some folks are meant to live a long time. I just happen not to be one of them. I love you like a brother and I'm really going to miss you, but I can't do this anymore.
Chris

I miss him terribly. I'm still mad at him for leaving me because we'd made such a connection.

ADRIAN BURROUGH
(Friend, former employee)

Years ago, I got into the same trouble Thomas was in once. I got crazy. My sister, who was also a flight attendant, ran into Thomas and she told him about my problem. He gave her a tape, "Sobriety Is An Option" to give me.

I had only been clean for 11 months. I listened to that tape and it changed my life. I'd never heard anything like it. The humor in the film made you feel like there was hope for me, too. It was going to be a struggle, but it didn't have to be the hand-wringing struggle I thought it would be. It was one of the saving graces of my life.

I called Thomas. Out of sheer desperation I needed to do something, so I had moved from Houston to live with my parents in Fort Worth. Thomas offered me a job. I'd been a business administration major. I'm getting ready to open a film company, he said. Why don't you come down and work for me?

"Thomas," I said, "I don't have any money."

He said, you come on to Austin. You can stay in my house for a month. I'm getting ready to go to Mexico. I have a car you can drive. I'll give you $500. So I went to Austin and began working as sales and marketing director of Specialty Films. We had a small company, only four of us, and I ended up bringing my daughter to be with me.

That was the start of knowing the new Thomas. He was a kind and helping person. I saw day in and day out where people would come in and ask for some kind of help. There was hardly a time that Thomas turned anyone down.

Also at that time Thomas became a single parent. He got custody of Thomesa. I think she was 14, my daughter was 13, and they sort of grew up during that time like sisters. I would keep Thomesa when Thomas went out of town. He was on the road a lot, speaking and promoting his films. I saw him as a caring, disciplined father. Thomesa changed his life even more when she came to stay with him. I thought he did a wonderful job being a single parent.

Thomas also sent me to school to become a licensed chemical dependency counselor. I had to take 270 hours of classes at Austin Community College to earn a license, and he paid for it. When I stopped working for Thomas and went to school fulltime, he gave me a lead on a job. Texas War On Drugs was looking for an assistant criminal justice coordinator, he put in a good word with Dan Bowie, the executive director, and I got the job.

I'm now with the Dallas County judicial treatment center. We get people on probation who have one more chance to go through a six-month program before they're given the option to go to prison. As for me personally, I've been clean since July 21, 1991.

I've been asked what makes Thomas tick. I think it was his conviction to do the right thing. He'd done the wrong thing for so long. You really must have a conviction. You really have to say, I want to change my life. I want to do something different.

Self-centeredness is the core of the disease of addiction. When you get away from yourself and start to help others it does something inside of you and you want to do it more and more. I never thought I'd get that feeling by helping others. I always thought I needed it all for me. The minute I started to say, let me help you, let me do this for you, a whole different person developed. I think that's exactly what happened to Thomas.

Thomas has always been a confident person and a self-promoter. He got the idea somewhere that his films would help others. It's probably one of the most dynamic treatment tools that treatment centers use today. I know a lot of people who are in prison or in trouble say, oh, gosh, that's Thomas Henderson and he's not like me. But he was. He was exactly like those people sitting there watching it. Sure, he had a name but he destroyed that name. He came back as a completely different person.

Thomas has been like a big brother to me even though I'm a few years older. He's my grandson's godfather.

A friend told me Thomas had won the lottery. I called on my cell phone and he said it's true. I'd bought Thomesa's old Blazer from Thomas and still owed him $1,500 on it. He said, "Tell your daughter that car is hers and you don't owe me a penny."

One day he said he had something for me. My sister was in town, he picked us up and we went to Ruth's Chris steak house. Sitting over a very tender steak and some creamed spinach, he handed me a $10,000 check.

He's a magnificent person, he really is. I knew the old Thomas and he was something else.

CHAPTER TWENTY TWO

HALL OF FAME, GRADUATION AND...
(Harry Truman?)

It came to my attention during the mid-1990s that Langston University, my alma mater, was planning a Hall of Fame for sports. When I heard about the project I thought, wow, I probably...no, not probably...I will be...

I know I'll never have a bust in the Pro Football Hall of Fame, although my name is there as a member of a Super Bowl winner. I've been to Canton and seen myself in a picture of the 1977 Cowboys who won Super Bowl XII. I didn't have a bust. I thought all the busts were unattractive anyway.

So I called Langston and asked, what's up with the Hall of Fame? I was told you had to be nominated and they'd send me a couple of necessary forms to fill out. That gave me a solid idea. I decided to contact Big Daddy, Roosevelt Nivens.

Big Daddy was my defensive coordinator and had been an all-America defensive tackle at Langston. He could have played in the NFL in my opinion. But through a series of incidents he never got the opportunity, didn't put himself in the right place to do it or just didn't go after it. Now he was coaching in Austin at Austin High School.

Here's a quick story about Big Daddy. When I went to the Cowboys in 1975 that was the first season Langston moved to the Southwestern Athletic Conference. I was with the Cowboys when Big Daddy and Langston went to play Grambling. Of course, I was excited about how the game would turn out. I looked in the paper the next day and saw that the score was Grambling 68, Langston 0.

I called Big Daddy and said, "What in the world happened to you all down there?"

"Tommy Wayne," he said, which is what he always called me, "we kicked off and all hell broke loose." That was his whole explanation. Langston kicked off and all hell broke loose.

Anyway, here are two All-Americans from Langston in Austin. I was first team all-America, No. 1 draft choice, defensive player of the year and member of the 11-0 team at Langston in 1973.

After the forms arrived, I phoned Big Daddy and said, "I'm going to nominate you. Why don't you nominate me?" He agreed, and I'm thinking, this is a no-brainer. We both fill out the forms. He gets his paper to me and I ship it overnight express to Langston to qualify us for that first class of inductees.

I didn't hear anything from Langston for days...weeks...months. Finally, about a week before the first induction ceremony, I called the university and spoke to a member of the nomination committee. He said the applications Nivens and I submitted were incomplete. Naturally, I started breathing fire through my nose. I can smell bullshit when it hits me in the face.

The bottom line was that I'd been to prison for some shameful situations. Coach Nivens had been fired at Langston and there was bad blood about that. So we both had different types of problems with the institution. Mine was that I'd shamed myself, my family and probably them to some degree. However, I never understood there was any sort of moral clause connected with being an eligible candidate.

I think there should be standards and if I don't qualify under those standards I'm capable at this stage of my life to understand the consequences. But if these standards are unwritten, if they are not in the by-laws, then my heart tells me this is prejudicial. This is political. And the word that sums all that up is bullshit

I thought about it for a second. They have a Hall of Fame. I was a member of an undefeated team at Langston. I was the Oklahoma Collegiate Conference defensive player of the year in 1973-74. I was NAIA first team all-American in '73-'74. Walter Payton was on those teams. So was Ed (Too Tall) Jones. I was selected Little All-American in '73 by The Associated Press. I was the No. 1 draft choice of the Dallas

Cowboys. I played in Super Bowls X, XII and XIII and was a member of the Cowboys who won XII. I made the Pro Bowl in 1979. Who has a better resume than that?

I called Langston president Ernest Holloway, who was a dean when I was a student. We'd become friends over the years. That didn't stop me from lighting into him about what was going on. There's a Hall of Fame and I'm not on the first ballot!

President Holloway explained patiently and in great detail that the committee decided to start with athletes from the 1920s, some of the founding football coaches, and then those in the 30s and 40s on up to the moderns. One of the first inductees was Marcus Haynes, the famous Harlem Globetrotter dribbler, who played basketball at Langston. (He also happened to be Drew Pearson's father in law).

I had no issues over who went in. They had standards and methods about how they select a Hall of Fame. I just happened not to be 80 years old for induction with the first class. After the second and third classes were inducted I called Dr. Holloway again.

Dr. Holloway never told me that it was my past that had caused them to pass me over. But he did say he felt my anger and frustration. He said there would come a day when he'd call me to be inducted and I'd be the only one honored at the ceremony. He and I had been long-time friends, but I still felt slighted. I also felt responsible for any questions about my worthiness for induction. It goes back to what I'll say over and over during my life. There's a time when one of the greatest comforts and moments of clarity for a person in good times, bad times and times of crisis, is the ability to say, okay, I need to understand rather than be understood.

Part of my growth in terms of functioning in a sane manner is that sometimes I relapse into a self-willed internal riot. I heard about Wilt Chamberlain declining to go into the Kansas Hall of Fame for many, many years. I thought, now that's a guy I admire. So I swore, well, when they ask me, I ain't gonna do it.

The other side of that debate is, who says they're ever going to ask you? So whenever someone mentioned the Hall of Fame I'd say if they do induct me, I won't show up. I'm not going in.

After I won the lottery in March of 2000, I really expected to hear from Langston, but I didn't. I was relieved not to be contacted because it wouldn't have sounded legitimate. Now that I'm a millionaire your standards have been modified? Because you hope I'll make a nice contribution to the institution? That would have been my impression. I was even expecting a phone call to tell me, Thomas, you know we made a mistake because of the issues and controversies in your life. The silence was deafening.

I didn't get the call until August or September of 2002. The message went something like this: Thomas, the board voted and we would be honored if you would accept induction into the Langston Hall of Fame No! My anger and resentment flared. Boy, if they want me now I ain't going. That lasted about eight seconds. Of course I'd go. All I wanted to know was how fast they wanted me to be there.

The ceremony was scheduled for an October homecoming weekend. I would be honored on campus, at halftime of the football game and during a luncheon roast. Since Langston was short on funds, they wondered if I knew anyone in Oklahoma City who would sponsor the luncheon. I put aside my anger and false pride and accepted although mildly put off by having to find a sponsor for my own luncheon.

One of the fortunes of time was that I knew a great Oklahoman, Jack Cooper. He owned car dealerships and was a longtime supporter of sports in Oklahoma, particularly the Oklahoma Sooners. When the Cowboys picked me No. 1 in 1975 after the Sooners' won the national championship, it confused Cooper that the first player drafted out of Oklahoma was Thomas Henderson from Langston.

Cooper hunted me down and put me in my first car, a 1975 Oldsmobile. He didn't give it to me but he did sell it for a very cheap price, same as the car I bought for my mother. I did a TV commercial with him and he took me on my first trip to Las Vegas. I've kept in touch with Cooper through good and bad times.

I put Cooper in touch with Langston and he spent $12-15,000 on a luncheon for about 200 people. Friends are forever, and that's when I understood that Jack Cooper was not only a fan of mine but a friend of mine. Barry Switzer roasted me. So did Marcus Haynes and Too Tall Jones. Beasley Reese, a former Cowboys teammate who made good in television sports on the East Coast, sent a funny tape talking about how much hair

I'd lost and how much weight I'd gained. I thanked Langston, Jack Cooper, the fans and Switzer for telling how he missed recruiting me at Douglas High School in 1971.

In the midst of the roast Dr. Holloway got up to speak with some papers in his hand. He had a special announcement to make. As president of Langston it was within his authority to grant credit hours toward a degree on the basis of life experience. Therefore, for building a football stadium and track, charity work in Austin and with his films in prisons across the country, he was authorized to grant me 12 hours toward a degree. So next spring at Langston University, Thomas Henderson would march as part of the graduation class in May of 2003.

I sat there thinking, Okay, I'm going to graduate from college! I thought it was cool until I got a letter from the registrar's office that included a bunch of forms. They'd given me 12 hours for the work I'd done over the past 28 years and then said in order for me to graduate I had to take an American History class. I knew there was a catch. Thomas Henderson had to go to class.

So what did I do? Sometimes my ego creeps into what should be a reasonable reaction. I've learned to call sponsors and mentors such as Chuck Denmark or Robert Spellings about a decision I'm about to make just to hear some feedback. One of the other lessons I've learned is to do nothing. Doing nothing is one of the best actions we can take sometime. So I sat with this for three or four days and then said to myself, "Hey, goofball Thomas, egotistical Henderson, why don't you take the class? Why don't you just go through the process?"

I contacted Huston Tillotson College in Austin and was put through to a professor in the history department. We settled on a correspondence course for three credit hours. My assignment was to pick a person or event and submit a 6-page, typed report with documentation of sources.

I picked Harry Truman and read David McCullough's biography of the former president. I should have chosen William Henry Harrison as my subject. He was the president who kept talking for hours in the cold during his inauguration and died a month later from pneumonia. Harrison's story would have been less than 992 pages in the Truman book.

Yet the more I read the more fascinated and interested I became. Truman was a simple man who was marginally educated and attended what amounted to a community college where he took an accounting course. He worked at a bank and a railroad, had multiple failures selling men's clothes and somehow fell in with the political machine of the Pendergast family. Truman wound up a county clerk or commissioner, and still helped his father on a farm. He was not the brightest color in the crayon box.

What I discovered about Truman was that he had the most instinctive common sense of any human I ever read about. People forget that Franklin D. Roosevelt dumped his vice president and picked Truman to replace him but never talked to Truman about anything important. FDR didn't tell him about a nuclear weapon we were developing. He didn't update him about Europe or Stalin, Churchill or Japan, our diplomatic work or our secrets. When FDR died, Truman was down the street and around the corner. He had to meet with Stalin and Churchill and hold his own while making some of the most important decisions in our nation's history.

I got hooked on Truman, this simple man who loved his wife and daughter and didn't like profanity. History will judge that he failed to stop some Communist infiltration into our government, but to my mind he was one of the greatest presidents of our time.

Nor do I believe like some people that Truman was a racist. He was just raised at a time when using that sort of lingo was the way they described blacks. I remember a story about Adam Clayton Powell who said something bad about Truman's wife, Bess. Truman said, "Well, that nigger will never come to the White House."

When Truman first went to Washington as a senator he looked for something to do and started auditing government contracts. He found all this waste, where contractors were getting millions of taxpayer dollars but were building on the cheap or not at all. He knew that business because he'd built the county courthouse in Missouri. So he went on a tour around the country in his car and drove thousands of miles checking on defense contracts and saved the government millions in overcharges.

One day he came across a budget for a mystery project and asked what is this for? Well, we can't tell you, they said. What do you mean, you can't tell me? It's a secret.

Here's what I meant about Truman having great instincts. Someone

277

whose judgment he trusted told him, "Don't look at it. It's secret. Don't worry about it." He never did. It wasn't until Truman was president of the United States that somebody finally said, "It's a nuclear bomb, Harry."

Then think about the decisions Truman made with that weapon. He didn't hesitate to drop it twice on Japan to end World War II. But he used restraint and refused to use it during the Korean Conflict for fear of starting WW III with the Chinese.

Thomas Henderson talks American history – that should rattle the 8-ball down at the pool hall. I finished my paper and received a 'B' because I didn't attend class. A 'B' is an 'A' when you take a correspondence course. I was proud of the paper and what I learned. I got ready for graduation day.

I got in my Range Rover in mid-May and drove 7 hours from Austin to Oklahoma City. The last time I'd been there was after the Murrah Federal Building had been blown up. Donald Burns, my high school coach, was working with the Housing Authority in that building. He perished along with scores of others.

When I heard he passed away I called Mrs. Burns, who I didn't know, to get her address so I could send flowers. I told her I was coming to the funeral to pay my respect to Coach Burns. Would she give me the date and time of the memorial service?

"Thomas," she said, "I want you to do me a favor."

"Of course."

"Would you eulogize him for me?"

I don't know why she chose me. No telling how many people asked to do the eulogy, from ex-players and coaching colleagues to the mayor and police chief. Coach Burns wasn't the only person I knew who died in that explosion. There were 15 or 20 that I knew from high school or in the Oklahoma City community. There were funerals all around town.

I eulogized Coach Burns with respectful humor. I told how he watched me play basketball and knew I was an athlete. He asked one day which position I played in football. I told him I was a quarterback so on the first day of practice he lined me up with the other quarterbacks. Truth is, I was more of a bootleg, option-type QB and not much of a passer.

Coach Burns told a receiver to run a post route and I would throw him a pass. I took the ball from center, backed up five steps and threw the ugliest, wobbliest football you ever saw. It looked like someone punted it.

"You ain't a quarterback. Get over on defense," Coach Burns said. He put me at defensive end and the rest is history.

Now I was back in Oklahoma City, spending the night before my Saturday graduation in a hotel. I had my cap and gown. I was going to graduate. Next morning I drove the 35 miles up I-35 north and got to Highway 33. Langston is 10-12 miles down the road. As I turned into this meandering, curvy two-lane country road the '70s came back. I remembered all the trips I'd taken down this road, when my car had broken down and where I'd stopped to get a candy bar or gas. I pulled into the campus full of melancholy for the past.

But I didn't know what to do. I'm a doofus. I never graduated from college. I didn't know where to go or who to talk to or what line to get in. I got out my robe. I saw other people with robes on so I thought, okay, that must be a sign. I put mine on. I put on a little graduation cap. Someone noticed the tassels were wrong and said, hey, move it over to the left side. I went to the auditorium to check in. I got in the proper line, the procession began and moved toward the stadium.

We were handed programs en route. There's only one thing I wanted to know. Was I in it? Did I fill out all the documents? Did I send in all my information? I opened the program and looked under the list of names under Bachelor of Science and there it was: Thomas Henderson, Bachelor of Science, Health and Physical Education. I started crying. I got out of line. This was real. Not only was I graduating, I was in the program.

We marched into the stadium and I sat down with a bunch of 21-year-old kids. It's been 28 years, from 1975 to 2003, and I was finally graduating. Dr. Holloway got up and said, the first thing we're going to do is graduate our alumnus, Thomas Henderson. So they made a presentation to me before the procession starts.

"May I say a few words?" I asked.

"Take a few seconds," said Dr. Holloway, who knows I can talk. I took three minutes. My words were full of gratitude.

Now it was time for each row of graduates to walk up and receive their diplomas. I already had my folder with a degree in it but I wanted more. I was having so much fun that I got up and went across the stage again. The crowd loved it. I couldn't get enough of graduating.

In the past, when I filled out forms in a doctor's office, for employment or a bank loan, I'd get to the part of the application and hesitate where you filled in the blank that read: college graduate.

I didn't know whether to fudge it or write, Okay, I did four years in college, when the question really was, did you graduate? I never felt bad about not graduating or that I couldn't answer that question on all those forms I've filled out for years. But now I understand what that pause was all about. It represented some unfinished business.

I think when I check that I've graduated there will be no more pause. Another piece of my unfinished business has been finished. Another transformation of Thomas Henderson has been completed along my never-ending journey.

Cap & Gown.
College Graduation 2002, Langston University, Langston, Oklahoma

CHARLIE WATERS
(Former Cowboys teammate)

I played in the NFL for 12 years and kept my eyes open all the time. What I saw happening during that time was the influx of a physically different player to our team and the league. By different, I mean athletes with a superior dimension of talent.

There were three who joined the Cowboys and influenced me to think, holy cow, we are moving into another dimension of football player. This game is going to be played at a higher plateau of skill. Tony Dorsett with his bursting speed was the first. Then Randy White with awesome strength. The third was Thomas Henderson for sheer athleticism.

The first time I met him I had to look up because he was about two or three inches taller. He flashed a smile at me, and I'll be damn if he didn't have a gold tooth. I thought, "Holy mackerel, we've created a monster."

I found out Thomas had created that monster his whole life. He was tops at stealing attention for himself. Like he did during the 1978 NFC Championship in Los Angeles between the Cowboys and Rams. I had one of my best games with a fumble recovery and two interceptions.

People don't remember what happened other than Thomas intercepted a pass with a minute left to play, ran 70 yards and then spiked the ball over the goal post. Everyone else could barely have gotten to the end zone because they're so tired. Not only did Thomas take it all the way, he leaped and slammed the ball.

We won, 28-0, and scored three of our four touchdowns in the fourth quarter. The first two were set up by my interceptions that turned momentum around. We scored another touchdown later. Then Thomas applied the exclamation point and THAT'S what everyone remembers!

I'm going to say something that might be wrong, but here it is. There were lots of people who helped Thomas when he had success with our team. He teased me about him making me the strong safety that I was because he'd come off his job to knock down the tight end that I was responsible for. I'd always tell him before the play, "Thomas, make sure you jam the tight end."

Telling this story is to say I always told Thomas what to do, what he didn't need to do, and what plays to expect. I feel like I played a big role in keeping him in check. I don't think anyone else could have played the same role when he started going off the deep end.

I was his conscience on the field. That little guy on his shoulder saying,

"Don't do that! Do this!" But off the field, there wasn't a person like that. After I retired, I don't think he even got that on the field. I don't think there was anyone who befriended him or knew his personality. They all thought he knew what to do. And he did know what to do. If he'd applied himself he could have known everything.

I thought there was no chance that he'd make anything of himself based on the reports I was reading. There was no first hand information, so I should have called Thomas directly. But with all he had, and to blow it, I didn't give him a chance in hell to come out of it.

I even questioned when I heard he was sober. I didn't believe it. I thought, he's the biggest con man to walk the earth. I thought he wound up conning himself. He spent enough time with himself to ask, who am I really? I felt for the longest time he was in la la land where he didn't know who he really was. He created something in his mind about whom he wanted to be and, by God, he made it. He became that person.

Today, I love him as much as I loved him when we first got together. Maybe more because I know what he's been through. I still think he's a bit of a con. That has a negative connotation and it might be a little rough, but he has an angle all the time. Thomas is always trying to convince someone to sell something or to sell himself.

I was disappointed in myself that I thought he wasn't sober. But I understand it was because he had a track record. I went one play at a time with Thomas on the field, and I'd go one moment at a time in life with him. I don't think about what he's done in the past, and I don't want to hear about what he was going to do in the future. I just want him to do what he does well the next moment I'm around him.

That thought fits the story of the first time I met Thomas after he'd won the lottery. It was spring of 2003 and he was being inducted into Langston Hall of Fame. I flew to Oklahoma, and he hustled me backstage before the ceremony began.

He asked now much my plane ticket cost. I told him $196. And the cab fare, he said. About $15-17, I said. Thomas pulled out a roll of $100 bills that took both his hands to circle. He handed me three $100s.

I said, "Thomas, I don't want your money."

He flashed that bright, twinkling smile. Then he winked and said: "Charlie, take the money. I'm RICH!"

We laughed and hugged each other. That's Thomas. You gotta love him. He's led such a surreal life.

282

CHAPTER TWENTY THREE

ACCEPTANCE

God grant me the serenity to accept the things I cannot change, the courage to change the things I can, and the wisdom to know the difference.

I try to live by these words. They sound plain, but they embrace a whole philosophy of living, and it is a damn healthy philosophy. Sobriety is a delicate, day-by-day deal. There are no guarantees that every day is going to bring a new level of bliss. Shit happens. Life can get and be complicated. Recovery is a simple process for complicated people. The Serenity prayer gives me a way to sort out things. It clearly helps me accept my powerlessness. I put things in piles. The piles help me do my dealing. One pile is the stuff I can't do anything about. The other pile is stuff I can do something about. The wisdom comes in finding out how the hell to keep the piles from spilling into one another. Because sobriety is so delicate is why my piles are important.

If I'm pounding my head against the wall over something that I can't change, I'm throwing away a piece of my life, tossing it right into the cosmic garbage can. I'm pounding and pounding, getting nowhere. It makes me frustrated because I like control. When it doesn't go my way, it makes me angry, bitter and gets me feeling victimized and usually sends me into a funk of self pity. Defined its called co-dependency. The upshot is danger for my sobriety. Experience has taught me that when I'm churned up inside and there's noise in my head, that's when I'm most vulnerable to relapsing. The calm decision is to accept that I can't change it and let it go. I often use the oldest short version of acceptance

283

– fuck it. Much, much easier said than done. I've learned to let go in stages. The work goes on.

One of the items in my 'can't change' pile was a deal I got into with the Denver Broncos and the NFL. It happened at the Super Bowl a few years ago. After I got in trouble, some people dumped me like I was a green piece of meat. They gave me a big leaving alone. Dan Reeves wasn't one of them. He was a friend and he stayed my friend. When I was in jail, he wrote to wish me well. When I got out, he sent me money to help me get on my feet. I'm truly grateful to him for that. Dan and I go back to our years in Dallas. He was a former player for the Cowboys and then an assistant coach to Tom Landry before he took the head-coaching job with the Denver Broncos. He's a kind, generous guy, in my eyes.

I was out a little over a year when I got a call from him. "Thomas, I'd like to invite you to go with us to Cleveland and be of support to one of our players," he said. "It would mean a lot to him and me, and, of course, we'll pay all your expenses." The Broncos were about to play in the AFC championship game. This wasn't about linebacking work. It was about drug and alcohol work. On my own time, I had spent some time a few months earlier when the player had been in treatment. I visited with him and shared my story and recovery with him. I told him the hell I went through and that staying sober was working for me. We got along well. Dan was thinking the guy could use some support with play-off pressure and media madness beginning to mount. "It would be my privilege," I said to Dan. I was fifteen months removed from jail. A coach on the verge of one of the biggest games of his career was seeking me out to help a young guy who was also young in his recovery. Dan believed I was sober and could help. That made the commitment to stay sober worthwhile at that moment. The gifts of sobriety. Most coaches in the same situation would not have even considered calling me. I felt important. I felt needed.

The nicest thing about that incident was that it wasn't anything I was angling for. When I was using, I was a master manipulator. My life was an ulterior motive. But this was a totally unexpected deal. The attending doctor called me and said he had an athlete in treatment and asked me to speak at the facility and I did. I noticed the big athlete so I hung around and visited with him. I asked him could I come by and see him sometime. He said yes. During his thirty-day stay, I probably came by ten days to visit and share.

I was playing golf in Arlington, Texas, when we stopped after nine holes to get coffee and snacks. I was playing with my good friends B.J. and Jimmy. I called home to get my messages and Dan Reeves was on my answering machine. After talking to Dan and agreeing to go to Denver and Cleveland, I shared the news with B.J. and Jimmy.

I had worked the process of recovery honesty, gotten up every day and lived a sober life, and here was a hell of a reward. A top coach wanted me, the Super Bowl Snorter, to carry forth the message of sobriety. And all I was doing was sharing with another alcoholic on my own time. That's how I keep what I have - I give it away.

Everything went fine in Cleveland. The Broncos won. I flew to Denver and caught the team plane to Cleveland. I spent some quality time with the player. We shared. I felt like part of the team for a moment. I stayed with them, hung around with them, went to practices.

The next stop was Pasadena and the Super Bowl against the New York Giants. Dan said, "I really want to thank you. I think you did him a lot of good." We were heading west. I was going back to the Super Bowl. This time my inhaler would not be making the trip.

A few days later I got another call from Dan. "Thomas, the League office called my staff. They don't want you on the sidelines during the Super Bowl so I'm getting you two tickets." The League office staff had seen me with the player in Cleveland, and worst yet, had seen me on the field the day before the game. They didn't want me around. I knew why. The NFL, for good reason, obsesses about its image the way a model obsesses about her figure, and they were afraid it wouldn't look too swift for Hollywood Henderson to be milling around the Super Bowl sidelines in full view of a hundred million television viewers. Nothing personal, just business.

Nobody from the League ever talked to me. There wasn't much dialogue with the Broncos, either. Dan was almost apologetic for the League. The NFL just wanted me to evaporate; that was all. I was there for the most benign reason possible – giving support to a young player early in his recovery. They like to punish.

In my own small way I may even have been helping the NFL steer clear of yet another drug casualty. But the dreaded image bruising was the issue here, so the NFL stance was "We don't want Henderson anywhere near the cameras." I had to do some work with my piles. My first reaction was outrage. I was hurt and wanted to lash out. Didn't they know I was a changed man? Didn't they know that I was working my ass off at sobriety? Didn't they know I was only trying to help, be of service to an alcoholic and addict? I wasn't getting paid for it.

For a few days, at least, it screwed me up big time. I couldn't stop thinking of how the NFL tried to squash my effort. I kept focusing on the disregard they had for me and kept imagining how they sat around and said, "Hey, let's call the Broncos and tell them to give Hollywood a one-way ticket back to jail."

I went to a meeting and shared about it. I can't express how much it hurt. I talked to my sponsor and a few other recovering people. They told me it was none of my business what the NFL and its staff thought of me. What I thought of me was what was important. They told me I couldn't control what anyone thought of me. I needed to hear that. I started working it through. I kept sharing my feelings. I felt myself obsessing about it. The issue was setting up house in my head, picking out curtains, planting tulips, and getting ready to screw up my sanity and sobriety.

It was nothing new. I hang on to things. It's not hard for most alcoholics to do that because, for a lot of us, it's part of the package. We spend years obsessing about our drug of choice, clinging to it even as life is becoming a holy hell. We are thinking about it when we're not using, figuring out how we'll get more. We dream of how great it'll be when we get away from the world with our next shot, toot or hit.

The obsessing is contagious. It spilled over into other parts of my life. Like lying, it became very easy for me. Talking about it got me out of myself. This belonged in the pile of things I can't do a damn thing about, I told myself.

What was I supposed to do, piss in a cup and Federal Express it to the Commissioner's office in New York? Hand in forty-four character references attesting that I was a different man than I used to be? I couldn't climb into their heads. I couldn't make them change their attitude about me overnight or ever, for that matter, or convince them this wouldn't tarnish their image.

The Super Bowl is the NFL's show. It was mine in '79. I'd been part of X, XII and XIII so I'd been at enough of them to know that if they didn't want me around, that was the end of the story. Slowly, I let the resentment go.

Every day in sobriety I believe that I have choices. If I choose to stew about something I can't change, dwell on something that's already done, the day is going to be pretty shitty. I'll be restless and agitated. This thinking and behavior is dangerous to my sobriety and well being.

The tantrum passed. I began to think of where I'd come from. I made a decision, right then, to cling to it, embrace the hell out of it, as hard as I've ever clung to anything in my life. At first, I had a brutal time admitting there were things I couldn't change. Hell, I had spent years feeling like I was one of the indestructible forces on the planet. I not only felt all-powerful, but half the time I felt like the Power, the One and the Only. I was reckless and I got away with it.

Once, I went to the Bahamas for a superstar competition. I brought along a few drugs for a few days: two ounces of coke, an ounce of high powered Thai stick and thirty Quaaludes. Stuck all of it in my carry-on shoulder bag. Didn't bother to hide it. I did a few toots before we landed, grabbed my bag and headed for customs. I had just turned the bag over to the guy, this jet-black Bahamian man in a customs uniform, when my clouded brain cleared. What the hell have I done? How could I have been so stupid? Because you are!! I'm thinking life's over, straight to jail, shit, I've screwed up.

The guy recognized me. I was international by now. He talked a little football with me and then he began rummaging through my bag. I could barely stand to watch. I saw his hand go into the sides, the zippered compartment, then he opened the main part where all my drug baggies were sitting in a pile, right on top, like I'd just gone shopping. I was counting the seconds, as my heart pounded, to the end of my freedom.

Waiting for him to bust my ass. Terror coursed through me, one fast, frenzied wave after another. I'm looking over in my bag with him. He looks at my Baggies and patted them, letting me know he knew. The prosecution rests, I was thinking. He looked up at me. I looked back, eyes pleading. A small smile crossed his face and he zippered the bag closed. He had a lilting, British accent and said "Hollywood, I see you've brought everything you might need. Enjoy your stay on our island." Superman strikes again. I'm bulletproof. I had no reason to think it would ever end.

But it did, of course, with a crash. I hit bottom and came face to face with my powerlessness over drugs and alcohol. Suddenly, with my crutches gone, I was more vulnerable than I ever felt before. As I spent more time with people in recovery and kept hearing about letting go of things I have no power over, I was told how important it was to keep the focus on my own stuff, not get side tracked by trying to change others. They urged me not to spend life worrying about what others might say or do because I couldn't control that, anyway, just as there were lots of things in my life I couldn't control. They warned me about my co-dependency. Co-dependency was explained to me this way: it's when your happiness is contingent on what someone else does or doesn't do.

They were talking about me finding some peace and solutions, but that wasn't what I was hearing. I was hearing that they wanted me to be a damn bystander in my life and therefore give up the control I thought I had. I was a doer. I was a linebacker. What I knew was chasing, smacking, confronting, sweating, and getting it done. It was all too much. I was powerless over this, powerless over that. Going from Superman to Superpansy in one shot. It felt like they were telling me to curl up in a corner and wait for my time to be up. What they were suggesting was that I change.

I was thinking, "Do you have to be a wimp to be sober?" I found out that to stop drinking and drugging was but a fraction of recovery. Living was the bulk of the process. Nobody was trying to make me a wimp at all. They were just trying to help me become a healthy, growing, recovering person; trying to help me learn the life skill of focusing my energy on places where it can do some good. Change the things I can, I kept hearing at the meetings. It began to make sense. I started to realize that I was giving away my serenity awfully cheap if I got beat out of shape every time something didn't go my way.

I don't want to give away my sobriety. I don't want to let my state of mind on any given day be hanging on whether someone else is going to do what I want them to do. That's simply not a good place to live. I don't want to require my life to be perfect because it never will be. I want my serenity to be much sturdier than that. I want it steady and reliable, with me all the time. Putting it simply, I just want to be okay.

A friend in the program told me that whenever he needs to let go of something, he tells himself "that train has left the station". You can stand on the platform and stomp your foot until it breaks or haul your ass down the tracks trying to grab the caboose. You can sulk or yell or feel like a vic-

tim because all the shit ain't going your way. None of the above is changing the fact that the train is still gone. The sooner you're able to come to
grips with that, the better your day, week, month, year and life will be. We
absolutely must let go.

Sometimes the hardest thing for an alcoholic and addict to do is nothing. I've learned that doing nothing can be one hell of an action – the best
action, a lot of times. My first impulse, when confronted with a situation
not to my liking, is to find a way to get in there and fix it, force a solution.
I'd do whatever it took. Sometimes doing nothing is the answer. Letting go
is healthy and gentle. Alcoholism is sick and hard.

With the help of my friends at the 12-step meetings, I've been able to
find the courage to accept the things I cannot change. I was able to accept
my sentence because I had accepted my crime. I was wrong. Sex for drugs
is wrong. After the NFL situation, I was able to understand rather than be
understood. They didn't know my recovery was real. What's important is
that I knew and I keep walking the walk. Almost every day I see how much
better I am at accepting things and living a new life. But I still screw up
sometimes. I haven't threatened to hijack a plane, assaulted anyone or
robbed anyone in years. I haven't written any hate mail to the IRS lately
either. One other clear statistic is I haven't been arrested since 1983. That's
the real measurement.

I had a brutal time dealing with the IRS decision to seize the house I'd
bought my mother. I owed them money and I'd tossed those yellow
envelopes, and so they showed up one day and basically said, "Mrs. Rivers,
the street is out that way." I was heart broken. A heart break hurts. I didn't
accept this at all. Had to do something. Had to get even. I just felt so shitty
and guilty about it that the disease was running wild, screwing up my serenity, screaming at me, "Go get those bastards! Show those fuckers who they're
messing with." I sat down and wrote a letter to the IRS agent in charge of my
case. Writing for me is therapeutic. It has often helped me process my feelings, given me clarity and helped me vent feelings if I was upset about something. This time it didn't help at all. My pen was smoking.

It was the most vulgar, vile thing I have ever written. Every third word
or so was four letters, and that was in the mellow part. I began, "Dear
mother fucker, you no good mother fucking, cock sucking, s.o.b." and
went from there. A real feelings love letter, this was. I was in jail at the time

and I stuck it in the mailbox about noon. By 8:00 PM I wanted it back. This letter was about self-loathing. It was about my feeling terrible that I would let such a thing happen, and my taking it out on this guy who was merely doing his job. I directed my rage at the agent because it was less painful than directing it at myself. This was my fault. At the time I didn't know how to own it. I had screwed up when I didn't pay my taxes, and screwed up just as badly when I sent this revolting letter. Writing down my feelings was fine. Mailing my feelings was a mistake. I support writing down feelings, good and bad.

I had to write a letter of amends. I said I was wrong to write such a letter to him. I asked his forgiveness and tried to explain. I wrote, "That letter had nothing to do with you. It had everything to do with me. I know it wasn't your fault or the IRS' fault that my mother's house was taken and sold. It happened because I was irresponsible. I didn't pay my taxes. The only person at fault is me."

There have been many lessons in my years before and during my present never-ending recovery. It's damn easy to get complacent, arrogant, and even after you have some years of sobriety behind you. You might go to few therapy sessions or 12-step meetings or spend less time with your recovering friends. You might think, "I've got this thing licked," and believe that alcoholism has little to do with your life anymore.

It's true that I have a better recovery now than I did a few years ago, but I don't ever want to forget that I didn't just cut the disease out of me in 1983, as if I had an appendectomy or something. I am not recovered, past tense. I am recovering.

So the old image sticks, just the way it did with the NFL at the Broncos vs. Giants Super Bowl. They remember my big mouth, my coke habit and my going to jail. My new friends know a nice man who knows how to be a friend. Sometimes it hurts like hell that the past won't go away. Sometimes I feel like tossing a few things in a knapsack and going door to door, stopping at every home in America and saying, "Excuse me, I'm Thomas Henderson and I'm not like that anymore." Sometimes I wish I could change people's thinking, give them current information. I even wish I could change what already happened. But I can't.

Lots of people probably think I got what was coming to me and don't give it another thought. That's my burden, the result of my drug and alcohol addiction and my wrong doings, and in sobriety I'm just working as hard as I can to accept that I can't change it. I accept it and then move on. When I meet new friends, especially women, I give them a copy of my first book Out of Control. They either accept me the way I am or don't call.

For me, looking back is the most dangerous thing of all. There are so many regrets, so many misgivings. I hit bottom and it was like a plane crash. Nothing was left except this little black box, a tiny fragment that somehow stayed intact; the fragment I built my sobriety from.

For my sobriety, for my life today, I need to see that to beat up on myself for my wrongs would do nothing but make it a hell of a lot more likely that I would start using again, and start perpetrating a bunch more wrongs. I feel tremendous remorse about a lot of my past, but I've done as much as I can to clean it up. For today, self-torment would do nothing but harm.

I also need to accept where I am today. I am no longer a major media event or even a minor one. I live in a modest condo in Austin, Texas. I threw away a great football career and snorted away more than a million dollars up my nose. These things are facts that I can't change. So I pray for the courage to change the things I can, instead. I work on my piles.

For years I set grand dreams and high expectations, but I would never feel good about it, even if I met them. There was always some place higher I had to go. I was restless. It was never enough. I was never enough. No matter what people saw on the outside, I felt I could not measure up on the inside.

Today, I try to accept what I have achieved and feel good about it. I try not to dwell on what I haven't done. I don't shoot for the sky because I think it's better for me to stick with the heart. I try to nurture myself, not tear myself down. I wake up every day and I try, more than anything else, to take care of my sobriety for that day. I talk it, and more importantly, I walk it.

Life is hard sometimes. So is sobriety. There are injustices and wrongs, setbacks and tragedies, and lots of other stuff that isn't pleasant. The better equipped you are to deal with it, the better your sobriety and your life will be. Like anything else, letting go gets easier the more you do it.

It gets to be something you want to do because you see how much better the results are. The bottom line is; it works. You feel better. It's all about being good to yourself, being kind and gentle, accepting that you're not perfect and life's not either, and going from there. Perfection is an awful lot to ask. I know a lot of people who have made their lives miserable insisting on it. I was one of them. I got tired of it. I changed.

I live in an imperfect world and I accept that now. Because I accept it, there's a huge difference in my life. I like this way much better.

Hit it, James Brown – I feel good!

PAT TILLMAN

I didn't know him personally but that's not important because I know what he did. My heroes used to be athletes and entertainers but I now know that athletes and entertainers are not heroes. Pat Tillman is now my one and only hero. His picture should be next to hero in every dictionary in the world. I couldn't have done what he did. I wouldn't have done what he did. It takes a special human being to put their life on the line for a cause.

He was driven by his patriotism and need to serve and protect his country.

Thanks Pat.

CHAPTER TWENTY FOUR

POLITICS AND POLITICIANS

A good way to stay sober is to give sobriety to another drunk. Although I felt my charitable work was important, it was not helping other drunks. In the course of giving speeches and attending 12-step meetings, I met an energetic woman named Ann Richards during the early '90s.

She was Texas state treasurer when I met her, and a recovering alcoholic. We'd see each other at recovery meetings and drink coffee, laugh, swap stories about our drunk and drug-a-logs. At these 12-step meetings we also talked about the problems of prison, and how drugs and alcohol accounted for a significant amount of crime and created a significant number of criminals.

One night I gave her a small unsolicited check toward her campaign for governor. She went on to win the election. With my new friend Ann's support I launched a program, "Sobriety Is An Option," geared toward teaching convicts that they didn't have to live the way they lived, that sobriety could help them change and lead reasonably functional lives.

It was a simple message but an important one. Too many of our youth are never told that sobriety is an option. Most adults don't remember who gave them their first drink. They don't even remember making the choice to drink. Drinking alcohol is thrust upon us and the act glamorized through advertising, movies and television.

Through that relationship with Richards, and her knowing what I did, I was allowed to put together a program for Texas prisons. We were funded through the Texans War On Drugs. I spoke at every prison in the state over a four-year period, with the emphasis on recidivism. My message to inmates was to try to convince them they could have a life if they took that first right step out of prison, the only step that I knew worked for me. I could never tell anyone to do anything I hadn't done my own damn self.

That was the only thing I had. My only piece of gold, my only stock was this summary advice: "Here's what I can tell you. I think you will make better decisions if you are sober than if you're not sober. If you are criminally challenged, that's a whole different story. But if alcohol and/or drugs has anything to do with your incarceration, I suggest with my experience and results, and with all my heart, that if you stay sober you can be free."

We gave convicts and those leaving prison on parole a booklet that showed them where to locate social services, shelter and food, legal advice, medical and dental help if they needed it. The booklet listed 1-800 numbers for social services they wouldn't ordinarily know about. We had 30 versions printed for different counties.

If a guy leaves prison in Texas without street clothes and no one brings him some Nikes and a nice pair of jeans and shirt, he gets prison industry Wranglers. The taxpayers add $100-200 to our booklet with a map of services.

On some occasions our program featured former convicts as speakers, including myself. Attendance at my talks was strictly voluntary. There was no guard racking the bars and saying, "Henderson is here tonight. Get your ass out of this cell and get down there and listen to him."

I'd get on average about 55 percent of the inmate population to hear what I had to say. If there were 1,500 prisoners, about 800 would come sit in a hot gymnasium and listen to me. Part of the attraction was the celebrity of being a former Dallas Cowboy, but more than that, it was about a man who was sober, and by then had been clean and sober for about 10 years. He had also been an inmate himself.

We have more than two million people in prisons around the country, and the recidivism rate is close to 50 percent. I want to reduce that number. My aim and purpose since 1986 has been to affect the recidivism rate in prisons. I couldn't do that as a Christian, and wouldn't try. I couldn't have done it as a great person. I couldn't be Roger Staubach. All I could be was me.

My experience was that alcohol and drugs were the catalyst that put me in prison, despite the charge that sent me there. I wanted to carry that message to prisons around the country. In some way, I have a presence in all U. S. prisons. My films are used every day in state prisons, federal prisons, county jails, drug rehab centers, and juvenile detention centers across the land.

But in 1996, George W. Bush defeated Richards to become governor of Texas and our funding was immediately cut off. I contacted Ron Wilson, a Texas legislator from Houston, the only politician I know who will wear leather pants to the capitol. He's my kind of guy. I asked Wilson if he could get me a meeting with Bush. He wound up getting me two.

I didn't know much about George W. I was aware that he'd been in the oil business in west Texas and owned a piece of the Texas Rangers baseball team. I liked and respected his father. I liked Ronald Reagan as well, and I'm a Democrat. There was something fatherly about Reagan. I actually supported George Sr. when he ran against Reagan, before Reagan picked him as his vice president.

So I went to see George W. I thought we had something in common. Since he, too, once had a drinking problem, I thought we could have a conversation about recidivism and the success of our program.

The purpose of my first meeting with Bush was to try to save the program. My pay was $20,000 a year, which barely covered expenses to go to Amarillo and other prisons around the state. Other staff members were making $26-28,000 a year. My part had nothing to do with Thomas Henderson making money. It was something I felt that I owed. It was my own answer to the question, How do I give back? How do I share the experience of incarceration and let people know they don't have to go back?

I went to see George W. thinking we had some common experiences and ideas. I was completely wrong. We exchanged pleasantries and visited about football, baseball, the Cowboys and Tom Landry for a few minutes. Then it was down to: "Governor, our funding has been cut off. The chairman of the Department of Criminal Justice doesn't want to fund us. Here is what we do."

I told him that we were affecting 85 percent of the prison population at the point of release. We were affecting recidivism by offering hope and change and restitution and sobriety to every inmate leaving the Texas department of criminal justice. We were providing more than 100 lectures about sobriety and recovery from former felons, people who'd been out of prison for 15 or 20 years, people who were productive citizens, taking care of their families and paying child support. They were tax-paying Texans.

I told him our budget was $300,000 and we wanted to continue. We knew his chairman was getting millions of dollars to lock up felons in Texas. We didn't want to influence that. We wanted to affect prisoners coming out of the gate.

As I was talking to George W., I noticed something. He wasn't listening to me. He was sitting there, looking at me and preparing to rebut. I can tell when I'm not being listened to. He was raring to talk. After I made my case, he said, "Thomas, what do you think about faith-based initiatives? It is my administration's view that we should be using faith-based treatment for alcoholics. That's what worked for me."

I said, "Governor, that's fine, but it's completely different from what we're doing. Faith-based is good, but we're dealing with agnostics and atheists and muslims and Jews. Although the Christian angle is a good one, it misses too many people who may not want to praise Jesus. I believe we have a generic form of reaching people that doesn't miss anyone. That is, God is how you understand him. That means if I have a felon who's a Jew, he may become more involved with his Judaism. If I have an agnostic, he may find his way to a higher power through sobriety. If I have an atheist, well, at least he has a belief system. He doesn't believe in anything religious."

Bush said he'd like to think about it before making a decision, which came down to approving our program or sticking with his chairman. I left the meeting knowing that I'd spoken to a man who didn't listen. He couldn't hear me or didn't want to because our views clashed on this issue.

About a month later, I went back to see George W. I guess he thought I was profiting because he said, "Thomas, why don't you volunteer?"

"Give us the funding, governor, and I will volunteer," I said. "And by the way, Governor, I was only making $20,000 and it barely covers my expenses. I have three or four people who need these jobs and they're doing excellent work for the state of Texas. If you fund us you can take my expenses out of the budget." I called his hand.

George W. finally said, "Thomas, I'm going to stick with my chairman. My advisors tell me faith-based is the way we want to go."

Lo and behold, about six months later, the chairman resigned amid charges of fraud and mismanagement. Why did Bush turn us down? I think he was just politically confused.

But the man has a heart. He has a family. He recognizes good work. I say that after what happened while I was fasting seven days to raise $300,000 and add a track to the football stadium I'd already built. To my surprise and delight I received $500 from the personal checking account of George and Laura Bush. I give him and her credit for the donation because they didn't have to do it. At that moment I sat back and thought, you're doing pretty good, Thomas, when you get a Republican governor and his wife to write you a check.

That's the sort of unsolicited trust and respect I began to receive through my works. It wasn't what I said or what I promoted. It was what I did with blood, sweat and tears.

* * * *

Rick Perry, another Republican, succeeded George W. as governor of Texas. And in August of 2003, the state announced that it would eliminate 62 of 153 prison chaplain positions. The budget cut of chaplains whose salaries ranged from $28,740 to $34,308 a year amounted to 40 percent of their remaining workforce.

So much for faith-based. There's another way to interpret that philosophy: We take care of the rich and let churches take care of the poor. I'd been aware of that trend from an earlier conversation with the Director of Treatment and Counseling Services for the Texas Department of Criminal Justice. I had done business with him for years, selling him films for the program and doing speeches for inmates. I'd just made a new film, but in so many words he told me not to bother sending it, that even if they liked it they might buy only one for the whole state. He said more than half of all drug and alcohol treatment programs in Texas prisons already had been cut.

"Look, Henderson," he said from Huntsville, "they're going back to just straight- up punishment, warehousing them and letting them go when it's time to let them go. I'm a Republican, and from working inside I see they want to go faith-based and move away from treatment. So they cut to where we are more administrative than treatment- conscious now. So here's my definition of compassionate conservatism. It goes like this: You are out of a job and we're sorry about that.

* * * *

I never saw anyone more authentic or sincere about a cause than the late Barbara Jordan, a Democrat Congresswoman from Houston. She was especially relentless about the integrity of the office of President of the United States. Much of her fame came from calling out Richard Nixon during the Watergate business. When they were going after Bill Clinton for impeachment I didn't hear or see a Republican whose motives were as pure as Jordan's on the issue of presidential integrity.

When Barbara retired after three terms in the House of Representatives, she moved to Austin as a professor at The University of Texas. I'd been in her company at some events but we'd never been formally introduced. I knew Ann Richards loved Jordan, and I knew she'd had an elementary school named after her.

One day I was flying back to Austin from a lecture and lo and behold, Barbara Jordan was on board this DC-10. I walked back to her seat and said hello. She didn't know me from Adam. I introduced myself and it was one of those uncomfortable moments: "Hi, I'm Thomas Henderson. Remember I used to play for the Dallas Cowboys?"

I seldom do that kind of awkward introduction, the kind where I say, "I'm Hollywood Henderson, former Dallas Cowboys linebacker. Played in three Super Bowls. Hey, remember me?" I don't do that anymore, and I probably shouldn't have done it with her, but I did. Not that it helped.

We landed in Austin and as I was walking off, one of the flight attendants stopped me. She said, Mr. Henderson, we can't get Miss Jordan's wheelchair back to her seat. Can you help move her to the front of the plane? Illness had robbed Barbara of movement in the lower half of her body. She had multiple sclerosis and would die in 1996 from that and complications from leukemia.

I said, sure, I'll do it, not only because I respected Barbara so much. She was up there with Martin Luther King and Gandhi in my estimation and even if she wasn't, she was a person who needed help. But the job of lifting her probably needed three people or a dolly. I don't mean the slightest disrespect when I say that Barbara was indeed a large woman.

At the time I weighed about 250 pounds, 30 more than my playing weight. One of my best attributes used to be upper body strength, and at one time I could almost clean-and-jerk as much weight as Too Tall Jones and Randy White, two of the strongest Cowboys when I was there. I never could do bench presses or had any endurance in weightlifting. But I was strong. I had that raw Jethro Bodine kind of physicality.

"Barbara, I've come to help move you," I said.

"Do you think you can hold me?" she asked, worried.

I'd estimate Barbara weighed a minimum of 300 pounds. She only had the use of her upper extremities. She was dead weight from the waist down. She was unable to take a step, so her legs had to be moved by an outside source...me. Her biggest fear, I found out halfway down the aisle, was that I'd drop her.

I got behind her and, with a bear hug, I put my arms under her arms and pulled her out of the seat. I got her straightened up, but I knew I had too much weight in my arms. My ego, my manhood and my constitution wouldn't allow me to say, "I've got to put you down."

So I'd kick her right leg from behind with my right leg. Then kick her left leg with my left leg. Meanwhile she was fighting me. Her fingernails were digging into my forearms. She was afraid I was going to drop her. I understood. I kept saying, 'Relax. Don't fight me, Barbara." The DC-10 was a big plane and I had to pass six seats, then the closet and through the galley to a waiting wheelchair.

Once I get that far, I had to hold her and turn myself around, back up and get her into the chair. It's not like I could push her forward into the chair. Halfway through turning her around, one of my vertebrae said, Thomas, what are you doing to us? I was 6'3" when I began to move Barbara. When I finally got her in the chair I know I was 5' 11".

Her people were waiting at the top of the tunnel and as they pushed her through the terminal I kidded with Barbara. Girl, I said, you broke my back. She had a car picking her up. So here comes a skycap bringing her two small bags. Barbara rummaged through her purse and gave him $5.

I reflected on that leaving the airport in my car. Five bucks for two little bags! I thought, Barbara, you could have given me a tip.

Helping Barbara paid off later when I released my first film for distribution in prisons. I called Barbara and asked if she would review it and then endorse the contents. Bless her heart, she wrote:

If you want to be inspired about the power of an individual to overcome self-imposed destructive tendencies watch Thomas Henderson's Staying Sober & Staying Free. I consider him the world's greatest role model.

I'm glad Barbara used the word "power." That's what I needed to carry her off the plane.

DARRELL ROYAL
(Retired University of Texas football coach)

Thomas Henderson is a lot mellower today. I would be a lot more mellow, too, if I won the lottery. I wouldn't be nearly as grouchy.

The present day Thomas is financially secure and more laid back. He doesn't have that pressure to succeed financially. That's improved his demeanor to the point where his true personality comes out. He's interested in politics in the city. I think he feels indebted to the neighborhood where he grew up and really wants to help out those people

I've been asked if I had reservations about dealing with Thomas. No. I didn't get to talking to him until he was sober. Our friendship developed over athletics and golf. Besides, he overlooked my warts, and I overlooked his warts.

Golf got us together through charity and celebrity tournaments. I knew he was promoting his video on drug abuse. He was trying to make a buck, and you've got to admire him for that. Lately, our friendship has grown and expanded into the political. He's taken an interest in politics in his hometown, which is good.

He's trying to get something done on the east side, where I've been involved for a long time. We had a charity golf tournament here and I put all the proceeds into Eastside Youth, which is the same thing Thomas is working on. He's also built a track and sports facility over there.

I go to the east side to eat all the time. I love Mexican breakfast. While I was over there I could see the poverty and need. I thought there wasn't a better place you could put your money for youth looking for a chance. They had some nice programs over there, but they needed funds to run those programs and encourage young boys and girls who were mainly Hispanic and Black.

I drew a map around the area where the money had to be spent so that none of the funds leaked out. I think we've put close to $4 million over there. People put in an application for their particular program. I have a committee that I trust to use good judgment on where the money goes. I served on that committee for a while and when I got satisfied with the committee I quit serving. I figured I was raising the money and getting it over there.

If there was any negative talk when Thomas came back to Austin that was all washed away when he won the lottery because a guy that rich does-

n't need to be hustling anybody. *I never saw any rejections prior to that. But he caused some people to shy away when he was aggressive and trying to make a buck.*

Do I see a link that a football background influenced his self-discipline to stay clean? I never have been much for that. You get those instincts and qualities from your parents or grandparents, from somebody in your family when you're young.

There was something he picked up from his background. You know he loves his step dad. Somebody, a citizen over on the east side, an older guy, somebody took an interest in him. Someone guided his natural instinct to compete in football. And football is not meant for everybody.

Football bruises you and exhausts you and makes you thirsty. Hell, you wonder why a guy plays it. There is something in the early days that I think hones the competitiveness that causes you to do it. I felt like his influences started earlier than football, that's my point. His self-discipline may have been honed by competitive football, sharpened by it, but there was something in his life earlier than that. Thomas hasn't talked a whole lot to me about his past. He didn't have to because I knew it all. As for mention of him playing for the Cowboys, probably a time or two. It's not something he talks a lot about or promotes.

He's turned out to be just one of the boys. That's it. He had a rough go as a young kid. Then he really had a rough go when he got into drugs. Now he's a good citizen of Austin, concerned and involved in the process.

He has a good story and shares it with people to encourage them to get off drugs. He made a talk the other day. I went over for a luncheon and fund raising deal at Austin Recovery Center and he told his story. To come off the floor and do what he's done is remarkable.

He's turned out for the better.

CHAPTER TWENTY FIVE

MAMMA AND STILL WORKING ON ME:

At some point in my recovery years ago, I read a quote from Albert Einstein that stuck with me as I navigated through life. This is what Einstein said:

"You cannot solve a problem with the same mind that created it."

I was 36 years old, back in Austin and there were still problems in my life. I was around my mother again. I was around my brothers and sisters. Their lives were going in unthinkable directions.

I was in a bookstore one day and picked up a book, entitled, The Flying Boy, by John Lee. It was an autobiography by a therapist who wrote about being emotionally unavailable because of traumatic events and relationships he had experienced. Whenever things would get just right, he would fly away and sabotage the peace. The book knocked me out.

I went looking for Lee and found him in town. He knew of me. I found out he met with a group of 13 men in Austin every week to help them purge psychologically damaging events from their past. Most of the horrors still clinging to these adults had occurred during their youth.

They spoke of childhood traumas – being sodomized by their father, hating their mothers, confusion over sexuality. They were the most courageous, gut-wrenching confessions you could imagine. The process took a man into the depths of his agony and distortion, his illness and resentment. The group would be there with him and share his moment of pain.

This was no collection of street bums or derelicts. The men were government officials, attorneys, doctors and lawyers. It was an upscale cross section of mentally ill people. I sat in front of Lee as if he were Muhammad Ali. I joined the group early in 1991 and was so transfixed by what I saw and heard that I didn't say a word for two months.

Each session lasted about two hours. Part of the process included the use of a baton. Recounting traumas of the past brought rage, anger and disappointment to an emotional peak. This was when the victim was encouraged to strike a large pillow, a futon, with the baton to expel those intense feelings.

I have seen men wield that baton with such ferocity that it scared me. They were in a coma of pain, oblivious to where they were as if everyone in the room had disappeared. There were times when I thought guys were going to hit me with the bat. I joined this group to do more work on me and my soul. This work was with men.

I have cried many, many times during my recovery. We whose lives have been so dysfunctional have earned a good cry. The work was good. What I understood about being a recovering alcoholic, drug addict and felon is that I need to keep moving toward solutions in my life.

A significant moment with my mother happened soon after. I made a habit of going to her house every day. My mom was still very poor. I had started buying her appliances and furniture and helping to fix up the house. I'm still doing all I can. At first I didn't have enough money to buy her another house, which is still a sore subject between us. I'm embarrassed and ashamed that I lost her house to an IRS foreclosure when I was in prison. She is mad and resentful that I lost her house. Out of love and guilt I was doing all I could otherwise. I bought things like new carpet or a new bedspread, whatever there was that I could afford. The sessions with John Lee were still fresh when I visited my mother one day.

Everything that I thought I was mad about went away. We were sitting and talking. She was in a grateful mood. "You know you've been good to me," she said. "You've been kind and nice and given me more money than I ever gave you."

At that moment I remembered something that set me free from my self-made trap of resentment I had about her. I remembered being 12 years old and wanting to go to the Border Olympics in Laredo. I loved track and field, and local schools had great runners like John Harvey and other track stars from Anderson High School. I remember going to where my mother worked to get $12 to pay for the bus ride to Laredo.

This was one of many times I went to her for money, but this one came back to me clearly. With that memory came an understanding of how misinformed I was about the anger I felt toward my mother and the conditions under which we lived when I was growing up.

I left school that day because I had a two-hour deadline to raise $12. Remember, this was 1965, and $12 to my mother was a lot of money. I caught a bus downtown to the little fried food restaurant where she was a cook and waitress.

"Mom, I have to have $12 by 3 o'clock or I can't go," I told her.

I watched my mother reach into her left pocket. She pulled out three or four wrinkled dollar bills. She went to her right pocket and started counting out dimes and nickels. Then she got down to pennies. Finally, spread on a stainless steel table in a restaurant kitchen was $12 – four one dollar bills, no quarters, the rest dimes, nickels and pennies. I think she put a single penny back in one pocket.

Twenty-five years later, I heard her say that I had given her more than she had ever given me and I said, "That's not true, Mother, because on many occasions you gave me all you had."

I forgave her and I forgave myself for being such a creep about how I perceived my childhood. My mother did the best she could. Today I'm grateful for what she did for me as a child. She did her best with what she had.

But I had always compared what we had to others, and we didn't have very much. Somewhere my unreasonable ego kept saying, "Why didn't she go to college? Why didn't she have a degree? Why doesn't she have a new car? Why don't we have television? Why don't we have a telephone? Why do we only shop once a week on Friday and the groceries are gone by Sunday?"

You have to grow up at some point. In the recovery field we find that children of alcoholics, alcoholic children or recovering alcoholics resent their parents for something. I got caught in that conviction, So that's part of the problem...your parents were no good...your father was this and your mother was that.

My mamma was special and could be unintentionally funny. Such as after I won the lottery and wanted to invest $1 million to build about 15 affordable homes in my neighborhood. I wasn't giving the money away. I figured to break even financially and do a community service. The deal never came off because I wouldn't fill out all those Requests for Proposals forms from the city. The city sends those out when they don't want to do business with you.

Ever see those government forms? In my amateur status as an architect, contractor and city planner, I couldn't fill out an RFP. They wanted plans, and they wanted site studies and they wanted how much lumber and…it was nuts. I refused to do it.

Mamma had heard about my plan when it went public. About a week later I visited her and she immediately began to cry. Now this was after I bought her a new Lincoln Town Car, given her lots of money and had helped buy her a new home.

"What's wrong?" I asked.

"Well," she sobbed, "I feel like if you can give the city one million dollars you can give me a million."

It took half an hour to explain to her that what I planned to do had nothing to do with charity.

Then there's Mamma's infatuation with playing bingo. I got a lot of bingo-related calls from her. They kept coming after I spent $3,000 on her trip to Las Vegas in the spring of 2003 where, of course, she lost. I knew what was coming when I got a sweet-talking phone call.

"Hi, honey, how are you doing? Are you busy?"

"No, mamma."

"Are you sure you're not busy?"

"No, mamma."

"Would you like to send your mamma to bingo?"

"Yes, mamma."

I'm thinking I'd rather give her $100 for bingo than have her blow another $3,000 in Las Vegas. So over the next two or three months she lost $800 to $900 on cards, pull tabs and anything else. She owed three or four friends, even the bingo operator, $20, $40, $60 over the past month. I think Mamma does math in her head like all the bingo regulars. It goes like this: I lost $1,000 but I just won $250, so I'm ahead.

When you are mature enough, I think you can look back and even if your parents made mistakes, they didn't abort you. They put a roof over your head. They put food in your mouth. If they screwed up in some way it was probably because they weren't ready to become parents themselves. There is no course in parenting.

I'm blessed today to have the 12 steps. They give me a road map. They give me instructions and solutions. Coupled with the Ten Commandments, in my estimation they serve as a strategy for living that's mentally sound. It will work if you implement it and believe in the process.

So I'm running around my hometown still searching for answers but doing well. I'm having a ball with my work. I made my first film, Staying Sober and Staying Free, and others, that are seen in about 90 percent of all prisons in America.

* * * *

November 15, 10:30 a.m., 2003, my mother was 66 years old. She had given birth to me 21 days short of her 16th birthday in 1953.

I got a call that morning from the hospital where she was being treated. The doctors and the staff wanted me to come over immediately. I knew why they were calling. She was being kept alive by life support and medicine.

I didn't rush over. Instead I took my time. Took a shower. Brushed my teeth. Fiddled. Flossed my teeth. Put out the trash. Got on the computer for a few minutes. I had to ready myself for such an awesome confrontation. I had been given medical power of attorney and I didn't want it. I got on my knees and prayed for guidance and strength.

This woman gave me life during a time when forced adoptions and coat hanger abortions were fairly common for 15-year-olds. She protected me, and all of her children. She birthed me, fed me, clothed me and sheltered me. She never made more than minimum wage her entire life. Somehow she raised five kids and none of us ever went hungry. We always had a place to stay and a place to call home.

I thought about how hard it must have been for her. She gave us all she had. There was heroism in this woman. She never had the finer things in life until her first-born bought her a house and gave her money and other worldly goods. And I took her for granted. I went to the hospital.

I was told she wouldn't make it without those machines. Part of me wanted to keep her hooked up forever. But after consulting with her husband and my brothers and sisters, we decided to let her go to that place beyond life.

I feel like I grew up with her. She's 66. I'm 50. I needed to say some things to her. I didn't get the chance but this is what I would have said:

Mamma, you took care of all of your kids against all odds. You did without so we could eat and be sheltered. You loved us all the same. We are all here because we know you are the best mamma, grandmamma and great grandmamma in the history of the world. We love our kids because of the way you loved us.

They pulled the life support systems just now. They brushed your hair back on the pillow. They washed your face. You look so pretty. You look so peaceful. You just stopped breathing. Your eyes rolled toward me and gently shut.

Your strength, family tradition, charity and love will stay with me forever. We will tell everyone about you forever. You were tough as nails and as kind as Mother Teresa. From all of us, thank you for being the woman you were. I will never get over not being able to call you and hear your voice anymore. I'm mad about that. But I'm happy that I can still hear you in my heart. Goodbye, Violet Faye. I'll see you over there.

FRANCHOT GRAY RIVERS
(Family member)

I am the younger brother of Thomas Henderson by 10 years. I don't know if you want to call it the southern side of the family or the northern side because we have different dads. His brothers on his father's side are up north and everyone on his mom's side is down south.

I've broken down my relationship with Thomas into three phases. There was early childhood, the Cowboys years and the adult life that followed. As for early childhood, he was your typical big brother. The only thing different was when he left to live with my grandmother in Oklahoma. I'm pretty certain he was 16 so I was six when he went away. Of course, he would come back to visit and we'd go up there to see him.

I didn't like it at all when Thomas left home. When you're a kid growing up in a tough neighborhood your big brother was a security blanket. I loved him for that, but I didn't want to see him go because I thought we needed him to look out for my other brother. James Rivers is our middle brother. There's me, James and Thomas. James is 42, two years older than me. So it made a big impact to have Thomas leave. It was a treat when he came home and it made us sad to see him go. To some degree we knew that Thomas was trying to do something to better educate himself and get out of this rat hole.

The Cowboys years came next. Those were tough years because I met a guy I didn't like too much. His name was Hollywood. Drugs changed him. He wasn't nice to be around a lot of times. He was often edgy and bitchy. Like, "You guys get up and clean house," or "Go do this...Go do that." It was spur of the moment stuff. We saw real sporadic behavior. Some of those years were dark and not the greatest of times. But there were good times, because this is the same guy who took us into his home.

Yes, he did. A 25-year old kid by himself, making the most money he's ever made, his name blowing up everywhere, the Hollywood status going and he takes 15 and 17- year old boys to raise. He moved us to Dallas, put us in high school and showed us the finer side of life. He had us hanging around a bunch of Cowboys and rich people.

As far as house rules, hell, he was worse than my dad. We had curfews and chores. Even though he had money he only gave us what we needed. I think that was to assure we didn't have extra money to do crazy stuff. We had the whole nine yards...the car had to be in by a certain time. We even had a weekend curfew.

There were times that he'd call us from on the road. They'd be playing the Giants in New York and he'd call home to make sure we did our homework and that everything was okay. So go figure. He was probably doing cocaine when he called to say, "Get your homework done, damnit!" All in all, though, he was a good guardian or father figure.

James and I lived with Thomas for three years. It would have been four, but he got fired in Dallas and had to move to San Francisco. James had graduated and left by then. A family put me up for last year of high school so I stayed in Dallas and finished my senior year there.

I was still naive as far as big time drugs. I knew Thomas had a problem and that problem was going with him from Dallas to San Francisco and Houston. But it took me years to understand how deep and bad the problem was. I was a dumb 17-year old. But I knew that drugs were involved because we saw evidence. Like cocaine residue on the dresser. You saw white powdery substance and then there was his attitude.

His jail time was tough as far as the family goes. You couldn't go to the local store because everyone knew us. We still supported Thomas. I think my mom wrote him every week. He was still my brother. I had a couple of fistfights with guys telling me my brother was this and that and has sexually assaulted someone. People were just cruel.

I had no contact with Thomas while he was in prison. I left Austin. I did a stretch in the military and was gone for 11 years, give or take a visit or two. I heard he was doing fine. I talked to him a couple of times after he left prison and got married in California.

We got back together in 1990 when I moved to Austin. Thomas was already there. One of the first things we did, and it was his idea, was to rebuild Yellow Jacket Stadium. He made me project manager. I watched Thomas throw dirt and use a shovel, things I'd never seen him do before. I'd never seen my brother work like that.

He was focused. He was determined. I mean totally different. He reminded me of the old Thomas. To me there was a Thomas period, a Hollywood period and then a Thomas period again. It was good to see him return to the Thomas side. He's been a father figure to me since I was 15. It was good to have someone that I could talk to when I had troubles. Thomas was caring and compassionate. He listened to what you had to say.

Our father passed away going on three years ago. Thomas has taken over as the figurehead of the family and he's doing a great job at it. What can I say? He's my big brother. I love him.

CHAPTER TWENTY SIX

TOM LANDRY

Now that I have matured as a man and a father, I can reflect on who I think he was and who I knew I was. Tom Landry and I came from very safe places; he from Mission, Texas in the Rio Grande Valley and me from Austin, Texas. I was raised in a safe segregated community. So was he.

My childhood didn't take place in Mississippi, Alabama or Georgia. In Austin I was never humiliated for being black. I was never called "nigger." I was never put in my place. I was a free man. I didn't connect to racism or to the civil rights movement of the '50s and '60s, frankly, because we didn't have a television or a telephone. I was insulated, protected and segregated most of my young life.

I remember going to a Black Muslim meeting in Oklahoma City in 1970 when I was a junior in high school. I was searching for some sort of identity or to hear what the latest struggle was all about. I listened to Malcolm X and the local Minister X. I understood and sympathized with their jargon but had no personal identification with the struggle.

They preached about more segregation, the white devil and to get rid of your slave last name. I sat there thinking, "Well, I'm already screwed up. My daddy's last name is Goree. My last name is Henderson. Now you want me to change it to X?"

I couldn't become a racist by osmosis. I'm not a racist today. Members of my family are racist. I know white racists. I think it's such a waste of energy. It's such an emotional waste of intellectual energy if you have any.

As for Landry, and this is only my opinion, when he played for the New York Giants in the 1950s the only black men he met knew their place. I didn't have a place, let alone know my place. I didn't know that because of my color I couldn't express myself. I had no fear. I didn't know what

Cornell Green, Don Perkins or Mel Renfro may have been through because they were five or 10 years older than me. I didn't know they had been called "nigger" and couldn't do anything about it. Or they'd been called "boy" and that was just the way it was.

I think Landry's confrontation with Duane Thomas in 1970-71 was his first encounter with an angry black man. I believe Duane knew racism and he was angry. I think Duane knew where his place was supposed to be and that made him madder.

I believe the difference between Duane and me was that Duane had racial contamination. I felt like Kunta Kinta from the TV show "Roots." They'd have to cut off my feet to put me in my place. I was never angry. I was just proud. I was arrogant, free and uncontaminated.

I put my relationship with Landry on an employer-employee basis. Let me do my job. Get out of my face. Let me stack these boxes. Let me wash these dishes. What are all these special rules just for me? Landry made up certain rules that I thought were aimed at me and were out of line. I would ask him, "What are you doing?" I never disrespected him but I would sit there unafraid and challenge his regulations. Landry already had a giant book of rules, and made up some more just for me because I didn't know my place. One said that if you missed practice you didn't start.

That was a Thomas Henderson rule, because I was not a lover of practice. I was a football player, not a football "practicer." I knew it had a place in conditioning and figuring out what was going on, but I hated practices and frankly did everything I could to get out of them. Landry saw the pattern. He also knew how much I loved to be introduced at Texas Stadium or any place we played so he thought, okay, the punishment was that I wouldn't start and be introduced. But even if he wouldn't start me he'd put me in the second series.

Landry and I had a tense moment the morning of a game in Pittsburgh in 1979, about three weeks before he kicked me off the team. Our trainer, Don Cochran, had let me miss practice earlier that week because I had the flu. Landry came to the breakfast table and said, "You know you are not starting today. You know what our deal was."

But the trainer had told me to take off. It wasn't me. So I said to him, "Well, Coach, if I don't start then I'm not going to play today." That created a problem because I said it in front of Bob Breunig and other players, so it wasn't a private moment. It wasn't between Landry and Thomas anymore.

And I wasn't going to play. I wasn't getting dressed. I sat in my locker without any pants or shoes, waiting on the call. Maybe Landry checked with Cochran. I don't know what changed his mind but he came by a few minutes later and said, "Okay, you win. You start."

I think by that fifth season Landry realized that he couldn't handle me in a reasonable conversation. I assumed and expected respect and frustrated him in conversations because I wasn't afraid to speak up for myself. I'm not sure he wanted a "fear" sort of respect from me, but I think he expected one. He had never experienced a spirit like Thomas Henderson.

Should anyone wonder, Landry's name would not appear on my list of racists. I never saw him treat black players different than the whites. He was as distraught about cutting Ken Hutcherson as he was about cutting any player. I never saw him as emotional about releasing someone as he was with Hutcherson, and Ken was blacker than some Stacy Adams shoes.

But I do think Landry picked and chose which players he liked and adored. He loved Randy White and Roger Staubach, Charlie Waters, Cliff Harris and Breunig. I saw that and I was sort of jealous. I suffered from his lack of adulation because I was nonconforming. We clashed from the beginning when he told me I needed to shave my beard at my rookie training camp. I thought, "What does that have to do with anything? I don't like to shave. What do you mean shave? I came here to play football, not join a barber college."

This wasn't the United State Army and he wasn't General Eisenhower. So I didn't. I didn't shave, so he withheld recognition. I wanted my accolades. I wanted my compliments. I'd gotten that in college – "Thomas, you played a great game... you helped us win." I only heard that once from Landry, after one game when I played whip-ass on Russ Francis, the star tight end for New England.

Even Mike Ditka, the special teams coach, withheld accolades and game balls. I'd go down and make almost every tackle on kickoff and punt coverage and some other guy would get a game ball or an award for making one block and one tackle. They'd get up in front of the team and say,

"Bruce Huther really had a great game." Even though I won the Headhunter Award many times, when they gave it to someone else it bothered me.

Sure, I wanted to win it every time. Why not, if I set the standard and out-perform everyone else? I came along before specialty team guys got a shot at the Pro Bowl. If there were a Pro Bowl for rookies in 1975 I would have gone as a specialty team player. I was the only linebacker covering punts from a split position and nobody out there could block me. Benny Barnes wasn't bad, either.

There was some sort of friction between Landry and me from the get-go. I don't think he understood the new black man. The black man who is not angry, not contaminated, who's not afraid and doesn't know his place.

Finally, an issue arose where I felt he disrespected me in my heart. It was a moment when I got angry with him, and I don't think I stopped being mad at him while I wore the Cowboys uniform.

This happened coming into my third year. I had been patient playing behind D. D. Lewis. I thought I could play linebacker better than him. Mentally, I didn't care about the Flex defense and all that. Just let me play. During my second year I played on the nickel packages and covered the best receivers in the NFL. In my third year, D. D. was still there and they really didn't know what to do with me. I was 210 pounds, 6' 2" and skinnier than anybody.

Jerry Tubbs, the linebacker coach, told me they wanted to try me at Sarah linebacker on the Strong side. I thought, "Damn, now I've got to wrestle with tight ends and tackles and guards." At the same time they didn't know what to do with Randy White, either. He was trying to play middle linebacker and also wasn't a starter.

So in 1977 they moved Randy and had us going for the same position, strong side linebacker. Being a far more fluid athlete I had the upper hand in covering tight ends and backs out of the backfield. Being more powerful, very fast and tough as nails, Randy had a slight edge on me in terms of playing the run.

Truth is, we were both out of position. I only played my natural position, at weak side linebacker, during my rookie year. When it became apparent Randy wasn't linebacker material, I used the occasion to ridicule him. Whenever Randy would blow coverage or the tight end or back ran past him to catch a touchdown pass I'd shout, "See, he can't play that position! I am the man! Get him out of here! I am your Sarah!"

Randy got mad, but that was okay. If it weren't for me he wouldn't be in the Pro Football Hall of Fame. I put his ass on all fours as a tackle in the defensive line. He owes me for that bust.

Then here comes Landry. I had clearly won the strong side linebacker slot. But instead of Landry saying, "Thomas, get in there, work hard, you got the job," he says in front of the team and then Tubbs reiterates it, "Thomas will be competing with Mike Hegman for Sarah linebacker. We won't announce a starter until the beginning of the season."

Here I'd been fighting my heart out, studying and working.. That could have been my finest training camp where I sort of shut up. I did the pull-ups for coach Jim Myers. I hated them. I used to cuss him out all the time. "Bleep you, I ain't doing no damn pull-ups today." But Landry hurt me. The day Randy White went down on all fours at tackle, I should have had the starting job. Now he was saying it was between Hegman and me. Hegman was a decent football player, but he wasn't Thomas Henderson. So I got mad at Landry and never, ever stopped being mad at him while I played for the Cowboys..

All of which preceded our meeting in Landry's office on Monday after we lost the 11th game of 1979 in Washington. Each thought the other had better hurry up and show some respect. Neither knew or understood what to do next. What became clear in this last meeting was that we were so far apart that there was nothing to say. The meeting was worthless.

I walked into his office and sat down. I was under the influence of cocaine. I had decided to do some coke on the way to his office, so I had my nose packed. Landry began to say things like, "You know we had a deal in training camp...You know this is not working..."

Then he said, "I'm going to have to put you on waivers." The first words out of my mouth, which was a mistake, was to snap back, "You can't put me on waivers. I'm not going to let you put me on waivers. I quit!"

That was the extent of our conversation. The meeting lasted about a minute. As I walked down the hall I was hoping to see general manager Tex Schramm or Clint Murchison, anyone who might support me. I even drove to Clint's house a few days later but the Cowboys owner wasn't there. I was just hoping someone would come to my defense. But I didn't have any allies.

I think one reason Landry stuck to his decision to fire me was because I didn't attempt to defend myself. I didn't ask for a second chance. I didn't fall on my sword. I did nothing to help him change his decision. I practically made him do it. My defiant attitude left him no other choice.

He could have said, "Thomas, I need you to behave, I need you to come to Bible study, I need you to respect me." I did respect Landry but I didn't cower before him. To me he was like any other employer I'd ever had, from dishwasher to oil rigs offshore. Just because he was Tom Landry, that didn't give him any more authority over me than my fifth grade teacher.

I left Landry without any wiggle room to alter his decision even though Tubbs, the linebacker coach, called me at home the next day. Tubbs asked me if I'd behave if Coach changed his mind. As if there was a chance after I'd told him he couldn't put me on any waivers because I quit.

Landry usually made decisions on the basis of the team rather than an individual. I still think firing me affected the team. He could have fined me or suspended me or done a couple of other things, finished the year and then run my ass off. The Cowboys didn't go back to the Super Bowl in '79; in fact, lost the first round of the playoffs. I could have helped that team. Personally speaking, I think he made a mistake. I think firing me shocked and contaminated the team. And in spite of what anyone thought, I was a serious contributor to the success of the Cowboys for five years.

Years later, I made amends to him for being such an ass. I wrote a long letter, apologizing for the hard time I'd given him and letting him know how much I admired and respected him.

In the end he apologized for not helping me. And best of all, he did it during a toast-and-roast in Austin to celebrate my 10th year of sobriety.

I wondered if Landry, my old coach, the man whose life I had made uncomfortable, would accept my invitation. I wondered how many of my old teammates would appear, men I had badly abused during my drugging years. D. D. Lewis headed the list of those who had reason to despise me. D. D. and I once came close to fighting in the shower until I decided I didn't want to grapple with a naked man. D. D. came, and spoke good-naturedly.

"Sometimes our greatest defects become our greatest asset," he said. "Thomas's mouth got him in trouble. Now it's his greatest asset." Roger Staubach told a story about how after a game I invited an attractive lady to my hotel room-champagne and hot tub at the ready. I looked into her eyes and told her she could have anything she wanted. To which she replied: "Well then, I want Tony Dorsett."

Landry had arrived. I spotted him in the audience looking fit as always and impeccably dressed in a well-cut leather jacket. Then it was his turn at the podium. I knew he would not be unkind. Landry had been hard as a coach, but he had not been unkind. He was a true Christian who practiced his faith. He believed in forgiveness, too.

"It's great to be a part of this," he said, and then began to almost apologize to me! Actually, he was apologizing to all the athletes who had suffered from drug addiction, explaining that he had been unprepared for the problems that began appearing in the late '60s and early '70s, that he had never even seen drugs back then.

"We just didn't know how to handle it, and I think that was the most disappointing thing," Landry said. I nodded to myself thinking that even today, so many years later, neither the NFL nor society knows how to handle drug problems. Addicts are tossed in jail like common criminals, when they need programs to cure them of their addictions. Then we're surprised when they use again and get jailed again.

"I just didn't know what to do to help Thomas," Landry went on. "I guess we ended up saying, well, we need to get rid of him because we had no way to take care of him. But to come here tonight and see what Thomas has done with his life is remarkable. He has a great heart, and that's awful important in life. He cares about people."

I don't think Coach Landry spoke for more than five minutes, but they were five minutes that I treasure to this day. I sat there, smiling, realizing that Tom Landry had come, he had spoken and he didn't hate me. He understood that I had been sick and that society was ill-equipped to deal with this new disease. Actually, crack cocaine wasn't really a new disease but just an old disease-alcoholism-in a different form.

Part of my response was meant as a personal message to Coach Landry. "When I met people like Coach Landry and Staubach, men who had God in their lives, men who were family oriented, I didn't understand them. I didn't understand their commitment. I didn't understand their morals or their principles," I began.

Looking directly at Landry I said, "I got some of those today, Coach. I used to not have them. When I used to think you and Staubach were squares I thought something was wrong with you. But something was wrong with me. I didn't know how to live.

"Through therapy and counseling and my willingness to change, my life has changed. I am a changed man. You don't have to believe it, but it has already taken place. What you think of me is none of my business. What I think of me is paramount. I love me. I like who I've become.

"I am father to that 14-year-old girl sitting over there. I pray to my higher power. I'm a giver. How did I get there? I don't know, but someone said to me recently, 'Thomas, if you could change anything about the life that you had, what would it be?'" And I said, "Nothing. I would not change anything. I like where I have landed. I have friends today, people who love me. I had the same kind of friends most dope addicts do. I had friends who would steal my dope and then help me look for it."

The next time I saw Coach Landry was during a Fellowship of Christian Athletes golf tournament at Barton Creek a few years later. A bunch of former Cowboys were standing around talking and all of a sudden Coach Landry walked up and said, "What's going on, guys?"

Everyone looked stunned. He had never asked us what was going on before. I think he was always afraid to ask me what was going on when I was with the Cowboys. I would have told him more than he wanted to hear. I had to walk away and laugh. Coach Landry never had been sociable with us or ever said, "What's going on, guys?" as if he were one of the boys. Nobody uttered a word. Later, I said to Robert Newhouse, "Did that blow you away? I didn't think he even knew the words."

Time passed, and I heard that he was ill. I talked to Staubach one day and he said, "I don't think Coach is going to make it." I didn't know you could live to be 76 years old and get leukemia. I thought it was a young person's disease.

The news didn't affect me emotionally. I wasn't worried about experiencing trauma or an emotional outburst. I thought. Coach has lived his life and he is obviously going to heaven. He was always a good man.

When I heard he passed away in February of 2000 I knew I would attend his funeral. I didn't go to the public memorial service because Charlie Waters had been assigned to pick the speakers, and I wasn't chosen. That pissed me off. I told Charlie I wanted to say something but he told me they had picked Staubach, Rayfield Wright and so on. It was one of those political moments that I resented. I wasn't in the same loop with Lee Roy Jordan, Cliff Harris and Roger. I wasn't one of the leaders in the locker room. Understand rather than be understood.

If I'd had a chance to talk I would have told Coach Landry how I was dressed. Let me explain why. We had a dress code when the Cowboys traveled. Players were required to wear a tie. The first time I got on an airplane I had on a white shirt and a shoestring-like bolo around my neck. Landry said something to me about it and I told him, "You don't know anything about fashion. This is a tie." He didn't agree and damned if he didn't add an entry in his rulebook to describe what constituted an acceptable tie.

So what I wanted to say to him was:

"Coach, I have a tie on that you would approve. And I wore a suit just for you."

The gravesite rites that followed were private, restricted to family and players. I found myself beginning to miss Coach Landry. He was so far removed from me. He never really talked to me. The only thing Coach Landry ever talked to me about was, "Thomas, you have to stop doing this," and that related to some disciplinary thought or a fine. He never asked me, "How is your mom?" or "How are you feeling today?" Nothing personal ever passed between us.

I didn't think I had any emotional connection to him until I got to the gravesite. Then I began thinking about the opportunity to be a Dallas Cowboy. To have been exposed to a man with strong moral and spiritual values and no-nonsense management style. I learned so much from him even though I fought every rule that he laid down until he fired me.

Landry's services were held on February 16, 2000. That was the last day that I cried.

I'd cried at Sue Stripling's funeral, but that had been almost 25 years ago. She was the mother of my college roommate, Oliver Stripling, and had been a surrogate parent while I was living with my grandmother in Oklahoma. I knew Mrs. Stripling from Bible study at church and I'd spent weekends at her home. She died after a long illness, and I went to the service.

The family knew how long she'd been sick but I didn't. They were sort of ready and relieved when she passed on, but I wasn't. When her body was lowered into the ground I started weeping uncontrollably. I walked from the burial site to a rock chalk road in the cemetery and kept walking. I stopped only to bellow some more. At some point my grandmother pulled her white Chrysler behind me about 50 yards and coasted along. She let me cry and cry. I finished and got in the car. She never said a word about it to me.

When I was in prison I got a phone call that my younger brother on my DNA donor's side had committed suicide. I was on the pay phone in a prison wing, and hit the floor. I bawled and cried so hard that they took me to the infirmary. It occurred to me later through therapy and counseling that on those two occasions I was crying for me. I wasn't crying for them. It was about all the things I needed to cry about. Sometimes you get triggered and cry and sometimes if you haven't cried for a long time you can't stop because you have to get it all out.

As I stood at Landry's gravesite I felt like the stepson who really did love his stepfather but never told him and now it was too late to say, "Coach, I really loved you and I learned so much from you. Although it's late in life and I've had to change a lot about me, I finally get it."

I held my composure until the flyover started. All of a sudden four jet fighters roared overhead and made a huge noise. I was still okay; hadn't been emotional or cried. Then the B-17 aircraft that Tom Landry himself had flown during WWII came over and I lost it. I started to weep. I took another of those cemetery walks. I didn't want anyone to see me cry. It wasn't about, "Oh, my, did you see Hollywood cry?'" It was about missing him.

I cried so hard I almost threw up. In the end I loved and respected that man. I got more from Tom Landry than any man in my life, including my stepfather. Despite my resistance, things he tried to teach me actually stuck and I was able to retrieve them later. I've applied some of those lessons to my children, my business and my personal life.

I've employed quality control, which is a huge concept. And being prepared in the things I do. Landry gave me back the ability to study. Charlie Waters will probably argue with that but at the end, by the time I was in my fourth or fifth year with the Cowboys, Charlie still was never sure I knew what I was supposed to be doing. But I did and you know what? It was none of his business.

Landry was always concerned about me but he wouldn't have played me in critical places if he didn't have faith that I'd do the job. He always liked the results of my play rather than the technique of my play. Sort of like Duane Thomas when he wouldn't talk and no one knew if he knew the play and then he'd run for 135 yards. I knew what I was doing. I never really wanted Landry to be comfortable that I did know what I was doing.

This was the man whose memory sent me walking alone in a cemetery, bawling like a child. At some point my sorrow began to lessen and I thought, "What are you crying about?" And the answer was that I loved him. The reason I loved him then and love him to this day is that Tom Landry was exactly who he said he was. He was a Christian, a devoted father and a husband, and I never saw a chink in his armor.

ED "TOO TALL" JONES
(Former Cowboys teammate)

I'm embarrassed to admit I lived with Thomas for two years and didn't know he was using drugs. That's how naive I was when we were teammates with the Cowboys during the mid-70s. Plus Thomas never used drugs in my presence, something I respect him for to this day.

Thomas knew I didn't do drugs and I didn't approve of them. We actually used to sit around and talk about people who did. So he knew not to bring it or anyone who was doing it with him around me.

The second year we roomed together, my brother was visiting me. One day he said, "Hey, you're gonna get busted leaving that stuff lying around like that."

I said, "What are you talking about?"

"Drugs," he said, and he could tell by my expression that I didn't have the faintest idea what he meant.

"Ed, let me show you something," my brother said. The door to Thomas's room was open and there was a vial lying on his dresser. "That's cocaine."

"You gotta be kidding," I said.

Thomas always had sinus problems, so I thought the vial was an inhaler to help his sinuses. Since I learned more and researched the subject, I know drugs were the issue. The stuff was being cut wrong and it was eating the cartilage in his nose.

I thought if something goes down in this house there was no way I would ever be able to explain that I didn't do it. All five of my sisters are educators. I was speaking at their schools in Chicago and Tennessee. So I said to myself, I'm getting out of here.

I didn't tell Thomas why I was leaving. He was a grown man. It was his life. I was not going to butt into someone else's business. He was a dear friend, but I knew you had to watch out being around that stuff. I just said I'd found a place to buy and moved out.

I realized later Thomas was having a bad time with drugs after he married his first wife, Wyetta, who was a flight attendant. I introduced Thomas to Wyetta, who's like a sister to me. We grew up together in Tennessee. Wyetta would tell me everything that was going on between them..

I still didn't want to butt into his business. The first time I did he was in denial. I found out through research that addicts deny, deny, deny. My lawyer came to me one day and said if I didn't make an effort to straighten up Thomas, and something happened to him, I'd regret it the rest of my life. That's when I went to him again, but the next thing you knew he was gone. He'd been released from the Cowboys. So he wasn't around. What shocked me was when I found out the coaches didn't know, either.

I'll never forget years later when we roasted Thomas in Austin and Coach Landry came. We were sitting around and talking, one of the first casual conversations I ever had with Landry. Landry sat right there and said to Thomas, "I feel bad because had I known I would have made every effort to get help, not only for you but for everybody." He looked Thomas right in the eye and said, "I didn't know."

How good a player could Thomas have been? The best way to put it is to compare him to the guy who is considered the best: Lawrence Taylor. Thomas was faster even though Taylor had great speed. Thomas was quicker. Probably nobody at his position could cover a back out of the backfield or, if they had to, a receiver, like Thomas did. The sky was the limit for him if he had stayed straight.

Thomas wanted to win as bad as anyone. He had a mean streak you need at linebacker. I've never in my life seen anyone who could turn on for a game, then turn off, as quick as Thomas. Soon as the game was over, he left it on the field. He was ready to have dinner and move on.

I didn't think he'd make it back because of everything I'd read and heard. I also knew his problem wasn't social. He had a dependency. My doctor, who's a friend of both of us, said that 97 percent of addicts relapse within three years.

When my doctor told me that, I thought I'd get a phone call one of these days about Thomas. I thought when you hit rock bottom like he did there wasn't any hope.

He used to write me from jail. He apologized for being who he was, his actions, being in denial. It was as if he sat around reminiscing about those he hurt who were close to him. Thomas was and still is almost like a brother to me. When he'd write those long letters, you started feeling sorry for him again. Your first thought was that when he got out you'd make every effort to make sure he stayed straight.

I wasn't afraid for him when he went back to Austin. His problems didn't start there. I know Austin. I've been to his home. His mom cooked for him and a sister there loves him. He didn't run with anyone in Austin who had a drug habit that I was aware of.

I didn't like it when he was in Houston, Los Angeles and Miami. That's where his peer pressure came from. You couldn't tell me he didn't do it in those areas. Drugs are plentiful there and those people wanted him right back on the stuff.

Of course, he was in Austin when he won the Texas lottery. I was in Atlanta at a black-tie event with Gerry Cooney, Ken Norton, Aaron Pryor and Michael Spinks when my cell phone vibrated. Thomas was on the line and said, "Ed, can you believe I just won that $28 million jackpot lottery in Texas?"

"Yes, I can believe it," I said, "because I've been to Las Vegas with you. You don't know how to gamble yet you always win. Congratulations, I'm proud of you today. But 18 years ago I would not have been proud, because then you probably would have killed yourself."

Thomas agreed. Then he said:

"Ed, I'm getting ready celebrate. I'm going to my refrigerator for a cookie and glass of milk."

CHAPTER TWENTY SEVEN

PARDON...ME?

The word sober was not part of my vocabulary until I was 30 years old. I didn't know what sobriety meant since I'd never used it in a sentence in my life. No one ever heard me say, "Oh, what a sober thought," or, "What a sobering day."

The same is true of pardon. The only way I heard that word expressed was when someone would say, "I beg your pardon," or "Please pardon me." I never dreamed that pardon would mean something quite different to me after I became part of the criminal justice system as an inmate in California.

Upon my release from prison in 1986, it was time to build a new life and try to get it right this time. I was 33 years old and hadn't gotten it right the first time. Crash and burn was the story of an earlier life that had included an NFL career and Super Bowls.

For 17 post-release years from prison I just wanted to do the right thing with society, with parole and with my children. I wanted to make restitution. I wanted to atone. I walked a certain path that I picked out and along the way met good people and I stole every good thing that I saw. I stole every ethical point that I could because I was learning how to live and I was paying attention.

And I was behaving. I was doing the right thing when nobody was looking. I wasn't under any fog of illusion when I put my name in the ring to run for the Austin City Council. I don't know why I made that decision. I wanted to represent a certain part of town and would probably do well at it now that I had grown up.

That's when they told me, "Thomas, we like you here in Austin, you're a good guy, but you can't run because you have a felony on your record in California." A newspaper article reported that the only way I could become eligible was if I were pardoned. That was the point of the application for pardon I filled out several months after I found out I couldn't run.

In the meantime I won the Texas lottery, which didn't make me a better guy. Seventeen years of life as I had lived it was the point.

Because of who I have become, this is a difficult subject to talk about. If I determined I deserved a pardon it negated the sorrow that I felt for the victim of this one night in my life that I cannot and will not rationalize, justify or even try to explain my mistake. Just say it was a culmination of '70s sex ideas and crack cocaine and an atmosphere in which bad things happen.

I was wrong, and I felt so bad for my children, for my grandchildren and family and friends who had to endure these mistakes I made over the years. It's a horrible thing and there's not a day that goes by that I don't think of what I did.

So how do you reply to the question on an application for pardon that asks in effect: "Why should we?"

The first thing you have to report is, "Here are the facts. I pleaded 'no contest' to one count of sexual assault and two counts of false imprisonment." Then you add, "They found a big bag full of crack cocaine pipes and residue and paraphernalia in my apartment on the date of the offense. Time served: 28 months."

When were you on parole? You put down the dates.

Then you write, "I entered treatment for crack cocaine addiction three days after the sexual misconduct and have stayed sober ever since." After that you continue, "Since my release I have lived a life free of crime and have tried to give back by sharing my story, as sordid and dark as it was on a few occasions, in high schools, colleges and prisons. I produced films, and many have been used for years in California prisons and all over the United States."

My work as a consultant in the alcohol field: "I worked in the state of Texas under Governor Ann Richards. My non-profit foundation in Austin raised more than $1 million and built a football stadium and a track for kids. I fasted for seven days to raise $300,000 to finish the project. I have two children, I am a grandfather and..."

I could go on and on about how I'd been living a lawful life and had demonstrated a real change from the incident that sent me to prison almost 20 years ago. My addiction to crack cocaine and the predictable behaviors therein caused unfortunate situations. I made a mistake but I am not my mistake. I am who I have become.

You go on and on until at some point you feel embarrassed. You feel self-serving. Then I had to go into when I saw a psychiatrist and psychologist and underwent a series of tests. (The results determine the chances of becoming a repeat offender through three categories: high, medium and low. They asked me sexual questions about men, women and children. At the end of the day they determined that I wasn't a predator or a habitual sex offender.)

Then you have to go to people like former Governor Richards and ask them to write a nice letter to the governor of California and say: "I've never recommended anyone for a pardon but if anyone deserves your full consideration it is Thomas Henderson."

Then you get your psychiatrist, Dr. Joseph A. Pursch, who's been your doctor for 20 years and by now has become a friend, to write a letter to the governor of California. He explains meeting me in 1983 and about me as a patient and recovering person. His letter says:

"Clinically, the classic sex offender, according to psychiatric literature, commits sex offenses on many occasions over a period of years and almost always when there is no alcohol or brain-altering chemical involved. By contrast, the behavior by which Mr. Henderson was charged in November of 1983 occurred in a setting when he was on a cocaine binge. Also, such behaviors are very common among drug addicts and alcoholics when they are toxic.

(In other words, Thomas Henderson was Chernobyl.)

"This kind of behavior has never occurred in the life of Thomas Henderson prior to his arrest nor has it occurred since then, a period of more than 20 years. In my clinical opinion, Mr. Henderson has never been what psychiatry defines as a sex offender. He is a successfully recovering alcoholic and drug addict. He presents no danger to the public whatsoever."

You send a copy of this multi-page form to the district attorney of the county where your case was heard and a copy to the office of the governor. Mine was mailed to California in the summer of 2000. A staff member told me this would be about a two-year process. I thought that was a long time.

So I said, Okay, I'll go through the process. At some point maybe I will go to California for a Pardons & Parole Board meeting or some sort of hearing. They'll look at my record and I'll get a reply from the governor's office saying, "He qualifies," or "He doesn't qualify," for consideration for a pardon. Keep in mind that the governor of California has absolute power to pardon anyone he chooses.

I'm not going to sit on a throne of righteousness and suggest that it is not a serious, serious consideration to pardon anyone who has a sex offense. There are rapists and child molesters who will repeat their vile acts on a regular basis if given the opportunity. I'm fully aware of that. It's a tough call. Because it's a tough call you do your best, even when you're feeling a little embarrassed and uneasy about promoting yourself.

I live in a Christian society and I'm a Christian-albeit a closet Christian – and forgiveness is something we preach in the Christian family. We forgive. We don't forget, we hold people accountable, but forgiveness is part of what we do. But when you add government to the situation I'm not sure that government forgives.

So two years go by and...nothing. Three years go by...nothing.

I've called. I've written. I've e-mailed. I've yelled. I've beat drums. I got into a hollering contest. There came a time where I started to call on every friend, every politician I knew. I called on these people but because my case was sex-related they didn't want to touch it.

The only information I've gotten from the governor's office in California is that as far as anyone could tell, then-Governor Gray Davis had never pardoned anyone and he'd been in office what...five years? It was like, "You sure you want to continue with us?"

Here's something I can talk about without shame or self-serving ideas. Whether it's for murder, manslaughter, bribery, white-collar crime, no matter what the offense, there is a pardon process in a state. That is law. Part of what the state or the governor or the Pardon & Parole Board does is to require people to go through this exercise. But to not make a decision, to not complete the process is wrong.

So my main objection is that they make you jump through hoops but don't deliver a yea or nay. I've never gotten past the initial letter that said my application had been received. That's the only response so far from the state of California.

At the time I'm sure Governor Davis had heard from thousands of applicants. I sent his office a full set of my films to preview, and information that the entire prison system in California uses them in their programs. I've been of service to the state.

An extremely high official in the Democratic Party told me, "I'll go to Gray Davis and try to help you, but can you get a letter from the victim?"

At that moment I thought, I would give anything to atone, to apologize, make amends, to see what I could do for that young lady and her family and kids. But I can't invade anyone's privacy for my own interest and say, "Hey, come here. Can we talk? And by the way I want you to help me get a pardon." I can't do that. I won't do that.

If there were something I could do I would do it. But I won't do it for the purpose of helping me get a pardon. My principles won't let me do that. I still wake up feeling bad about that incident every day of my life. And if I received a pardon, I'd still feel bad about that every day for the rest of my life. The new Governor Arnold Scharzenegger responded to my pardon application. It's finally under review.

I am still one of the luckiest men in the world, but I wouldn't want what happened to me to happen to anyone. Someone asked me if I could change anything would I? I said no, because if it took what it did to get me here I liked the journey. Prayer works and I pray.

It reminds me of a story of a missionary in Africa. He took a long walk in the jungle and it had almost gotten dark when he noticed 12 female lions following him. He was too far from camp to get back. He knew just enough from watching Wild Kingdom to know he was about to die. He took off running, fell into a bundle and looked up to God.

Please God,, he said, fill these lions with Christianity. God answered his prayer. All 12 of those 300-pound lions stopped a foot short of him, crossed their paws and bowed their heads. Then in unison they purred: "Thank you for the food we are about to receive for the nourishment of our bodies...."

So prayer works. Just be careful what you pray for.

ROGER STAUBACH
(Former teammate)

I really didn't understand Thomas's addiction until after I retired from the NFL and realized that it played a big part in the changes in his behavior from 1975 to 1979. Thomas probably gave up being a Hall of Fame player for us because of it. Addiction is a crazy disease. Once you are addicted, it's like going from a tadpole to a frog.

You can't go back again.

I appreciated his athletic skills and I liked him, but I didn't hang out with Thomas and he didn't invite me to the drug stuff. I had a good relationship with him when we were players. I got involved with him as a friend in the early 80s after I retired. He needed money and I helped him. I didn't know I was enabling him. I've been involved with a number of players, and I'd do anything for my teammates.

You help teammates, but unless they recognize their problems, you're only enabling them. Thomas told me he had this financial problem. He had a house in Dallas and needed money to pay off the mortgage or something like that. I don't know what he did with the money. He might have bought drugs with it. He gave me a lot as collateral. I finally got rid of it. I didn't know what to do with it so I gave it to charity. Thomas was still living in Dallas then, but before he got in all that trouble and went to prison.

I wouldn't try to help anyone other than through counseling or paying for treatment. Giving money to addicts is not helping them. They have to confront their woes and get help. Thomas took a long time to figure that out.

If you look back on his story you would say it would not have been impossible for him to get turned around. He had an analytical mind. I mean Thomas was a smart guy. That doesn't mean smart people don't stay addicted. But I could see the change in him figuring it out and facing the challenge. I saw something in his character as a player that made me think he could come back.

That's what drove me crazy when we were teammates. I kept thinking, why is this smart guy doing these things? He kept pushing the envelope until finally in '79 it wasn't just one incident but a combination and you're thinking, what is going on with this guy? But look at the behavior of some players and it isn't just their egos or their success. If there's a chemical component involved, they change drastically.

I think Thomas would have been an unbelievable player because he was that good. He would have been successful, as he is now, through that whole period of time if he hadn't been involved with drugs. You could tell that Thomas was sharp and had things figured out until addiction complicated his life and screwed it up.

I've been disappointed in other people. It's not that you don't want to give someone another chance. But you have to feel the person is facing his challenge. Once I was convinced that Thomas was dealing with his addiction, that he was the Thomas everyone saw potential in, I got involved with him in a number of programs. Most of it was funding. We bought some land together. That's how much I trusted Thomas.

Many people have asked me about Thomas since the lottery days. He's still part of the Cowboys aura because he was there for three Super Bowls and the victory over Denver. I say he has a great story. Yet it's a story that if you get your life out of balance, especially with an addiction, you can destroy your best qualities. That's what happened to Thomas. Thomas recognized he had to deal with it and he did, and it's a fight every day. I tell everyone it's a wonderful story because Thomas was giving back time and effort to good causes before he won the lottery.

I'm proud of him, and think he's made a difference in the lives of a lot of people, whether it's a prison he visited or a youth group. You have to say, here's a guy who's got it all together. He could have ended up in the gutter but he didn't. He's helping people in a sincere way. You know good evangelists can help people in their spiritual lives. Bad evangelists can screw up people. If you preach virtue but don't walk the talk it can hurt. After 20 years Thomas is walking his talk. Winning the lottery gave him more flexibility to do good things. It hasn't screwed him up, that's for sure.

Thomas was always the life of the party, but he also was the party. He still has the same personality to be the life of the party. But he has his life under control now so he's not the party anymore.

Chapter Twenty Eight

FINAL THOUGHTS ABOUT...

Relationships

The hardest part of forming a relationship for me was being found out. I can't count the times I sabotaged potential relationships just to keep the secret. The secret was that I didn't know how to be intimate, honest or committed.

The intimate part involved allowing someone to see me being myself. That scared me. I felt like if you really knew me you wouldn't like me.

The honesty part was about truth, the whole truth and nothing but the truth. I wasn't capable of rigorous honesty. Lying and covering up had become a full-time reaction to truth.

Commitment involved too much labor. To commit to something or someone other than myself was literally and figuratively impossible.

For years my mother never knew who I really was. We had a complex mother-son relationship based on fear and love. Fear was based on the memory of my mother whipping me. I outgrew that fear, and she was the last person ever to whip me. Yet I loved her no less.

When it came to women and intimacy, I never had a clue on how to behave with integrity. Because of what I had seen in my home as a child, I thought that deception was normal. I lied repeatedly to girlfriends and the women I married.

It is difficult to have friends if you are not one yourself. I had been in the company of many well-balanced people who would have been great friends. But what did I do? I sought lower companions who were just like me. As I've said before, I had friends who would steal my dope and then help me look for it.

This sort of behavior eventually hurts. You find yourself alone and disconnected from people and family. You wander aimlessly through life meeting new victims.

My pattern was to take an acquaintances to a certain point and abandon them before they found out I was an imposter. I wasn't who I said I was. I don't mean I wasn't Thomas Henderson, the athlete. I'm talking about integrity and truth. I've never been mean or violent but I was an accomplished liar.

I would lie for no reason. Or I would lie for any reason. I thought that lying sometimes protected the innocent. The truth was, lying protected the liar. I just didn't want to be found out, the inner me exposed.

The best identity I ever had was as a Dallas Cowboy. Celebrity became my disguise. But celebrity is not intimate. It's public fantasy. When this was removed and my life ruined by alcoholism and crack addiction, my cover was blown. With nowhere to hide, I was naked.

Losing the cover of celebrity became my worst nightmare because it magnified my disgrace. Now it was public knowledge that Thomas Henderson had self-destructed. That was something I knew all along. Now everyone else knew. It didn't matter that alcoholism, crack addiction and a sex charge ousted me. The word on me was out.

To rebuild your life from such a low point is difficult in itself. I knew I was alone. And I really didn't know how to proceed.

At 30, I began a new look at life with me in it. The first thing was to sever my long-running relationship with alcohol and drugs. Oh yes, it was definitely a relationship. Alcohol and other drugs never disappointed or failed me like humans had. As destructive as they were, they were the best friends I ever had. This was why divorcing from them was the hardest relationship to end.

My vision slowly focused on learning how to live. Being sober and learning how to live became my mission. Other people with the same goals contributed. Everything that's good about me today came from other alcoholics and addicts trying to live their lives differently. Every good decision I've made about love, my children and friends, I stole from people I respected and wanted to emulate. I wasn't capable of figuring that out on my own.

I learned how to be honest, intimate and a friend, and it's made me joyous. It's a pleasure to be blunt and frank without intention to harm another person, rather than deceiving through a lie. What I learned since 1983 was that life is fun, short and complicated. So, today I have healthy relationship with my daughters, girlfriend and many friends. My friends expect total honest from me, and I expect the same from them. Loving friends and family surround me because I've made myself available emotionally and intimately.

I owe everything to recovery and the recovering community. Left on my own, I'd still be smoking crack in a back alley with all those lose souls of addiction and dysfunctional lives. I look forward to tomorrow because today was so good.

The first step toward honesty has to be to oneself. I don't lie to myself, so I don't have to lie to you anymore. Relationships helped save my life. The very relationships I ran away from in the past are my greatest treasures. Remember that in order to have friends you have to be a friend. In order to have solid relationships you have to bring honesty to the union. In order to be happy, joyous and free, you have to commit your most personal resources to the quest. That means your touch, your time and most of all, your love. My significant other is Linda. I respect her and love her. She's my best friend and I can count on her.

* * * *

Prevention

I was 30 years old before I understood that sobriety was an option. Where I grew up, I saw my mother, step dad, uncles, aunts and neighbors drinking alcohol and sometimes getting drunk.

Never during childhood and into my early 20s, from elementary grades through high school and college, was there mention of alcohol or drug prevention education. That wasn't anyone's fault. It's just a fact. It occurs to me now that kids and adults alike should be exposed to that course of study. Just saying "No," isn't enough.

Our culture conditions us to drink when we turn 21. Yet it's the age that a person could decide not to drink. I've met people who've never used alcohol or drugs. But most begin with using alcohol at some point in their lives, and don't know why they started. It's often peer pressure or strangers involved at the beginning. Few people consider the long-term consequences of alcohol use before they start using it. They wouldn't start if they did.

Alcohol and other drugs are mind-altering chemicals. It doesn't matter to what degree your mind is altered. It is altered. There are actions, decisions and choices made in an altered state of mind that millions of people regret for the rest of their lives.

When I discovered that I didn't have to drink to have fun, it gave me a feeling of euphoria. I can't remember who told me that drinking was a good additive to having fun. Whoever did was wrong.

The consequence of beginning and maintaining a relationship with alcohol or other drugs is like playing with a time bomb. It will explode someday and anyone nearby will be harmed. Health and social affects are as numerous as economic concerns. I have seen failed marriages, sick relationships, abused children and dysfunctional families caught in this tragedy. College students leave school because the party ended, but they kept going until they flunked out. Thousands die every year in alcohol-related traffic accidents. The price is too high to pay.

I can't think of a single positive aspect to drinking alcohol and using drugs. Heavy drinkers suffer blackouts caused by an over consumption of alcohol. A person in a blackout stage walks, talks, dances and even has sex. They awake the next day and can't remember anything they said or did the night before. They can't even remember driving themselves home.

I met a man in prison serving three life sentences for a triple murder. One of many nights when he was blacked-out drunk, he went home and killed his wife and two children. Then he got in bed and went to sleep. He awoke from his blackout the next morning unaware of the carnage he had created.

Blackouts aren't cute or amusing. They are one of the clearest signs that a person is drinking addictively and is on his way to an awful place. Chugging beers and downing multiple shots of hard liquor is the most dangerous drinking in the world. Anyone with these habits is a certain candidate for failure involving his or her profession, family and health. Alcohol is that cunning, baffling and powerful.

Teenagers harm their undeveloped minds by using alcohol too early and too often. Unfortunately, many parents introduce alcohol in the home. Children see their role models drinking alcohol. They think it's what their parents do and what they will do when they grow up. The problem is that kids grow up at 10, 11 or 12 years old and will sneak beer and even liquor. I know I did.

Alcohol and drug prevention education shouldn't be restricted to kids. It's useful to anyone at any age who has never told that sobriety is an option. I know that not drinking and using drugs was the best decision I ever made.

* * * *

Recovery

Trouble got me into recovery. Some people enter recovery because they have a moment of clarity and decide to leave their cycle of pain, which most often is self-imposed. Whether it's alcohol, drugs, food, gambling, or another compulsion that rules their lives, once the decision of free will is made they begin recovery.

Then there is Thomas Henderson and many like me. We are silly, insane, contaminated with false egos and confused. We see sign after sign of addiction and suffer small but indistinct consequences. This can go on for years. And then it happens. We somehow get sick and tired of being sick and tired.

My moment of clarity came when my lawyer, Arnie Gold, found me in an unfurnished apartment in Long Beach, California, shortly after I had run out of crack cocaine. I remember it vividly. He looked at me with disgust and sorrow. I'd never seen anyone look at me like that in my life. I was facing serious moral charges and my first impulse was to buy crack cocaine and keep on smoking. It was his idea, not mine, that I was taken to a treatment center in Orange, California, on an afternoon in early November of 1983.

There had been signs of my decline since late in 1979 when Coach Tom Landry fired me from the Dallas Cowboys. My wife had divorced me. Coach Bill Walsh later asked me to leave the San Francisco 49ers after seeing me loaded in my locker with my uniform on. In all insane honesty, I never connected the dots that drinking and drugging was the reason my life and career was falling apart.

Somehow in early 1981, I found myself a patient at a psychiatric drug clinic in Scottsdale, Arizona. With the wreckage of my life in full view it still never occurred to me that alcohol and drugs were the issue. I refused to admit there was an issue. I blamed my wife, the Cowboys, 49ers, the NFL and all the conspirators for my demise. Meanwhile I figured I would return to playing football and all would be well.

No one in my family or close friends knew the extent of my abuse of alcohol and crack. In a covert manner, I slipped deeper and deeper into the sordid life of an absolute addict. I passed in and out of consciousness for months. I got loaded when I was awake.

Coach Don Shula signed a full-blown crack addict to the Miami Dolphins in the summer of '81. Football became my ticket for drugs instead of a career. But in August of '81, I broke my neck in a Miami uniform. The remainder of '81 and deep into 1983 became a crack cocaine blur.

After I was arrested on sexual misconduct charges in '83, I hit bottom. That was my wake-up call, the moment to look at where I'd been and who I had become. The shame, degradation and consequences of years of drug abuse became clear. I asked myself how and why I had done this to myself. Well, I started drinking and using other drugs to have fun. From a state of absolute shame, I couldn't remember the last time I had had an instant of pure fun.

Arnie Gold picked up my pitiful and sorry ass and drove me to the place where my life began anew. If not for that ride I don't know where I would be today. I don't remember why he came to my apartment that day. I don't know why I even answered the door. I only know that my recovery began when he broke through my denial with his disgust of my predicament.

Recovery has been an education for me. You can't take back all the wrongs you committed, but you can begin again. You can have a clean slate if you trust the process and stay the course. Recovery is as fragile as a newborn baby. It must be handled with utmost care. You must feed it, hold and comfort and obey it. Most of all, you must love it.

My recovery began before I entered prison. I was seven months clean when I became a guest of the California Department of Corrections. There was no denial anymore. I was finally living the consequences of my actions and behaviors.

Most people would think that my incarceration was horrible. But in all honesty I needed time to sit, think and ponder life. The 28 months I served rescued me for a time. Before I did time in prison, when I was alone, I was in bad company. But now, clean and sober, doing time alone with myself made it okay to be alone. I left prison in 1986 still clean for almost three years.

Recovery became my substitute for football. It's my most important life skill. I realize that if I'd not in recovery I don't have a life. I can't be father, grandfather, friend or neighbor without recovery. I can't have relationships with other people. Recovery is therefore more vital to me than my children, because if I'm not clean I have nothing.

I have been clean and sober since November 8, 1983. That is my identity. That is who I am. Recovery has given me a life I never had before. I used to think football, money, property and prestige were my ultimate goals.

I won millions a few years ago in the Texas lottery. I would give all of it away if the choice came down to my recovery or the money. When recovery means that much to you...you will be free. Recovery is my wealth. I can always make more money. I don't think I could recover again.

* * * *

AARP Material

On March 1, 2003, I turned 50 years old. I considered it a miracle, because I didn't think I'd live to see 31.

Some people make a big deal about turning 50 and celebrate with a party. I've never thrown a party for myself in my life. I take that back. I have thrown parties, but never one that I would invite my mother.

Earlier that year, my girlfriend Linda stole my day planner and phone book, and started calling my friends. She sprang a surprise birthday party on me at the Omni Hotel in Austin. I walked through the door of the ballroom and there stood more than 200 of my friends and family. Among them were my mom, my children, sisters and brothers, former teammates, colleagues, business partners and former bosses.

Congresswoman Eddie Bernice Johnson was there and others I hadn't seen in years. Freddie and Janice Ferriell had flown in from Florida. Bill O'Donnell, John Schmitz, Judy and John McCaleb were my employers when I worked for Sierra Tucson during the early 90s. They had come from Chicago, South Carolina and Arizona to celebrate my birthday.

Darrell and Edith Royal came, as did Don and Gini Riddle from Houston, family members from New York and my brother, Duane Bell, from Philadelphia. Too Tall Jones, Drew Pearson, Beasley and Paula Reece attended. The room was decorated, there was a cake and buffet of food, and the band played on.

There is a point to all this name-dropping. I've heard that if you have four or five good friends, you are lucky. I must be the luckiest man alive to have had so many people spend money and travel long distances to share my birthday.

The party and attendees gave me a memory that will remain close to my heart. They gave me unconditional love that only true friends can offer. Linda did something for me I would never have done for myself. I'm eternally grateful to her and I love her.

I received a letter from the American Association of Retired Persons (AARP) shortly after the party. It welcomed me to the senior citizen community and asked me to join the group. I declined, because I don't see age 50 as a monumental moment in time. I quit drinking and drugging when I was 30. Mentally and physically, I believe the clock slowed on my aging. I don't feel 50 and have been told I don't look 50.

As for the party, it showed me where my real wealth lay. It's with my family, friends and relationships. As a recovering addict I accepted the party as a reflection of how I have treated myself and, more importantly, how I have treated others.

It is clear to me that I have done something right in public, private and intimate relations. Treating others respectfully and going that extra step to be nice and compassionate has worked well for me. It's been an easy behavior for me. Rigorous honesty in all my affairs has paid huge dividends. My friends trust and respect me. What more could I ask?

* * * *

Regrets Are Avoidable

I believe most people who make mistakes eventually regret them. Of course, there are some cold-blooded and mean-spirited people who cannot feel remorse. They are exceptions.

Our nation's courts and prisons are choked with people who momentarily lost control of their temper and sanity and committed crimes against people, property and society. While in prison I never met anyone who did not regret his or her crime, although there were some who simply just hated being caught.

Normal people wonder why a man would hit a woman. Or how parents could beat and mistreat their children. As long as these things are done in a covert, unreported fashion, there are no consequences and these intimate crimes continue. It seems that only when someone is caught in such despicable acts do they express regret.

Some people are constitutionally incapable of changing. Many convicts told me how they assaulted or murdered someone because they felt disrespected. They blamed the victim. They said, "If he hadn't done that I wouldn't have killed him."

I've seen hundreds of cases of all sorts of crimes from celebrities to common folk and always wonder: Was their regret avoidable? Yes, most of the time, and often because they didn't think before acting. There are basic thou-shall-nots' such as murder, assault, child abuse, acts of terror, sexual crimes and so on. Our prisons house more than two million guests who did not think before they acted.

When I spoke to the NFL rookie symposium in 2000 the title of my lecture was, Regrets Are Avoidable. I spoke of how alcohol and drugs had the potential to sabotage their jobs and lives.

When crimes of violence, passion and stupidity appear on television, normal thinking people shake their heads and ask, "What were they thinking?" Obviously they didn't think. Thinking is a must to prevent avoidable regrets.

If what you are about to do makes you feel uncomfortable, stop and think. Most of us have those instincts. I learned over the last 20 years to do the right thing even when no one was looking. I've had many regrets that were avoidable. Today, I chose to think, live a good life as a clean and sober man, father, grandfather and friend. I think it through and have avoided many regrets.

* * * *

Yes, I'm Still Clean

Being perfect is a hard thing to maintain in almost everything. Being clean and sober is the only perfect thing I have done. There was a time in my life that if I was awake, I was drunk or loaded with drugs. Stopping the use of alcohol and drugs was the best decision I have ever made.

This was no big deal to some. It was a matter of life and death to me. I thought my chances of getting clean were well below average. I had a long-standing relationship with alcohol and drugs and, frankly, I liked drinking and drugging. The habit became part of my persona. Happy hour was fun and crack houses were a way of life. It did not matter how drunk I got or how paranoid I became, the relationship was a constant for many years.

The culmination of being fired from the Cowboys, my wife leaving, loss of money, property and prestige never caused me to think alcohol and drug abuse had anything to do with it. I still don't know why I decided to get clean and then stay clean for 20 years. I just know now that I go to bed clean and wake up clean.

Whenever my mind romances the idea that I can drink alcohol, smoke weed or crack, I reverse the tape and play it all the way back. When I play it that way I see myself broke, in prison and insane in the end.

I have not relapsed since November 8, 1983, because I am scared. I am frightened of alcohol and all drugs. They scare hell out of me. I'm not scared to use. I'm scared that I still have a choice. I'm scared of what would happen to me, and my children. My fear is based on the dark remembrance of the life I endured under the influence of alcohol and drugs.

Anyone who has used and abused alcohol and other drugs can tell of great fun and wonderful parties. But they usually don't recall the bad days and nights in detail. What they lost, who they hurt. The things they did that they wished they hadn't. The shame of their behavior mingling with regrets. Conversations of consequence about these events don't occur unless the addict seeks treatment and group therapy.

I wish I'd never started an alcohol and drug relationship. Alcohol and other drugs brought me nothing but loss and pain. The relationship was never manageable for me. There was never enough to satisfy my thirst. As painful as it was, I feel joy and gratitude for the opportunity to be a clean and sober man, father, grandfather and friend.

I am clean because I got tired of being high and drunk. I am clean because I want to be. I am clean because I'm still scared. I am clean because I was lucky.

Some people think I won the lottery twice. I did. In 1983, when I got sober, I won my life back. And in 2000 I won the money.

* * * *

Southern Baptist

The subject of religion and/or faith has been a confusing issue for me during my entire life. I was raised and baptized in the church at age six. As a black southern Baptist in my youth, I heard great singing, praying and preaching. But over the past 44 years I have sort of faked my way through the maze of religion and faith.

The Bible has always been a complicated document to me. When I read about Job, Daniel, David and others, I took issue with God. I was especially upset by the story of Job where God had a conversation with the devil. And God basically said to the devil, "Destroy everything Job has. Just don't hurt him."

That bothered me. Why would God partner with the devil to make Job's life miserable? I could see Job walking down the street saying, "Hey, God, I'd just as soon you left it the way it was."

During my early religious training, I had questions. I was told to believe every word or else. But since I didn't believe every word, for my whole life I felt that I was going to hell. Therefore for the longest time I have been a closet Christian.

I read enough of the Bible to lock on to a scripture in the Book of Matthew that said a person of faith could do his praying privately. He didn't have to show off by praying publicly to God. I embraced that form of worship, so that I won't appear on national television or a public forum and declare myself a Christian.

The only time I ever really prayed was when I was in trouble or needed something. I never prayed thankful or grateful prayers. But I've always believed in God and his son, Jesus Christ. Then I learned that Jews didn't recognize Jesus as the Messiah. That confused me. I had more questions. Jews were there with Jesus and didn't believe he was sent by God the Father?

My grandmother was a shouting, talking-in-tongues holy roller. I had questions for her, too. Then in college I thought I had the answer to it all. It seemed to me that God was there to make humans fearful.

Kings and their armies ruled the long-ago world. People worshiped statues, symbols and monuments. The strong dominated the weak. Slavery was common. I surmised that right and wrong were issues absent from everyday life.

By creating God, heaven, hell and consequences after death, it made some people behave with humanity. Before then, no one knew what to expect when they died. Going to hell and living in fire for eternity was a frightful threat. Now there was good and bad to be had in the hereafter. I was smoking marijuana and hallucinating on LSD when this theory arose.

When I began recovery I was introduced to the theory of "God as you understand him." What a relief. For the past 20 years I have prayed thankful and grateful prayers. I have never denied my faith as a baptized Christian. I still think the bar is too high to publicly state that I'm a Christian. Therefore, I'm a closet Christian.

Recovery is a religious experience. I believe faith is a private matter. So I have a personal relationship with God, as I understand him. I know that God loves me and has a sense of humor. I can relate to Job and understand his love of God despite the tragedies he endured. God picked me up, sobered me up, showed me love and gave me all that I have. I love God with all my heart.

My daily prayer...

God, thank you for letting me laugh and smile again, but please, God, don't ever let me forget that I cried.

CHAPTER TWENTY NINE

PASSING IT ON AND RECOVERING FRIENDS

As an author, lecturer and treatment professional, I'm often asked where an alcoholic, addict or family member should go when they need help or information about where to get help.

My first recommendation is that if a person has health insurance, they go to a family of origin model treatment center to start their recovery. This model of treatment is for the whole person, not just the abuse symptoms.

If a person has no insurance or finances, I support them going to Alcoholics Anonymous and the free support groups that were born from the 12-steps of recovery philosophy.

There is Cocaine Anonymous, Narcotics Anonymous, Over-eaters Anonymous, Gamblers Anonymous, Co-dependency Anonymous, and Adult Children of Alcoholics, Al-Anon and other 12-step groups. These and more are the programs people are referred to following their initial treatment program stay. They are referred there because these programs absolutely work. People who can't afford treatment have walked off the streets into these 12-step programs for over 50 years and are living clean, sober and free from their addictions. Aftercare and continuing care are vital for long term recovery and good solid sobriety. These 12-step groups work no matter how you get there. Just get there and stay.

These 12-step groups are free. The only requirement for membership is a desire to stop drinking, using or abusing chemicals or self. The irony here is that the best treatment in America is free. That's right, free. 12-step programs are expanding and are used in conjunction with most successful addiction treatment programs. All 12-step programs are based on the principles originally outlined in the book Alcoholics Anonymous. Buy a copy.

With my over 20 years of sobriety, I still do not have all the answers to a problem that has been ravaging human beings for centuries. There is no painless way. If you're looking for "Drug or alcohol Free forever in 30 Days," it isn't gonna happen. The advice I do have is the insight and experience of my own struggle in recovery, and the willingness to be totally honest about it. I went from being a football star and magazine cover boy, a guy who was rich and adulated and moved with the pretty people, into a broken-down lowlife and convicted felon who did twenty-eight months in prison. I know something about falling, and about self-destruction. I also know something about the slow, arduous process of picking yourself back up, of rebuilding an entire life.

I believe that the process of recovery is a very misunderstood thing. I believe that's because not enough people recognize that it is a process, a day by day journey, a gradual unfolding of a healthier way of living. You don't get cured of alcoholism or drug addiction. Once you have it, you have it for life. I still am an alcoholic and drug addict. But I am recovering. The disease is there its just in remission.

Many people don't really grasp this. Their approach to addiction is simple and clear-cut; you stop using, the problem goes away. Nice and tidy. Struggle through withdrawal, rid yourself of the physical craving and go about your business. If only it were that simple.

You don't just stop drinking or taking drugs, and then get better, any more than you can just stop cancer or any other disease. Being addicted to drugs is having a physiological compulsion, but it is more than that, too. It is also a psychological, emotional and spiritual illness, one that attacks you in any number of ways. It is very deep-seated stuff. It is about self-loathing and self-deception. It makes you think nothing of lying and cheating and manipulating the hell out of family and friends. It's a disease that is one, huge, insidious lie, and the lie being this: you're sure, I mean 100% positive, that your cocktail or your line of coke (or whatever your drug of choice is) is the only thing that is keeping you afloat and able to cope in this world. The truth, of course, is that it is the one thing that is keeping you from coping. The truth is that it is killing you. That isn't melodrama; it's fact. And it's just as true about alcohol as about cocaine or any other so-called hard drug. There's a tendency in our society to put these things in very different categories. Alcohol is legal and socially sanctioned. It is everywhere. Parents who would probably be ready to slit their wrists if they knew their kids were doing coke are the same folks who roll out the keg for the graduation party. Alcohol is advertised and glamorized. Hell, it's even passed out in clubhouses. You don't have to call your dealer or meet under the bridge in the fog to get drunk; you go to your corner bar and say, "Give me a double," and off you go. It's very easy to take alcohol less seriously than other drugs, to think it is less dangerous. It is not. It is every bit as dangerous. It may not take you down the road to ruin as fast, but it can take you down every bit as far.

There's a saying I've heard among people who are in recovery. They say, "If you give it away, you get it back even more." They're talking about giving away their experience, strength and hope, so that those who are struggling, who are just starting to try to live without alcohol or drugs, will feel heartened and fortified and able to stick with it. In this book, my aim is to give it away. Writing has given me that much more to keep. What a great deal that is.

I have written this book to help people better understand the process of getting sober, and to help them realize that it isn't a quick-fix proposition. I've also written to let you know that there is no such thing as a hopeless case. I don't care if you're the most far-gone alcoholic or drug addict in the annals of intoxication. You must know this: THERE IS HOPE! You can do it. You can be sober. No matter how low you feel, no matter how useless and worthless and out of control you think you are, you can get better. You can take the first step today, right now, by choosing not to pick up a drink or a drug, by picking up the phone instead, and getting help. Call Alcoholics Anonymous or Narcotics Anonymous, or call a local hospital or rehabilitation or detox center. Call somebody. Ask for help.

The disease wants desperately for you to believe it is hopeless; that there's no point; so screw getting better and bring the next round of chemicals. As I said before, this disease is a liar.

I was a hopeless as cases get. I got help. I got better. And day by day, each day that I choose not to use, I am continuing to get better. Today, because I am sober, I am contented and grateful, and I am able to write this, to give something away that may help save a life, just as other recovering people helped save mine. Considering where I was just a few years ago, it's a pretty remarkable achievement. It's a miracle. It's the gift of sobriety.

Passing on information to suffering alcoholics, addicts and family members is my job. I've made it my job. Working with recovering people is my mission in life. I carry this message to alcoholics and addicts — that every day and every night, sobriety is an option. Carrying the message of hope in sobriety is what I do just by living it.

Other issues that devastate individuals and family systems are co-dependency and adult children of alcoholics' syndromes. We all have a little of both, I suppose. If we are dysfunctional, what's clear to me in my experience is that we all can heal and change our course of functioning and purpose. We have to change. I've lived a change so I know it works. Living it has given me a perspective of reality I never knew possible. I'm finally free. I've become totally focused in my work. I know what my purpose is. As time ticks away and my life cruises along, I just hope I can make a difference in the lives of addicted people, recovering people, and our young people who haven't used yet. Sobriety is an option.

Being focused with a purpose makes my work come easy. I love it. I figure I'll end up working in treatment centers, prisons, jails and institutions for the rest of my life. I'd like that very much. That's where folks like me end up. I want to be there to tell them they don't have to live like this anymore. As I wrote this book, I wondered where and how it would end.

So, not knowing how or where to stop, I asked some of my recovering friends to share their experience, treatment, recovery and continuing care with you. My recovering friends come from a cross-section of Americans: male, female, black, white, brown, alcoholics, addicts, co-dependents, overeaters, sex addicts, incest survivors, etc.

We recovering folks can help when no one else can. By sharing where we've been and where we are now is how we help those in pain. They identify with our past problems and believe they too can recover. Being helpful is our only aim. That's why we share our recovery.

If you are the mother or father of an alcoholic or addict, the wife or husband of one, or the girlfriend or boyfriend, know there is help for you, too. Often times the significant other of an alcoholic and addict becomes as sick (or sicker) than the person they want to fix. Get help for yourself if you are involved with a practicing addict or alcoholic.

This recovery deal has processed me into the man I want to be. I can cry, care, love, and express myself. I'm no wimp or sucker by doing this. I'm more of a man now than I've ever been.

Relax and read what some of my good friends have to share about their experience, strength and hope. I'm truly proud to know these people. I respect them as I respect myself. I hope one or more of these true intimate sharings will touch, inspire or help you.

LAST WORDS FOR NOW

My self imposed addiction to drugs and alcohol was not a necessary journey. But if trouble and pain is the intervention that paves the way to a better life its been worth it.

The hurt and pain I caused some will never be forgiven. But I stand ready to apologize, make amends and atonements for the rest of my life.

There are people who don't know me and have never met me but don't like me. This is due to football crap and the case that sent me to prison. What they think of me is none of my business.

In these instances, I must understand rather than be understood. It is not my desire to be liked. I just want to live out the rest of my life in complete contrast of my addictions and bad behaviors.

My recovery is all I've got today. Its the stable foundation that I stand on and live for.

* * * *

Pat B.

Who would ever thought I would become an alcoholic? I have never seen my mother or father drink, but I do know that alcoholism was in my family. I remember the first time I drank. I also became drunk. It was great. I discovered very fast that I could change the entire world in five minutes. You see, my main problem all my life has been my feelings. I really didn't know how to deal with them so I did the next best thing – I suppressed them. Alcohol gave me permission to live in this world and be comfortable at the same time. I loved it. In my desire to suppress my feeling, alcohol did many things for me. Eventually, it did many things to me.

My first drunk was as a student nurse in Oklahoma City. I was 18 years old and in those days Oklahoma was a dry state and we had to get alcohol from a bootlegger. That tells you how old I am. We were drinking alcohol and chasing it with beer and boy did I ever get sick! I made a statement that every alcoholic and addict has made before: "I will never do that again." And of course I did.

For the next several years I did very little drinking. I had a tour of duty in the Navy as a nurse. I got out of the Navy on a hardship release to care for my brother-in-law who was dying of cancer. Later I was off to the Missions. I was a lay missionary in Tanzania, East Africa for about 3 years. Then back home and back in the Navy.

When we frequently say 'take a trip or not take a trip', it never occurred to me not to take the trip. Always restless, on the go, looking for God knows what, trying to fill the emptiness within. Alcohol solved that problem, but only on a temporary basis.

While stationed at the Naval Hospital at Bethesda, Maryland, I began to drink alone. I lived in the BOQ (bachelor officer quarters) and was beginning to experience some depression. So after 3 years there I prayed to get out. Be careful what you pray for, you might get it.

Time to take another trip. I got orders for Vietnam. I served aboard the hospital ship, USS Repose. I drank on that ship and for that I am very ashamed. After I returned home, I began to drink on a daily basis that would eventually lead me to consume a fifth of alcohol a day. The more depressed I became, the more I drank. The more I drank, the more depressed I became. Up on speed, down on alcohol, and level off on Valium. I was caught in the box.

I was stationed in San Diego after my return from Vietnam and worked in the operating room. Once again, I was ready to move on. Restless, angry, depressed and lonely, I was a full-blown alcoholic. I left San Diego in a total blackout.

By the time I reached Newport Naval Hospital in Newport, Rhode Island, I had reached the attitude of "I don't care." But the alcoholic never dances alone. Low and behold, I found another drinking partner, a Navy physician who was also an alcoholic. So I began my decline into incomprehensible demoralization.

In the fall of 1972, very intoxicated, I loaded a revolver and placed the end of the barrel tight against my right temple. I slowly pulled the trigger. The gun clicked. I was so angry that I couldn't even kill myself. After drinking more, I raised the gun towards my head and again pulled the trigger. I blew a hole in my ceiling and passed out. The next morning I found the shell in my bed and realized that I had missed a chamber when I loaded the gun.

The next week I did what I said I would never do – I went in the operating room toxic. At last the Navy said treatment or face a possible court martial. Now that is an awakening.

I was the second Navy nurse ordered in for treatment and I arrived at Naval Station, Long Beach, California on Christmas Eve, 1972. I was hostile, depressed and very ashamed. There were about 60 military men in treatment and me. I was so very afraid someone would see the real me. Inside, my feelings were as a child. After 5 weeks, several of us patients went to the Mission, a skidrow meeting place in Los Angeles. An elderly man was leading the meeting and insisted I get up to the podium. When I looked at those people, I finally realized that I, too, was an alcoholic. My denial was broken at a skidrow meeting. A 12-step program really saved my life. I remained in treatment for 3 months. After 18 plus years of sobriety, I fully realize the greatest thing to happen to me was the 12-step program. I got myself back and I am free.

* * * *

Anonymous

I was always searching for glamour and excitement. Instead, I found myself desperate and scared. I lost my soul, my spirit, my self-respect and my morals to cocaine and alcohol. Cocaine and alcohol were my lovers and best friends. I was their slave.

I grew up in California during the sixties and seventies as an only child. My parents are artists and had many hippie friends. There were lots of wild parties with pot smoking and drinking. I was always that cute little blonde girl among all the craziness. I hated seeing my parents under the influence, especially my mother. It really hurt me to see her out of control. I never imagined I would turn out to be just like her. Because my family is different from most, I always felt like I was on the outside of the world.

I would fantasize about the family I wanted to be in. When I got to junior high school, it became very important to me to be popular and part of the cool crowd. I began smoking pot and drinking. I was always the one who got too drunk and who didn't remember what she did the night before. I was always shy and reserved, but when I was drunk I became a flirt. By the time I got to high school, I had a reputation for being a loose chick. I hated having this reputation, but once I started drinking I always got drunk and then lost control. I would wake up feeling ashamed, remorseful and disgusted with myself.

After high school, my cocaine use escalated. I had a boyfriend whom dealt coke and hated to see me drunk. The cocaine would keep me in check. I could balance out my drinking with the blow. I always went for the slick, hustler type of guy. I found them to be sexy and exciting. I especially loved cocaine dealers.

When I was 19 I moved to New York to become a fashion designer. I graduated from college and got a good job. I worked hard, traveling all over the world for my company, but I led a double life. During the day, I was the successful designer who wore nice clothes and seemed to have a nice life. After work, I would hang out in sleazy bars and after hour's joints and use coke. I lived with a man for 4 years who abused me both mentally and physically. I couldn't get out of the relationship though because I couldn't face being alone. I was miserable with him and with myself. So drugs and alcohol were the answer. I was cheating on my boyfriend and stealing cocaine from my friends in order not to face myself. It got so I couldn't look in the mirror. I hated myself and the person I had become. I started to freebase because sniffing wasn't getting me high enough. My nose was eaten up inside. Big scabs would come up every morning and my nose was in constant pain. Freebasing took me to another level of addiction. My boyfriend said he couldn't watch me kill myself any longer and moved out. After he left, I had no one to answer to and I would stay out for two or three days at a time. I was begging people for hits off their pipe, something I swore I would never do.

I started to get very frightened. Several times I had taken hits off a pipe and my heart seemed to stop beating (and probably did stop) and I thought I was having a heart attack. But I still couldn't stop getting high.

Finally, coming home from a business trip overseas, I began to pray to God that I could stop getting high. My prayers were answered because when I got home, I called a 12-step program and asked for help. This was the scariest thing I ever did. I never thought I could live life sober. I never wanted to, but I didn't want to go on the way I had been. I admitted that I was a drug addict and alcoholic and realized my life was unmanageable.

I was miserable for a long time in sobriety. I couldn't sleep and had constant headaches, but I prayed to God that He help me stay sober. I'm so thankful to be sober today. Sometimes I can't believe it's been two years. I have a full life today and I have good friends and a relationship with God. I try to help other addicts and alcoholics. These are the important things in my life today. Money and success never filled up the empty hole inside me. That hole is slowly getting filled up as I keep praying and putting sobriety as number one in my life. Since I've been in recovery, I got laid off from my job and it's been tough. But today I can face that difficulty with hope and faith and sobriety.

* * * *

Buddy W.

I am 26 years old, an alcoholic, drug addict, an adult child of an alcoholic, and I am currently serving a prison sentence for murder. This crime was a direct result of my disease of addiction.

I come from an upper-middle class family in a small town in Alabama. Both my parents work and are successful at what they do. They are wonderful people that I love very much, but together they were simply incompatible. Our family was clearly a dysfunctional one. My parents divorced when I was 12 years old and eventually got back together "for the sake of the kids," but it didn't work. I remember staying away from the house as much as possible and hanging out with the boys. My first experience with alcohol was in my home. There was always a supply of alcohol kept in the house and my first drink was out of curiosity at a very young age. When I was 13, I was turned on to pot. By the age of 14, I was drinking and smoking pot on a regular basis. The first day of high school I arrived ready to meet the new situation – high on pot. That set the tempo for the next 4 years of school. I began smoking pot every day, all day long, and drinking whenever I got the opportunity.

I was always very involved in sports. I became a pretty good athlete and enjoyed the acceptance and approval that came with it. I wasn't very big in stature, but I played with a lot of heart. I loved to win and I played like I lived, wide open. One particular evening, I smoked a few joints just before our football game and played the best game of my high school career. Needless to say, that just added to my justification that drugs are all right and was doing me no harm.

When I was a sophomore, I fell in love for the first time. She was a beautiful girl and tried to convince me that drugs and alcohol were not the way to go. Her words fell on deaf ears. Things were definitely going my way, I had all the right answers, and besides my drug and alcohol use were only recreational, or so I told myself. That year turned out to be one of the toughest years of my life. My best friend was killed in a hunting accident, my grandfather passed away, and the young lady I was in love with died in a car accident. I was devastated and my use of drugs and alcohol escalated. I turned to pills and hard liquor to ease the pain and escape from reality.

I finished high school with a minimum of effort and lettered in football, baseball, and track, and I was a full-blown alcoholic and drug addict. I just didn't know it. The athletic scholarship I had dreamed of didn't materialize but I was fortunate that my father was able to send me to college. I enrolled in an Alabama college that was known to be a party school. A lot of my friends were attending there, along with a young lady that I started dating. The first year of school I managed to make decent grades and joined a fraternity. I met some people who were into big time marijuana growing so I had a steady supply for the next several years. I started using cocaine on a regular basis and it soon became my drug of choice. Before long, I was selling coke to support my own habit. The following 4 years of college were pretty much a blur – endless days and nights of selling dope, drinking, taking pills, smoking pot, doing coke and partying. The cocaine use increased steadily and I was soon going through several ounces a week, selling just enough to make the next deal the following week.

By the time I was a senior in college, I had come close to getting busted for drugs on several occasions. I had almost died many times from my drinking and drugging. I lost my girlfriend of 5 years, quit hanging around my fraternity house, flunked out of school, and had gone through a small fortune in drugs. I was completely hooked.

I had been locked up in my apartment for several days doing coke and one morning my brother and an old girlfriend came by to see if I was still alive. I was, but just barely. At this point I honestly believed there was no way out other than just doing the coke until it finally killed me. I thought I was too far-gone. They persuaded me to call my mother and try to get some help. I made the call and told her that I had a problem that was bigger than me and I needed help.

My mother convinced me to enter a 28-day drug and alcohol program. My addiction had robbed me of everything worthwhile in my life – relationships, friends, education, goals, dreams, health and values. Fortunately, my family still had enough love and faith in me not to give up.

During the first week of treatment, my mind and body craved the drugs and alcohol that had become a part of my daily life over the past 10 years. I learned a lot about the disease of addiction and I was introduced to the 12-steps of Alcoholics Anonymous and Narcotics Anonymous. I began attending AA and NA meetings and meeting people who had the same problems I had. Things started looking up for me again. But I made a common mistake that sabotaged my recovery. I had a deadly hidden agenda. I thought that if I could just get off cocaine, I could still handle a cold beer and a joint every now and then. I still had reservations about using anything heavier, but I couldn't accept the fact that I could never drink or get high again. Somehow I stayed clean and sober for 6 months just going to meetings. I wasn't working the 12 steps like the program suggested and I didn't even talk with a sponsor. I wanted to be in control. Finally, I decided I didn't need AA or NA. I could handle it myself. So I quit going to the meetings. Within a month I was drinking and smoking pot again. I was working as an estimator for my father's construction company and had started dating a woman I had known for a long time. She didn't drink or smoke and I that thought maybe she could keep me off drugs and my drinking to a minimum. I was badly mistaken.

I managed to maintain my work at the office during the day, but my nights soon became filled with drugs and alcohol again. The more I used, the worse I felt about myself. In turn, my addiction progressed back to the point where I left off, plus some. I kept my cocaine use to a minimum, but my drinking accelerated tremendously. I started taking pills and smoking pot daily. My health declined and my nerves were shot. The young lady that I was seeing left and I drank even more. This went on for several months.

One night a friend and I went out to a bar. We drank several beers on the way and arrived in time for the 9-11 drink special . . . one-dollar drinks for 2 hours. I had several drinks and an old friend came up and handed me 3 10-mg. valiums. I swallowed them without even thinking twice about it. Soon after, I became tired and ready to head for home. The friend I had come with decided to stay there and told me to go ahead. So I left, alone. On the way back home, I fell asleep at the wheel. I was awakened by a terrible crash. I was treated at the hospital and carried straight to jail for DUI. The next morning the officers read me my rights and informed me that I was being charged for the murder of the young lady that was in the car I had run over.

I can't seem to come up with words that would describe my feelings on that day and the many months after except to say that the pain, remorse, guilt, fear and depression were more than I thought I could live with.

That was 26 months ago. As I write this story, I am incarcerated in the Alabama Department of Corrections. By the grace of God I made it back to the fellowship of AA and NA. I have had a unique situation to sit down and meet the real Buddy W. and look at my past and come to terms with it. I have allowed myself to change by working the 12 steps of AA and NA. Today I have a program of recovery. Today I choose not to use. The 12-step program enabled me to work through the pain, guilt and depression and all the other defects of character that keep my addiction alive. I found out that I wasn't a bad man trying to be a good man. I was a sick man trying to get well. I was sick with cocaine, alcohol and all the other drugs. I also learned that it wasn't just a drug and alcohol problem. It was a life problem. This program is teaching me to live because I never really knew how. I am learning to share with others, to be a real son to my parents and a brother to my brothers and sister. I am starting to love myself and to love others, unconditionally. The program has helped me grow in all aspects of my life – physically, mentally and spiritually.

AA and NA tell me not to worry about tomorrow because it hasn't come yet; not to worry about yesterday because nobody can change it. Live one day at a time, they say. And it works.

* * * *

Jack P.

When Thomas Henderson asked me to write how the 12-step programs saved my life, my first thought was how Thomas himself had intervened to lead me into recovery from drug and alcohol addiction. I still remember clearly. It was on February 14, 1981, that I read a short article in the local newspaper about Thomas' battle with cocaine addiction. He had gone into treatment and when a reporter asked about it, Thomas said, "Because of cocaine, I've lost family, friends and career." For me that statement was the turning point in my life.

I had been actively and openly using cocaine since 1973 and my life had gradually fallen apart. Once a prominent and wealthy attorney and business entrepreneur, I was now living over a garage, having sold my home, my furniture and my car to raise money to support my addiction. I was facing 10 years in prison stemming from my arrest in the fall of 1979. It never occurred to me that drugs were the cause of my downfall. 'Family, friends, and career,' I thought. My family had disowned me when I was arrested. My children had apparently written me off. The only friends I had carried guns and most of them were already in prison. I was a millionaire 15 years earlier and now I was $450,000 in debt.

Six days later I entered a residential drug treatment program where I stayed for the next two months. Dealing with life without drugs to numb my feelings was very painful for a while. Without my white powder friend, all the fears I had stuffed during the past years came up. I couldn't sleep and wanted to die when I was awake. I was terrified of prison, had to acknowledge that I was broke, and missed my children in the worst way. Looking back now, I thank God for AA. Every day, as part of treatment, I was required to attend an AA meeting for an hour and a half. Although I was a novice at feeling and understanding my feelings, I was able to acknowledge that during an AA meeting I felt safe and loved. I didn't understand it, but each day I looked forward to my AA meeting.

When I was discharged, it was my AA meetings that kept me sane. I would get into my office at 8:30 a.m. and by 11:30 I was so filled with fear that I couldn't work anymore. I would dash out to the local noon AA meeting and run into my friend Rick, who was going through similar feelings. We would spend the rest of the afternoon together at a coffee shop, supporting one another. After dinner I would head out to the 8:30 p.m. meetings, going to sleep that night clean and sober for one more day.

Gradually, my life came together again. As I got more involved with the 12-step program, my self-confidence and self-esteem returned. When I was sober 9 months, I had to face up to my 1979 arrest. As part of the plea bargaining, I had pleaded guilty. The prosecutor would ask that I am incarcerated for 18 months to 5 years, and my lawyer would argue for a lesser sentence. The man who had me arrested showed up for the sentencing to make sure they followed his recommendation to "lock me up and throw away the key." The courtroom was also filled with many of my new AA friends who came to support me during this most difficult day.

After the prosecutor made his argument, my lawyer presented witnesses who told the judge that I was doing well with my own efforts to rehabilitate myself from drug addiction and alcoholism and that prison would only hurt my recovery. As the judge was about to pass sentence, the man who had me arrested stood up and said, "Your Honor, I would like to address the court. My name is ___ and I know a great deal about alcoholism and drug addiction. I am a physician as well as a recovering alcoholic myself. I have just talked with my wife and we've changed our mind about Jack. We also feel that prison would hurt his recovery and therefore we don't want him to be incarcerated." A ray of hope hit me and when the judge gave me a suspended sentence, I knew it was only because I was a member of AA.

AA is a spiritual, but not a religious program. Things started happening to help me believe that if I was to "let go and let God", as AA suggested, my life would become more manageable.

When I was sober about a year, I had to fly to California on business. Financially, my life was still a disaster. The IRS was chasing me, and I had thoughts that if I got drunk in California, no one would know. While waiting at the airport, I looked for a paperback book to read on the flight. My eyes focused on a book with a sexy girl in a bikini on the cover. I pulled the book from the rack for a closer look and all of a sudden I'm holding a book entitled God Is For the Alcoholic. And, there's no girl on the cover! I go back through the rack, book by book, and there's no girl in a bikini on any of the books. Then it occurred to me that this "higher power" stuff AA talk about might just be something real and perhaps my higher power wants me to read this book I'm holding. I bought the book and read it on the flight to LA and lost my desire to get drunk. Whew!

By now my life has turned around. I've paid off a huge chunk of my bills, the IRS is out of my life, I own a profitable business, and I see my sons regularly. All my recovering friends are wonderfully loving, compassionate people. My AA friends would tell me things like 'the joy is in the journey,' and 'live in the now.'

So I tried that. They told me to let go of resentments, make amends and to think loving thoughts about everyone. So I gave that a shot, too. My friends told me God is love and love is the glue that holds it all together. I know today that this is all true.

If I spend my day focusing on what is right in front of me, and if I practice the principles of love, patience and tolerance, I can look back at the end of each day and suddenly realize that I was truly happy and peaceful that day.

My friend Jack relapsed. He's back in the program and has a little over a year clean now. His story is still important. Just because you get many years clean and sober doesn't mean you're cured. Jack found that out the hard way. Jack, welcome back. TH

* * * *

Kathryn

My name is Kathryn and I'm an alcoholic. I was born in the hill country of Southwest Texas on a goat and sheep ranch. Neither of my parents was alcoholic, but one of my grandfathers was a heavy drinker. He was German and I loved him very much — hard working, rough talking, free spending. He drank too much but stopped when he realized what he was doing to Gran.

I lived in a one-room house with my mother, father and 4 siblings. I had two sets of grandparents who were loving and parents who were dedicated to us. My childhood was happy.

My first drunk happened when I was a freshman in high school. I was simply curious about it, but the remorse and guilt I suffered afterwards was terrible. I promised my mother and myself that I would never do it again.

My first taste of drugs came in my junior year. I had been up late one night playing basketball and was too tired to get up for school the next day. My mother, who was always watching her weight, gave me one of her diet pills to get me through the day. It was wonderful! I fell in love with the powerful feeling and from that point my disease progressed.

I went on to college and received a degree in education. I began teaching school in small towns in Texas, pulling periodic drunks. If I received one complaint I'd pull up and go somewhere else. Finally, I migrated south to Mexico City where I met and married Bernardo. His family was socially affluent. His mother had been protocol secretary to President Aleman and his father was from a famous family. Dazzled by the glamour, I tried to be someone I was not and lost what little self-sense I had. Bernardo was also an alcoholic and I really learned to drink with him. After seven years of marriage, we moved to Dallas and hit bottom. I was so tired of fighting with the world, drinking, speeding, drinking some more to come down from the speed. The glamour was gone from the partying games. All that was left were the bleakness and despair of broken dreams and monotony and boredom interspersed with bewilderment, frustration and despair. No one could stand Bernardo and me and we couldn't stand us. But we found AA. I took to it like a drowning person seizing a lifeboat.

Bernardo didn't seem to need the support of other AA members like I did, but I hung in there anyway. The compulsion to drink was lifted from me early in the game, but high-strung nervous energy replaced it. I found physical sobriety, yet fear dominated those early years. My wonderful sponsor and dear friend was central to me during that time. She made me stand up for myself as I pounded away at the 12 steps. I said my prayers and talked to God, even when I didn't think He heard.

Finally, I realized my marriage was a farce and was given the strength to leave Bernardo. My co-dependency had kept me in this relationship long after it had died.

Through AA, I am now a sober alcoholic. I came, came to, and then came to believe. My relationship with my Creator is deep and meaningful. I work the steps of AA, go to meetings, to go church, teach school, exercise, and am of service to God and my fellow man. I still have much to learn but I've come a long way from the self-willed, wounded, egomaniac with an inferiority complex that I once was.

If you are an alcoholic, as I am, there is no better way to live than the AA way.

＊ ＊ ＊

Leo H.

I came from a dysfunctional family. In fact, I came from a dysfunctional neighborhood. Everyone drank. The priests drank, dogs drank, cats drank, loan sharks drank, and bookmakers drank. If you didn't drink, we didn't have anything to do with you. Alcoholism didn't run in my family and neighborhood – it galloped!

I crossed the line into alcoholism with my first drunk at age 13. At that age, I was 5'6" and weighed 200 pounds. The first time I got drunk, suddenly I was transformed into a 6', 175 pound, handsome hunk. But after staying up all night puking my guts out, I was once again the 5'6", 200-pound shmoe I had been the day before. That was the start of the cycle. The way I felt when I was high was worth the wretched state of my body after being drunk.

A couple of months later, my mother took me to a doctor who gave me diet pills. Over a period of several months I lost 60 pounds and grew 5". I stopped taking the diet pills and quickly gained back all the weight. The lesson was there again – better living through chemistry. I vowed to take diet pills for the rest of my life and for the next 18 years I took 1-5 pills a day.

Over the next 15 years I tried every form of experimentation and self-deception trying to prove to myself that I wasn't an alcoholic. I got married, changed jobs, changed addresses, changed clothes, changed drinks – beer only, white wine with fish, red wine with meat, spritzers, vodka with vitamins A, B, C, D, B6, B12, niacin, etc; and, when I claimed I wasn't drinking, I drank beer. As I look back on my life it wasn't unmanageable it was unbelievable.

I made my first 12-step recovery meeting in 1964. The only reason I went was to get my wife back. In my neighborhood it was a disgrace to be an alcoholic. So I went to this meeting in a disguise. I had on my black gangster suit, black gangster shirt, black tie, black hat, and black sunglasses. I looked like Zorro coming into this meeting. Today they have young people's meetings. This was an old people's meeting. The average age was 55 but they all looked 105. I was 25. I looked around and saw all these crazy signs: "Easy Does It," "Live and Let Live," "Be Nice," etc. Then I saw the sign I liked. It said "Exit." So in and out I went for the next 9 years. All this time I never once stopped drinking so sobriety was never there. Finally, in 1973 I hit bottom.

Since then, thanks to good sponsorship, good fellowship and a day-by-day working program, I have not found it necessary to pick up a drink or drug. I have all the usual problems associated with daily living in recovery – no job, too many jobs, no money, car accidents, kids not listening, etc., but I was taught one thing early on, a drink will never fix anything. It will only make it worse. In recovery, I've met a host of new friends. Life has taken on a new meaning. All the promises in the big book come and go according to how hard I work on my program. My life statement now is "If I work my program hard, my life goes easy. If I work my program easy, my life goes hard."

* * * *

Jimmy

My name is Jimmy and I am an alcoholic and drug addict. I have been clean and sober since June 10, 1982. I was born in Moorman, Kentucky and raised in the housing projects of Louisville, Kentucky. My mother came from a pretty dysfunctional family and carried it into her own family. I was raised without ever knowing whom my father was. I am the second of ten children. In my early childhood I always felt lonely and alone. I also felt ugly because of being so poor. Two things stand out in my mind that it seemed I was supposed to learn: one was to learn to be a REAL MAN. The other was to MAKE IT. I still don't know what either of them mean, but when I was eleven I set about trying to do it.

I started drinking at this age and it changed me. It took the pain and loneliness away. I quit school when I was 15 and got a job in a dental laboratory and started a rock and roll band. I got married when I was 19 and by the age of 20 I was a full-blown alcoholic and drug addict and was about to start on a prison career. For the next 12 years I was in and out of prison 4 times for forgery, burglary armed robbery and larceny. This career in crime was the direct result of my disease of addiction. I have come to know that when the phenomenon of craving takes over in an alcoholic or drug addict, there is nothing in God's world that will stop him or her from finding a way to feed this craving. It is the deadliest symptom of the disease of addiction.

I got out of prison for the last time on March 17, 1981 and headed for Dallas to live with my brother, who I was in prison with in 1980. I planned on just drinking, drugging and doing whatever I felt like because God made doctors, lawyers and all other kinds of people and then He made poor, lonely people like me who spent most of their lives behind bars and couldn't do anything about it. I really didn't know how to quit doing drugs and alcohol and therefore how to quit stealing to support my habit.

I was driving around one afternoon trying to figure out what to do with my life because I knew I was in deep trouble. I knew I was very close to going back to prison for the rest of my life. I had been told that as a four-time loser my chances to stay out in society were very slim at best. I stopped at a track field and began to run. I ran and ran until I finally fell down on the ground and started crying and cursing God. I cursed Him for everything — never having a father, losing loved ones, for the loneliness I had felt all my life.

I don't know how long I lay there, but shortly afterward I found myself at the doors of a 12-step group and they had a little sign that said "Only 12 More Steps To Go." I didn't know that those people and those 12-steps were to lead me to true transformation, liberation, and eventually to know the true meaning of the word freedom. They taught me that freedom, peace and plenty are not dependent on circumstances or conditions. Freedom is a condition of the soul.

So I started out on a journey to find out who I was and what the problem was in my life. I found out through these people and the 12 steps that I was powerless over drugs and alcohol; that the difference between me and a normal person was that the phenomenon of craving does not take place in them; that the disease is mental, physical and spiritual and what was missing was a higher power to change me. That power came through the people who had already made the journey through the 12 steps and they passed it on to me and opened me to a truly higher power. And it was all free.

I have since discovered that I was suffering from a disease that only a spiritual awakening and experience can conquer. When you get straight spiritually, you automatically straighten out mentally and physically. All my life I had heard from people that I was bad and needed to get good. But I learned another very powerful thing — that I was sick and could get well and recover if I could walk all the way through the 12 steps and get in touch with spiritual principles.

Today I consider the love of my friends and family my most precious gift of sobriety. I have more than I ever dreamed possible. My business is doing well because I go to work every day and work instead of talking about it. I voted in our Governor's race. I pay taxes and have probably paid close to enough taxes to take care of the cost of all the years of my incarceration. That is a good feeling. It makes me smile. But perhaps the greatest miracle is that through the 12 steps and the help of my friends I proved a lot of people wrong. I proved it wasn't true that I could not live out here in society with the rest of you. Thank God I proved them wrong.

* * * *

Gayle B.

The picture looked idyllic on the outside – husband, a West Point graduate and highly successful corporate vice president, handsome, witty and world traveled; wife, graduate of Eastern girls school, petite, pretty, president of PTA, home economics teacher, innovative dresser, decorator and entertainer; kids, 3 good looking, intelligent pre-teens doing well in school and outside activities.

In fact, all was quite splendid until Gayle B, the wife and mother – me, took that first drink of wine, beer, or my favorite, a Gimlet or Bloody Mary. What happened after that was anyone's guess. Maybe I would not drink another or maybe I would sneak drinks, lie about them and continue to drink until I blacked out or generally acted out in ways I wouldn't normally do. That is the way my alcoholism manifested itself. It was never daily, often unpredictable, and sometimes very much within the confines of social acceptability. The difference for me was that I could not safely predict my behavior after the first drink even though I retained a reasonable amount of personal control.

For example, I never acted out at a company sponsored event but the entire time I was obsessed with the drinking process – lining my stomach before I drank, pacing myself, choosing drinks that would effect me less, etc. Basically, I was trying to drink like other people and get away with it.

Despite all my obvious drinking behavior, no one ever said much to me about it. My husband manifested displaced anger towards me, but never while I was drinking. My father, a proud and respected doctor, just kept insisting that I'd be OK if I only drank 2 drinks. My brother, also a physician, never berated me, even for 3:00 a.m. collect, incoherent phone calls. My kids just silently and sullenly went on with their lives. Alcoholism has sometimes been called the elephant in the living room that no one talks about.

Everyone, including me, believed that if I just displayed more will power, all would be better. We all truly felt that "next time I would be better." None of us knew that I was in the grips of a progressive disease and that I was an alcoholic.

It took a very painful and embarrassing public experience to cut through my delusion and denial. I fell down the stairs at an impressive social function in a mansion in fashionable New Canaan, Connecticut and cut my head. It bled a lot. The man I was dancing with, who was also drunk, punched three people. Not a very classy ending to a first class event, but precisely what I needed to bring me to a point of asking for help. As a direct result of that experience, I began my now 21-year tenure in a 12-step program.

I thought that was to be the end of my fun and a sentence to a boring and meaningless life with a bunch of "winos." But recovery for me has been about beautiful beginnings, growing up, facing reality, and reevaluating my life, searching for deeper meaning to my life. It has been one day at a time, sometimes slow like the little engine that could, and often times at an incredibly fast pace. It has shown me how to face my fears, that I am never alone and that almost anything can be done or undone with faith in a higher power and help from other recovering people.

Perhaps the greatest single lesson I have learned is to let people be there for me and that there is nothing that a valium and a drink won't make worse. I learned that through a relapse I had 14 years ago. It didn't last long and did no permanent damage, but it unconditionally taught me and my family that I am not and can never be a social drinker.

I wish I had gone to a treatment facility for my alcoholism. It would have made it so much easier for my family and me. They would have learned the facts about my disease instead of operating from stigmatized ideas and believing they should be ashamed because I am an alcoholic. They would have learned about their own co-dependency and how we all played a part in my alcoholism. I believe that anyone who can should seek professional help. A properly conducted treatment center benefits everyone.

My life in recovery has not been easy. Whose life is easy? But a sober life has definitely been worth it. I gave up so little to gain so much. My motto has become a quote by Winston Churchill, a hero of mine and one with whom I share a birthday, "What is the use of living if it is not to make this world better for those who live in it after we are gone?"

"There were bets that I wouldn't survive. Here I am one day at a time for over 20 years. This story continues and gets better because I choose every single day to stay clean and sober. This simple decision make all things possible." TH

EPILOGUE

It is not often that a recovering alcoholic and drug addict gets to tell his story in book form twice. I am proud to be a member of the recovering community. There are millions of us worldwide. I am not a leader or spokesperson. I am in the rank and file. My story is unique only because I played for the Dallas Cowboys and was a member of a Super Bowl championship team. Otherwise my story is common in the recovering community.

I decided to add comments from family, friends, sponsors, mentors and associates about their experience and relationship with me as a person, my work and recovery. Their impressions and opinions of who I was and who I have become are shared throughout this book. I personally did not interview anyone. We believe that hearing from those who know me intimately would add substance and credibility to the story of Thomas Henderson.

My first book, *Out Of Control*, was published in 1988. As I have traveled the United States doing hundreds of lectures at rehabilitation centers, colleges, prisons, community groups, high schools and corporations, I've been asked, many times when I would write another book. It was as if *Out Of Control* left people wanting proof that sobriety and the recovery process do indeed work. They wanted to hear from me again.

I think they were trying to be nice by saying, "Thomas, you were really fouled up, and we hope you're better now. We want to hear more."

I am better now, and it is time to tell more of my story. I've been trudging my lane in life one day at a time doing my best as a member of a family and society. This thing called living is hard. Living is an everyday grind of survival.

A series of unbelievable miracles changed my heart and mind. Since November 8, 1983, I haven't used alcohol or drugs. I pay taxes, child support, own a home, am not currently in prison, haven't been arrested, am a member of golf clubs, give to charity, pray and have a valid driver's license. I have children, grandkids and friends. I even won the Texas Lottery to the tune of $28 million, which turned out to be $10 million after Uncle Sam took his. I still have most of that money.

I don't profess to be someone special. My story plain and simple is about the life and times of a survivor. I made up my mind to be different. I am not my mistake. I am who I have become. Today I share my experience in recovery with children, alcoholics, addicts, strangers, prisoners, athletes, entertainers, my community and the world in person or on film. This is my work. My life is my work.

Ain't I lucky?